SOCIAL ECOLOGY OF FOREST RESOURCES
A Study of a Tribal Region of Orissa

SOCIAL ECOLOGY OF FOREST RESOURCES

A Study of a Tribal Region of Orissa

Bibhuti Bhusan Malik

Publications

KALPAZ PUBLICATIONS
DELHI - 110052

Social Ecology of Forest Resources : A Study of a Tribal Region of Orissa

Rs. 850

ISBN : 81-7835-286-9

Published in 2004 in India by
Kalpaz Publications,
C-30, Satyawati Nagar,
Delhi-110 052
Email : kalpaz@hotmail.com

Laser type Setting by: ***Tact Computer Graphics***, Delhi
Printed at: Mehra Offset Press, Delhi

Contents

	Preface	7
1	Introduction	9
2.	People Tribe and Ecology	55
3.	Social Structure and Change	77
4.	Political and Legal System	105
5.	Religion and Belief System	141
6.	Culture Leisure and Communication	181
7.	Economy Ecology and Development	231
8.	Social Ecology and Forest Resources	283
9.	Change and Development	307
10.	Conclusion	335
	Appendix	343
	Bibliography	353
	Index	367

Preface

The book is an attempt to look at ecology and tribal life in its reciprocal symbiotic forms. The inter-relationship of physical, biological and cultural features of a region is the subject matter of social ecology which is the essence of this book. Human beings, especially tribals, try to adapt themselves to particular geographical and cultural environment and in doing so they try to control the environment according to their requirements. Every major achievement of mankind can, in fact, be traced directly or ultimately, to the influence of an organic community, that is, a community whose people are united by biological links as well as by common culture, tradition and ideals, and who have ecological roots in the land whence they derive their means of subsistence from. The interchange between man, his habitations, resources and technology and social habits and values is reciprocal and intimate. Sociologists exclusively study human society, its nature, forms, social structure, economy, polity, religion and culture. In this book a systematic approach has been applied to see the linkages of various social institutions or forms with reference to ecology. The sociology of social ecology has been exhaustively reviewed with special emphasis on conceptualizing and defining the concept itself as well as its theory and approaches. For a better systematic exploration this review has been categoried as non-Indian and Indian studies. The ecological infrastructure of human society consists of soil, water flora, fauna, climate, etc. In this work, forest has been taken as a single and only ecological criterion to explore the way of life, society and culture of *Saora* tribe of Orissa.

Forest-trees and common property resources are basic to tribal communities, directly benefit them like a foster mother, and fulfill their biological, cultural and emotional needs. For food, tribals are mostly dependent on forest by collecting nuts, wild fruits, vegetables, leaves, flower, roots, stems, honey, wild animal and insects, and so on. Likewise all cultural artifacts developed by them are mostly forest-based. They collect all raw materials like bamboo, canes, fibers, oil, *bhabha* gram, waxes, resins, gums, dyes and wood to construct their houses. The agriculture instruments and hunting weapons are also prepared from forest produce. The forest has also been closely associated with their life-cycle activities from birth to death; even the religion and folklore are based on the forest in which they live. Further, major tribal economic activities are based on forest—food gathering, pastoralism, shifting cultivation and settled cultivation. All these categories evolved around forest ecology and natural resources. The *Saora* tribe practices shifting cultivation by cleaning the forest patches and partially depending upon forest produce. An attempt has been made in this study to explore the inter-linkages and interdependency of varies institutions developed by *Saora* tribals on forests. Moreover, how far the symbiotic dependency of these institutions has been disturbed in due course of time has been systematically explored.

It is a matter of great delight for me to acknowledge my intellectual and academic indebtedness to my teachers at the Jawaharlal Nehru University, three of whom I would specially mention here: Professor Yogendra Singh who has not only taken personal interest in the completion of this study but also always favoured me in a great man's spirit and by his wise counsel. I owe a deep debt of gratitude to Professor K.L. Sharma and Professor Anand Kumar for their personal guidance, encouragement, assurance and advice.

I also wish to express my heartfelf thanks to Professor Ramesh Nanand Dwivedy, Prof. R.P. Jaiswal and Dr. Ravi Prakash Pandey of Department of Sociology Mahatma Gandhi Kashi University, Kashi Vidyapith, Varanasi for having rendered to me all kind of co-operation and encouragement towards the publication of this study.

Finally, I owe special thanks to Mr. B.P. Garg of Gyan Books, New Delhi, who found it relevant to publish this work.

Bibhuti Bhusan Malik

1
Introduction

Tribal communities live in forests, and therefore, in India they are called *jan jatis* (forest dwellers). Their socio-cultural life is mostly woven around nature. The geographical and climatic conditions around the indigenous communities inform their ways of thinking, living and acting. Tribals' cultural and religious symbols are centred on the natural habitat. Culture here stands for both the material and non-material aspects of it. The indigenous communities, whatever they find from their surrounding, try to use that for their day-to-day life activities. Eminent anthropologist Hersokovities stated that culture is man-made aspect of environment. Household assets, instruments for agricultural purposes and use of tree leaves in the tribal religious and cultural festivals form the part of culture, which is mostly determined by the natural resources available in their surroundings. In case of *jan jatis*, their culture is more defined by nature and less made by man.

The indigenous people nowadays are increasingly being cut off from their traditional symbiotic relationship with forests. With the use of more, and more alien technology and new development projects, the natural surrounding is losing its cultural and occupational links with the life-ways of the tribals. This has been the experience in most cases where new, planned development projects have been put in use for the advancement of the locals. Unexpectedly, perhaps, most of the development models have failed to address the needs of the locals, causing in the process ecological disasters and occupational displacements, sometimes, of colossal proportions. In a nutshell, development projects, planned and implemented by the administrators from plain areas and with no sensitiveness to the value systems of the indigenous people, have in most of the cases disrupted the traditional sources of livelihood of the inhabitants, leading to displacement, migration and refugee or slum settlements around urban centres.

This alienation, resulting in the tribals because of government policies also has a great impact on natural environment. In this context the traditional culture, economy, polity, social structure and society of *Lanjia Saora* have changed. These changes induced by modernisation and economic liberalisation, and their relationships with social institutions in the tribal societies have been traced in this study in order to arrive at a sociological understanding. Environmental degradation and occupational changes occurring in the tribal societies and the causes behind them have been systematically explored. This study also goes into the effects of cultural interaction with those emanating from outside, that is, through migration and mass media.

Statement of the Problem

Tribals have been seriously affected by degradation of forest land, commercialisation of forest and their reduced accessibility to forest resources on account of government control and new forest laws, which in most cases have denied access for the tribals to jungles. The functional and symbiotic dependence of the tribals on forest is under threat. Degradation of environmental surroundings and rigid forest laws have adversely affected the food accessibility, livelihood option and quality of life of local communities, who have been traditionally dependent on these natural sources for their fuel and livelihood. Such degradation has often caused periodic phases of hunger and malnutrition in the absence of supportive means for acquiring basic essentials of life.

Forest-trees and common property resources are basic to tribal communities, directly benefit them like a foster mother, and fulfill their biological, cultural, religious and emotional needs. For food, tribals are mostly dependent on forest by collecting nuts, wildfruits, vegetables, leaves, flowers, roots, stems, honey, wild animal and insects, etc.

In the culture context, all the culture artifacts of the tribals are mostly forest-based. They collect all the raw materials like bamboo, canes, fibers, oils, *bhabha* gram, waxes, resins, gums, dyes and wood to construct their houses. The household assets, which they use for their day-to-day life, are also made from the forest produce. The agriculture instruments and hunting weapons are also prepared from forest products. Even tree leaves are essential for their life. For example, Shal leaves are used by the *Lanjia Soara* to make food-plates and bowl. They prepare indigenous cigar beedi out of this leaf. In the social and religious practices, Shal leaves with a few rice coloured with turmeric on it are used as invitation letter for deities' invocation worships.

As in the case of other tribal communities, the religion and folklore of the *Lanjia Saora* are based on the forest. The forest has been closely associated with their various life cycle activities from birth to death. *Lanjia Saora* use some trees and perform certain ritual under the trees. Lots of references can be found in their folklore, as will be clear from subsequent paragraphs.

The emotional need which is fulfill by the tribals from the forest becomes also evident as that they feel happy when they look at green pastoral which brings peace to them. This sentience (capacity for sensory experience) is also in a dying state.

There are four major tribal economic activities based on forest— food gathering, pastoralism, shifting cultivation and settled cultivation. Though classified, these are not exclusive. All these categories evolved around forest ecology and natural resources. The *Lanjia Saora* practice shifting cultivation by cleaning the forest patches and partially depending upon the forest produce.

After Independence, especially in the recent decades, the tribal areas have been exposed to outside contact. That is because of the development plans, laying of roads and railways, connecting inaccessible terrain and dense forests with plain areas. As a result, cultural contact and migration has taken place in these areas. The migrants from the plain areas try to exploit the abundant natural resources to their personal profit, while the same were traditionally a common source to fulfill communitarian requirements for the tribals. Increasing commercialisation has replaced barter economy by paper currency. An organised clique of traders has emerged in the tribal areas, which buys their local produce at lower rates and sells it at higher prices in urban markets, the resulting competition has left behind the locals, and cooperative experiments have not been successful either.

The essentiality of forest for needs is one aspect of the story. But the indirect benefits which the whole surrounding was benefited has become degraded. The indirect benefits such as preventing soil-erosion, conserving moisture, water, recycling nutrient, preventing drought or reducing its impact, providing leaf mour, fixing nitrogen by leguminous trees, regulating climate and rainfall, providing greenery and beauty, reducing pollution, etc., have been adversely affected.

In this backdrop, this study would seek to find out the reasons for some of the pertinent problems, which are as under:

1. The forest that was providing alternative source of livelihood and offering coping strategies to the local communities is no more easily accessible to the tribals. This brings out the most basic question of survival of indigenous people. In other words, their economic activities, culture, social structure and religious beliefs, are under threat.

2. Diverse functions of forests eco-system such as watershed properties and microclimatic regulation have been adversely affected, thereby affecting lives and livelihood of local communities.

3. Exploitation, expropriation and threats from outside agencies have increased and local communities have been forced to forfeit their lands. This has swelled the ranks of the landless labour in these areas.

4. The constitutional rights of local people are being violated most often and in practice, the tribals stand to lose in the existing socio-economic and political setup, which tends to be repressive and most often works to their disadvantage at least, that is how the locals feel.

5. Large areas of forest have been formally kept out of reach of indigenous people, who have tended forest for subsistence and income. Such actions or policies have led to tension in social control of forests and social unrest has become sharp in some areas. Increased pressure on forest and new laws denying access to forests have led to firewood and fodder problems for local communities. Social and economic problems of the locals have multiplied, widening the areas of conflict in the tribal societies.

Objectives of the Study

This formulation of research problem in connection with *Saora* tribes of Gunupur area of Orissa's Koraput district has the following objectives.

1. How far the dependency on forest of tribals has been affected by deforestation and modernisation and has disturbed their social and ecological settings? Here, the focus will be on their cultural, religious, economic and social structure, which have been traditionally dependent on nature.

2. To study tribal perception about nature: whether they themselves perceive forest as a source of livelihood like a foster mother or something similar?

3. How far *Lanjia Saora* tribals understand the environmental process and manage their scarce resources? The environmental process, in this context, means how the non-human factors affect the society and society affects nature and is affected by it.

4. To what extent the environmental degradation and deforestation have affected on the autonomy of the local people: whether they are still dependent on forest or migrating to the nearest town areas?

5. What are the various representation of nature in their folk cosmology and art? And what kind of knowledge (Traditional Forest Related Knowledge—TFRK) the local communities had of their natural environments, e.g., ethno-botany, ethnozoology.

6. What are the functions of caste and village institutions in regulating the use of forest, water and other common resources? This study will also focus on the role of leadership in social development, especially the role of village head in maintaining the symbiotic relationship with the forest.

With these above-mentioned objectives, this study seeks to highlight the interrelationship between ecology and society. Here, ecology has a single perspective, that is, the forest and society is of the *Saora* tribe. Therefore, for conceptual clarity and disciplinary requirement, we need to see the growth and development of ecological discipline.

Ecology : A Concept

The word ecology is derived from the Greek words: 'oikos' meaning habitation, and 'logos' meaning discourse or study, implying a study of the habitations of organisms. Ecology was first described as a separate field of knowledge in 1866 by the German zoologist, Ernest Haeckle, who coined the word oeckologie to mean "The relations of the animal to its organic as well as its inorganic environment, particularly its friendly or hostile relations to those animals or plants with which it comes in contact."

Ecology is one of the main divisions of biology, the other two being morphology and physiology. The emphasis in morphology is on how organisms are made, in physiology how they function, and in ecology how they are related to environment.

Ecology has been variously defined by other investigators, as "scientific natural history", "the study of biotic communities", or "the science of community population"; probably the most comprehensive definition is the simple one most often given: a study of animal and plants in their relations to each other and their environment.

Ecological studies by zoologists and botanists have established in numerous field studies that organisms, whether plants or animals, establish viable relationships with environment, not independently but collectively, through the mechanism of a system of relationships. Bioecologists were thus led to employ a set of concepts and techniques of investigation that imparted a markedly sociological coloration to their work.

The ecological approach was introduced as human ecology into the field of sociology at a critical period in the development of this discipline. When a balanced web of relationships is viewed in a specific local area, it presents the aspect of community—a concept with obvious appeal for students of human social life. This can be easily traced by reviewing a number of studies.

Review of Literature

As we have discussed briefly the meaning of ecology in biology, botany, sociology and social sciences, it is pertinent to trace the development of ecology in the field of social science research. In social science research, geographers, economists, psychologists, sociologists and social anthropologists abroad and India—have elaborately given a theoretical understanding to the study of social ecology.

The ecological approach was introduced in social sciences research in general and sociological research in particular as human ecology. Sociologists made free use of the analogy and borrowed heavily from the concepts of the plant and ecology. For better understanding and clarity these contributions can be examined and interpreted by which a sociological meaning can be derived and a theoretical approach can be developed. At the outset the attempts made by scholars to analyse ecology, human ecology and social ecology can be produced as Indian studies and non-Indian studies.

Non-Indian Studies

H. Hawley in his book *Human Ecology: A Theory of Community Structure* (1950) tried to develop a full, coherent theory of human ecology. His argument begins with the contributions of plant and animal ecologists, which have a sociological bearing in the development of the fundamental aspects of community structure. Very often, ecology is viewed as an all—inclusive point of view—a study of all of life in relation to all of environment. This is no less true of its application to human social phenomena than of its use in the study of similar matters involving other forms of life. A view elaborated that the application of concepts from plant and animal ecology to the human community carries the implication that community is essentially a natural phenomenon. This means that it has developed independently of plan or deliberation. Thus, human ecology was interpreted as the study of the biotic or sub-social aspect of human social organisation (Park, 1936).

Marston Bates discusses in *Anthropology Today: Selections* (1962) that the concept of "environment" is certainly difficult and may even be misleading, but we have no handy substitute. It seems simple enough to distinguish between the organism and the surrounding environment and to separate forces acting on an organism into those that are internal and inherent and those that are external and environmental. But in actual practice, this system breaks down in many ways, because the organism and the environment are constantly interacting so that the environment is modified by the organism and vice versa (1962 : 224).

In the case of man, the difficulties with the environmental concept are compounded because we have to deal with man as an animal and with man as a bearer of culture. If we look at man as an animal and try to analyze the environmental forces that are acting on the organism, we find that we have to deal with things like climate, soil, vegetation and such factors common to all biological situations. But we also find very important environmental influences that we can only class as "cultural," which modify the physical and biological factors. But man, as we know him, is always a bearer of culture; and, if we study human culture, we find that it, in turn, is called by the environmental factors of climate and geography. We, thus, easily get into great difficulties from the necessity of viewing culture, at one moment, as a part of the man and, at another, of the environment.

This perhaps helps to explain the difference in materials, emphasis, and conclusions that one is likely to find between textbooks of human geography and textbooks of cultural anthropology. The geographer tends to regard culture as a part of the man and is, thus, preoccupied in describing and explaining the environmental relationship of the man-culture system. The anthropologist, on the other hand, is likely to be preoccupied with culture as a thing-in-itself, and he, thus, tends to describe and explain human behaviour directly in cultural terms. It may be that the chief virtue in stressing an ecological point of view lies in the consequent necessity of reconciling these apparent differences: of treating culture in one context as a part of the man and in another as a part of the environment (*Ibid.* : 224).

The difficulties introduced by cultural factors are apparent in the studies of the effect of climate on man. The biologist can study the temperature conditions of the normal habitats of his organisms in nature and can check the effect on them of other temperature conditions in laboratory experiments, thus arriving at a description of the optimum and limiting temperatures for various species or for particular kinds of activity. But with man the variable of culture is always interposed between the climate and the organism—clothing, housing, and custom must always be taken into account (*Ibid.* 225).

By relating environment with the culture, the author tried to define the concept of community. No organism does live in isolation, nor is the behaviour of any organism understandable without reference to other organisms. The oak tree, the cricket, the nitrifying bacterium, the mushroom of the fairy ring—all are involved with one another in complicated patterns of food and energy relations, of protection and support, of competition and co-operation. But these relationships are not diffused at random through the biosphere. Closely associated organisms tend to form systems of relationships among themselves, forming patterns that are relatively complete and independent of other similar aggregations. Such associations, which go to make up a particular kind of forest, a pond, a bog, a coral reef, or tidal flat, are called "biotic communities."

The study of such communities is a major preoccupation of biological ecology. I cannot see, however, how this study can carry over directly to the human field. The human community is a very different thing from the biotic community and must be studied by very special methods. It is an accident of language convenience that we use the same word for both concepts. A biotic community is perhaps more properly called a "biocenosis" or "biome" and with such labeling the semantic confusion disappears. (*Ibid.* : 228).

Post-Neolithic man has come to form a biological community system of his own, with his domesticated plants and animals, his parasites and hangers-on, like weeds and rats and cockroaches; and the relationships among these organisms make an interesting and important field for study. But it is biological ecology as much as human ecology. When we move on into the field of social relations within the human community, to the study of Miami or of a Seminole village, we have moved into a field where biological factors are so completely swamped by cultural factors that we had better frankly admit that we have moved into a whole new area of science, where even analogies may be dangerous. Yet, man as a bearer of culture has developed from man as an animal, and his biological inheritance is still with him. The ecological point of view may be useful in trying to understand this biological basis of human nature.

Man is definitly a social animal—that is, he customarily lives as a part of aggressions that are larger than the family (parents and immediate offs-ring). The simplest known human economies are based on groups of several families, and it seems probable that man has been a social animal for a very long time. The fossil record gives some evidence of this, though necessarily indirect. It seems to me probable that man was a social animal before he became a bearer of culture, since I cannot imagine how the primordial elements of culture could have arisen in a non-social animal (*Ibid.*: 229).

Raymond F. Dasmann in his book *Environmental Conservation* (1968) discusses the need for an integrated approach to the problems of human environment. He says it has become apparent to the various specialists in environmental management, and is being demanded from many quarters. Conservation has become popular, and even the word "ecology" appears in the daily Press and is heard on commercial television. Is there a cause then for rejoicing? Unfortunately, no. The reason for the acceptance of the concept of conservation lies in the rapid deterioration of the human environment. It, therefore, expresses the opinion that in any planning for the future of man on this earth, we must also plan for the wild land and wild creatures which have been a part of his heritage and which must remain a part of his life if such life is to have much meaning (1968:ix). This book is an attempt to look at our environment and human problems from the viewpoint of conservation. It is an attempt to provide a factual basis on which action to improve the environment can be taken. Action without information usually leads to a worsening of the situation.

Thomas R. Detwyler points out in his book, *Man's Impact on Environment* (1971), that man-environment research has been neglected since the 1930s, when the flaws of "environmental determinism" became widely recognized. For the preceding several decades the occurrence of many of man's cultural characteristics were largely attributed to the nature of the environment where they were found, often without much evidence. This idea, promulgated by Friederich Ratzel, Ellsworth Huntington, Ellen Semple, and others, became firmly entrenched in anthropology and geography before it was gradually discredited and replaced by other explanations. The important point here is that in reaction to environmental determinism, these disciplines dampened all kinds of physical geography. This book squarely focuses on answers to the question "What is man doing to environment?"—revealing the wide spectrum of environmental changes brought by man.

Present processes of change: What human activities cause environmental change, and how? What are the basic and detailed causes for different changes? Which are deliberate and which inadvertent? *Environmental effects of man's activities*: Solutions to problem arising from such activities are treated only incidentally because (a) solutions must follow awareness and understanding of the problems (and there is no room to treat both adequately, and (b) feasible solutions to most environmental problems are a complex blend of environmental understanding, politics, economics, social attitudes, and technological capability. *"Detrimental" effects which cause or probably will cause problems for man*: A claim might be made that coverage is one-sided. However, in general, "good" effects are publicized and well known; "detrimental" effects are not and they merit attention because of possible grave consequences for man. *Complexity of change within systems*: Man's initial actions commonly trigger a chain of cause-and-effect relations and synergistic feedback within the total environmental system. These second, third, and higher order effects are usually unanticipated and often threatening to man. This book does not treat man's direct effects only (e.g., effects of smoking), but many indirect effects of man's health, economy and culture are discussed. *The scale of man's impact varies from the molecular to the global.* How do processes occurring at different scales in space and time interact? *The temporal and spatial trends of environmental modification are important*: Many of man's effect are intensifying and spreading (e.g., lead pollution from auto exhaust, now detectable on the Greenland icecap). Today, man's overall impact is greater than at any time in history. The force of man now rivals the strongest of nature's other forces. With this power comes the responsibility to understand the extended consequences of man's actions if his children are to have a life worth living.

In the book, *The Ainu Ecosystem: Environment and Group Structure (1972)*, Hitdshi Watanabe discusses the system of social solidarity between man and nature where it starts from Radcliff Brown's theory of totemism, and worked out an important basic concept of the subject of relation in myth order (Radcliffe-Brown, 1952 : 130-3). The recognition of the concept leads to that of various processes by which the natural order is brought within the social order. The subject which has been discussed here is the degree and kind of interest taken by a people in spatial orientation of natural phenomena around them, and its role in the process of bringing the natural order within the social order.

No attempt has been made of analyze the beliefs and rituals of the Ainu as integral of the system of relationships between their group life and their habitat or, in other words, as the system of social solidarity between the people and the natural world which works as counterpart to the ecological system. Yet, such analyses are thought to be essential to the understanding of the Ainu territoriality and, concurrently, of the distribution and workings of Ainu groups. The author tried to conceptualize the notion of solidarity by elaborating an example that, in the case of gathering, either fishing, hunting or collecting, in the territory of a different river group, one had to get permission from anyone of the headmen in the river valley, regardless of the method of one's fishing or hunting. Such permission was given on the performance of a ritual for local *kamui*-spirits concerned, but not always, because assurance was required that the fisherman on hunter be faithful to the local *kamui*-spirits concerned. The discoverer of any trespasser must bring him to his headman or some headman available at hand in the river valley, to make him apologize as soon as possible to the local *kamui*-spirits of the river concerned. Also, the discovery of such evidence of trespass as salmon bones thrown in the mountains of the river was a cause for serious issue, for it meant a grave offense to the *kamui* spirits of the river from which the people of the river or the river group received exclusive favour and which they guarded with greatest caution. The Ainu express the maintaining of their territory, that is, the territory of the river group, by the words 'the guard of our *iworu* owning *kamui* spirits'. Their territoriality was actually activated not only by economic interest but also by their system of social solidarity with nature as such. The Ainu world was full of divine visitors: all the natural resources exploited by them were *kamui* spirits in temporary guises. In consequence all their gathering activities implied social intercourse with *kamui*. Moreover, each *kamui* had its own function in relation to the economic and social activities of the Ainu. Thus there was close interdependence between Ainu and *kamui*, and their rituals and taboos were an expression of this relationship. The relationship, that is, the social solidarity between Ainu and *kamui* was established on the principle of coresidence of local contiguity. Ainu cosmology emphasized its component of spatial orientation; nature, i.e. *kamui*, was ordered on local basis. The effective ritual relationship between those spatially oriented *kamui* and the Ainu was in the hands of the matrilineal kin group of males which formed the basis of the Ainu local organization.

Robert A. de J. Hart in his book *Ecosociety : A Historical Study of Ecological Man* (1984), discusses that one of man's main hopes of surmounting the basic challenges of this most crucial era in world history must lie in an international programme of comprehensive resource development schemes, designed to meet essential human needs and to solve the problems of environmental pollution. Those people have built up a vast capital of survival techniques, based on personal observation of local soils, climates, crops and livestock which has been almost entirely ignored by the urban intellectuals who provide most of the administrators in the 'developed' and 'under-developed' nations alike. Far-sighted people admit the need to build up more ecologically adapted societies than the urban conglomerations, often with their squalid fringes of 'shanty-towns', which are mushrooming in countries where the dominant objectives are those of economic growth (1984 : l). Despite disasters of all kinds due to natural causes, wars, oppression and exploitation, it has been the family farm, the village, clan or tribe 'hefted' to its own piece of land, which, by its endurance, perseverance, skills, ingenuity, improvisations and continual creativity has maintained the fabric of human existence and the essential basis of civilisation. Every major achievement of mankind can, in fact, be traced, directly or ultimately, to the influence of an organic community, that is, a community whose people are united by biological links or by common culture, tradition and ideals to each other, and who have ecological 'roots' in the land whence they derive their means of subsistence. No man is an island. By giving the examples of many greatest geniuses of world culture, of whom Shakespeare, Leonardo da Vinci and Beethoven are three have been of peasant or yeoman stock. Their works have grown out of their native or ancestral soils and cultural atmospheres, which have provided both the emotional stability and stimulus, which are essential to the development of superior talent (*Ibid.*: 2).

There is an age-old peasant philosophy, derived from direct experience of natural laws, from the necessity of finding means of subsistence out of often intractable soils and from overcoming the ordeals of drought, flood, fire, storm, wild animals and human aggression. The two basic tenets of this philosophy are self-reliance and mutual aid. The earliest agricultural communities were groups of kinsfolk, members of extended families, clans or tribes and the principle of family responsibility remains the backbone of all vital peasant communities today. The orphans, aged and afflicted are not left to fend for themselves or become wards of the State, but are cared for by the community as a whole. Mutual aid is, in fact, the basic law of life. Every living being—micro- organism, plant, animal or man—comprises a complex of cells, all fulfilling their individual tasks in co-operation with each other. When one group of cells ceases to act co-operatively or seeks to assume a dominant role, there ensue disease, disintegration and death. Ecology studies the operation of this law within natural communities. An ecological community has an innate design, which seeks to sustain the laws, energy and processes of life. If allowed to develop its potentialities unhindered, it progresses from simplicity to complexity. The ecological climax to which most plant communities aim, where soil and climatic conditions are favourable, is the mixed forest, whose trees and other forms of vegetation provide 'niche-structures'—stable wombs in which the mobile entities, animals and human beings, can find refuge and shelter. Through the efforts of human beings the wild exuberance of the mixed forest is transformed into simplified and disciplined systems of agriculture and horticulture. Where these efforts have been carried out with wise husbandry and understanding of ecological laws and relationships, maintaining a wide variety of plants and livestock, the energy and productivity of nature has been conserved and even enhanced; but where wholesale destruction has been followed by monoculture, as has been the fate of so many wild areas subjected to Western technology, the result has too often been desolation, erosion and land-death (*Ibid.*: 3). It is sometimes possible to detect plant, animal and human forms, and they are believed to symbolise the complex interrelationships between different natural organisms and to represent an ecological view of man's place in nature. The author explains it by giving the example that, the science of ecology dates back a little more than a hundred years, but the peasant, living in the midst of nature and almost operating as a natural force himself, has always had an understanding of ecological relationships, derived from intuition, observation and experience. He has been, and is, the true ecological man (*Ibid.* : 4). In these days of 'Women's Lib.' it is of interest that, from the earliest times, women have generally enjoyed full equality, if not taken the lead, in peasant and tribal communities living in close ecological relationship to the soil. Their maternal instincts and commonsense have given them special aptitudes for recognising the nutritional and curative value of wild plants, for horticulture, for the rearing of animals, and, above all, for dealing with the psychological tensions implicit in organic, communal living. A notable example from modern China was the achievement of a Mongolian woman named Bolortoi in leading a successful reclamation project in an area of shifting sand-dunes in the Maowusu Desert.

Ecology and conservation, caring and sharing, are essentially feminine concepts, in contrast to the masculine instincts of domination and exploitation which have been responsible for so much of the spoliation of natural resources with which the Western world—and much of the rest of the world too—is faced today. The modern American Indian, in his reservation, surrounded by evidence of the effects of the most advanced industrialism, such as open cast mining, nuclear installations and the effects on wild life of pollution and poisonous sprays, still clings to his traditional faith in the Earth Mother and his profoundly ecological view of life. In an article in *Kainai News*, an Indian named John Smith wrote: The Indian relates to all living things; the grass, the trees and the animals. He sees the roundness of things, the cycles of nature, and how he himself fits together along with everything else at the breast of the Earth Mother (*Ibid.* 7).

In chapter one of the same book 'The Womb of Nature' it discuss that the early development of man, with his extreme vulnerability, highly complex nervous system and a brain more elaborate than any computer, must have taken place in particularly favourable environmental and social condition (*Ibid.* : 8). Man, in his early naked, homeless, relatively helpless state, must have grown to maturity in a temperate, 'natural orchard' landscape, with and abundance of wild fruits, nuts and edible shoots and leaves, and with few natural enemies in the form of savage animals or disease germs. He must have lived on good terms both with his environment and his fellow beings, animal and human, and this must have enabled him to enjoy long periods of physical and psychological security, without which normal development is impossible. In fact, those aspects of nature that are associated with the maternal, *yin*, principle must have been predominant in his life. With extraordinary foresight, nature provides 'nurse' conditions for the advent of higher, more delicate and sensitive organisms. This can be seen by examining the processes of ecological succession wherever life starts to colourize a hitherto barren landscape, such as the volcanic island, which recently arose from the sea off Iceland (*Ibid.* : 9). Hundreds of millions of years before the advent of the first man, nature seems to have prepared for that event by establishing the principle of the protected seed. The first manifestation of that principle was in those higher plants which provide for the perpetuation of their species by having their seeds embedded in fruits or nuts attractive to animals, thus ensuring that seeds are widely distributed together with manure to facilitate their germination and growth. By this means, also, ecological associations were built up between higher plants and higher animals—not only mammals and birds, but also the social insects, like bees and wasps, which are responsible for pollinating blossom. The most advanced form of the protected seed principle is the implantation and development of the ovum within the mammalian body (*Ibid.*: 9).

It is impossible to believe that early man adopted the unnatural habit of hunting until some change of climate impoverished the edible vegetation in his environment and made him desire the flesh and warm coats of his animal neighbours. But early man must also have eaten many vegetable products, which we, with our excessively refined tastes, would not find palatable today. Many North American Indian tribes have, throughout their history, eaten a wide variety of wild fruits, nuts, seeds, leaves, shoots, saps and tree barks which we would only tolerate as 'survival foods', and have shown great ingenuity in preparing them for consumption (*Ibid.* 10). The evolution of man's higher qualities was also facilitated by the unique characteristic of human family life. The close and lasting co-operative links of monogamy, with the husband constantly available to protect and support his wife during her periods of vulnerability, constituted a continuum within which the young human animal could progress slowly to maturity and learn the lessons and skills of life by direct contact with his elders. At an early stage, also, the qualities of responsibility and compassion, which are more highly developed in human beings than in any of the animals, led the nuclear family to expand into the extended family—which is still characteristic of peasant communities in many parts of the world. By this means, not only were havens of security provided for the orphan, the sick and the infirm, but the younger people had the continuing benefit of the wisdom and experience of their elders, at a time when the only storehouse of knowledge was the human memory. From the pre-literate period of human development stems the great epics, such as the *Finnish Kalevala* and the *Odyssey*, enshrining deep wisdom in symbolic forms, which were handed down from generation to generation by word of mouth (*Ibid.* 10).

The basis of human development was thus the ecological community: the group of human beings united by blood and affection and rooted in the environment which supplied all its physical needs, gradually discovering and developing wider potentialities in itself, in its members and the natural resources which surrounded it. Such a community provides not only a secure and stable framework but also continual stimuli for development, from contact with other human beings and from nature, including the birds and animals which existed in unimaginable abundance and were doubtless generally tame and friendly before the advent of hunting. From observing the habits of animals, early man must have learnt which plants were good to eat and also those that had curative powers. This practice of learning from animals has been continued by people living in close ecological relationship to their environment up to modern times (*Ibid.* : 11). It is not, of course, to be imagined that all communities of early men lived in perfect harmony within themselves, with their neighbours and with nature. There must have been many species and tribes of men and sub-men who, like the Neanderthal, died out because they lacked the qualities necessary for survival and evolution.

With the discovery of fire-making, the early cultivators must have initiated the 'slash-and-burn' system of shifting cultivation which is still followed in remote forest areas today, and was even practiced in parts of Finland not very long ago. This consists of burning down an area of forest and then sowing seeds in the wood-ash-enriched soils for a number of years, until the land begins to become exhausted and infested with weeds, when the area is left and the cultivators move to another area and start the same process. After the first area has been allowed to rest for a number of years, and its fertility restored by the natural processes of leaf-fall and managing by animals, the cultivators will return to it; so shifting cultivation can be a cyclic process covering a wooded area by static population living at its centre.

In chapter three of this book 'Tribe and Clan', the author discusses that— many tribal societies have lived—and some still live—nomadic or semi nomadic lives—ranging over wide areas with their flocks and herds, hunting, fishing, gathering wild plants or engaged in shifting cultivation. These societies seldom possess permanent settlements with substantial dwellings and well-defined areas of land under continuous occupations, but dwell in tents, tepees or huts that can easily be dismantled and moved.

In the Highlands of Scotland many clansmen used to live in cabins made of sods, which were periodically pulled down and spread on the land as manure. These societies often enjoy intense ecological relationships with the soils, plants and animals of the territories over which they roam, based on expert and intimate knowledge of their qualities and used as well as religious convictions concerning their spiritual essences and the hidden powers that regulate them. However, their stability and integrity do not depend on concepts of land-ownership but on close-knit ties of kinship, real or fictitious, often governed by complex traditional rules administered by the elders (*Ibid.* : 35). The author cites the example of Indians who spread across the hemisphere and their numbers multiplied, so they split up into tribes, which adapted their ways of life to their chosen environments. Some continued a mainly nomadic existence, as hunters and gatherers of wild plants, roaming wide but defined territories, notably in the areas of the Great Plains and the Great Basin of the West and Middle West of the present United States. In the South-West the Navajos adopted a largely pastoral life, as sheep and goat farmers, becoming the 'Bedouins of North America' in the deserts and arid plateau where their reservation—the largest in the United States–still exists in the states of Arizona and New Mexico. In what is now the Mexican border area, the Papagos and Pimas, like the Pueblo Indian, became desert farmers, acquiring advanced skills in cultivating and irrigating arid land and making the fullest possible use of cacti and other wild desert plants (*Ibid.* : 36).

The intense tribal solidarity of peoples such as the American Indian is something of which individualistic urban man has little conception. The sense of intolerable isolation experienced by tribal man when attempts are made to 'assimilate' him into a 'civilised' way of life, and he finds himself forced to live in some shanty suburb or skyscraper with thousands of other rootless human beings like himself, causes lasting psychological harm. To such a man life apart from the organic grouping too which he belongs has little meaning; man can only attain his full potentialities within the group framework. There life is not lived for oneself alone but for all; it is a life of 'caring and sharing', of mutual responsibility. Society accepts responsibility for the widow, the orphan and the aged; this knowledge gives a sense of security far more real than any afforded by state institutions or insurance schemes. It also gives rise to a rich and satisfying inner life; Ruskin wrote: "Intensity of life is intensity of helpfulness." In the larger

Indian tribes and nations the cohesive principle was manifested in a complex pattern of interwoven relationships, ranging from the nuclear family to the extended family and clan, and including religious groups, warrior societies and other organisations. These gave every individual a strong sense of significance, of belonging, of his own indispensability to the smooth running of the groups as a whole—something which urban man, with his fragmented lifestyle, has lost and seeks to replace by sporting loyalties and other artificial expedients. But in any society cohesiveness is not a matter of institutions but of deep-seated psychological controls, of an abiding sense of duty and discipline; and it is towards the development of these that the main emphasis of education is bent in any truly organic community (*Ibid.* : 40).

This fact has been clearly brought out in two studies of a tribe of the Amazonian rainforest, the Ye'cuana, characterised by a complete absence of centralised control. The first of these, by a Venezuelan anthropologist, Nelly Arvelo Jimenez, is called *The Dynamics of the Ye'cuana (Maquiritare) Political System: Stability and Crisis.* (IWGIA, Copenhagist, 1973). In it the author writes, "It has been suggested for such societies (lacking centralised power) that, in the absence of secular mechanisms for socio-political control, beliefs and institutions, which are primarily religious in nature, take their place and exert indirect control over the social behaviour of individuals?" The structural unit of Ye'cuana society is the evolving autonomous village—no higher authority exists. Within the village are a number of 'official' individuals or groups, but the offices of none are of long duration except that of the village headman, who maintains his position, not by legal sanction but by wisdom, tact and strength of character. His main functions are to uphold harmonious relations between families, take a lead in executing decisions reached by the senior-male circle and act as an ambassador in dealing with other villages. The senior-male circle consists mainly of heads of families who are brought together for ad hoc meetings on the initiative of the headman; any head of household has the right to veto any decision affecting the whole village; otherwise all decisions are by consensus. No formal procedure exists for dealing with disputes, crimes or moral offences, but these are settled by social and psychological processes of great subtlety, which are far more effective in healing, discordant and violent trends than the more severe and harsh legal procedures of 'civilisation'. In particular the accumulation of evidence and examination of motives are carried out by women's deliberation groups. A device frequently employed is temporary banishment or ostracism of an offending family or individual—not so much by way of punishment as to give the person or persons involved an opportunity to ponder their position and problems and regain psychological equilibrium. Where this device fails, the offenders' entire extended family may decide to secede from the village and either form a new village or seek to engraft itself on to another. Each village prizes its identity and, while relations with other villages are kept peaceful and subject to strict rules of etiquette, certain formal rituals of hostility are enacted during festivals in order to 'beat the bounds'. The central feature of each village is a round-based communal house, symbolising and reflecting the Ye'cuana concept of the universe; by virtue of this, the village, self- sufficient in the principal necessities of life, is regarded as a micro-cosm, a miniature replica of the universe. No clearer indication could be given of the village's claim to political autonomy (*Ibid.* : 41).

The age-old Ye'cuana system—doubtlessly typical of many societies living in Stone Age conditions —was subjected to a major test when the tribal territory was invaded by a nomadic group, the Guaharibo, at the end of the last century. Despite their stability and profound conservatism, the Ye'cuana adapted themselves to the challenge with great efficiency and worked out a harmonious and constructive solution. They split into small mobile groups, which melted into the depths of their forest environment-whose trails and remotest recesses had become familiar to them as a result of centuries of hunting expeditions. Unseen by their opponents, the Ye'cuana watched them and assessed their strengths, weaknesses and aims. At a strategic moment they then attacked the Guaharibo by surprise and succeeded in inflicting considerable losses, thus demonstrating their military superiority. In the subsequent peace negotiations, however, the Ye'cuana made no attempt to impose vindictive terms, but worked out a symbiotic lifestyle with the Guaharibo to the two tribes' mutual advantage. In exchange for certain tasks performed freely and seasonally for the Ye'cuana, the Guaharibo obtain industrial products for which they crave and which the Ye'cuana are able to get from Creole traders by bartering their fine craft-work, such as canoes, paddles, woodwork and basketry. The tasks performed by the Guaharibo include gathering forest products such as resins and fibers for the Ye'cuana in the course of their nomadic treks, and clearing land for fields, tracks and village sites by burning areas of forest (*Ibid.* : 41).

In 1969 the Ye'cuana experienced the most serious threat to their ecological way of life that they had ever had to face. The oil-rich Venezuelan state decided to 'open up' the southern jungle provinces of Bolivar and Territorial Amazons inhabited by the Ye'cuanas and other Indian tribes by means of an ambitious programmed with the grandiose title 'Conquest of the South'. Prospectors penetrated into the forests seeking natural resources and schemes were promoted for colonisation by white or half-cast Venezuelans. The Ye'cuanas' reaction to this crisis was a series of village fissions and fusions; old villages were split up and new ones formed; for the first time in their history, the cohesive solidarity of Ye'cuana extended families was infringed. Whether the tribe will succeed in establishing a new equilibrium and reverting to its traditional life style, as it has been following previous alien incursions, remains to be seen. To the Ye'cuana, freedom is a supremely important value—many of them committed suicide rather than submit to enslavement by white rubber prospectors at the beginning of the century. But in the latest crisis their extremely de-centralised political system is proving disadvantageous, as they have difficulty in finding Spanish-speaking leaders capable of negotiating with the authorities at Caracas and stating the case of the tribe as a whole. It is to be hoped that, with their genius they will succeed in working out a solution to their problems based on a closer on a political cohesiveness of the entire tribe.

The author referred to a study on Ye'cuana is contained in a remarkable book, *The Continuum Concept* by Jean Liedloff (Duckworth, London, 1975) which deals largely with child upbringing. Strangely enough the author never gives a precise definition of the Continuum Concept, but by giving numerous examples of its working, largely drawn from Ye'cuana life, she makes its nature clear. It is nothing less than a development of maternal-mammalian protectiveness and stimulus, which has been the main biological mechanism responsible for the evolution of higher animals and man, into the sphere of communal living (*Ibid.* : 42). The essence of Continuum, as manifested in Ye'cuana life, is mutual support, the confidence felt by every member of the villege, of every age, that he can count on the spiritual backbone of the community in any emergency. This starts at birth. "From birth", Miss Liedloff writes, "continuum infants are taken everywhere before the umbilical cord comes off, the infant's life is already full of action. He is asleep most of the time, but even as he is becoming accustomed to the voices of his people, to the sounds of their activities, to the bumping, jostling and moves without warning, to stops without warning, to lifts and pressures on various parts of his body as his caretaker shifts him about to accommodate her work of her comfort, and to the rhythms of day and night, the changes of texture and temperature on his skin and the safe, right feeling of being held to a living body." As a result of this uninterrupted contact with his mother's body and activities, the Ye'cuana child quickly imbibes an intimate understanding of his environment and a knowledge of basic skill. These developments are furthered by the parents who, on the one hand, allow their children the utmost possible freedom to gain their own impressions and experiences, while, on the other they maintain their children's balance and assurance by being available in emergencies. "A daily bath is routine from birth, but every infant is also dipped into fast rivers; first only his feet, then his legs, then his entire body. The water goes from swift to swifter and on to plunging rapids and falls, the times of exposure lengthens too as the baby's response reveals growing confidence. Before he can walk or even think, a Ye'cuana baby is well on the way towards expertise in judging the force, direction and depth of water by sight" (*Ibid.* : 43). The principle of potential support continues throughout life. The main group within the Ye'cuana village is the extended family of at least three generations. All of them, young, old, strong and weak, are prepared to put forth a great concentrated effort to help any of their member who is in serious difficulty, and any man or woman who commits a crime or in any other way comes into conflict with the village as a whole can be sure of the collective support of his entire extended family. Social responsibility rather than competitiveness characterises the whole of Ye'cuana life, and as everyone, from earliest childhood, is expected to act altruistically rather than selfishly without compulsion, the wheels of life within the village in general turn with incredible smoothness (*Ibid.*).

In reference to another study the author states that "The traditional African family lived according to the basic principle of ujamaa. Its members did this unconsciously, and without any conception of what they were doing in political terms. They lived together and worked together because that was how they understood life, and how they reinforced each other against the difficulties they had to contend with—the uncertainties of weather and sickness, the depredation of wild animals, (and some times human enemies), and the cycle of life and death. The family member thought of themselves as one, and all their language and behaviour emphasised their unity.... They lived together and worked together; and the result of their joint labour was the property of the family as a whole" (*Ibid.* : 44). "This pattern of living was made possible because of three basic assumptions of traditional life. The first of the basic assumptions, or principles of life, I have sometimes described as love, but that word is so often used to imply a deep personal affection that it can give a false impression. A better word is perhaps respect, for it was — and is — really recognition of mutual involvement in one another. Even the most junior wife in a polygamous household had respect due to her; she had a right to her own house and in relation to her husband, and she had full access to the joint products of the family group. Within the extended family, and even within the tribe, the economic level of one person could never get far out of proportion to the economic level of others.... Inequalities existed, but they were tempered by comparable family or social responsibilities, and they could never become gross and offensive in the social equality which was at the basis of communal life. It is a necessary principle that everyone had an obligation to work" (*Ibid.* : 45).

Another African writer, Jimoh Omo-Fadaka, writes in a UNESCO publication, *Impact of Science on Society* (Vol. XXIII, No. 2, 1973): "The people were bound together not only economically and politically, but religiously and socially by a system of collective activity and mutual help which extended from the family to the ethnic group as a whole. It was a give-and-take policy, with a sense of belonging and brotherhood serving as the cornerstone of Tanzania's traditional extended family system. In crisis or hardship, the individual could depend on the family of clan for help. The extended family scheme constituted social security which followed the natural pattern of personal relationships.... The strength and number of social ties between members of the same family, clan or age group and between different families and clans meant that the community could be very easily mobilized for co-cooperative activity. The building of houses, fences of bridges, cultivation and harvesting, even sewing, were usually group activities"(*Ibid.* : 46).

In many African ecosocieties, as in those of other continents, the spirit of co-operation extends beyond the social and natural environments to the supernatural—the 'happy hunting grounds', of the tribal ancestors.

To the Shona tribe as to the people of other ecosocieties, the essence of life is unity. They are bound by a complex of ties—to their families, extended families, clans, tribes, nation, ancestors and land. These ties are not regarded as inhibiting their freedom, for along them, as along a coil of electric wires, there passes a continual stream of vital force, which is stimulating, healing and stabilising in its effect (*Ibid.* : 46).

Carolyn Merchant in his edited work *Key Concept in Critical Theory: Ecology*, states that domination is one of our century's most faithfu l concepts for understanding human-human and human-nature relationships. The theme of domination and its reversal through liberation unites critical theorist and environmental philosophers whose work spans the twentieth century. When the domination of nonhuman nature is integrated with the domination of human beings and the call for environmental justice, Critical Theory instills the environmental movements with ethical fervor. This book brings together the Frankfurt school's analysis of domination with the insights of today's deep, social, and socialist ecologists, ecofeminists, people of colour, spiritual ecologists, and postmodern scientists. There is much disagreement over why and how nature and humans are linked and what to do about changing those linkages.

From the 1920s, the Institute for Social Research in Frankfurt had attempted to develop a multidisciplinary theory of society and culture that would bring together critiques and alternatives to mainstream social theory, science, and technology and address social problems. They expanded on Marxism by extending its analysis of political economy to the interconnections between and among the spheres of nature, economy, society, politics, psychology, and culture. They characterized their approach as a comprehensive, totalizing theory of dialectical interactions among the various aspects of society. They were deeply concerned about the problems they associated with modernity—the period from the Renaissance and Reformation to the era of state capitalism in the twentieth century—and the concept of enlightenment that epitomized the modern world. Horkheimer and Adorno exposed the Greco-Roman roots of individualism, science, and the domination of nature that reached a crescendo in the eighteenth century's Age of Enlightenment. Rather than seeing the progressive aspects of modernity in which science, technology, and capitalism increasingly improve on the human condition, they emphasized modernity's dehumanizing tendencies, its destruction of the environment, its potential for totalitarian politics, and its inability to control technology (1994: 2).

Critical Theory drew its initial inspiration from Marxism. Karl Marx and Friedrich Engel's nineteenth century critique of the inequalities created by industrialization's separation of capital from labour, entrepreneurs from working people, mind from body, and humanity from nature went to the heart of the problem of social justice. Under capitalism, justice and equality for every person could never be achieved because of the structural constraints built into capital's need to expand its sphere continually, by using nature and humans as resources. While Marx and Engel's displayed an extraordinary understanding of and sensitivity towards the "ecological" costs of capitalism, as revealed in the selection of their work edited by Howard Parsons, they nevertheless bought into the Enlightenment's myth of progress via the domination of nature.

Working in New York City and Los Angeles, California in the 1940s, Horkheimer and Adorn turned their attention to the problem of the domination of nature and human beings. In the ancient world the emergence of a sense of self as distinct from the external natural world entailed a denial of internal nature in the human being. Tribal societies pursued their needs through the imitation of nature. Human beings became as much like the animals they hunted as possible. Power over nature, hence self preservation was achieved through imitative magic. Enlightenment thinking disenchants nature by removing that magic and turning the subject into an object, and that process of objectification distances subject from object. In the early modern era the domination of nature reached a new level in the thought of Francis Bacon. In the early seventeenth century, Bacon advocated experimental science that put nature on the rack and tortured "her" to reveal "her" secrets. Power over nature was subsequently extended to mathematics and physics by Rene Descartes and Isaac Newton (*Ibid.* : 3).

The disenchantment of external nature was achieved by despiritualizing a human being's internal nature. Bourgeois society lived according to quantification, calculation, profits, exchange, and the logic of identity. But so deeply imbedded does this way of thinking become that it is presumed to be reality by mainstream society. So powerful is the mystique of reason as instrument in the control of nature and human bodies that it banishes other modes of participating in the world to the periphery of society. Logic and mathematics along with the calculus of capital become privileged modes of thought, defining the very meaning of truth. The identity "a = a" in logic and between the two sides of an equation in mathematics allows instrumental reason to describe the natural world. Describing the world through logic and mathematics, in turn, leads to prediction and hence to the possibility of controlling nature. Instrumental reason and enlightenment are thus synonymous with domination (*Ibid.* : 4). The domination of external nature by internal nature exacts a cost. The repression of human emotions and animal pleasures leads not to human happiness, but to anguish. But the tighter the rein, the greater the potential for rebellion. The revolt of nature is thus contained within the enlightenment project. Internal nature rebels psychically, spiritually, and bodily. External nature revolts ecologically. Here Critical Theory and the ecology movement intersect.

Horkheimer and Adorn in their book *Dialectic of Enlightenment* emphasize the flux between mimesis and enlightenment. Mimesis, like enlightenment, depends on identity. Identifying with another subject through imitation allowed for self-preservation in tribal societies. Naming of plants and animals entailed the identification of characteristics that remain constant through change. Names in turn bring power in ritual magic. Yet at the same time, mimesis retains its original sense of participation in nature. On the other hand, enlightenment is also myth. Its historical specificity, its contextuality within modernity, and its limited truth domain destroy its claims to absolute knowledge. The myth of enlightenment is the guiding story of modernity.

The domination of internal nature makes possible the domination of external nature, which in turn leads to the domination of human beings. The relationship between the domination of nature and the domination of human beings was explicitly stated by Adorn in a 1955 essay on the German historical Oswald Spengler: "The confrontation of man with nature, which first produces the tendency to dominate nature, which in turn results in the domination of man by other men, is nowhere to be seen in the *Decline of the West.*" The domination of external nature therefore proceeds, and is a condition for, the domination of human beings in society.

Horkheimer and Adorno's analysis of the dialectics of various forms of domination—internal, external, human and nonhuman—thus sets up a problematic for future work on the roots of the ecological crisis. It opens room for discussion of the many aspects of the relationships between domination and the life world—women, minorities, technology, economy, justice, spirit, and science.

Herbert Marcuse in his books *Eros and Civilization* (1955), *One Dimensional Man* (1964), *Counterrevolution and Revolt* (1972) applied critical theory to social reproduction by examining the role of mass media, the control of information, and the decline of the family in maintaining the culture of needs necessary to the success of capitalism. Although Marcuse was not an ecological philosopher, he did address the issue of ecology in a special symposium on 'Ecology and Revolution' published in *Liberation* magazine in 1972. He saw ecology as a revolutionary force of life; against which the counterrevolutionary forces of ecocide were destroying "the sources and resources of life itself" in the service of monopoly capital. Writing in the context of Vietnam War, Marcuse connected the genocide and ecocide in North Vietnam, which at the time were being carried out through modern science and technologies showcase weapons—the "electronic battlefield" and chemical defoliants—with the wider war against nature. Similarly, the same process that transforms people into objects in a market society also transforms nature into commodities, leaving little natural beauty, tranquility, or untouched space. The ecology movement exposes this war against nature and attacks the space capital carves out for its own. William Leiss published a major treatise, on *The Domination of Nature* (1972) where he explores the legacy of Horkheimer and Adorno, who had returned to Frankfurt after the War. Elaborating on the role of Francis Bacon in setting the modern agenda of power over nature through science and technology, Leiss analyzed technology's role in mastering both the external world of nature and the human being. "In the process of globalized competition men become the servants of the very instruments fashioned for their own mastery over nature." The result is the revolt of nature, both internal and external, in a "blind irrational outbreak of human nature" and the concomitant collapse of ecological systems (Leiss: 1972).

According to Eckersley, political theory needs to move towards an ecocentric approach to the human-nature relationship. "Ecocentric theorists", she writes, "are concerned to develop an ecologically informed approach that is able to value (for their own sake) not just individual living organisms, but also ecological entities at different levels of aggregation, such as populations, species, ecosystems, and the ecosphere". (cited, *Ibid.* : 6)."

In this connection economists like While Daly set out the conditions for a sustainable economy, sociologists like Len Doyal and Ian Gough delineate conditions for a socially just society. The new reality is that the awareness of the delicacy of the biosphere must now go hand in hand with democratically planned production for human need (Doyal and Gough 1986). Fulfillment of basic needs entails individual human health and autonomy. For individual needs to be fulfilled, societies have to be able to reproduce themselves. They have to produce the basic needs of material life—food, clothing, shelter, and energy and to provide the conditions for physical and emotional health. Children must be socialized, educate, and taught to communicate in order to become independent adults, and there must also be some means of maintaining social order. Social justice involves a guarantee of basic liberties, such as free speech and the right to assemble the removal of social inequalities that prevent equitable distribution of social goods, and equality of opportunity. How these basic needs are to be satisfied in a sustainable world entails the relationship between the state and human liberty and the problem of liberation of nature. One avenue for bringing about a sustainable society and socially just world is through green politics. Creating a green future starts at grassroots level with individual empowerment, coalition building, and living within the means of the bioregion. The green programme for change is based on four pillars: ecology, grassroots democracy, social justice, and nonviolence (*Ibid.* : 8).

To overcome the deeply engrained anthropocentrism at the root of the domination of nature requires a new philosophy and ethics. Deep ecologists argue that mainstream environmentalism is limited and incremental in scope and that what is needed before real change can occur is a transformation in consciousness. Fundamental to the deep ecological approach is the need to overcome a narrow anthropocentrism dominant in Western culture. Yet deep ecology's focus on anthropocentrism also masks the role of capitalism and political economy in the domination of nature and human beings (*Ibid.* : 8).

An alternative to deep ecology has been developed by Murray Bookchin. He argues that as opposed to deep ecologists, critical theorists, and

Marxists, the domination of human beings is historically and causally prior to the domination of nature. For example, the early tribal societies were basically egalitarian and lived within nature, the increasing prestige of male elders created social hierarchies and inequalities that led to power over other human beings, especially women, ultimately over nature. The growth of ancient city-states, medieval walled towns, and state capitalism depended on increasingly entrenched hierarchies of elders over other tribal members, men over women, and elites over labourers and slaves. This social domination led to the domination of people over nature. The goal of social ecology is to remove hierarchy and domination from society, including the domination of people over nature. Bookchin's ecological anarchism envisions an ecological society to be achieved through reliance on the resources and energy of the local bioregion, face-to-face grassroots democracy within libertarian municipalities linked together in a confederation, and the dissolution of the state as a source of authority and control (*Ibid.* : 9).

Indian Studies

Ecological analysis has been further focused by a classical and pioneering Indian social scientist Prof.Radhakamal Mukerjee. His pioneering work, *Man and his Habitation: A Study in Social Ecology* (1968) defines that, the methods of plant and animal ecology "greatly help towards a scientific study of the spatial, occupational and temporal relationships of human beings". He further says that "symbiotic relationships between different groups of people with their different modes of exploitation of resources and social habits develop so that the region becomes an assemblage of ecological patterns" (*Ibid.* : v). Here exclusively he has dealt with "the study of the human individual in his reactions to the environment, physical and organic; his adaptation to soil and climate as well as his structural and behavioural responses to his habits and occupations, and to his relations with other individuals of his own or other communities" (*Ibid.* : v). The interchange between man, his habitations, resources and technology and his social habits and values is reciprocal and intimate. Mukerjee gives the example of crowded plains of India and South-East Asia, as it is "subject to intensive, one-sided exploitation and depletion for successive generations". He further shows his concern that the new technology and new economic and ecological planning will have to be aided and reinforced by the human community's recovery of its ancient sensitiveness and responsiveness to Mother Nature and Mother Earth. Therefore, social ecology has tremendous practical significance for modern urban-industrial culture that has spread as a global pattern in East and West (*Ibid.* : viii). Ecology being a comprehensive science, it opens out many approaches to the study of man's social orientation and behaviour. Mukerjee in his *Regional Sociology* (1926) defines the scope of human ecology "as a synoptic study of the balance of plant, animal and human communities, which are systems of correlated working parts in the organisation of the region" (*Ibid.* : ix.). Therefore, social ecology stresses the ever-complex give-and-take between man and the region, and attributes the present social disorganization as much to the ecological unbalance of the region, and between different types of habitations as to the sophisticated habits and artificial patterns of living of the population.

Kidar Nath Thusu and Makhan Jha have conducted an ethnographic survey and its report is entitled as *Ollar Gadba of Koraput* (1972). This, ethnographic survey of the selected tribes of central India, was assigned to carry a field work among the group of people called the Ollar Gadba of Koraput, Orissa. A detailed comparative study on different aspects of the life of these two neighbouring and linguistically related groups of people will be fruitful in more than one respect. It may be remarked at this stage that there are some common oral traditions that are still in practice among these groups of people, respectively, known as the Dhurwa (Parja) and the Ollar Gadba.

The book, *Anthropological and Sociological Theory: Approaches and Applications* (1984) by R. S. Mann, describes about 'Ecology and Society in Ladakh'. Some accounts of Ladakhi life and culture are revealing of the fact that there is a substantial contribution of eco-system in the make-up of Ledakhi way of life in particular forms. Sometimes, the eco-system attributes can be seen in a way as if they are the determinants of particular life-styles. They have certainly, had their say in the shaping of some social relations. At times, it appears as if the ways have been conditioned by the external ecological factors (1984 : 290). However in certain other spears, more related to material culture, instances and explanations have been put forth which indicate that there has been conspicuous element of adaptability in the interaction with eco-system. Ways could be devised to take maximum advantage of the surrounding conditions. In such cases, one carries an impression that the Ladakhi society has adapted itself to the eco-system prevalent around. Thus, in the building up of certain aspects of Ladakhi social structure, the adaptation and 'conditioning or determinant' variables, in respect of eco-system, have been involved. There has been a sufficient inter-play between eco-system and the Ladakhi society and its specific cultural patterns.

By describing the village settlement in Ladakh, the author states that the villages are either in and along the valleys, or on the foot-hills. Such valleys are along riversides. The foot-hills, as sites for village settlement, are mostly those where the hills above remain covered with snow (*Ibid.* : 293). The author gives an example of adaptability, which is reflected through a particular kind of house design. This is primarily to overcome severe winter of Ladakh. In the first floor of Ladakhi house is kept an apartment used as latrine. The kitchen, in a big hall, is again in the first floor and keeps the air warm inside. All family members sleep around the fireplace to protect against the severe chill (*Ibid.* : 294). Among the Ladakhis, there are two major divisions of household. One is known as *Khangchen*, and the other as *Khaon*; *Khangchen* is the ancestral house, occupied by the married sons and their wife/wives and the children. A *Khangchen* is more important as it retains family worship room, and the family name, too, goes with it. In case of Ladakhis where a son or sons get married and beget children, the parents, with their unmarried daughter or son, if any, leave the ancestral household and start living in a separate house which is called *Khaon*. The separating parents are also allotted some land to bank upon. Such a separation or division of family is not for the sake of privacy or to avoid conflicts. Rather, it is because of the hard conditions under which the people have to earn their living.

Because of extreme cold and arid climatic conditions, special kind of food and clothing were required by the people, and the same were locally managed. The source of livestock has been greatly tapped for the purpose. To overcome arid conditions, and also for energy purpose, the Ladakhis drink butter-tea. Depending upon the economic position of the family, a Ladakhi may consume as much as twenty cups of this tea a day. That means the butter requirement is very high. This is procured from various animals domesticated by the Ladakhis. Then, because of high altitude, one feels breathlessness while walking fast or carrying load. To carry load, especially the compost from house to the fields, every Ladakhi family keeps a donkey. For clothing and shelter too, the Ladakhis procure material from the livestock. From Yak's hair are prepared the ropes and tents. Woollen clothes are made from the wool of sheep and goat. The people themselves do the spinning and weaving. A major part of fuel, required in extreme winter, is obtainted from the animal dung. The skin, worn by the women on their backs, a very common feature, is the goat or sheep skin. Such a wear is partly the matter of pride, and partly serves as a device for the protection of garments worn by the ladies. The sole of the shoes, that Ladakhis wear, is made out of the woollen threads, properly knitted and weaved. The height of this shoe sometimes reaches up to the knee (*Ibid.* : 296).

The author describes that the pattern of social grouping, beyond the level of family, is also essentially an outcome of the compulsion of eco-system. Such a grouping is different than extended family or lineage groups, which are essentially based on kinship. Because of hard and difficult conditions, there is the requirement of co-operation and interdependence among the people. One source of cooperation is that the persons are related through blood and marriage ties. The other are those who are members of the same *Phasphun*. The latter is a group not necessarily based on agnatic or affined links. Rather, its formation is sustained on religious binding (*Ibid.* : 300). It may however be stressed that eco-system, society and its culture are greatly inter-linked. The former can have say in the shaping, in particular forms, of social and material life, especially in ecological settings as that of Ladakh. Certain areas of social structure, thus, can be better understood and explored through eco-system, in addition to the use of other tools for social explanations (*Ibid.* : 310).

Moonish Raza has written in an article 'Ecology and Development: Synoptic View' in H.S. Sharma and M.L. Sharma's edited volume *Environmental Design and Development : Conflict or Harmony ? (1987)* where he notes that the realms of nature and culture or between the worlds of man and that of his non-human environment lead to a situation wherein each segment of knowledge ends up, in its own specifically sophisticated manner, with an aspectual, distorted and limited vision of that which is, definitionally, mistaken for the integrated, living, ever-changing system of interdependencies (1987: 1). The essentiality of man and nature is based on "man as a natural being and nature as a human reality". Since the naturalization of man and dehumanization of, nature proceed simultaneously through man's interaction with nature, human history may be viewed as to continuance of, and a qualitatively new stage in natural history—the two constituting a differentiated unity. Nature comes within the orbit of development primarily as a constituent element transforms it, and itself gets transformed in the process. In the process of transforming nature and himself, social man moves from the realm of necessity to that of freedom. Freedom should not be confused with the "self-determination of the spirit" or the so-called "freedom of will" which puts it outside the purview of the compulsions of nature. Neither should of necessity be equated with mechanistic determinism, which negates the role of human will and considers the action and behaviour of man as the function of objective nature alone. "Necessity is blind only insofar it is not understood". As man marches onwards on the basis of understanding natural laws and systematically making them "work towards definite ends", he steps into freedom though continuing to be within the gravitational field of necessity, which no longer remains blind but becomes an instrument of conscious social practice. The realm of freedom is the Noosphere, the sphere of the planet earth which has been "humanized" by rational human activity. The traditional division of the planet into the lithosphere, hydrosphere, atmosphere and the bio-sphere may interest the geologist, the hydrologist, and the meteorologist, but these layers enter into the development process not separate from but in intrinsic relationship with each other. In order to be able to interact effectively with nature through the use of the instruments of labour, man has to come to terms with other men, and, as a consequence, has to build a system of institutions–economic, social and political. The latter constitute facets of a complex sub-system, integrated the eco-system with every fiber of its being, this makes social life possible, and the process of humanising nature to proceed in desired directions (*Ibid.* : 4).

Nature provides the bases, lays down the limits of freedom and indicates the direction along which optimum appropriation through social labour is possible in the long run. Technology aids natural processes, bends them to human (or shall we say humane) purposes, modifies them and thus extends the range of freedom. Institutions are either conducive to or restrictive of man-nature interaction. The development process unifolds itself through, integrating the anthropogenetic and the non-human components into a system of interdependencies. Unless the concept of the eco-system, as a holistic complex of interdependencies, subsumes within it this anthropogenetic component, operationalised through the triangle of force in the development process, it would cease to be the concept of the system and would flounder in the quick-sands of its own inadequacies. The concept of the eco-system has arisen as an intellectual construct as a timely corrective to the academic tradition of the post-industrial society based on the disagregation of the totality into facets, aspects, parts or fragments for deeper study and analysis, thereby engendering the knowing of more and more about less and less till, as a wag remarked, one finally ends up by knowing everything about nothing. The gap between the essentially holistic character of the objectively existing system and its fragmented cognition through disaggregated analysis has already become serious constraint on and had led to a crisis in knowledge. Like all the significant ideas of science, the scientific conceptualization of the eco-system, which is a recent product of the intellectual crisis of the post-industrial society, is rooted in a pre-scientific tradition of great chronological depth and is, in fact, embedded in the basal psyche of the homo sapien (*Ibid.* : 5).

However, the social sciences have moved towards a certain degree of internal cohesion, the world of non-human nature is still alien to it, at best producing unnecessary noise in their sophisticated computer programmes. Let us reiterate that development is operationalized through a triangle of forces, where in nature lays down the limits of freedom and indicates the direction of optimal advance, wherein technology extends the area of freedom within the general orbit of necessity; and wherein institutions are either conducive for restrictive to man's interaction with nature through technology (*Ibid.* : 6). Moreover it is only by viewing the development processes that we can steer clear of two erroneous strategies: first, the strategy of "development" at all cost, leading to eco-destruction; and second, the strategy of rejecting development in the name of ecology.

Within the conceptual frame presented above, the ecology-development contradiction is a false contradiction. The laws of nature not only impose constraints on but also point to the direction of optimal development. Unless this dual relationship between the ecological correlates and the development processes fully recognized, it tends to get neck deep in the morass of "hippie" ecology— the spurious environmental concerns of the "flower people for whom nature is a virgin which should not be violated through human intervention. The author states that our concern with ecology within the framework of an eco-systemic approach is directed to optimising (and not maximizing) development so as to extricate people from the vicious stronghold of hunger and poverty; or, in the Third World, hunger continues to be a most potent pollutant—an eco-destructive force of tremendous magnitude. It destroys man, the crucial component of the contemporary eco-systems (*Ibid.* : 7).

However, there is no essential contradiction between development and ecology, there is no essential contradiction between urbanization and ecology either. Urbanization is intrinsically linked and irrevocably intervocable, intertwined with the development process, and should be viewed as an essential element in the anthropogenesis component of eco-systems. The lesson that the developing countries have to learn from the historical experience of the development ones does not lie in the rejection of urbanisation but in its regulation not through the market mechanism but through social controls, not through the maximization of private profit but through the optimization of social benefits. The hiatus does not lie in technology but in social organization, which has shown a unique incapacity to implement these technically feasible solutions. Let us save ecology from development no doubt at the same line, let us save development from ecology, as well.

This argument is further developed by another eminent geographer and social scientist of M.H. Qureshi in his paper entitled, 'The Interactive System of Man and His Environment–An Appraisal' where he focuses that, all human societies owe their economic development to the interactive dynamism between 'untiring man' and 'ever-changing earth'. This interactive is regulated through man's labour and through which he transforms the environment, and in turn, he gets himself transformed (*Ibid.* 21). The environment, besides indicating the direction of development, sets limit on the extent of development. This limit varies from society to society and region to region depending upon the level of technology available to them. Further, this limit is not fixed, rigid or permanent. The man's relationship with environment is a relationship of mutual interaction and mutual transformation. We cannot think of 'non-humanised nature and non-naturalised man'. "He (the man) alone among the known species of the planet, just does not adapt himself to nature but is an actually interacts with it; who is not only a passive element but is an active factor in the eco-system; who does not only vegetate and survive within the orbit of blind necessity but operates with in a realm of freedom;

cognising laws of nature so as to transform it" (*Ibid.*: 22). Man's tool of transforming the nature has been the technology available to him. Hence the shackles of environmental factors have been strong and persist to remain strong in those societies where technology is backward. This has brought heterogeneity in the level of development of various regions. It does not mean that the process of brining sophistication has stopped. Man has always endeavoured to modify and refine the available technology in order to achieve higher efficiency, to reduce the drudgery of the work and also to obtain longer periods of leisure fulfill his higher needs (*Ibid.* : 22).

The technology might be primitive or sophisticated depending upon the level of intellection and the intellectual attainment in different societies. The technology is not ubiquitous. There is a definite lag in its invention and diffusion. It has its own peculiar characteristics, which are responsible for uneven adoption and consequent inequality in the same society. The characteristics lead to inequality within the same society because of the owners of better technology and have larger freedom, and it becomes unavoidable where private ownership is prevalent. The situation can be corrected only by the social checks provided within an institutional frame. The unsuitable desire to enter into the realm of freedom leads man to more inventions. The new vistas of development are opened, new means of subsistence are unwilled and man moves towards larger freedom taking advantage of his new searches. The light of knowledge reveals the darkness of unknown and the horizons of known expand (*Ibid.* : 23). The author cites empirical studies of two districts selected for illustration in the present paper which lie on the western margins of Rajasthan State, sharing the international boundary with Pakistan. In spite of this similarity, there are glaring differences in the levels of their economic development. The human intervention through the technology at its command has mainly been responsible for this difference (*Ibid.* : 27).

Veena Bhasin in his book *Ecology, Culture and Change: Tribals of Sikkim Himalayas* (1989) studied two tribals *Lepchas* and *Bhutias* of North Sikkim and their relationship between man and nature has been examined to show how and where eco-system and socio-cultural factors are interconnected. The ecological perspective was essential, since both these people, though living in North Sikkim, show socio-economic features, which are sharply contrasted, yet display certain similarities. They are situated in distinct physical environments, and it appears reasonable to assume that geographic factors may be a major cause of their distinctiveness. The *Lepchas* of Dzongu live in hilly-forest terrain; the *Bhutias* of Lachen-Lachung are inhabiting a high-altitude environment with scanty vegetation and a few domesticated plants. The study pursues cultural adaptation in forest-hilly environment in Dzongu as well as the process of change in Lachen-Lachung after the closure of border trade and re-orientation of the existing economic resources. Different ecological factors are responsible for economic arrangements improvised by the population. *Lepchas*, living at lower altitude practice agriculture, and *Bhutias*, at higher altitude mix farming and pastoralism, though in varying degrees. *Lepchas* are the original inhabitants of Sikkim, while *Bhutias* came from Tibet and Bhutan. Both the areas have remained isolated for long periods. This isolation was not complete. Isolation of a region, community or individual promotes self-sufficiency. It is equally true that self-sufficiency can promote isolation by making it unnecessary to seek elsewhere for goods or assistance. Isolation was thus a feature of environment, political subjugation and a matter of choice based on these considerations.

Likewise the work of Ramachandra Guha—a social historian—who has firmly established the field of social ecology in India, by choosing to follow an illustrious sociologist, Radhakamal Mukherjee's approach. In the book *Unquiet Woods* (1989), Guha tries to bring out an ecological perspective in sociology by the study of agrarian history and peasant resistant movements. He is concerned that the Indian historians neglect the relation between colonialism and ecological decline. He says the important consequences of the colonial rule were the system of "commercial forestry it introduced". Guha's work falls in the area of historical sociology or social history.

C.V. Rajashekhar in his edited work *Environmental Factors in Economics and Industrial Management, Vol. IV* (1992) observes that the state of the environment today is but an indicator of the crucial juncture at which mankind stands in its path of development, progress and prosperity. The breakdown of societies and governments the world over, is reflected in the destruction and gradual elimination of the ecological system that has sustained, nurtured and fed human beings for centuries untold.

Development is today symbolized tragically by the thousands of millions of factory chimneys that spew out poisonous gases into the atmosphere, river tributaries that carry millions of tonnes of toxic substances into the sea and barren slopes of hitherto green-clad hills and mountains denuded by greed, want and wastefulness of a so-called civilisation that actually has lost sight of all that is truly valuable and precious, not only for ourselves but for the generations to come. The environment and the ecosystem are being polluted beyond repair and all of mankind seems to be oblivious of the monumental catastrophe that awaits our unborn children (1992: preface).

In tropical regions of the world, growing populations in rural areas, including those in India, burn forest wood as domestic fuel and also burn forests to clear the land for grazing and cultivation, releasing more carbon dioxide to the air. The gas has accumulated more rapidly than it has been absorbed by natural processes, reacting a kind of "dirty window" over the planet Earth. Its effect is similar to that of a greenhouse, which allows visible light from the sun to reach and warm the earth's surface but prevents infra-red energy from radiating back into space (*Ibid.* : v). Even virgin forests are not free from the pernicious effects of man's mindless activities in the name of industrialisation and development. Not only does man litter, at the least, but also cuts, chops, slashes, slices, shreads and destroys. This applies particularly appropriately to his depredations of the forests all over the world for profit. Large tracts of virgin forests in Europe and North America are now withering because of airborne pollution as instead of the life-giving showers, what falls gently from the heavens is without mercy, that is acid rains. There are reports that there are several species of plants sensitive to sulphur dioxide and these plants have stopped flowering in areas close to industrial centres and on city pavements and sidewalks (*Ibid.* : vi). The author notes that the ecological study is confined to in the context of Darwin's theory of organic evolution. The development of ecological analysis in the present century has been fast, and also comprehensive as well as controversial. One has to be cautioned that ecology does not simply mean "living with the land and its resources"—rather it goes beyond this to encompass a greater goal, that is, living for the land (*Ibid.* : vii).

Like other countries India too faces a wide array of environmental problem, which affect the well being of its citizens. While for developed countries environmental problems are largely due to pollution caused by resource wasteful lifestyles. The stresses on India's environmental resources come mainly from the pressures for satisfying the basic human needs of a large and growing population. The Secretary General of the Indian Environmental Society once wrote: "Physical growth cannot go on indefinitely on this finite earth and the explosion of human population and its increasing indiscriminate encroachments on the biosphere poses a grave danger to main's own survival". In another publication it has been stated: "Conservation and improvement of the environment are vital for the survival and well-being of mankind. National resources of land, and water have to be used wisely as a trust to ensure a healthy environment for the present and future generations"(*Ibid.*: viii). According to the author the current plan of environmental problems in India can be grouped into two categories: (a) Those arising from conditions of poverty and under development; and (b) those arising as negative effects of the process of development (*Ibid.* : viii). "The first category has to do with the impact on the health and integrity of our natural resources (land, soil, water, forest, wild life, etc.) as a result of poverty and the inadequate availability for a large section of our population, of the means to fulfill basic human needs (food, fuel, shelter, employment, etc.). The second category has to do with the unintended growth and development. In the latter category would fall the distortion imposed on national resources from poorly planned development projects and programmers, as well as from lack of attention to long term concerns by commercial and vested interests." Thus it would be clear that environmental conservation is an integral part of the total development effort.

Ramchandra Guha's well acclaimed edited work *Social Ecology* (1994) gives a comprehensive analysis to the ecological and environmental problems. According to Guha the first decades after Independence were an age of 'ecological innocence' —circumstance that helps to explain why environmentally oriented thinking found such little resonance in intellectual and political life. We had to wait till the 1970s for a systematic development of environmental sociology. Likewise Western sociologists are also not taking interest in responding to environmental degradation. Guha points-out two basic reasons for this, "The Judo-Christian ethic of man's mastery over nature" and "the fact of social sciences themselves being formed in an epoch of unprecedented economic prosperity". In case of India, after

Independence "it was viewed above all as a collective national endeavor to reduce the gap between India and the industrialized countries of the west. In the circumstances, any talk of ecological constraint would have been irrelevant" (1994: 2). Guha points out that, sociologists implicitly work within four board parameters: the economy, the polity, the social structured and culture. The economy incorporates, in the Marxian sense, the forces and relations of production, or from a more conventional viewpoint, questions relating to the production, distribution and allocation of goods and services. The polity refers to the relations of power and authority between different social groups, as well as to the institutions, which regulate power relations—notably, the law and the state. By social structure he means those social arrangements that are critical to the reproduction of social units, for example, family and kinship (including gender relations), caste and community. Finally, culture embodies characteristic forms of collective self-expression (e.g., ritual, music, art as well as ideas and ideologies) which influenc social life, whether religious or otherwise. But Guha adds a fifth dimension, which he calls "ecological perspective". However, ecological perspective needs to be understood on the basis of ecological infrastructure. The ecological infrastructure of human society consists of soil, water, flora, fauna, climate, etc. While humans are unique amongst the earth's creatures in their elaborately developed culture(s), they do not stand above or apart from nature. "The ecological infrastructure powerfully conditions the evolution and direction of human economic life, political relations, social structure, and ideology. At the same time, human interaction itself reshapes the natural environment in its own image" (*Ibid.*: 5).

To define social ecology, he says it "rests on the awareness of the interdependence of the biophysical and socio-cultural domains". Juxtaposing the ecological infrastructure to the economy, polity, social structure and culture gives us the following five-fold schema, labeled by him as Culture (the arts, religion, ideology), Polity (relations of power, law, the state), Social Structure (family and kinship, caste community), Economy (forces and relations of production, trade); and Ecological Infrastructure (soil, water, forests, etc). The task of an environmentally oriented sociology or social ecology is the study of the reciprocal relations between institutions in the one hand and ecological infrastructure on the other (*Ibid.* : 5). He also focuses on how the elite (high class) manipulated the natural resources "for their own benefits but only at a substantial cost to the environment and disadvantaged social group". In the rising conflict, he says that there was conflict over forest in seventies and eighties but now there is conflict over water by giving the example of Sarover dam in Narmada river (*Ibid.*: 11).

Methodology

This study is mostly based on primary sources of data. In this regard an intensive fieldwork was done in the Summer of 1999. In the fieldwork, observation, focused interview and interview schedules were the tools of data collection. Basically it is an explorative and analytical study. However, this researcher also consulted the secondary sources of data. The studies conducted by various sociologist and anthropologist have also been referred.

Sample Size

In this study, total 230 samples were selected for interview out of 2,578 population. The sample have three broad variables like age, religion and occupation. To explore, these variables have been divide to young, those who fall between 15 years and 35 years; this is 58.7 per cent of the total sample. Likewise the tribes who fall in the age group of 36 to 49 years are grouped as middle age group; this is 27.4 per cent of the total sample. The tribes who are above 50 years have been classified into the old category. This is 13.9 per cent of the total sample.

Secondly, the sample has been further classified on the basis of their religious beliefs and practices. Here, out of 230 tribes, 109 are referred as Hindu and 121 as non-Hindu, i.e., Christian. The total sample size of Hindu believers is 47 per cent and 53 per cent for the Christians.

Thirdly, the sample has been further classified on the basis of occupation. Occupationally, we have the tribes who practice agriculture and depend mostly on forest. Their sample size is 158, i.e., 69 per cent of the total sample size. In the same way the tribes who're involved in other than agricultural occupation like government job or business, etc., have been categorised as non-agricultural group. Their sample size is 72, i.e., 51

Chapter Scheme

This study has ten chapters including introduction and conclusion. The first and introductory chapter contains the problems and importance of the study. In this chapter, the researcher has reviewed the existing literature to define nature and scope of social ecology, which gives theoretical base to this study. Social ecology is the interdependent of bio physical and socio-cultural domain. These biophysical features like water, soil, forest defines the way of life, customs, and institutions. Society is existing because of the interactive result of bio physical and socio-cultural domain. In this chapter the methodology is also discussed. The researcher has used interview schedule, observation and explored various published and secondary matters. The sample size has taken of 230 tribals of *Saora* tribes of Orissa.

In the chapter 'People, Tribe and Ecology' I have explained the universe of the study, i.e., Orissa with relation to the *Saora* tribes and their ecology and natural surroundings. The approach here used is of F.G. Baily. Orissa has been seen as macro area of the study, whereas Gunupur tahsil and Sagada panchayat has been the micro area. This chapter highlights the people of Orissa in general and tribals in particular. The Orissa society is the conglomeration of many castes groups. It has 62 tribal communities. Orissa has full of natural resources. The interaction between the natural resources and people has established culture and way of living. Orissa has many common characteristics with the *Saora* land with few exceptions.

In the chapter 'Social Structure and Change' it has discussed about the structural elements of the *Saora* tribe. The *Saora* tribals have their own lineage known as *birinda*, which governs the activities of the villages. Tribals do not marry in their own *birinda*. These *birinda* systems govern their marriage and kinship rule. Nowadays this is changing. The *birinda* rules and regulation are no more rigidly followed so as the family and marriage rules. Mostly tribals are going for love marriage in the Church without any traditional flavour of feast and music. These changes have also affected the forest resources, as there are changes in family and family occupation. Apart from this other development plans also responsible for change in forest resources.

The chapter 'Political and Legal System' discusses the legal and political life of the *Saora* tribes. How the traditional and modern means of governance are different from each other and in which they are helpful for their smooth governance and sustenance. The comparative analysis of traditional and modern leader reveals that traditional political and legal system was more prone to nature and willing to safeguard the nature. The contradiction is resulted because the modern political system has brought changes and development in other sphere of tribal life. Due to panchyat raj and economic development the tribal to have a different socio-economic, cultural and legal set up now.

In the fifth chapter *Saora* 'Religion and Belief System' has been discussed. Basically most of the tribals have changed their religion. Here the traditional and changing aspect of the religion and ritualistic believe has been focused. The traditional aspect of religion reveals the great belief of *Saora* on supernatural and ancestral spirits. Due to Christianity changes have come but many aspects of *Saora* beliefs is as it is. It can be called as Hinduised converted tribals. This change has come because of change in forest resources. The pertinent question of forest and *Saora* religious practices has a close relationship, which has also been examined with special relation to change and religious conversion.

In the sixth chapter, 'Culture, Leisure and Communication' system of the *Saora* tribe has been studied, The culture as a concept has been defined and how the tribal culture has changed, has also been traced. Their means of entertainment, and adaptability to modern practices, garments and music have also been explored with caution and care. The *Saora* culture, basically the material and non-material culture have changed. *Saora* consider leisure as profane as they always prefer to do the work than leisure. Their communication is of symbolic in nature, as they believe to listen Radio, TV attracted towards modern music and garments.

The seventh chapter is 'Economy, Ecology and Development' where it focuses on the economic practices of *Saora*. Traditionally they depended on minor forest collection and shifting cultivation. Even today they do practice terrace and shifting cultivation. Here, we have seen the trend of migration, urbanization and how these social factors are influencing tribal life; and their nature bounties and ecology has been examined.

Chapter eight, throws light on 'Social Ecology Forest Resources'. Here, the relationship between forest and its social history has been examined. The new forest policy and the tribals' opinion regarding the government intervention is also under focus. How the natural resources have been disturbed because of the change in the attitude of the tribals has been examined in this chapter. The main conclusion is that the government policy and intervention is the cause of change in the social ecology.

The chapter ninth contains a discussion about the ' Change and Development '—how the developmental initiative taken by government has influenced tribal life and ecology. The important aspect of development, i.e., education has been taken into consideration from developmental and ecological perspective. The reasons like, poor attitudes of parents, economic backwardness are the main causes of backwardness in education. The finding shows that improvement in education will bring change in ecology.

The tenth and conclusion chapter summarizes the findings of the study. It is evident that the dominant attitude of man over nature is very pertinent. This is because of the change in attitude of people and government. Practically the whole human civilization is looking forward, at the cost of nature, ideology and feelings.

References

Bates, Marston, 1962, *Anthropology Today : Selections,* New York.

Bhasin, Veena, 1989, *Ecology, Culture and Change: Tribals of Sikkim, Himalayas, New Delhi,* Inter India Publications.

Bookchin. Murrary. 1989, *Remarking Society : Pathways to a Green Future,* Montreal. Blackrose Books.

Bookchin, Murrary, 1990, *The Philosophy of Social Ecology : Essays on Dialectical Naturalism,* Montreal, Blackrose Books.

Bookchin, Murrary, 1991, *Towards Ecological Society,* Montreal, Blackrose Books.

Bookchin, Murrary, 1996, 'The Concept of Social Ecology' in Carolyn Merchant (ed.), *Key Concept in Critical Theory : Ecology,* Jaipur & New Delhi, Rawat Publication.

Dasmann Raymond F, 1968, *Environmental Conservation,* USA, John Wiley & Sons, Ins.

Detwyler Thomas R, 1971, *Man's Impact on Environment,* New York, McGraw Hill Book Company.

Guha, Ramchandra, 1994, *Social Ecology*, New Delhi, Oxford University Press .

Guha, Ramchandra, 1989, *Unquiet Woods*, New Delhi, Oxford University Press.

Hawley. A. H., 1950, *Human Ecology: A Theory of Community Structure*, New York, The Ronald Press Company.

Hart, Robert A. de J, 1984, *Ecosociety: A Historical Study of Ecological Man*, Dehra Dun, Natraj Publisher.

Horkeimer, Max and Adorn, Th. W., 1972, *Dialectic of Enlightment*, New York.

Jimoh Omo-Fadaka, 1973, *Impact of Science on Society*, UNESCO Publication Vol. XXIII, No.2.

Jimenez, Nelly, Arvelo, 1973, *The Dynamics of the Ye'cuana (Maguiritare) Political System: Stability and Crisis*, Copenhagist, IWGIA.

Kidar N. T. & M. Jha, 1972. *Ollar Gadba of Koraput*, Calcutta, Anthropological Survey of India.

Leiss, William, 1972, *The Domination of Ntaure*, Not avilable.

Liedloff, Jean, 1975, *The Constinuum Concept*, London, Duckworth.

Merchant, Carolyn (ed), 1994. *Key Concept in Critical Theory: Ecology*, New Delhi, Rawat Publication.

Mukerjee, Radhakamal, 1926, *Regional Sociology*, Bombay, Popular Prakashan.

Mukerjee, Radhakamal, 1968, *Man and his Habitation: A Study in Social Ecology*, Bombay, Popular Prakashan.

Mann, R. S. 1984, *Anthropological and Sociological Theory: Approaches and Applications*, Jaipur, Rawat Publication.

Marcuse, Herbert, 1964, *One Dimensional Man*, Not available.

Marcuse, Herbert, 1972, *Counter-revolution and Revolt*. New York.

Marcuse, Herber, 1955, *Eros and Civilization*, Not available.

Park, R.E., 1936, 'Human Ecology' in *Amercian Journal of Sociology*, Vol. XLII, pp. 1-15.

Qureshi, M.H., 1987, "The Interactive System of Man and His Environment—An Appraisal", in Sharma & Sharma (ed) *Environmental Design and Development: Conflict and Harmoy* ? Jodhpur Scientific Publisher, pp. 21-27.

2
People Tribe and Ecology

In the panoramic India, Orissa, the land of Oriyas can be depicted as a kaleidoscope of colourful scenery much like the Jewels of the bridal attire. Its history, geography and culture represent a unique yet vibrant aspect of social existence and a different yet dynamic way of life. Endowed by nature's bounty, vast stretches of clean and virgin beaches, serpentine rivers, breathtaking waterfalls, rugged hills, miles and miles of rolling forests, lush green country sides, fabulous wildlife, colourful tribes and vivacious virgins, Orissa, the eastern state of India is still rich by its great tradition, architecture, monument,sculptura l art and the finest of its filigree and antique workers. Handicraft has been a royal road to Orissa's long and enriched cultural legacy.

Archaeology and monuments have been the treasures of Orissa tradition. Their pristine beauty and marvelous design simply takes the mind to another realm—a realm of dream of cultural paradise. The entire length and breadth of the state is dotted with a large number of standing monuments and archaeological sites. The great tradition of 80 monument building which is as old as the recorded history of even older, finds an echo in the religious and cultural life of the people even today.

History

When we turn to the pages of history we are confronted with the great Kalinga War of Ashoka in the third century BC which formed a turning point in his life, in the history of Buddhism as well as in the history of Orissa. Since the carnage at the foothills of Dhauli, the mountain, Orissa has been ravaged and ruined by mercenaries of blood, and misery with intermittent epochs. In it all are recorded, rather vividly among these mountains. Various regions of which is the modern Orissa is, were parts of the kingdoms of Kalinga, Kosala, Utkala and Odradesha in historical times. Whether politically united or existing in a large number of princely states, the region of Orissa has been known since the Mahabharata. Kalinga was a name to conjure with during King Asoka's historic campaign and his conversion to Buddhism.

Physiography

Location

Orissa as situated to the east coast of India, located in the east coast of India with the Bay of Bengal forming its eastern and south-eastern frontiers and lies between 17.48 degree and 22.34 degree North Latitude and 81.24 degree and 87.29 degree East Longitude. With an area of 15,5,707 square Kms. Orissa is the tenth biggest state in India. As per the census of 1991 Orissa has a population of 31.7 million. The state contains 4.47 per cent of the landmine of India and accounts for 3.47 per cent of the population of the country. Geographically speaking, it is bounded by the sea Bay of Bengal, on the East, Madhya Pradesh on its West, Andhra Pradesh on its South, West Bengal on the North-East and Bihar on the North.

Topography

Geographically, Orissa may be divided into five regions: the coastal plains, the middle mountainous country, the rolling uplands, the river valleys, and the subdued plateau. The coastal plains stretch from the Subarnarekha River in the north. They are narrow in the north, widest in the middle, narrowest on the coast of Chilka Lake broadening further to the south. The delta formulation of the rivers falling into the Bay of Bengal and the vast arable tract are distinguished by the endless stretch of rice land. The Eastern Ghats constitute the middle mountainous zone. The mountainous regions cover about three-fourths of the area of the state, cut by deep and broad valleys of the important rivers, of which the longest is the Mahanadi. The Mahanadi flows From Bastar in Madhya Pradesh and almost cuts the state into two. The south most of Koraput district, the western portion of Ganjam district, Phulbani district and large portions of Kalahandi and Balangir districts form a continuous zone of hills and plateaus merging into the rolling uplands. In the north the hills and plateau of the Mayurbhanj, Keonjhar, Sundergarh and portions of Sambalpur and Dhenkanal districts again form a continuous mountainous zone which spills over into the coastal plains. The rolling uplands are lower in elevation than the plateau. The major river valleys in Orissa are the basins of the Mahanadi, the Brahmani and the Bansadhara rivers. The subdued plateaus are almost flat and resemble the peninsular tablelands, which are higher than the rolling uplands.

Lake

The state has a number of saline and sweet water lakes and waterfalls, which adds to its picturesqueness. The Chilka Lake along with the seacoast is a unique phenomena and is quite large. It has an area of 1100 sq. km., the largest blackish Water Lake in Asia.

Forest

About 36.0 per cent of the total area of the state is covered by the forest. Spread over unevenly across the state its cover comprises large tract of evergreen and temperate forests. They provide the state with timber, bamboo, tendu leaf, sal seeds and other minor forest produce and contribute a major share to the state exchequer.

The total area under forest in Orissa in 1981 was 59,963 sq. kms, which accounted for about 38 per cent of the geographical area of the state and 8 per cent of the total forest area in the country. During 1993-94, the forest area was reported to be 57,184 sq. kms, which was 4.63 per cent less than the area in 1981. This has further declined to 56059.52 sq. kms during 1995-96. Out of the above total forest area of 56059.52 sq. kms. In the state the area under reserved forests demarcated and protected forests, un-demarcated forests and unclassified forests accounted for 26331.15 sq. kms., 15432.69 sq. kms., 14280.50 sq. kms. and 15.18 sq. kms. respectively. Though the forest cover is unevenly distributed, the coastal districts with which much higher population density have comparatively less forest area (Economic Survey1996-97: 52).

Orissa is also home to a variety of wildlife. Some forest areas of the state have been declared as sanctuaries by the state government. So far 17 sanctuaries and 2 proposed National Park have been notified in the state.

Rainfall and Irrigation

The Gross Cropped Area (GCA) of Orissa is 92.70 lak hectares, of which the irrigated area is 20.88 hectares, slightly more than one-fifth. The average rainfall is 150 cm. in Orissa. The southwest monsoon brings much of its rain and the rest comes from the northeast monsoon especially during its retreat. On an average the rainy season in Orissa extends from June to September. Saınbalpur, Sundergarh, Keonjhar, Mayurbhanj, Baleswar and Cuttack experienced heavy rainfall in the month of June, July and August and remaining districts experienced it in the month of August and September.

Soil

There is various soils sub- order association that prevails in Orissa. The most common and widely spread sub-order associations are Ustalfs, Ustalf-Orchrepts, Ustalf-rchrepts acquepts, Ustalf-Rock Ontcrops, Ustalf-Aqualfs-Ochrepts, and Ustalf Orchrept- Orthents. These are high base status soils and are mainly red in colour with varying texture of loam and sandy loam. These soils are especially suitable for cultivation of paddy, fruits, vegetable and mustard. These soils cover almost all districts of the state.

Mineral

Orissa has a large variety of minerals, including chrome (98 per cent of country's total reserve), nickel (95 per cent), bauxite (70 per cent), iron ore (26 per cent), and coal (24 per cent). Yet the level of industrialisation and urbanisation is quite low. The state continues to retain its predominantly rural character. There has been a small increase in its urban population, from 11.8 per cent in 1981 to 13.3 per cent in 1991

Language

Oriya, the regional languages, belongs to the great Aryan family of languages and is closely related to Assamese, Bengali and Maithili, as a direct descendant of eastern Magadhi. Under the influence of neighbouring regional languages of the Aryan and Dravidian families, as also that of the austric group of language current among the tribal groups, Oriya has developed many linguistic variations.

Demography

Orissa's population increased by about 20 per cent, to 31.7 million, between 1981 and 1991. The population density rose from 169 persons per square kilometer to 203 persons during the same period.

Table 2.1 Demographic Indicators of Orissa

Year	Orissa			All India		
	Birth rate	Death rate	Infant mortality rate	Birth rate	Death rate	Infant mortality rate
1951	25.7	21.6		13.9	27.4	146
1961	26.2	13.4	124	41.7	22.8	146
1971	34.6	15.5	127	41.2	19	129
1981	32.7	13.1	115	37.2	15	110
1991	28.2	12.7	126	29.5	9.8	80
1992	27.8	11.7	115	29.2	10.1	79
1993	37.3	12.2	110	28.5	9.2	74
1994	28	11.1	103	28.6	9.2	73

Source: Directorate of Health Services, Economic Survey Report, 1995-96, Govt. of India.

Orissa is also home to a vast number of Schedule Tribes and Schedule Castes. Schedule Tribes constitute 22.43 per cent to the total population of the state as against the national average of 7.76. Similarly, 14.66 per cent of its populations are Scheduled Castes. Most of them live in the relatively underdeveloped districts of the state. Thus huge concentration of marginalised sections an the state as stated to be reason behind the backwardness of the state as the socio-economic standard of these people are very below compare to others.

Despite, these obstacles, the literacy of the state increased from 47 per cent for male and 21 per cent for female, to a repeatable 63 per cent for males to 35 per cent for female in 1991. Though the overall literacy rate of 49.1 per cent lags behind the national average of 52.1 per cent. Even this small progress is not uniform and has a high degree of regional and community variation.

Some demographic indicators of the state are rather alarming. For instance, although Orissa's population growth rate is fourth lowest in the country (19.5 per cent in 1981-91), the infant mortality ratio at 7.4 per 1,000 live birth is also the highest in the country. However, the total fertility rate in Orissa is lower than the national average by 15 per cent. Orissa has also the dubious distinction of having maximum death rate due to cerebral malaria, with the number increasing over the years. Other diseases those are found among Orissa's populace are tuberculosis, leprosy, elephantasis, gastro-entireties and yaws. Skin infection such as scabies, and eczema are common among the tribal population of Orissa.

Table 2.2 Literacy Rate (in Percentage)

Year	*Orissa*		*All India*	
	Total	*Female*	*Total*	*Female*
1961	21.7	8.6	24	12.9
1971	26.2	13.6	29.5	18.7
1981	32.4	21.1	36.2	24.8
1991	49.1	34.7	52.1	39.4

Source: Census of India, 1991.

Socio-Economic Situation

Orissa's economy is predominantly agrarian. The share of population depending on primary sector continues to be very high, despite a surge of spate of industrialisation in recent years. In 1991 more than three-fourth of its working population were engaged in agricultural activities as against two-third of its share at the all-India level. Correspondingly, the shares of workers in secondary and tertiary sector are less than that of national average. Large proportions of its women workers (82.7 per cent) were engaged in agricultural activities. Between 1981 and 1991 census period the share of activities had declined and that of agricultural labourers has increased. This shows the increasing pauperisation of the state over the years.

Table 2.3 Percentage Distribution of Population by Sector of Activity

Sector	*Orissa 1991*	*All India 1991*
Primary	75.8	67.5
Secondary	7.5	12
Tertiary	16.1	20
Total	100	100

Source: Census of India, 1991.

Table 2.4 Work Participation Rate in 1991

Sex	*Orissa*	*All India*
Male	51.6	53.8
Female	22.3	20.8
Total	37.5	37.5

Source: Census of India, 1991.

In fact, poverty continues to pose serious problems for the state. Agriculture absorbs 80 per cent of the labour force in Orissa, but the annual rate of growth in food production is less than 3 per cent. Nearly, 38 per cent of the total population were put in the category of workers in 1991 census, of whom 44.3 per cent were cultivators, 28.7 per cent were agricultural labourers, 3.1 per cent household workers and 23.7 per cent were classified as other workers. However the size of land holding has declined during 1981-1991 showing the increasing dependence over agriculture and subsequent stagnation of economic growth. The poverty of Orissa is further bolstered by statistical sources from various governmental agencies. As per the Planning Commission estimates, the rural poverty in the state in 1984-85 was 48.4 per cent as against 33 per cent at the all India level. As per the expert committee estimates of 1993, nearly 65 per cent of the rural population live below the poverty line. A recent report shows that 55 per cent of Orissa's population live in poverty. Further, the per capita income of the state in 1991 was only Rs. 1615 as against the national average of Rs. 2239.

Administratively, Orissa became a separate province in 1st April 1936 and following the independence all the princely states of Orissa joined in the state and with the state reorganisation Orissa got its present shape. Initially, the state was divided into 13 districts, but the reorganisation of 1992 added 17 more districts to the existing total. It now has 58 Subdivisions, 314 Community Development Blocks and 50,972 villages.

Culture

In the nature of cultural development of any region or of any people at any time in its history, such cultural inflow and outflow in many directions is the rule rather than the exception. The racial differences among the people are not insignificant. Most of the tribal people and much of the population in Orissa belong to the Australoid group in racial history, while most of the general population belongs to the broad-headed Alpinoid type. Besides this, a sprinkling of Mediterranean types is also found in the general population. But these racial barriers or the more powerful linguistic barriers as between the Aryan speakers, Dravidian speakers and Austric-Mundari speakers have never stood in the way of cultural communication.

Another facet of the cultural life of Orissa adds to the complexity and brings in another dimension of cultural differentiation. We refer here to the regional differences within Orissa. Broadly speaking, we may think of four cultural regions within the present boundaries of Orissa. The northeastern areas bordering on Bengal have been influenced in dress, food habits, language, social customs and festivities by Bengali culture and language. The southern parts of Ganjam and Koraput districts have a sizable Telugu speaking population and have been influenced in language, food habits, and dress and marriage customs by the Andhra culture and language. The western districts of Sambalpur, Bolangir and Kalahandi may be said in many ways to be a cultural and, to some extent, linguistic continuum with the region of Chhatisgarh of Madhya Pradesh just beyond the border, where many Oriya-speaking castes live even at present. The fourth region may be said to be the distinctive or typical, or at least the tone-setting one, in cultural institutions, social customs and linguistic and literary sophistication. This region comprises roughly the coastal districts of Balasore, Cuttack and Puri and portions of adjoining districts. The remaining areas of the State extending from the northern districts of Sundargarh, Keonjhar and Mayurbhanj to the southern tribal areas of Phulbani, Ganjam and Koraput districts, to a large extent, can hardly be pressed to the confines of a more or less homogeneous cultural region. The only common feature of these areas is that these are inhabited by tribal peoples who account for more than 50 per cent of the total population. Each of the tribal communities has its own languages, whether Mundari, Dravidian or, in some cases, the regional language, Oriya. Each of them, again, has its own tribal religion, assimilation to a larger or smaller degree the local cults of Hinduism. Besides, in the pattern of dress, food habits, drinks, house, architect, village organisation and other social and economic characteristics, they differ from one another. Some of the tribes, like the *Kondh* and *Saora* have developed internal social differentiation along occupational specialisation, as potters, weavers and basket makers. Some of the tribes, like the *Bhuiyan*, the *Gond* and the *Binjhal* (Hinduised) and their status is equivalent to that of the clean Hindu castes from whom water is accepted by the Brahmin.

Tribal Orissa

The Scheduled Tribes (communities) are concentrated in two belts. The northern belt comprises the districts of Mayurbhanj, Keonjhar, and Sundargarh; the southern belt consists of the districts of Koraput, Ganjam and Phulbani. A large percentage of the tribal populations in these districts have their own oral tribal languages and they do not know Oriya. The most important of these languages are Mundari, Santali, *Saora* and Kui/Kuvi.

Since pre-historic days various people have inhabited the land of Orissa. Stone Age remains have been discovered along the Burhabalanga, the Brahmani, the Mahanadi and its tributaries like the Tel. Recently, prehistoric remains have also been found in the interior of western Orissa and in the river valleys and plateau of southern Orissa. Although the prehistoric communities cannot be identified, it is well known that Orissa had been inhabited by tribes like the *Saora* or Sabar ("Suari" according to Pliny, the Roman historian) from the Mahabharata days. To this day the *Saora* in the hills and the Sahara and Sabar of the plains continue to be an important tribe distributed almost all over Orissa. In the earlier centuries the proportion of the tribal people to the general population in Orissa must have been much. However, remote the habitat of the tribal people may be in the recesses of the jungles and hills, the influence of Hindu religion, mythology and even the Hindu concept of ritual purity and pollution have reached them.

In 1928, N.K. Bose had noted the use of sun-dried rice in the Juang rituals and the worship of Lakshmi as the goddess of fertility, though accompanied by blood sacrifice (Bose, 1967). The influence of Hindu-society was not only restricted to the fields of religion and customs. It extended to the formation of caste-like social and occupational differentiation on the lines of the local caste system. But the interaction between Hindu society and tribal society was not a one-way affair. In language, and perhaps in many customs of marriage and funeral ceremonies, the strong influence of the tribal neighbours, particularly in those regions where they constitute the politically dominant society, may be perceived on the non-tribal society.

Table-2.5 List of Scheduled Tribes

1.	Bhagata	32.	Kisan
2.	Baiga	33.	Kol
3.	Banjara. Banjari	34.	Kolah Loharas. Kol Loharas
4.	Bathudi	35.	Kolha
5.	Bhottada. Dhotada	36.	Koli. Malhar
6.	Bhuiyan. Bhuyan	37.	Kondadora
7.	Bhumia	38.	Kora
8.	Bhumiji	39.	Korua
9.	Bhunjia	40.	Kutia
10.	Binjhal	41.	Koya
11.	Binjhia. Binjhoa	42.	Kulis
12.	Birhor	43.	Lodha
13.	Bondo Poraja	44.	Madia
14.	Chenchu	45.	Mahali
15.	Dal	46.	Mankidi
16.	Desau Bhumij	47.	Mankirdia
17.	Dharua	48.	Matya
18.	Didayi	49.	Mirdhas
19.	Gadaba	50.	Munda. Munda Lohara. Munda Mhalis
20.	Gandia	51.	Mundari
21.	Ghara	52.	Omanatya
22.	Gond. Gondo	53.	Oraon
23.	Ho	54.	Parenga
24.	Holva	55.	Paroja
25.	Jatapu	56.	Pentia
26.	Juang	57.	Rajuar
27.	Kandha Gauda	58.	Santal
28.	Kawar	59.	Saora. Savar. Saura. Sahara
29.	Kharia. Kharian	60.	Sahabar. Lodha
30.	Kharwar	61.	Sounti
31.	Khond. Kond. Kandha. Nanguli. Kandha. Sitha Kandha	62.	Tharua

Source: Planning Commission 1969.

District Profile : Koraput

Location

The district of Koraput is located between 17°50' North and 20°24' North latitudes and 81°24' East 84 °2' East longitudes and is the southern most district of Orissa. On the extreme north it is bounded by the district of Kalahandi and the state of Madhya Pradesh, on the west by the state of Madhya Pradesh, on the south by the state of Andhra Pradesh and on the east by the state of Andhra Pradesh and the districts of Ganjam and Phulbani of Orissa.

Area

The area of the district is 26,961.0 km. It is largest district in Orissa and also one of the largest districts in India. Being irregular in shape, the district resembles in form the letter 'Y' its southeastern boundary runs roughly parallel to the seacoast and its shortest distance to seacoast is 42 miles. The remote corners of the district are more than two hundred miles apart.

According to the 1981 Census, the population of the district is 2,484, 005, comprising 1,246,378 males and 1,237,627 females. In order of size and population it hold the first and fourth places respectively among all the districts of Orissa. The density is 92 persons per km^2, which is the second lowest in the state.

Administration

There were, at the beginning, two subdivisions Rayagada and Koraput. Koraput subdivisions comprised five taluks, namely, Koraput, Pottangi, Jeypore, Nowrangpur and Malkangiri. The Rayagada subdivision had three taluks Ryagada, Gunupur and Bissam Cuttack.

River

A large number of small rivers and rivulets drain the district. Among them the Nagavali, the Indravati, the Kolab, the Vamsadhara and the Potteru rivers are important. The district has varied geological formations which range from Archaean through the lower and Upper Proterozoic successions to the recent alluvium.

Soil

The humid climate and the variations in geology have effected largely the distributions of soils in Koraput. Accordingly the soils in the district are classified as Aqualfs-Aquepts-Udalfs, Aqualfs-Ustalfs, Ustalfs-Ochrepts-Ustalfs-Ochrepts-Aquepts, Ustalfs-Rock-Outcrops, Ustalfs-Ochrepts-Orthents, Orthents-Tropepts-Rock Outercrops and Orthents-Ochrepts-Ustalfs. Koraput is a part of the Southern Orissa Highlands which is sub-divided into nine sub-micro regions on the basis of geology, soils, topography, climate and natural vegetation.

Table 2.6 Area, Number of Occupied Residential Houses, Households & Census, Villages in Different Blocks/Towns/Districts, 1991, Census

	Name of the Blocks/ Towns/District	*Geographical area in Sq. K.M.*	*Number of residential houses*	*No. of Village*		
				Inhabited	*Uninhabited*	*Total*
	1	2	3	4	5	6
1	Rayagada	531.25	17,691	275	19	294
2	Kashipur	481.86	23,736	414	33	447
3	Kolanara	356.63	13.340	189	7	196
4	K.Singpur	420.63	11.622	238	17	255
5	Gunupur	1,241.39	11.874	121	6	127
6	Gedari	754.49	7,012	148	11	159
7	B. Cuttack	622.05	16.617	282	26	308
8	Chandrapur	432.63	5.698	195	24	219
9	Muniguda.	649.47	15.192	351	65	416
10	Ramanguda	849.59	10.208	118	5	123
11	Padmapur	860.24	9.721	114	9	123
	URBAN					
1	Rayagada(M.)	18.65	10.002	—	—	—
2	Chandili (C.T.)	5.17	3.567	—	—	—
3	Gunupur (N. A.C)	11.65	3.816	—	—	—
4	Gudari (N.A.C.)	2.28	1.438	—	—	—
	Total Rayagada District	7.580.0*	1.61.534	2.445	222	2.667

Source: District Statistical Handbook: Raygada. 1995

Rayagada : The New District

Location and Area

Rayagada is one of the southern districts of Orissa state. It is bounded on north by Kalahandi and Phulbani districts, on east by Gajapati district, on the south by Srikakulam district of Andhra Pradesh state and on the west by Koraput and Kalahandi districts. The district is spread over in an area of 7584.7 sq. kms. and the administrative headquarters is located at Rayagada town.

History

The district of Rayagada was carved out as a separate district in the year 1992 as a result of multi-division of Koraput district. According to the said division, four tahasils namely Kashipur, Rayagada, Gunupur and Bissam-Cuttack including eleven Community Development Blocks separated from its parent district (i.e., Koraput) to form this new district. At present, the district is comprised of two Sub-divisions, four Tahasils, eleven Community Development Blocks and equal number of Tribal Blocks. As it is stated, the present district of Rayagada was a part of Koraput district, its historical past is one and the same as of its parent districts.

Demography

Total population of this district, according to 1991 census, is 713984 persons (354911 males and 359073 females). Of these, 624658 persons (309229 males and 315429 females) from rural areas and the remaining 89326 persons (45682 males and 43644 females) from urban areas. The sex-ratio i.e. females per 1000 males of the district as per 1991 Census is 1012 as against the state average sex-ratio of 971. Community Development Block-wise population distribution of the district including those of Scheduled Castes and Scheduled Tribes population is given below in Table 2.7.

Geography and Physcial Features

River

The tract consists of two broad, almost parallel valleys of the rivers Vamsadhara and Nagavali running over levels varying from 300 ft. to 1200 ft. and with high and rugged hill ranges hedging them in.

Table 2.7 Demograhic Profile

C.D. Blocks/ Urban Areas of the District	*Total Rural/Urban*	*Total population*	*Population of*	
			Scheduled Castes	*Scheduled Tribes*
1	2	3	4	5
Rayagada	T	96107	100064	61695
	R	79956	7652	60291
	U	16151	2412	1404
Kashipur	T	101995	20333	62742
	R	101995	20333	62742
	U	—	—	—
Kolnara	T	59309	5413	40775
	R	59309	5413	40775
	U	—	—	—
Kalyaninghpur	T	50807	7125	32105
	R	50807	7125	32105
	U	—	—	—
Gunupur	T	54237	3582	38501
	R	54237	3582	38501
	U	—	—	—
Gudari	T	30120	3806	22552
	R	30120	3806	22552
	U	—	—	—
Bishama Cuttack	T	73276	12186	45579
	R	73276	12186	45579
	U	—	—	—
Chandrapur	T	25947	2705	18188
	R	25947	2705	18188
	U	—	—	—
Muniguda	T	65302	16120	21195
	R	65302	16120	21195
	U	—	—	—
Manguda	T	42259	4396	27336
	R	42259	4396	27336
	U	—	—	—
Padmapur	T	41720	5372	19533
	R	41720	5372	19533
	U	—	—	—

Note : Excluding the population of forest range(s) in the district.

C.D. Blocks/ Urban Areas of the District	Total Rural/ Urban	Total population	Population of Scheduled Castes	Population of Scheduled Tribes
1	2	3	4	5
Total Urban:				
(i) Rayagada (M)		48217	5714	7464
(ii) Gunupur (NAC)		18317	3680	1421
(iii) Gudari (NAC)		6611	1280	413
(iv) Chandili (CT)*		16115	2412	1404

Source: S.C. Bhat. The Encyclopedia. District Gazetters of India (ed). Vol.9. Gyan Publishing House 1998: 753

* Population of Chandili (CT) has also been shown under Rayagada Development Block as urban Population.

Minerals

The district is rich in mineral deposit. Among the minerals, fairly good deposits of iron, limestone and manganese are found at different places. Graphite in small quantity is found near Rayagada. In Rayagada and Gunupur sub-divisions the other mineral found is Kaolin.

Forest

It contains rich cultivated lands and good forests. Teak and sal, apart from bamboo and coarse grass are found predominantly in the forests of this tract.

Towns, Villages and Amenities

The district is at present comprised of two sub-divisions, four tahasils, eleven Community Development Blocks and equal number of Tribal Blocks and 140 Grama Panchayats. It has four towns and 2667 villages.

Communications

Rayagada is situated on the Raipur-Vizianagaram rail line of South Eastern Railways. There are total 10 stations on this line in this district and the line runs from north to south. It is a broad gauge line which was opened to traffic in 1932. Besides this, there is also a meter gauge railway line which runs from Naupada (Andhra Pradesh) to Gunupur in this district. This line traverses only about 3 to 4 kms. in this district and was opened to traffic in 1931. As regards waterways and ferries, floods in the rivers of the district appear and subside quickly. No regular ferry service is, therefore, maintained all the year round. During the rainy season, however, a ferry service near

Gunupur on the river Vamsadhara is maintained. Rayagada is located at a distance of 110 kms. from Koraput. Regular bus services are available between these two district headquarters. Road transport is the common mode of communication and all the tahasils/Community Development Blocks head-quarters and important places of this district are inter-connected with each other through transport services. State Transport Buses ply on all these routes. Nearest airport is at Visakhapatnam.

Fairs and Festivals

Important fairs and festivals organised in the parts of this district are Thakurani Jatra, Kalabandh Jatra, Jhankere Jatra, Dola Jatra, Ghanta Parva, Agni Kuanri Puja, Shivaratri, Ratha Jatra, Bali Jatra, Chaitra Parba, Radha-Krishna mela, Ramnavami and Gadagada Jatra. Apart from this the fairs and Festivals organised in urban areas of the district are : Kalasi Jatra and Ratha Jatra in Rayagada and Ratha Jatra, Ramnavami, Shivaratri, Dola Jatra and Bali Jatra in Gunupur area.

Education

The following table provides information regarding the type and level of educational institutions available in the towns of the district including the number of stadia and public libraries:

Table 2.8 Number of Educational Institutions

Name of the Towns	*Educational Institutions*	*Stadia*	*Public libraries (including reading rooms)*
Gudari	Higher Secondary or Secondary School (1) Primary Schools (5)	—	PL : 1
Gunupur	Higher Secondary or Secondary Schools (2) Junior Secondary and Middle School (1). Primary Schools (11)	—	PL : 2
Rayagada	Arts and Commerce College (1) Higher Secondary or Secondary School (3) Junior Secondary and Middle Schools (2) Primary Schools (13)	—	PL : 3

Source: S.C. Bhat, The Encyclopedia, District Gazetters of India. (ed), Vol.9. Gyan Publishing House 1998 : 756

Medical

The table given below provides information on types of medical facilities available in the towns of this district. It also indicates the number of beds available in the medical institutions.

Table No. 2.9 Number of Medical Institute

Name of the Towns	*Medical Institution*	*With number of beds*
Gudari	Health Centre (1) Family Planning Centre (1)	6
Gunupur	Hospital (1) Family Planning Centre (1)	10
Rayagada	Hospital (3) Family Planning Centre (2)	38

Source: S.C Bhat, The Encyclopedia, District Gazetters of India (ed), Vol.9, Gyan Publishing House 1998: 756

Gunupur : The *Saora* Land

This study was conducted in Sogoada panchayat of Gunupur Block and Tahasil of Rayagada district. Gunupur block and tahir has 1,241,39 Sqr km. geographical area and d11,874 houehold seattled in 121 inhabited and six uninhabited villages(see Table 2.6). This block has 54,237 total population consist of 26,853 male and 27,384 females. Among Scheduled Tribe population 18,958 male and 9,543 female. The total population of Sogoda panchayat is 2,578.

This panchayat has 19 villages consist of eight revenue and eleven hamlet village. This panchayat has 593 families.

The ethnic environment of the *Saora* is cosmopolitan. To the northeast live the 'Hindu' Oriya population who speak a language of the Indo-Aryan family and to the south live the 'Hindu' Telugu, belonging to the Dravidian family. To the northwest live the *Khond* or *Kond* whom, though they speak a Dravidian language, are also considered 'tribal' and whose culture is in many ways similar to *Saora*. The *Saora* sometimes think of them as adivasi, a pan-Indian terms for 'tribal'. The *Saora* in this study also refer to themselves as 'Hindu' in opposition to the enclavcs of missionaries Christian *Saora* in they're midst.

Types of *Saora*

The *Saora* perceives them as falling into several main divisions. The *Saora* groups in the plains, such as the *Sarda* (clean) and *Kapu* (cultivator) *Saora*, live by various occupations and resemble their caste-Hindu neighbours more or less closely. These groups remain virtually unstudied. The *Saora* with whom the researcher lived call themselves the *Lanjia Saora* and are also known variously as *Lamba-Lanjia*, Jedu (wild), *Mone*, and *Arsi* (monkey). The word 'Saora' were refers to these *Lanjia Saora*, who by any criterion can be considered the most isolated and 'tribal' of any *Saora* group. They straddle the mountain border between Ganjam District and Koraput District in Orissa, an area to this day made inhospitable to visitors by virulent malaria. I live mostly in *Saora* villages within a few miles of Puttasing, a settlement on the Koraput side which contain some assorted officials but is inhabited mainly by Pano (Dom), a Christianised group of Oriya dalits who live throughout tribal Orissa by trading with the tribals and lending them money at high interest.

Lanjia *Saora* territory comprises a series of mountains rising to 3,000 ft. Plains or river valleys bound it to the north by the *Khond* hills and on the other three sides. At the foot of the hills lie the towns of Gunupur and Parlakhemundi, containing a diversity of Oriya and Telugu castes as well as *Sara* and *Kapu Saora*. The path out of Gunupur towards the *Lanjia Saora* hills leads through fields of paddy and irrigated vegetables by the river Vamsadhara and past a village of *Sarda Saoras*.

As one draws away from Gunupur, certain contrasts appear between the *Saora* and the peoples of the plain. Many of the Oriya and Telugu castes and even the *Sarda Saoras*, have comparatively long-limited, dark, often almost ebony-skinned bodies and their men have a strong beard growth and hairy legs 'like a bear'. By contrast, the *Lanjia Saora* have short bodies, sometimes with a light reddish-brown skin, round faces, often with distinctly southeast Asian features, no beard growth and very little body hair. Among both men and women, the chest is usually bare when they are among their own kind. For men, the ankle-length lungi, dhoti or trousers of the plains give way to a cream-coloured homespun cotton loincloth exposing thin muscular thighs and buttocks or increasingly these days, to market-both khaki shorts. Whereas women in the plains wear saris, often brightly coloured; *Saora* women wear a knee-length wrap-around skirt, which is either homespun in cream or karket-bought in black. Instead of the vivid colours of plastic and nylon, virtually all artifacts in *Saora* homes have the colour of the earth, stone or dried vegetation from which they were made. *Saora* women wear none of the mascara or other cosmetics of the plains, through the faces of both women and to a lesser extent men have permanent tattoos, dyed with the juice of an indigo-coloured berry. The brightest colours are those of their jewelry in brass, silver, aluminium, gold and coloured glass, all made in the plains by Hindu castes using a technology of fire which remains a mystery to the *Saora*; brass water pots, though only in wealthier homes; and the red patterned bands in vegetable dye, used deliberately sparingly on the borders of homespun loincloths and skirts. Even in the markets the *Saora* choose cloth of khaki, black, white or dark blue and the merchants cater for them accordingly.

Historically, the evidence suggests that the *Saora* have been squeezed into their present enclave from a much wider area. Many villages along the coast from the Mahanadi valley well into Andhra Pradesh have *Saora* names but few of any '*Saora*' inhabitants. The *Saora* did not appear to practice human sacrifice and so did not attract the righteous British campaigns which were waged against the neighbouring Khond (Campbell 1864; Macpherson 1865; Padel 1987). Nonetheless the Puttasing area was brought under government rule in 1864-6 by an expeditionary force which executed and transported *Saora* resistance leaders and established a permanent police presence (Senapati and Sahu, 1966:72). Thereafter, the area has been suspended in permanent marginality between various distant centres (Elwin 1955: preface; Bell 1945). For much of the colonial period, this entire region lay at the far northernmost tip of the vast Madras Presidency. But the *Saora* live on the very boundary between the north and south Indian culture areas and this is now appropriately reflected in their division between two of India's modern states. If they go down the mountain one way, they enter the Indo-Aryan world of the Oriya-speaking State of Orissa; if they go down the other side, they find themselves in the Telugu-speaking, Dravidian state of Andhra Pradesh. Even within the state of Orissa, which now encompasses most of their territory, the *Saora* people live on either side of the border between the districts of Ganjam and Koraput. On the Ganjam side they were ruled in the British period through Oriya middlemen of Paik (Warrior) caste and khsatriya Varna; and on the Koraput side through *Saora* village Headmen

Headmen (*gomang*, also meaning 'rich man'), who were appointed by the British and collected revenue for the raja of Jeypore. Since the 1950s, the office of Headman has been officially suspended (though in practice it remains powerful) and the area governed through local councils (panchayat).

Conculsion

Orissa, the eastern state of India has many similarities and little differences with the district profile of Koraput, Rayagada and *Saora* land. The historical development of Orissa shows that different kingdoms have merged and given birth to today's Orissa. Therefore, historically Koraput and *Saora* land has not much differences, as both these areas were under Madras Presidency. Geographically, the location of Orissa and the Koraput district has not much variation, only of degree.

The topography of Orissa has five regions. The Koraput region has the characteristics of mountainous country. This region is full of hills and plateaus merging into the rolling uplands. There are various kinds of soil found in Orissa. It has many sub-orders which prevail all over Orissa. Orissa, Koraput, Rayagada, and *Saora* region has the similar kind of soil. Orissa is very rich in minerals. Likewise Koraput has the minerals of iron and manganese. The *Saora* region has the small quantity of graphite.

In the context of socio-economic phenomena, Orissa primarily is of agrarian economy. Agriculture is also the main source of living of the people of Koraput. But in *Saora* region tribals practice shifting cultivation and largely depend on forest resources.

There is a cultural difference between the pan-Orissan concept in comparison to tribal areas. The *Saora* tribe has their fair and festivals at different occasions of the year. Mainly the people of these regions speak Oriya but in their regional level they speak their own dialect of Koraputia and *Saora*. Many Saoras even do not know how to speak Oriya.

References

Bhat, S.C., 1998. *The Encyclopedia District Gazetters of India* (ed),Vol.9, New Delhi, Gyan Publishing House.

Bose, N.K., 1967, *Culture and Society in India*, Calcutta.

Bose, N.K., 1977, 'India's Eastern Tribes' in Romesh Thapar (ed.), *Tribe, Caste and Religion in India,* New Delhi, Seminar Publications.

Elwin, Verrier, 1955, *Religion of an Indian Tribe*, London, Oxford University Press.

Govt. of Orissa, 1996-97, *Economic Survey, Orissa,* Cuttack, Govt. Press.

Govt. of Orissa, 1995, *District Statistical Handbook: Raygata*, Cuttack, Govt. Press.

Govt. of India, 1995-96, *Economic Survey Report*, New Delhi.

Govt. of India, 1991, *Census of India*, New Delhi.

Govt. of India, 1969, *Planning Commission Report*, New Delhi.

Government of Orissa, 1989, *Scheduled Tribles and Scheduled Castes of Orissa*, Bhubaneswar, Harijans and Trible Welfare.

Government of Orssia, 1987, *Mineral Statistics of Orissa,* Directorate of Mining and Geology.

Government of Orissa, 1991, *Statistical Abstract 1991*, Bhubaneswar, Directorate of Economic and Statistics.

Macpherson, Willia..i, 1865, *Memories of Service in Inda : From the Correspondence of the Late Major S.C. Macpherson*, London.

Senapati and Sahu, 1966, *Orissa District Gazetters*, Cuttack, Govt Press.

Singh, B., 1984, *The Saora High Landers: Leadership and Development*, Bombay, Somaiya Publication.

Vitebsky, P., 1993, *Dialogues with the Dead: The Discussion of Mortality Among the Soura of Eastern India*, Cambridge, Cambridge University Press.

3

Social Structure and Change

Sociology of small societies remains inconclusive and bereft of perspectives without a note on the concept of structure. Social structure is the corner stone of any society and decidedly influences the pattern of behaviour, rules of governance and the scheme of interpersonal relationship. Though the term, social structure, ordinarily refers to the interrelationship and interdependence of various segments of society, it has deep meaning from the perspective of sociological analysis and therefore, requires substantive explanation. Basically a society functions-on the basis of a few basic prerequisites of society, which function in relation to others. This chapter discusses *Saora's* family types, their household pattern, marriage, kinship, their *birinda*, etc, on which tribal social organisation is based. The other perspective taken into consideration here is the ecology. How ecology and changes in ecology affected the social structure of the tribal social organisation? The objective of the study is to examine the social structure and social process among the tribal communities to find out how these contribute to accelerate or retard change in the *Saora* communities. We all know that tribal communities are closely knit and self-contained social units and their comparative identity and isolation from the mainstream of society enables them to resist the forces of change much more effectively than open society. Tribal societies are characterized by traditional values, use of primitive technology and non-rational behaviour patterns that are incongruent with the values, technology and behaviour patterns of the modern world. There have been governmental efforts to modernise them in an attempt to integrate them with the mainstream of social life. As a result, they have gone a long way in breaking the tribal isolation and changed some of the practices, which are out of tune with values of the modern society.

Therefore, here an attempt has been made at analyzing social structure of a tribal community with a view to identifying the social processes that have contributed to their modernisation. The factor of continuity and change can be well understood and delineated only if the elements of the tribal culture and tradition were examined in their pure and original form. Since here we are focussing on social structure and change, it is necessary to examine the concept of social structure and also analyse various perspectives developed by western and Indian scholars.

Social Structure: The Concept

Though the fashionable use of the term is a post 1945 phenomenon, the concept of social structure has a long history. In its original English meaning the word "social structure" referred to building construction. By the sixteen century, it was also being used to refer to the interrelations between the parts of any whole. It was, in fact, widely used in this sense in anatomical studies, which were in active development at that period. Its further extension from anatomy to Sociology, though delayed for several centuries, was a logical corollary of the very general use of organic analogies by political philosophers (International Encyclopedia of Social Sciences, Vol.14, 1968: 482).

The terms "structure" and "function" were inducted into social sciences literature by Herbert Spencer and were used to define the basis of human relationship later by Durkheim. From Durkheim the concept went into the hands of Radcliffe-Brown who extensively used the concept. In the latter half of twentieth century G. P. Murdock, Radcliffe-Brown and Levi-Strauss made pioneering effort in introducing a sense of purpose and potency to the term "social structure" and made it an important conceptual tool to understand and explain fundamental relationship among members in society.

Murdock's principal concerns were the ethnographic facts and the taxonomic classification of societies on the basis of manifest, readily describe characters. Murdock has compared societies systematically by analysing written source materials according to strictly uniform procedure. It is presupposed that the tribal names, which appear in anthropological monographs, correspond to fixed, readily distinguishable social entities (societies, tribes, and cultures), which are fully described by using some of their attributes. Murdock's use of the word 'structure' implies either a building analogy (society or on assemblage of independent bricks) or a dead organic model dissected for demonstration.

In contrast Radcliffe-Brown presumes that society may be compared to 'a living organism' or a working mechanism. For Radcliffe-Brown, a society has a life of its own: it is not an object so much as a creature, so that the study of structure that is, the interdependence of component parts of the system is linked with the study of function, or how the component parts of the system work in relation to each other and to the whole. Although Radcliffe- Brown's views of social function depend upon a holistic view of social structure, his British followers have not, in general, concerned themselves with the analysis of total working systems. Radcliffe-Brown himself was engaged in comparative work and theoretical generalisation and encouraged his followers to concentrate on those aspects of social system which display clear cut formal characteristics and which reflect to a minimal degree on the interplay of personal rivalries. Scholars like Fortes, Evans-Pritchard and Ford have concerned themselves with only one formal aspect of society at a time like political structure, kinship structure and ritual organisation. They display this system as a set of rules, and discuss the mutual interdependence of the rules that fit between the society and its environment (ecology).

The idea of social structure took a definite and different turn in the writings of Levis Strauss. Levi Strauss's concept of social structure is rooted more in mathematics and linguistic than biology. His view of structure has been taken over more or less directly from linguistics, and it is because of this, his arguments often appear highly abstract when compared to the relatively empirical analysis of British structural anthropologists. Radcliffe-Brown conceived of the task of social anthropologists as that of establishing a kind of linnacan taxonomy of functioning social systems. In such taxonomy the difference between one society and another would be one of structure but this structure readily describes empirical characteristics of the system. In Levi-Strauss's analysis, on the other hand, interest in structure comes to the fore only when one system is contrasted with another. Levi-Strauss is interested in how far empirical systems correspond (or fail to correspond) with the theoretically possible transformations of a single (mathematical) structure; his structure thus starts with as 'models' rather than as empirically observed facts.

The term, social structure has nothing to deal with empirical reality but with models built after it (Levi-Strauss, *Structural Anthropology*). This should help one to clarify the difference between social structure and social relations. Social relations consist of raw materials out of which the models making up social structure are built, while social structure can, by no means, be reduced to the ensemble of the social relations to be described in a given society. Levi-Strauss opines that structuralism is different because structures are models—formal properties which can be compared independently of their elements. The structuralism's task is thus to recognise and isolate levels of reality which have strategic value from his point of view, namely, which admit of representation of models, whatever their type. It often happens that the same data may be considered from different perspectives embodying equally strategic values, though the resulting models will be in some cases mechanical and in others statistical.

Levi-Strauss then introduced the notion of time dimension in structuralism. For him time must be a parameter in a kinship model, not because marriage, birth, aging, and other activities have temporal duration but because the relationships are expressed in the model between one generation and other and between older and younger siblings with an intrinsic temporal component. The time dimension in a model may be either reversible or irreversible; it may be straight, circular, progressive, empty, cumulative or statistical; there is also micro-time and macro-time. The significance of different kinds of time in indigenous thinking and in social analysis has been familiar to Evans-Pritchard, Levi Strauss acknowledges, and Fortes. There is also a distinction between synchronic and diachronic model as the temporal dimension is concerned. When the model has a historical dimension it becomes diachronic and when it is a historical it becomes synchronic.

Structuralism is the study of the order of orders. Levi-Strauss writes that an anthropologist considers the whole social fabric as a network of different types of orders. The kinship system provides a way to individuals according to certain rules; social organisation is another way of ordering individuals and groups; social stratification, whether economic or political, provides us with a third type and all these orders can themselves be ordered by showing the kind of relationships existing among them— how they interact with one another on both the sycronic and diachronic levels. Mayer Fortes has successfully tried to construct models valid not only for one type of order kinship, social organisation, economic relations, etc., but where numerous models for all types of orders are themselves ordered inside a single model.

However, from a significant departure to the study of linguistics Levi-Strauss employed his theory in the study of kinship, myth and totems. In his study of kinship he used the structural analysis by opposing nature with culture. Describing marriage system as a form of communication and reciprocity, he narrates that nature allows physical relationship between opposite sexes but culture prohibits by thrusting incest taboo. According to him to avoid intra— and inter—group conflict exchange of women was evolved as a pragmatic solution and the forms of exchange namely, restricted and generalised determined the structure of kinship. For him, the kinship structure rests upon the fundamental unit of family, which is constituted by the woman, her brother, husband and child. It emphasises on the relationship— of sibling, of affinity, of alliance. Here is a relationship of oppositions, between the relationship of consanguinity and affinity. He goes on to describe various permutations and combinations and their inter-connectedness.

Social structure is also defined in terms of social institution, which refers to a network of relationships. In other words social structure exhibits the existence of comprehensible enduring sets of relationships. So, when we speak of the structure of some particular element of society we mean such things as the number of people who normally compose a family group; the kinds of consanguine or conjugal relationships which are comprised in it—in short, the normal, regular and persistent characteristics of what may be called its 'shape' and 'size'. Secondly, when it is said that anthropologists are concerned with 'the social structure of kinship of primitive peoples, this means that they use normal and persistent characters of 'size' and 'shape' as criteria for classifying, and for making general statements about human societies. Some sort of notion of this kind whether clearly formulated or not; must be a necessary part of thinking and living.

Firth says that social structure is 'concerned with the ordered relations of parts to a whole with this arrangement in which the elements of social life are linked together'. Radcliffe-Brown puts essentially the same thing in a different way: he says that social structure is the complex network of actually existing in contrast to 'ideal' or 'right'— what takes place rather than what people say ought to take place. But he means also, not a particular instance—a particular family—but rather a general form of such relations. He distinguishes between 'social relations' by which he means the raw data and 'social structure', which for him is the general form. Like other terms of sociology, it is designed to give regularity and order to the raw data of observation. Radcliffe-Brown restricts the term social structure to actual social relations. As Firth points out, the study of social structure involves the consideration not only of those patterns of relations, which actually exist, but also those people believe to exist, and those, which they think, ought to exist. Indeed the essence of the concept of social structure, says Firth, is those social relations which seem to be of critical importance for the behaviour of members of the society, so that if such relation were not in operation, the society could not said to exist in that form. In this sense, we may know social structure as continuing of systems of expectations held by the people in a society, about the way things are usually, or ought to be done. Thus, Talcott Parsons tells: in 'the essential aspect of social structure lies in a system of patterned expectations, defining the proper behaviour of persons playing certain roles, enforced both by the incumbent's own positive motives for conformity, and by the sanctions of others'. The function of social structure is thus to analyse the varied potentialities of human nature.

As Robin Fox has stated in his book, *Kinship and Marriage: An Anthropological Perspective*, there is a good deal of the primate heritage that is relevant to any study of human society: dominance and hierarchy, territoriality, group cooperation, consort and mating behaviour, bonding behaviour, ritualization, etc, the 'facts of life' with which man has had to come to terms in the process of adaptation, and which are immediately relevant to the study of kinship and marriage (1967:31). This can perhaps be reduced to four basic 'principles' as he states: Principle 1: The women have children, Principle 2: The men impregnate the women, Principle 3: The men usually exercise control, Principle 4: Primary kin do not marry with each other. Gestation, impregnation, domination and the avoidance of incest, lie at the root of all social organization. The first two are unremarkable but unavoidable. The third is no doubt contentious, he feels that objections to it are some how unreal. For the greater part of human history, women were getting on with their highly specialized task of bearing and rearing children. It were the men who hunted the game, fought the enemies, and made the decisions (ibid:31). All this is possible at the level of social organisation.

Social Structure : Indian Perspective

Nearly half a century ago Rivers complained of 'the almost total neglect which the subject of relationship has suffered at the hands of students of Indian Sociology, (1914:27). A review of the subject written over four decades later contains the following apt observation: "In present state of knowledge, to write a book on Kinship in India is a daring venture. One would think that, for a general picture to be attempted, a number of intensive studies should first be written, and, apart from tribal monographs, we have very few of them indeed (Dumont and Pocock 1957: 44)". The earliest of these is the Srinivas's famous book on the Coorgs (1952). Though primarily concerned with an examination of the role of religion in social life, it contains a fairly detailed analysis of the Coorg joint family called the *okka*.

Gough's publications on the matrilineal Nayar of Malabar (Gough 1952a, 1952b, 1955, and 1959) are the most detailed analyses of marriage and kinship in an Indian community published so far. Equally distinguished, though not as detailed, is Mayer's excellent monograph on caste and kinship in Malwa (Mayer 1960). His interest in kinship derives from his interest in the analysis of the internal structure of caste. The only other book—lengthy study devoted exclusively to the Hindu family is by Ross (1962). It is not a fieldwork monograph in the strict social anthropological tradition, being based on case studies the data for which were obtained from 157 Hindu interviewees of middle and upper classes, representing three Dravidian and one Indo-Aryan linguistic groups (see Ross 1962). Besides the above, there are several papers and chapters in books devoted to other themes, but these are by their very nature limited in scope. Mention may here be made of Dube (1955), Dumont (1950, 1953 and 1957a), Gough (1956), and the relevant papers by Desai, Kapadia (1959) and others in the Sociological Bulletin.

Karve's Kinship Organization in India (1953) is the only general compendium of kinship terminologies and usages covering most of the linguistic-cum-cultural regions of the country (excluding the Kashmir Valley); but, as may be expected, not all of her material is based on intensive first-hand fieldwork (see Dumont and Pocock, 1957: 44).

Rivers (1924: 25-7) feels that had Morgan predicted, on the basis of the Dravidian kinship terms available to him, that cross-cousin marriage was the usage of which these terms were a social consequence, then kinship studies in India would not have suffered from neglect.

From the above discussion it is pertinent that social structure is one of the key characterstics of understanding social relation in real sense. Various anthropologist have put forth their view to conceptualise the very concept of social structure. As anthropology and sociology has emerged in west definitely the concept of social structure also gets its formation in the west. It is accepted that Indian sociologist and anthropologist have not done adequate work to formulate the Indian version of social structure. This following analysis may strengthen the social structure understanding from Indian perspective. Here the *Saora* social structure and their social organisation has ben discussed.

Traditional Social Structure of Soara Tribe

According to the Dictionary, kinship has to do with relationships by blood, or consanguinity; affinity with relationships brought about by marriage. In social anthropology, the two topics are very closely connected. All cultures distinguish various categories of kin and affines, and these categories, with their associated patterns of rights and obligations, make up what social anthropologists call kinship systems (Beattie, J. 1964:93).

Why is kinship so important in small-scale societies? The answer is that in all human communities, even the most technologically simple ones, the basic categories of biological relationships are available as means of identifying and ordering social relations. This is so even though some of these categories may be differently defined in different cultures. Everywhere people are begotten of men and born of women and in most societies the fact of parenthood and the bonds of mutual dependency and support that it implies are acknowledged. This leads to the recognition of other links, such as those between siblings (children of the same parents), and between grandparents and their grandchildren. So even in the simplest societies, kinship provides some ready-to-hand categories for distinguishing between the people one is born among, and so for ordering one's relations with them. Apart from sex and age, which are also of prime social importance, there is no other way of classifying people which are so 'built in' to the human condition (Ibid.: 93). A kinship system is not just a collection of distinct and mutually. exclusive terms, each denoting a different kind of genealogical and social relationship. It is rather a whole way of life, and it can be understood only by a thorough investigation of the language, values and behaviour of the people who have it. In many societies kinship is used to establish and define distinct corporate social units. In the conditions of simpler cultures it is essential for everyone to be a member of a co-operating, closely-knit group of people, upon whose aid and support he can depend in such vital activities as hunting, agriculture and herding and war.

Family and Kinship

The most remarkable thing about the organization of *Saora* society is its lack of organization. Its endogamous divisions are vague and often disregarded and, in sharp contrast to all the neighbouring tribes, it has no exogamous totemic clans, no pharatries, and no moieties. The one essential unit is the extended family descended from a common male ancestor, but there are also divisions into aristocracy and proletariat and by villages. *Saora* aristocracy consists of the families of the Chiefs and, where they exist, of the Buyya priests. The Chiefs are known by various names, the most common being Gamang—the word also means 'rich' and 'important'. But they may also be called Naiko, Janni, Karji, Dora; a Mandal may be the head of a village, or merely a Gamang's assistant. The Dhol-behera has an important, though somewhat subordinate position (Ewin, 1955:50)

The Gamangs and Buyyas are not only the wealthiest, but they are recognized by government, and in the old days used to receive an official turban which was greatly prized. The Gamang, the Chief, is of great importance, for the intermediary between Government and the people; it is by his orders that the villagers go to work for officials, or the Bissoyis; his presence is essential at all village functions; in Koraput he is the arbiter in matrimonial disputes; and in practice everywhere he has the final say in the allocation of land. Where the Buyya priest, in his secular capacity, is head of a separate quarter in a village, he may be of almost equal importance to the Chief himself. Below the members of these large families form the *Saora* aristocracy, are members of a large number of families who are called by the general term Poroja or Ryat, which simply means peasant. The heads of these families have no official standing, no representative capacity and are generally poor. But the shamans and funerary officials may be drawn from these or from any groups whatever their social or economic standing.

The family is called *birinda*, which is the one fundamental division of *Saora* society. It consists of all the descendants of a common male ancestor, 'men and women of the same blood'. This family group has no name and no totem. It is distinct from the hamlet, though only rarely from the village. Thus members of two families may live together in one hamlet, or members of one family may be divided between two hamlets. But nearly every family is to be found contained within the boundaries of a single village. The *birinda* family also controls the funerary arrangements. There are separate burning grounds and separate groups of memhirs for each family. Separate *Idaimarans* and *Idaibois*, who officiate at funerals, are appointed for each group and cannot, normally, function for others.

It is rare for a son or brother to migrate from his own to another village. If he does so, he retains the membership of his own family and when he dies his bones, or if possible his actual corpse, should be brought to his original home for disposal. Sometimes, if there is bad feeling between, say two brothers and one of them leaves his home and goes elsewhere, he may make a separate burning-ground and erect his own memhirs, but he has to abide by the marriage rules. The *birinda* also controls certain sacrifices, and in particular the ceremonial eating of food. The *Doripur* and *Ajorapur* ceremonies, for examples, are performed only for and by members of a particular family. At the great funerary rites of the *Guar*, *Karja* and *Lajap*, members of the family concerned eat their food in their own homes and get more; members of other groups eat out in the fields and get less. The family food is cooked in a new pot, other food in an old one, and the two lots of food must not touch and cannot be shared. At a funeral only member of the deceased's family attend.

Marriage

The *birinda*-group controls first of all the marriage arrangements of the tribe. 'We go by the blood', as a *Saora* once said to Elwin. That is the only real rule, breach of which is regarded as incest, as the ultimate taboo.

A youth can, if he tries, marry a girl of a different tribal type; he can elope with a girl outside his social class; he can marry within his own village or quarter but he cannot under any circumstances whatever marry a girl of his own *birinda.* And since the family boundaries are widely drawn, this means that he cannot marry his mother's brother's daughter or his father's sister's daughter, for both have his blood. Here is another remarkable difference between the *Saoras* and other Indian tribesmen: cross-cousin marriage, so popular elsewhere, is not allowed.

A very important fact is that a woman does not change her *birinda* by marriage; she does not join her husband's family but continues in the group of her birth till death. Theoretically, therefore, a man should be able to marry his maternal grandmother, his mother's sister, a widowed daughter-in-law, his wife's brother's wife, his wife's elder sister, his mother-in-law, his younger brother's wife and his father's elder brother's wife. But in practice, this is not allowed.

Marriage between the aristocratic and proletarian families is admitted only in a typically aristocratic way. The Chiefs will accept girls from the proletarian families, but will not give girls to them. Generally, however, the Chiefs prefer their sons to marry girls from the families of other Chiefs; *buyyas* like to marry *Buyyas*. *Mandals* like to marry Mandals. But there is no objection to a Gamang marrying a Buyya, or a Mandal or a Naiko, if they are sufficiently well to do.

While the village is the more important unit (people pay their taxes and celebrate most of their festival as a village), the quarter—especially if it is something more than a row of housed in a street—also has its significance. Many ceremonies take place within it for its own members who owe a special loyalty to their particular leader. Neither the village nor the quarter is an exogamous unit. There is no real territorial exogamy among the *Saoras*; there may once have been, but Fawcett, writing in 1888, says that' a *Saora* may marry a woman of his own village or of any other village'. But since most of the inhabitants of a quarter are generally of one family, it is natural for its men to seek wives elsewhere. But it is the family, not the quarter or village, which makes this necessary.

There is some disagreement as to whether a man may marry his stepmother. But some *Saoras* consider it is not improper for the son of a polygamous father to marry after his father's death one of the younger widows, a younger co-wife of his own mother. Elwin states that he knows a *Saora* who married a woman who had left her first husband by whom she had a daughter. The woman then died and the man married the daughter. 'There is no harm in it,' he was told, 'she was of different blood.' A *Saora* is expected to marry his elder brothers widow and even his father's elder brother's widow. The *Saora* marriage ritual has been studied in detail by Fawcett (1988:230). It is unusually secular in character, a business contract rather than a religious union. Its function is the stabilizing of society round the institution of the family and the canalization of sex into the fruitful field of child-production. *Saora* marriage, which takes place rather early, at sixteen or seventeen for the boy, fifteen or sixteen for the girl, does not initiate its partners into sexual experience, either generally or with one another. As in most tribes at this level of development, pre-marital life is fairly (though not exceptionally) free, but great value is place on the integrity of the marriage-bond.

The marriage ceremony and its preliminaries are simple and economical. It is curious that a tribe which never loses an opportunity for ceremonial display should surround this critical event with so little. The betrothal is effected by a series of visits (which may extend over many months) from the bridegroom's family to the girl's house; on the first visit the suitors take an arrow and a bangle and put them in the roof or, where the central pillar of the house has breasts carved on it, in the ground between them. Gifts of palm wine are made and the bride price is paid. The betrothal is important and should it not end in marriage, compensation must be paid by the family of the girl, if she is at fault, proportionate to the gifts that have been received. The actual ceremony is marked by a feast and a dance. The bride visits all the houses of her own village to bid farewell, and is then escorted by a party of relations and friends, with drums and trumpets, to her new home. There she is welcomed and taken into her husband's house. A priest or shaman makes offerings to the ancestors. There is plenty of eating and drinking, and a lot of noise. But there are none of the usual marriage rites observed by other tribes: no wedding furniture of turmeric or vermilion, no booth, no circumambulation of a pole, or tying the pair together. And there is no bedding of married pair as among Bondos, Marias and Murias. About a week after the marriage the young husband and wife go to the girl's house with presents for the parents. The father returns the betrothal arrow to the youth saying, 'I have given you my daughter; see, I also give you back this arrow'. After a marriage a man builds his own house and sets up a separate establishment as soon as he can.

There is very little religion in all this. At the time of paying the bride price, a shaman makes offerings to the gods and ancestors. When the bride is brought to her husband's house her father says to the boy's father, 'From today we give you our own life. Now our life has become yours. If the gods or ancestors trouble her, that is your affair. If she elopes with someone else, if she dies, that is your affair, not ours. You be happy; we will be happy.' When the bride cleans the house and cooks for the first time, her mother-in-law says, 'From today this will be your home. The pots and pestles are yours; the gods and the dead are yours. The seeds of rice and millet, pulse and beans are yours. We are old and ignorant; feed and take care of us.'

The nearest thing to a ceremony Elwin has recorded occurs when the bride arrives her husband's house. Bride and bridegroom stand before the door, and a priest or shaman puts *Bauhinia vahlii* leaves in their hands. He makes a libation of palm wine, puts a little rice into each leaf and says, '*O Kittung Mahaprabhu, you are Darammasum, you are Uyungsum*. You made the world. You know the fate of men. Today we have joined these two as man and wife. You are above; *Labosum* is below.' He makes a mark with rice on the foreheads of the boy and girl, and they salute *Darammasum*. Then they go into the house, carrying the rice in their hands. There they tie the rice up in the leaves and hang them in one bundle from the roof

The *Saoras*, like other tribesmen, have .the custom of engaging a suitable youth to serve for a period of years for a girl. This is usually done when there is no son in a household, or when the parents are particularly attached to a daughter and do not want her to leave them for another home. Marriage by capture seems to have been fairly common at one time; in fact Fawcett was told that 'formerly every one took his wife by force'. But even in his day this practice had become greatly modified, and now only occurs sporadically. A widow is expected to marry her husband's younger brother or one of an elder brother's sons, if there are no younger brothers. If she marries someone else; compensation must be paid to the husband's brothers.

Divorce is simple, though emphatically disapproved. There is no ceremony; it is effected by the payment of compensation, for no woman leaves her husband except for another man. The dispossessed husband has the right to follow his wife to her new home and kill and eat any goat or pig he can find there, whether it is the property of the new husband or not. 'A woman', says Fawcett, 'may leave her husband whenever she pleases... Formerly, it is said, if he did not pay up, the man she left would kill the man to whom she went'. Divorce usually comes from the woman's side, but a man may turn out a wife if she does not work properly, if she gives away his property to her own relations or a lover, or if he catches her in the act of adultery. Even then, if anyone marries her, the new husband must pay compensation.

Polygamy is fairly common, in Dodripanga, Elwin found every married man had at least two wives. Fawcett has some interesting remarks about the situation in his day. Men usually married their wives' sisters, as this was less expensive. 'In some places all a man's wives are said to live together peaceably. It is not the custom in the Kehalakot villages. Knowing the wives would fight if together, domestic felicity were maintained by keeping up different establishments. A man's wives will visit one another in the daytime, but one wife will never spend the night in the house of another. An exception to this is that the first wife may invite one of the other wives to sleep in her house with the husband: unless so invited the other wife will not go to the house. As each wife has her separate house, so has she her separate piece of ground on the hillside to cultivate. The wives will not co operate in working each other's cultivation, but they will work together, with the husband, in the paddy' fields. Each wife deeps the produce of the ground he cultivates in her own house. Produce of the paddy fields is divided into equal shares among the wives'. Elwin found much the same arrangement persisting to the present time. At Parisal, for example there, there was an old priest with five wives, his father had nine and each had her own house, and her individual pigs, fowls and swidden. The eldest wife arranged how the husband was to sleep; he usually had each wife four days at a time. When he was sleeping with a wife, he would take his food and spend his time in her house. If he spent a day or two too long with one wife, the others would abuse her saying, 'What god had carried him off? Was it *Mardisum* ? Was it is *Labosum* ?' After a husband's death, each of the widows retains her own house, swidden and domestic animals, but the fields are divided among the sons.

Social Structure: The Present Scenario

Family

Robin Fox's four basic principles where the first one 'the women have the children' highlights that of family. The family as the standard social unit has been found in one form or other at almost all levels of cultural development. The form and basis of familial groupings have varied from time to time and place to place. Different types of families have been observed in different structures and at different points of time and space. But as a basic social group family existed in all societies and all times.

According to Lowie (1950-215), the family may be considered as an association that corresponds to the institutions of marriage. Radcliffe Brown (1941: 2) includes in the family husband and wife and their child or children. But the tribal family will include not only the husband and wife and their minor children but also parents, in laws and wife / husband of sons and daughters. The *Saora* family presents most of the characteristics of the typical tribal family in India. While nuclear family is the main type that prevails among the *Saora*, other characteristics of compound, extended and joint family are also common. In terms of residence, it is patrilocal but the newly married couple have a tendency to build their own houses.

Table 3.1 Head of the Household

Category	*F*	*Per cent*
Father	51	22.17
Mother	15	6.52
Husband	149	64.78
Wife	4	1.74
Son	11	4.78
Daughter	0	—
Total	230	100.00

The Table 3.1 indicates the nature of household. It shows out of 230, 149 households have the husband as the head of household which shows, after marriage the couple build there own and separate house. This 149 is the 64.78 per cent of the total sample. This also shows the other types of household where father is the head of the family— it is 51 and 22.17 per cent of the sample. It shows that some sort of extended family is preferred after nuclear family. This father and husband head of the household shows the patriarchal family. In 15 households where only (6.52 per cent) mother is the head, in 4 households wife as head and in 11 households son is the head of the family. From the above statistics it is clear that mostly sons go to build a new house after their marriage and it is patriarchal family.

Table 3.2 Type of Saora Households.

Types of family	*No. of household*	*Per cent*
Nuclear	134	58.26
Compound	30	13.04
Extended	35	15.22
Joint	31	13.48
Total	230	100.00

In Table 3.2, it is clear that out of 230, 134 households have nuclear family, which is 58.26 per cent. After that 35, (15.22 per cent) households have the extended family. It means that as a second preference, tribals like to live with their parents. However, joint family is also prefered. Out of 230, 31 families, (13.48 per cent), have a joint family. This shows their influence by modern or Hindu culture where married sons generally stay with their family. N. Pattanaik in his study *The Saora* mentions that 'mostly the family is of nuclear type comprising of married couple and their unmarried offspring. The compound families having more than one wife and their children are most common among the well to-do *Saora*. The extended families having parents and their married sons and grant children living together are comparatively less. Joint families with several married brothers staying together are rarely found among them' (1989:30). As a solid social and economic unit, the extended family does not go on forever. When a man's sons start to raise families of their own, the extended family gradually begins to segment. When the family head becomes too old to visit the gardens, control over them passes to his eldest son, or in the immaturity of the son, to the head's younger brother. The old man and his wife will usually move out of their large house into a smaller one, and his successor takes over his house. By slow process, the family head is thus divested of former status and power. By modern ethices influences of missionary influences that— an old father or family head should be properly fed and cared for by his brothers and sons. Actually he sinks into a pitiable position; aboriginaly, his family might have killed him (Williams and Calvert 1859:144). However anthropolgists suggest that 'in any case the nuclear family is bound to be derivative and not 'basic'. The basic unit is the mother and her child, however the mother came in be impregnated. Whether or not a mate becomes attached to the mother on some more or less-permanent basis is a variable matter' (Fox, 1967: 39).

In this the compound family where two wives are present, the number is 30, i.e., 13.4 per cent which shows it is declining. Earlier this was the only type of family was very much prominent among *Saora*. Now this is decaying. It has many reasons. The first one is that people are influenced by Christianity. They have a fear always that if they go for more than one wife they will be out of the Christian *mandali*, they won't have much importance to express their opinion. Secondly, *Saoras* are influenced by modern culture where one wife system is preferred. It shows the influence of their outside contact. Thirdly, few people also hide this fact that they have more than one wife. It has been generally observed by the researcher that, the adult male used to have sexual intercourse with many girls but it does not materialise into marriage.

Table 3.3 Size of the Household

Number of Members	*No. of House hold*	*Per cent*
Below 4	35	15.22
5 to 8	121	52.61
9 to 12	53	23.04
13 to 16	18	7.83
17 to 20	2	0.87
20 to 25	1	0.43
Total	230	100.00

The nature and head of the household became more pertinent when we see the analysis of Table 3.3. This table shows the demographic trend. Mostly *Saora* families today are having 5 to 8 members. Out of 230, 121 or 52.61 per cent households have this size. After that, 9 to 12 members household is persisting which is 53 of 230, that is 23.4 per cent. The family of below 4 members - there are 35 or 15.22 per cent. Eighteen households have 13 to 16 member of this sample size, that is 7.83 per cent. Only one family is of 17 to 20 and has 20 to 25 members. This figure shows the population trend among the *Saoras*. This tribal community is trying to understand the small family norms and also the shortage and depletion of natural resources; which is forcing them to go for small family. N. Pattanaik (1989:30) states that 'the size of family is usually small consisting of 4 to 6 members'. It is also evident that household composition among farmers varies with the type and amount of labour required for effective crop production (Netting). Sahlins, in his article, "Land use and the Extended Family in Moala" (1957:449-62) have indicated the advantages of the extended family household for cooperatively exploiting widely dispersed resources and coordinating their consumption. On small-holdings in rural Ireland, the presence of a second male worker lowers individual productivity (Symes, 1972:25-38). Similarly the domestic unit of a mature man with one wife is considered best suited to the demands of mixed farming among the Haya (Reining, 1970:41-89). Plentiful land in northern Thailand may promote agricultural cooperation between brothers (Merman, 1968:227), while competition for scarce resources strains brotherly relationships in Ceylon (Leach, 1961:344), and the Pathan area of Pakistan (Barth, 1959:5-21) shows persisting rivalry over fields and irrigation water between close agnatic collaterals.

Table 3.4 Age and Sex Distribution of Saora Family

Age	*Sex*	
	Male	*Female*
0-4	109	110
5-15	249	234
16-35	246	314
36-50	50	79
51-65	43	73
66-above	6	8

Now let us examine the age and sex distribution of *Saora* family. This is shown in Table 3.4. which states that in *Saora* family the sex distribution among the members of 0 to 4 age group is 109 males and 110 females. It reflects that fertility rate is high. When we look at 5 to 15 age group it suggest that the female infanticide is more, as the number is less in comparison to male. This also shows the children population among the *Saoras*. Next figure shows the age group of 16 to 35, which has 246 males and 314 females. This is the working population among the *Saora* households. The members belong to 36 to 65 age group with 50 males and 79 females. In the age group of 51 to 65, there are 43 males and 73 females. The population of 66 years and above comprises of 6 male and 8 females. All this shows the demographic trend among the *Saora* tribes. The life expectancy is 50 years, as it is- evident the old population is less. After 50 years the age and sex distribution figure decreases. These are the age, sex and population trends among the *Saora* of Sagada panchayat. The neo-functionalists claim that the basic facts of technology, environment, and demography determine social structure and culture (Harris, M : 1968).

Table 3.5 Family Religion

Category	*F*	*Percent*
Christian	91	39.57
Hindu	84	36.42
Both Christian & Hindu	55	23.91
Total	**230**	**100.00**

In *Saora* family a typical trend has been observed regarding religious practices. It has been given in Table 3.5. Out of 230 families, 91 families are Christians where the whole family preaches this religion. This is 39.87 per cent of the total sample. In the same fashion 84 families are Hindu i.e.36.52 per cent. But there are families where they have the members of both Hindu and Christian faith. The figure is 55 out of 230, which is 23.91 per cent. It means there is a cohesion between tradition and modernity; as the yonger people are pracing christianity whereas the older are following their traditional practices. Mostly in families the old members preache Hinduism with a few exception from young and middle age groups.

Kinship and Birinda

After the family, it is important to see from where dose this family descended. This descendency is not the clan but it is different from it. It is called in their languages *Birinda*. The *Saora* are unique due to the absence of clan or sib organization, which is common to most of the tribal communities in the country. Their main exogamous unit is the extended family descended from a common ancestor. This unit is called *Birinda*, which is based on patrilineage. They have no phratry and no moiety. *Birinda* is equivalent to lineage, as marriage with any one which shares some amount of common blood, as in the case of the members of lineage, is considered to be incestuous and to be absolutely avoided. All the *birinda* members participate in *Guar* (second death ceremony) and *karjya* (final death ceremony). When one dies the *birinda* perform the funeral rites and participate in *guar* ceremony which is held to admit the deceased person to the under world. The *birinda* also inherit the property of hire-less members. A remarkable feature among the *Saoras* is that a woman belongs to her father's *birinda* even after her marriage. After her death the members of her father's *birinda* claim to perform her funeral rites and *Guar*.

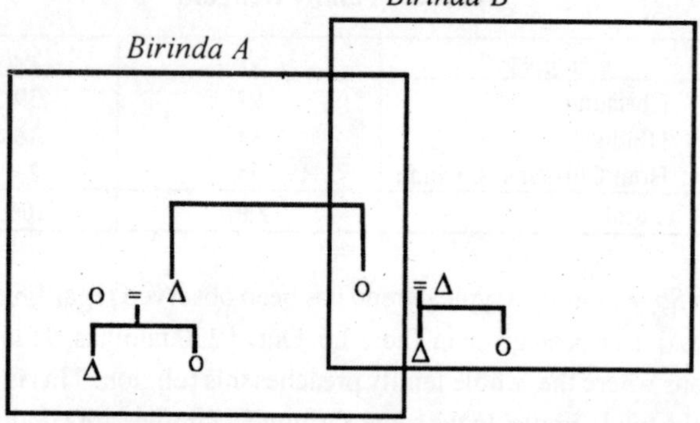

Figure-1. *Status of Birinda after marriage*

This above diagram shows that if a particular male of group-B marries in group-A, relation of this lady in group-A retains. And even after death of the lady, the funeral "will be done at both the places of group-A and group-B *birinda*. When somebody else also dies from her *birinda* A, she shares the ceremonial pollution. . Her brothers and sisters belong to her *birinda*, as also the children of her brothers. Her own children and those of her sisters do not belong to her *birinda*, Hence, her own children could be married to her brothers children— at least theoretically.

Nevertheless, *birinda* is not synonymous with clan or gotra where members living in far off places observe common rules of exogamy. *Birinda* members live in one village and its membership is limited to 4 to 5 generations. It resembles the Hindu *sapind* or *kutumba*. On rare occasions some one may migrate to another village but he retains the *birinda* of his own and after death his bones, etc. are required to be brought to his original village. It is likely that *birinda* may be confused with 'sib' which is briefly defined as a unilateral kin group. If a tribal is organized into further sibs, every child follows the father's sib and takes her father's sib name. A sib would include a common male ancestor (totemic in nature in most cases) with all his sons and unmarried daughters. Thus, the father's sib embraces a male ancestor, his children, male and female and the children of his male descendants. In sib organization, whether it is father sib or mother sib, any individual would take the patrimony on birth, preserve it till death and if a male, transmit it to his children; thus sib bond is permanent.

Table 3.6. Family Descended

Name of the Birinda	*No. of House holds*	*Per cent*
Gamango	46	20.00
Dalbehera	40	17.39
Karji	18	7.83
Badarahit	10	4.35
Sabar	87	37.83
Raikia	29	12.61
Total	**230**	**100.00**

In this connection a question was asked to know their *birinda's* name and how many types of *birinda* groups they have. This has been stated in table 3.6. Out of 230, 46 belong to *Gamango*, 40 *Dalabehera*, 18 *Karji*, 10 *Badarahit*, 87 *Sabar* and 29 *Raikia*. Traditionally, the *gamango* was powerful and they used to govern the society. Their traditional structure was like such that *gamango* use to solve the problem of that particular village with the help of *dalabehera*, *karji*, and *badarahit*. Even today with a few exceptional gamango still retain the power. People from this group mostly entered into national politics. In fact, when social anthropologists deal with kinship relations they are really dealing with relations of a very different kind, that is, with social ones. These may be relations of authority and subordination, of economic exchange, of domestic co-operation, of ritual of ceremonial. Thus, kinship relations are not special kind of social relationships, like economic relations or legal relations. Rather, the categories which kinship affords provide the context and the idiom for many different kinds of social relationships. By asking this question the aim is to know that after becoming Christian whether they continue to believe in this genealogical tradition or not, Our result shows that even many things have changed but their traditional kinship structure is almost same. It means that the impact of modernisation and Christianity is not clear in this structural aspect of the *Saora* community. This researche has noted no structural changes. But the flexibility has been found in this kinship and *birinda* structure. Kinship, ties become loose and people used to have sexual relationship in their own *birinda*. That is because of the influence of christianity and modernisation.

Marriage

Levi-Strauss in his study of kinship used the structural analysis by opposing nature with culture. Describing marriage system as a form of communication and reciprocity he narrates that nature allows physical relationship between opposite sexes but culture prohibits by thrusting incest taboo. The *Saoras* generally abide by the polygynous rules of marriage. Yet there are instances of both polyandry and monogamy. In a *Saora's* marriage negotiation starts from the bridegrooms side. Pre-marital relationships are not a serious offence in the society and a girl who becomes pregnant before marriage does not find it difficult to get herself married. Widow re-marriage and marriages after divorce are permitted. Bride price is paid in all cases of marriage. In most cases, polygynous marriages are of sorrel type. Cases of marriage by service are also seen among the *Saora's*. In some cases, the period of service is only two years and in other cases it is as long as five years. But generally it does not exceed six years. Those who are not able to pay the bride price resort to the mode of marriage by service.

Village exogamy was previously observed, because in the past, the village .comprised of one lineage. In recent years, the composition of the village has become multilineage. Hence, occurrence of inter-village marriages is not unusual. In *Saora* tribe polygyny is regarded as a symbol of special status for the number of wives one has; it indicates the important position of a man in the society. This practice is to derive economic advantage. Each wife in a polygamous household has her own house and establishment and her family comprises mainly herself and her children. Most often the compounds of the houses of the co-wives lie next to one another.

Modern Trend

Marriage pattern among the *Saora's* is changing. Now, most marriages are love marriage. And due to the impact of Christianity and modern liberal atmosphere, they prefer to marry to only one lady. But it is commonly observed that the extra-marital and pre-marital sexual relationship is widely practiced. Secondly, people are marrying in very early age around 13-14 for male and 10-14 by the females. This trend has developed because young boys and girls generally go to church, morning and evening they tend to develop an 'affair' and at the end they marry in the church. In this sample size of 230, Christians are 121 and Hindus 109. Mostly all these groups follow marriage rituals. Hindu marriage ritual is related with bride price and offering buffaloes and wine. In Christianity there is no bride price but they come to church and all the marriage work has been done by the *pastor* of that Church.

Forest and Social Structure

There is a close relation between the social structure and forest. As we have already discussed about the family and its changing trend, it is evident that tribals are now preferring nuclear family. A nuclear family and forest has a relation, as each and every family depends on forest. For example, firewood for cooking is required for each nuclear household and that all nuclear families go to forest to collect it. Exploitation of natural resources will be more. Social institutions are always adaptive to the environment. Steward regarded such features as the sexual division of labor, land tenure, family organization, group size, and political control as likely to be closely involved in the utilization of the environment (1938:120). His approach had the advantage of isolating the relevant or effective variables in the natural environment that had functional significance for human adaptation (Greez, 1972:23-40), extending the perspective to an intercultural environment that included the interactions of a group with its neighbours (1968:337-44), and including cultural, biological, and physical factors in a systemic model (Vayda: 1968,564).

In the same way the researcher have discussed the kinship and *birinda* system. It is evident from here that the traditional *birinda* members were concerned about the village and nature. With dying of this *birinda* system, the concerned for ecology or forest is also dying. *Birinda* and gamango system was functional to the maintenance of social ecology, which is heavily disturbed after the introduction of panchayat raj. Scholars like Fortes, Evans Prichard and Ford have concerned themselves with only one formal aspect of society at a time like political structure, kinship structure and ritual organisation. They display this system as a set of rules, they discuss the mutual interdependence of the rules, and that fit between the society and its environment (ecology). It is evident from all the discussion that change in social structure brings change in the state of forest.

Conclusion

Social structure is not something directly observed but an abstraction of structural forms from the actually existing relations, which are observable. These abstracted "Structural forms" or "normal forms of social relat ons" cannot be described or understood without reference to culture. Social relations are only observed, and can only be described, by reference to the reciprocal behaviour of the persons related. The form of a social structure has, therefore, to be described by the patterns of behaviour to which individuals and groups conform in their dealings with one another.

This concept was inducted into social science literature by H. Spencer by using the term 'structure' and 'function'. And latter Durkheim has used it on the basis of human relationship. Likewise G.P.Murdock, Radcliffec Brown and Levi-Strauss have also made pioneering effort in introducing a sense of purpose and potency to the term social structure. For Murdock, structure means building analogy but for Radcliffe-Brown it is compared to a 'living organism' or a 'working mechanism'. In contrast to this Levistrauss concept of social structure is rooted more in mathematics and linguistic than biology. In this connection he has talked of structural models rather than empirically observed facts. For him social structure is the orders of the order. Firth has taken the direction of Levistrauss by saying that social structure is concerned with the ordered relations of parts to a whole. With this arrangement the elements of social life are linked together.

With all this theoretical background *Saora* traditional and modern social structure have been discussed. The remarkable aspect of *Saora* Society is its lack of organisation, no clan, no *phratry*, and no *moiety*. There is a family hierarchy, as aristocracy their ranks are in superior position who looks after the village with the help of *Dalbeheara*, *Karrgi*, *Naiko* etc. All these groups are the members of different families i. e. called different *birindas*. They have descended from these families. On this basis they have their own specialized occupation in the village. *Birinda* is the sole basis of kinship and marriage.

Traditionally a member of same *birinda* can not marry in the same *birinda*; as it is their blood relationship. Traditionally aristocrat *Saora* families in exceptional cases can marry in their subordinate groups but they prefer to marry the other aristocrats. Like *gamango* chief with buyyas chiefs etc. The traditional marriages are celebrated with many rituals followed by feast and music. Traditionally divorce is emphatically approved. Divorce comes usually from women when the husband does not care money and property. Among the *Saoras* polygamy is fairly common as people marry more than two in many instances, but the wives do have good understandings and stay in different rooms in a single household. But in course of time this has changed and several nuclear family has come, by leaving back the traditional compound family. The husband is considered as the head of the family today.

The findings of this study shows that traditionally 100 per cent compound family has existed where as' today it 58.26 per cent nuclear family followed by extended family 13.04 per cent. So the whole family structure has changed in due course of time. This has a clear link with the family size as the maximum result is of 5 to 8 members in a family followed by 9 to 12. This means there is a change in demographic profile. The main causes are of single marrige system and adopting to small family norms. The result shows in connection with the demographic profile the female population is more than the male population. This is a general picture of many tribal society. Tribals do not have any complain related to male or female issues. The finding also reveals that *Saora* family believes in different religions. Members of two different religions stay together without any hassles. Most of the family religion is; Christian 39.57 per cent, Hindu 36.2 per cent and both 23.91 per cent. So the religion of *Saora* has a mixed result. Though they practice Christianity they are guided by the dominant culture of the society that is of Hindu Culture.

Birinda and kinship is on the verge of changing because of population growth. But still people prefer to live-in their own *birinda* and try to maintain the sanctity of these relationships. There is marked change in the marriage system of *Saoras*. Nowadays their marriages are only love marriage through exchange of garlands in the Church.

The above said changes are occurred due to the change in the ecology. Since the traditional authority system i.e. of *gomanga* rule has changed, so the taboos related to forest and nature have also changed. This is because of modern development plans. Likewise , since the family and marriage system has changed, the attitude of tribals towards forest has also significantly changed.

References

Beattie, J.1964, *Other Culture*. London, Rautledge & Kegan Paul Ltd.

Durkheim, Emile, 1925, *The Rules of Sociological Method,* Paris, Felin Alcan.

Dube, S.C., 1955, *Indian Village,* London, Routledge and Kegan Paul.

Damont, Louis, 1957, 'Village Studies', *Contribution of Indian Sociology*, No. 1. April.

Dumont, Louis and D. Pocock, 1957, 'For a Sociology to India', *Contribution to Indian Sociology* No. 1. April

Desai, I.P., 1964, *Some Aspects of Family in Mahua*, New York, Asia Publishinmg House.

Elwin, V., 1955, *Religion of an Indian Tribe*, London, Oxford University Press.

Evans-Pritchard, E.E., 1951, *Kinship and Marriage Among the Nuer,* Oxford, Clarendon Press.

Fortes, Mayer, 1949, *The Web of Kinship among the Tallensi,* London, Oxford University Press.

Forde, D., 1934, *Habitat, Economy and Society: A Geographical Introduction to Ethnology,* London, Methnen.

Firth. Raymond, 1956, 'Functions' in *Current Anthropology* edited by William. L. Thomas, University of Chicago Press. pp. 237-258.

Gough, E. Kathleen, 1952a 'A Comparison of Incest Prohibitions and the Rules of Exogamy in 3 Matrilineal Groups of the Malabar Coast'. *Institute of Archeological Ethnography*, 46, pp. 82-105.

Gough, E., Kathleen 1952b, 'Changing Kinship Usages in the Setting of Political and Economic Change among the Nayars of Malabar', *J. Roy Anthropological Institute*, 82, pp. 71-87

Gough, E. Kathleen, 1959, 'The Nayars and the Defination of Marriage', *J. Roy Anthropological Institute*, 89, pp. 23-24.

Harris, M, 1968, *The Rise of Anthropological Theory,* New York, Grorwell.

Kapadia, K.M., 1959, 'The Family in Transition', *Sociological Bulletin,* 8 (2).

Kapadia, K.M., 1958, *Marriage and Family in India*, Madras, Oxford University Press.

Kapadia, K.M., 1947, *Hindu Kinship*, Bombay.

Karve, Irawati, 1953, *Kinship Organisation in India*, Bombay, Asia Publishing House.

Levi-Strauss, 1953, 'Social Structure in A.L. Krober (ed.), *Anthropology Today : An Encyclopedic Inventory*, University of Chicage Press.

Levi-Strauss, C., 1963, *Structural Anthropolgy*, New York.

Mayer, Adrian C., 1960, *Caste and Kinship in Central India*, London.

Murdock. G.P., 1949, *Social Structure*, New York, Macmillan.

Netting, Robert McC, 1976, 'What Alpine Peasents have in Common : Observations on Communal Tenure in Swiss Villiage', *Human Ecology*, 4 (2), pp. 135-146.

Parsons, Talcott, 1949, *Essays in Sociological Theory: Pure and Applied*, Glencoe, Illionois, The Free Press.

Pattanaik, N., 1989, *The Saora*, Bhubaneshwar, THRT Publication.

Robin Fox, 1967, *Kinship and Marrtage: An Anthropological Perspective*. London, Penguin Books.

Radcliffe Brown, A.R., 1940, 'On Social Stuture'. *The Journal of the Roayl Anthropological Institute of Great Britain and Island*, Part-I.

Rivers, W.H.R., 1924, *Social Organisation*, New York, Knopf.

Ross, Aileen, D., 1962, *The Hindu Family in its Urban Settings*, Toronto, University of Toronto Press.

Spencer, Herbert, 1925, *The Principles of Sociology* (See Part II, 'Induction of Sociology), New York & London, D. Appleton and Company.

Srinivas, M.N., 1952, *Religion and Society among Coorgs of South India*, London, Oxford University Press.

Sahlins, 1957, *Land Use and the Extended Family in Moala*, Not available.

Steward, J.H., 1938, 'Basin-Platean' Aboriginal Socio-Political Groups, Washington, *Burean of American Ethnology Bulletin*, 120.

Social Structure, 1968, *International Encyclopedia of Social Sciences*, Vol. 14.

Vayda, A.P., (ed.), P. (ed.), 1968, *People and Culture in the Pacific*, New York, The National History Press.

4

Political and Legal System

Isolated from the mainstream of civilization for centuries together and accustomed to live in relatively small groups with their kinsmen, the identity that the tribes are evolving within the structure of a plural society passing through the processes of transformation into a modern nation state, is of great interest of sociologist, cultural anthropologists and to the students of politics.

As anthropologists analyzed political behaviour in the absence of overt political offices in many African societies of the past, they set up a dichotomy of 'centralized' and 'uncentralised' or 'acephalous' polities (Fortes, M : 1945, and Evans-Pritchard 1940). However, this dichotomy accommodated intermediate types (such as petty chiefdoms) rather poorly. Mair Primitive Government (1962) therefore suggested, somewhat later, a tripartite classification into societies with 'minimal government (such as family bands among hunters and gatherers); those with governmental functions 'diffused' among and embedded within social categories (such as age-grades or lineages); and those having a state organisation. Rather than dealing in such discrete categories, A.P. Cheater in his book *Social Anthropology* would like to suggest that the international and historical range of political organisation is best understood along a continuum, stretching from family bands to modern bureaucratic states. That way we can find a place for every variety and, more importantly, avoid endless disputes about taxonomies. Mair LP. (1962) in his book *Primitive Government* remarks: "there is no society where rules are automatically obeyed." The function of power is to defend society against its own weakness, to keep it in good 'order' and to adopt itself to the changes that are not in conflict with its basic principles. As soon as the social relations extend beyond kinship relations, a more or less apparent competition is set up between individuals and groups—each trying to influence the decisions of collectivity in accordance with his or its own particular interests. Consequently power becomes political and it appears as a product of competition and as means or containing it. (Pandey, 1989:2)

In case of *Saora* tribes of Orissa they do have a simple 'family band' by which they govern themselves. In the process of time, of course this has changed but even though the politics is governed by this traditional factor. In this chapter the day to day political activities of *Lanjia Saora* has been discussed. How these political activities changed their society and culture? While discussing the changes, it has been found that we will also focus how the traditional political mechanisms were functional to the *Saora* society. The discussion has started with some theoratical conceptualisation of political anthropology. The *Saora* political aspect has also of been discussed in details. The *Saoras* have their political life which is very much associatied with their social structure. For a better analysis discussion on the political life of *Saoras* have been divided into three aspects; the traditional, the modern panchayati raj system and the emering changes and contradiction. It has been observed that changes in political activities has also bought changes in the forest ecology.

Politics: An Anthropological Understanding

African Political Systems was the first attempt of British social anthropologists to isolate the political aspects of the societies they studied and present these in a form that would make comparison possible. Less than thirty years later Goody (1969: 11) can call for "a political sociology that does not limit itself to the party politics of the Western world", and Abner Cohen (1969:213) can describe social anthropology as "essentially a branch of political science" and social change as "essentially a change in the forms, distribution and exercise of power". As Tylor said, "Wherever you see a belief in spiritual beings, you know that you are dealing with religion," Radcliffe-Brown says, "Wherever you see recognized means of enforcing recognized claims, you are dealing with a political system".

Evans-Pritchard found among the Nuer no arrangements for the management of public affairs even at the village level (if we discount the minimal activity of the "man of the cattle" in opening and closing initiation periods). He did not use the phrase "political community", but called a Nuer tribe "the largest political segment" of a "people" defined by a common language and a sense of common identity. The tribe was the largest population who not only claims a common territory but "acknowledge the right of their members to compensation for injury".

More succinctly he says elsewhere that there is law within a tribe but not between tribes (1940:5,121). Law, as his account makes clear, is enforced by self-help; Radcliffe-Brown's definition is the only one in terms of which the Nuer could be said to have an internal political system. Evans-Pritchard remarks that their political system "includes all the peoples with whom they come into contact" (1940:5). He has little to say, however, about their dealings with their neighbours. Just as political scientists have rejected the idea that constitutions describe real-life interactions, so anthropologists have come to look at the process of adjustment of competing interests as well as—not instead of—stated norms concerning authority and obligation. One of the landmarks in this advance was Barth's (1959a) study of the formation of alliances among the Swat Pathans, a population among whom a unilateral descent structure identical with that of the Nuer is combined with other "constitutional" principles so as to produce oppositions of a completely different type.

Evans-Pritchard (1940b) traced from the remembered history of Anuak kings three stages in which the contest for the ritual emblems of kingship was conducted in different ways. Godfrey Wilson (1939) built from oral tradition an account of the transformation of the Ngonde divine king into a secular ruler. Southwold (1961) deduced from records of the clan membership of Ganda chiefs that there were periods during which they asserted hereditary claims to office and others when the Kabaka made appointments at his pleasure.

A new line was taken by Leach (1954) when he interpreted the history of the Kachins as one of periodic revolutions against chiefs who claimed more privileges than their subjects were willing to grant them. He made this the ground of an attack on the concept of equilibrium, that vague metaphor, hardly deserving the name of mode, which is sometimes taken to mean immobility; but Gluckman (1968) commented that the Kachin system, on Leach's own showing, oscillated between two poles and did not change cumulatively in one direction. A stronger stimulus towards the study of process came from Gluckman's (1955, 1963) treatment of conflict, although this too in its earlier form emphasized the function of conflict, not in producing desired changes but in maintaining stability. Gluckman rightly distinguished between a rebellion aimed at replacing the incumbents of established offices and a revolution seeking to change the whole political structure. His followers have concentrated attention not on actual rebellion, but on the various ways of manipulating inconsistent norms in the pursuit of political power on a minimal scale. This is what led

Easton (1959) to say that anthropologists treat politics as a dependent variable, and do not in fact examine or even identify political systems as he conceives them. Kuper's treatment of the Kalahari village explicitly follows Easton's schema, and makes policy-making its main theme rather than competition for office. Yet one of the two policy decisions that he deals with in detail is a contest for the lowly office of pumpman at the borehole, and the process followed out is a matter of rivalry between factions. Kuper uses the Easton vocabulary to show how demands and support come from different directions according to the nature of the decision to be taken, and how decisions react on the system as a whole. He does not convince that the Easton formula is more than a recipe for describing political systems. If the analysis applies to all systems of whatever kin, it offers no variable for comparison.

In the book *Tribes Without Rulers,* J. Middleton and D. Tait define 'political relations' independent of the forms of government that organize them. They qualify these relations by the functions they perform. They are relations 'by which persons and groups exercise power or authority for the maintenance of social order within a territory'. They distinguish them according to their internal or external orientation. The first operates within the political unit, ensuring its cohesion, maintenance or adaptation; the second operates between distinct political units and is essentially of an antagonistic kind. On the basis of his own experience in research—among the centralized societies of East Africa—and using an analytical method J. Marquet distinguished three orders of relations which may be found simultaneously in the political process and which have a common formal characteristic. Marquet constructs three rational models composed of three elements — the actors, the roles, and the specific content. He says these three models have a practical value.

Likewise Evans-Pritchard has studied the Lineage segmentation as political organisation where he has mentioned that, traditionally the matrilineal Nuer (calling themselves 'Nath': 'we, the people') were divided into some 20 different 'tribes', each subdivided into clans. Each tribe had a dominant or 'aristocratic' clan whose members claimed special prestige from living in their clan territory (which they lost if they moved out of it), but no other privileges. In turn, the clans were segmented into lineages of varying depth, from the largest (maximal) units in which members were able to trace their descent from a common ancestor, to the smallest (minimal) units not exceeding five generations in depth. Each local descent group, or minimal patrilineage, formed the agnatic core of a village. Neighbouring

Evans-Pritchard (1940) called the 'tertiary tribal section', the smallest separate territorial unit in the Nuer system. The tertiary sections were aggregated into secondary sections, dominated by a major lineage. In turn, the secondary sections were grouped into primary sections, controlled by maximal lineages or small clans. The primary sections were the largest sub-divisions of the tribal territory as a whole. Within the tribal territory, disputes were supposed to be settled by compensation. Beyond this territory, with unrelated neighbours, open warfare erupted, which, against the Dinka but not other Nuer tribes, often culminated in the acquisition of livestock, women, children, and even land by the victor. The disputed that gave rise to feuding (and occasionally warfare) often started in the dry season (between December and April) at the cattle camps. As the floodwaters receded, Nuer moved individually from their permanent villages on the inter fluvial ridges, to the permanent watering holes in the desiccating plain. As more and more people sought to water more and more cattle at these camps, treading on another's toes could, quite literally, spark off a fight, a homicide and feud among members to the same tribe. Feuds started in cattle camps among distantly related Nuer normally living well apart might smoulder on for years. In Nuer ideology, a feud never ended though it might be interrupted temporarily by the payment of cattle as compensatory blood wealth. Such temporary settlement of feuds was negotiated by the earth priest, who afforded the killer refuge in his homestead until the agnate of the deceased, seeking his life, dispersed home. Earth priests came from lineages monopolizing special ritual powers. As successful negotiators, they could achieve, off this ascriptive position, considerable prominence as informal leader, but they had no access to any instruments of force to make feuding disputants comply with their recommendations. The best they could do was threatened to curse the recalcitrant by the earth, to cause the fertility of their land, cattle and women to dry up, which normally resulted in cooperation and the acceptance of compensation.

Feuding created gross inconvenience when it polarized close agnates, affines and neighbours living in the same tertiary tribal section. Feuding at this level was, therefore, most easily settled by compensation, not least because there were built-in structural limits on the feud itself. These inhered in the relationships through which support was sought. Basically, the old Arab- proverb applied 'I against my brother my brother and I against my cousin; my cousin, my brother and I against all outsiders'. In words, agnatic proximity structured the support which feuding antagonists could muster. The more closely related they were, the smaller was the number of potential supporters, before they reached a common ancestor who united them with their antagonists. The more distant the relationship, the greater was the number of supporters who could be mobilized, before an ancestor many generations back defined the limits of recruitment. Evans-Pritchard (1940), therefore, in his structural analysis of this political behaviour, regarded it as part of and embedded within the genealogical relationships of matrilineal descent. At the same time, however, he emphasised that agnatic closeness also increased the intensity of the 'structural opposition' between lineage segments.

To understand Nuer politics fully, a supplementary analysis of informal leadership is also necessary. In addition to the earth priests as mediators in feuds, the village 'bulls' or 'big men', and the prophets possessed by sky-spirits (the sons of the High God, Kwoth), were important in Nuer politics. The prophets, in particular, organised armed resistance to both Arab and British colonisers, managing to unite men from different Nuer tribes into armies numbering up to 300 men. Not surprisingly, by the time Evans-Pritchard reached Nuer land in 1930, the prophets were maintaining a very low profile, some having been imprisoned for their military entrepreneurship. It is conceivable that, had their unificatory activities not been interrupted, these prophets might have created some form of divine kingship among the Nuer. Similarly, at the village level, the 'bulls' (especially where they were simultaneously earth priests and aristocrats) might have become headmen or even petty chief. They provided advice, guidance and assistance on both productive and judicial matters. Through their charismatic personalities and fighting prowess, these 'bulls' attracted non-agnates to their village. Their lack of political office, then, did not deprive the Nuer of informal leaders with political functions.

In contrast, the matrilineal Gikuyu arranged their society not on the basis of segmentary lineages, but into age-grades which accommodated political functions. By the age of twenty, Gikuyu youth (male and female) had been initiated, after which the young men entered the junior warrior sub-grade and became part of its 'council' (the *njama ya anake a mumo).* They fell under the military and social discipline of the senior warrior sub-grade, and its 'council of war' *(njama ya ita),* headed by the war priest *(mondo mogo wa ita)* who was presumably an elder. Some six years after initiation, a junior warrior moved up automatically to senior status, having served his military apprenticeship in the ranks, so to speak. The warrior age-grades, both 'officers' and 'men', were charged with defiance and raiding, under the control of the decision-making elders. The warriors were organised at village, district and national (or tribal) levels, with elected leader and spokesmen at each level. The Gikuyu transition from warrior to elder status was achieved individually by marriage, after which a man was required to join the council of the lowest of three sub-grades of elder hood, the *kiama gia kamatimo.* In this capacity he again became an apprentice, this time in judicial and administrative matters. Having spent fifteen or so years learning, as an observer, how to maintain and restore social order, when his first-born child was initiated, the junior elder was promoted into the 'council of peace' *(kiama gia mataathi).* Here he took part in the judicial process of resolving disputes (concerning land, stock, trade and marriage) brought before the village council. Finally, when all of his children had been initiated and all of his wives had passed the menopause, he could enter the third and highest grade of elderhood and become a member of the ritual council *(kiama gia maturanguru),* which sat in the centre of the decision-making village council, flanked by the senior and junior elders. Accession into a more senior age grade was, at all levels, accompanies by oaths swearing the newcomer not to reveal the secrets of that level of political responsibility to those junior to him.

In the pre-colonial past, individual mobility through the Gikuyu age-grades had been confirmed categorically, at the national ritual whereby authority was devolved from the retiring to the incoming generation of (senior and junior) elders. This ritual was last held in the 1890s, before its proscription by the British and the disruption of the traditional Gikuyu social order by white settlement on their land. Subsequently, the colonial government introduced chiefly office and selected incumbents on the basis of their leadership qualities demonstrated previously in their capacity as senior elders. After the Second World War, elements of traditional politics, notably woathing, were revived and incorporate into the anti-colonial, Gikuyu-dominated Mau movement. The Gikuyu were split into those opposing colonial rule, and 'loyalists', including chiefs, who were employed by it. This split rather than any traditional status within the defunct age-grading system, provided the fuel for conflict within the Gikuyu dominated Kenya African National Union, both before and after Independence in 1963. Notwithstanding Kenyatta's (1938) treatise, against the backdrop of colonisation, on the logic and desirability of Gikuyu tradition, politics in independent Kenya, as a centralised state dominated politically by the Gikuyu, apparently owes little to such modes. Pre-colonial politically by the Gikuyu, apparently owes little to such modes. Pre-colonial models of (male) democracy seem to have little attraction for those who attained state authority of the base of party organisation and universal suffrage.

Political Anthropology: Indian Context

With reference to these above studies scholars in India tried to see the power and kinship relationship among Indian tribes in the light of above discussed models. The Indian rural population has long been classified into tribes and castes by social scientists, administrators and others. Oddly enough, although many writers have glibly spoken of tribe and caste, few have ventured to state specifically how these two categories of society are to be distinguished. Risley and Majumdar characterize both types of social groups merely as endogamous collection of families without further elaboration of differences and similarities. Weber called attention to the relative economic self-sufficiency of a tribe vs. a caste, and pointed out that a tribe comprises people of social rank, while a caste is frequently divided into sub-castes, each with a different social rank. A caste is a social and occupational group forming part of a wider social community as a whole. Mandelbaum has characterized the Kotas of the Nilgiris as almost Hindu peasants, but also points out that in the 19th century they were a tribe influenced directly by literate peoples and cultures (as a low caste villages were). Their social system was not geared into the main system and was less elaborate. They were also relatively independent of markets and lacked the temples and deities of Hinduism. Most of the monographs on Indian tribes have dealt with whole tribal peoples and have not been studies of individual communities. The works of Elwin, Rivers and Roy may be cited in this context. Recent departures from this extensive approach have been intensive studies of single communities by Bailey and Sinha. Yet the published reports on these studies have been highly specialized in coverage and we do not have a comprehensive picture of the structure of any single tribal community.

Since independence the North Eastern region has experienced a bitter taste of insurgency created by the underground Nagas, the Mizos and the Manipuris demanding sovereign states of their own. The process of integration of the Nagas with the mainstream of national life is yet to be completed and subversive activities on the part of a few of them still pose a serious menace to the unity and stability of India. It is not only the intra-nationalism of the tribes that India has to encounter after independence, their sub-nationalism has also been perplexing (Sinha, 1972:410-22).

Following prolonged agitation by the All Party Hill Leaders' Conference, the Union Government agreed to create an autonomous state for the tribals within the State of Assam which involved a structural innovation in the federal framework of India. Subsequently it was invested with full status as one of the constituent units of the Indian Union. The creation of the States, viz., Nagaland, Manipur, Tripura, Meghalaya and Assam was a negation of one of the cardinal principles which had generally governed the establishment of any new state in the country, namely, that the state should be financially viable. The creation of five states and two union territories was a concession to their intense struggle for autonomy. "The Nagas fought for independence and got statehood. The Mizos rebelled and got a Union Territory. The Khasis and the Garos struggled for sixteen years successfully for Statehood. It was only Arunachal Pradesh which was constituted into a Union Territory without any serious agitation." (Rao, 1976:540)

Concept of Leadership

Leadership is the ability to command respect and honour and take a decision by virtue of some extra qualities of personality. Every tribal community has some tradition of leadership, its own ideology about a leader and the functional responsibilities associated with him (Naik, 1969: 170). This has been developed in the myths and legends, which largely define and interpret this concept and its functions. These legends and not historical records, which are almost non-existent for most tribal communities, provide an understanding of the traditional leadership (*Ibid*: 171).

Generally, four different types of leaderships have been suggested by writers as operating in a community. They are the Institutional Leadership, the Situational Leadership, Dictatorial Leadership and Creative leadership. These, in turn, give rise to three different types of leaders, as appointive, self-constituted and group-selected leaders. Persons holding office in a community whether elected appointed or otherwise designated to carry out routine functions are institutional leaders. Such leadership is rarely progressive and democratic. The primary functions of such a leader is to assist the community to maintain its customs, purposes and attitudes. Situational leadership may arise from within a community in a situation where the existing social structure becomes inadequate. They arise without a reference to the existing leadership pattern. Such leaders are, therefore, the products of a situation that may have required this leadership. In special circumstances, both the institutional and situational leadership may develop into a dictatorial form of leadership; the whole authority is here, devoted to and vested in, one single person of the community. Creative leadership is the ideal of democratic leadership. Its essential ingredients are a genuine vision of the potentialities of human society and a desire to encourage and help others to develop their own abilities.

Power is necessary, but is confines within precise limits. It requires consent and certain reciprocity. Accordingly this involves a network of highly varied responsibilities and obligations: peace and arbitration, defiance of custom and law, generosity, prosperity of the country and of individuals, agreements of ancestors and gods etc. In a general way, it might be said, that power must justify itself by maintaining a state of collective security and prosperity. This is the price to be paid by those who hold it — a price that is never wholly paid (Pandey, 1989:5). In one of the study 'Tikopia of Polynesia' Raymond Firth examines in great detail the problem of 'acquiescence' and effects of 'public opinion'. He reminds that power cannot be entirely autocratic. It seeks and receives a variable degree of support from the governed, either by routine apathy of inability to conceive of an alternative or acceptance of certain values regarded as unconditional. But in any case the governed impose limits on power; they try to contain it within certain bounds, by means of 'formal institutions' (chief's councils or nominated elders) or by 'informal mechanisms' (gossip and public opinion). We are back, then at the ambiguity already mentioned: power tends to develop as a relation of domination, but the consent that legitimizes it tends to reduce its control. These contradictory movements explain that 'there can be no equilibrium in any political system'. Firth states emphatically: "There is struggle,' there are alliances, there is respect for the existing system and desire to change it; there is obedience to the moral law and an attempt to get round it or reinterpret it to sectional advantage". Contrary to the Hegelian interpretation, a political system does not necessarily realize the transcendence of particularities and particular interests. (Pandey, 1989: 6)

Leadership in a tribal community is a specialized job; it requires a special ingenuity and skill in performing the duties and obligations in the various spheres of society. Hence, leaders are formed for every sphere of life; there are village leaders or what may be called administrative leaders, then there are social leaders, economic leaders and religious or ritualistic leaders. (Naik, 1969: 197)

Tribes of Orissa: A Political Profile

High concentration of tribal population is one of the important characteristics of backwardness of the Orissa State. Even though the total tribal populations of India constitute only 6.94 per cent, Orissa records the highest proportion of scheduled tribes, i.e., 23.11 per cent followed by Gujarat (13.9 per cent) and Assam (12.9 per cent). There are 62 tribal communities in Orissa constituting 6.07 million people out of a total population of 21.9 million. The Scheduled Areas constitute one-third of the total area of the State and comprise underdeveloped, inaccessible, hilly and mountainous terrain in the districts of (i) Koraput excluding Kashipur Tahasil, (ii) Mayurbhanj, (iii) Sundargarh, (iv) the uplands of the district of Ganjam excluding a small portion of the Soroda Taluk, and (v) Baliguda Sub-division of Phulbani district excluding Chakapad Block. The tribals account for 56.84 per cent of the total population of the Scheduled Area, which covers 56,553 square kilometres. (Mishra:648)

Socially, the tribals in most cases are well organised into many groups. Verrier Elwin says, "there is a regular village hierarchy. Every village has its own chief who is its spokesman and general organiser; in some tribes... he has great authority, in others he is mere figure head". On the social organisation of the *Khonds* it has been observed. "There is probably no old established community in the world which might with so much of justice appropriate the motto of liberty and equality; in their deliberative assemblies all voices are equal and each cultivator is the alluvial proprietor of the soil he tills". The tribal blocks of Keonjhar district are predominantly inhabited by the tribes such as the *Bhuyans, Juangs, Koths, Mundas* and *Bhatudis* out of which the *Bhuyans* and the *Juangs* are the most primitive tribes numbering about 30,000 who are on the decline. Their population is concentrated in a particular area known as *Bhuyan pirh* and *Juang pirh* which consists of six *pirhs* headed by a headman "Sardar", in each *pirh*. These tribes have multifarious history, culture, social customs and traditions of their own. In the district of Koraput "the typical agency village is a settlement of, from half a dozen to fifty families of one of the aboriginal tribes". The village is named after the name of a tree prominent in the village—Koraput, Dumuriput, Kendupada, Tentulikhunti etc. are examples of such names of the tribal inhabited places". In the past they used to acknowledge the leadership of the persons whom they chose themselves, independent of the appointment of *Mustarjar* made by the authorities of the Jeypore State. "The Savar headman is known as *Gomango,* the *Kandhs* call him *Samanto* or *Majhi,* the *Porojas Janni* or

Mudui and the *Koyas* call their leader as *Pedda, Goantia* or *Naik.* The Koraput District comprises greater part of the areas formerly known as the agency tracts of Visakapatnam which on account of the backwardness of the inhabitants were administered by the Collector with certain special powers under the Ganjam and Visakapatnam Act, 1939. The members of a tribal group are very much intimately bound to each other for a variety of reasons such as common livelihood and settlement patterns, common ancestry and common social activities. They believe in ancestral spirits and in a number of natural malevolent spirits. Common feast for the civilized people of the plains known as the *Dikus* is another unifying factor among them, which keeps them aloof from the mainstream of the society.

Political System of Saora

Traditional Political and Legal System

The *Saora* villages are as much social entities as they are political, with a good deal of cohesion and continuity. Every village is more or less an independent unit with little relationship with the more distant villages. But within the village, people lead more or less a collective life and usually act in common. During the British rule, *Bissoyis* were employed as government officers and stationed by one of the Paralakhemundi Kings at different places for keeping *Saora* under strict administration and control. As such during the British rule, the *Saoras* have lost the political influence and independence.

Prior to British rule the local-self government governed *Saora* villages. Every village was an independent unit with no connecting link with other villages. There was no links of bondage, for these villages, to live together. Rather, the nearby 5 to 6 villages at the most tried to have some sort of mutual assistance and cooperation with one another. Thus, it can be said that every village was a separate kingdom by itself. The people in a particular village owned their allegiance and loyalty to the village leaders, but did not claim individual rights or independence. (Patnaik, 1989:52) Among Saoras, no one would act independently on his own, but would always prefer to act in a common way with others in the village. All the persons in the village together can follow a new course of action or adopt a new usage or custom but no one would like to break away from others to follow his own course of what he likes. This shows collectivity in preference to the individual urges. This can be expressed in Durkheim view as collective consign and social solidarity.

In *Saora* village, the secular headman, i.e., *Gomango,* is synonymous with the lineage head. In the past, he was a man of great prestige. His powers are similar to that of magistrate. The second equally important is the village religious head, the *Buyya.* Apart from village governance *Buyya* has complete freedom in religious matters. The village administration rests with these two officers. (Singh, 1984:25). The offices of *Buyya* and *Gomango* are on hereditary basis and occupied by the members of one and the same family. Though the eldest son has the right to succeed to this office yet in case he does not have the necessary ability to perform these functions, he can be disentitled from occupying this post and the same may be offered to his younger brother. For the office of *Buyya* it is not sufficient to have a mere hereditary right, but he should also have a sound knowledge of the religious customs and practices. In addition to these offices which are indigenous, there is in some villages an astrologer called *Disari* and this post is achieved but not ascribed. The man who acquires requisite knowledge about stars becomes an astrologer. In most villages there is a post called *Barik* who acts as the village messenger (Patnaik, 1989:53).

The *Saora* society is democratic, and matters concerning the village are decided in the village meetings over which the *Gomango* presides and at which attendance of family heads is obligatory. Decisions are arrived at by consensus and not by majority vote (Singh, 1984:25). The *Gomango* and the *Buyya* remain present on every occasion of marriage, funeral and common festivals of the village. Matters relating to purchase, sale and mortgage of land and trees are decided in the village meetings presided over by these two officers and attended by other elders. Whenever the village assembly has to decide on any of these issues there are certain religious practices observed. Till about hundred-years back, this village body was even deciding murder cases presided over by these two officers (Patnaik, 1989:53).

In this connection a question was asked to assess the opinion of tribals regarding the *Gomango* governance system. Table 4.1 shows that out of 135 young respondent 74 said that traditional governance system was good, 44 said 'bad' and 17 did not respond. This shows the mentality of tribal, how they are adapting to changes. Those who say 'good' they are tradition bound and found some complex problem in relation to governance today. Those who say 'no' they are prone to change and modernity. They are more adoptive and critical about the drawbacks of *Gomango* governance which will be clear when we finally, analyze this

Table 4.1 Opinion on Traditional System of Governance

Variables	*Age*								*Religion*						*Occupation*					
Response	*Young*		*Middle*		*Old*		*Total*		*Hindu*		*Non-Hindu*		*Total*		*Agriculture*		*Non-Agriculture*		*Total*	
	F	%	F	%	F	%	F	%	F	%	F	%	F	%	F	%	F	%	F	%
Good	74	54.8	39	61.9	19	59.32	132	57	65	60	67	56	132	57	94	59.1	38	53	132	57
Bad	44	32.6	22	34.9	10	31.25	76	33	38	35	38	31	76	33	50	32	23	36	76	33
Can't say	17	12.6	2	3.2	·3	9.4	22	10	6	5.5	16	13	22	10	14	8.9	8	11	22	10
Total	135	100	63	100	32	100	230	100	109	100	121	100	230	100	158	100	72	100	230	100

table. Among 63 middle-aged respondents 39 said 'good', 22 'bad' and 2 did not say anything. More people among this age group are prone to tradition. Out of 32 old tribal respondents 19 said good, 10 bad and 3 did not say anything. This age group is also more prone to tradition as they used to get justice as and when they required it. When age is a broad category, out of 230, 132 were in favour of *gomango* governance system and 76 against it and 22 were in the category of can not say. When we found 22 can not say that means they are not able to adjust between the *gomango* governance and today's system, so we put it in negative point and it is 96 which is 43 per cent of the total sample who do not like it. But more people like the present system which shows that they are prone to change.

When we consider this question from religious point of view among 109 Hindu respondents 65 said 'good', 28 'bad' and 6 can not say. This also shows positive trend to change and reflect the negative aspect the traditional political culture of *Saora* tribe. Out of 121 Christian respondents 67 said good, 38 bad and 16 did not say anything. It shows a mix approach to the traditional system and modern system. The true sense of Christianity is not reflected. From religion viewpoint mostly people like traditional governance system. It shows religion does not have much effect on tribal in connection with political activities. Secondly tribals are not able to distinguish between traditional governance system and modern system.

When occupation was taken into consideration, out of 158 people engaged in agriculture, 94 responses were 'good' (59.5 per cent), 50 'bad' (31.6 per cent), 14, (8.8 per cent) can not say. More people are in favour of traditional system. Among 72 respondents who practice non-agricultural occupation 38, (52.8 per cent) said 'good', 26, (36 per cent) 'bad' and 8, (11.1 per cent) can not say. Here people engaged in non-agricultural activities are more prone to change. This trend shows more people are in favour of traditional governing system. This is because, traditional system was more democratic, easily accessible, not expensive, no complex system was involved. This trend shows a politically transitional period which exists among the *Saora* tribe. They are also not to completely forgo the traditional and accept the modern system. This fact will be more clear when we see the functional pre-requisites of the existing of traditional system. To know this, a question was asked, 'How far the traditional governing system was essential for the society'. Table 4.2 show that, out of 135 young people 66 respondents said (48.9 per cent) 'yes', only one 'no' and 68, (50.4 per cent) can not say. It is clear that most of the youth were unaware of the benefit of traditional governing system. It shows *Saora* youth do lack of political socialisation. Secondly they hardly try to know about the traditional system of governance. This is clear when we found out that of 63 middle aged tribal respondents 50 said yes 79.4 per cent, four said no and 9 said can not say. As we go ahead with age category, the awareness of existing traditional system became more evident. Out of 32 old respondents 27 said 'yes' (84.4 per cent), not a single 'no' five response was can not say. This means old aged tribals are tradition bound and found the *gomango* system of governance was essential for the sustenance of the society. This shows that it was essential for the sustenance of the society, as 62 per cent tribals prefer to say, yes. A large number of tribals are not able to understand the difference between present and traditional system, which shows the lack of understanding of the governance system. When religion has taken into consideration, out of 109 Hindu respondents, 72 responses were 'yes', 1 'no' and 36 cannot say. This shows more or less Gomango system was beneficial for the society. But many tribals are not clear what to say regarding traditional system. In the same way out of 121 Christian respondents, 71 said 'yes', 4 able 'no' and 46 cannot say. But it has same trend as Hindus. This is clear when out of 230, 143 respondent were said 'yes' and 5 'no' and 82 cannot say. This shows the trend of not distinguishing between the beneficial and essentiality of the traditional Gomango system as shown in Table 4.1, where 57.39 per cent, respondents were in favour of it.

To consider it better when we see from occupational point of view out of 158, agriculture practicing respondents 96 said 'yes', 4 'no' and 58 cannot say. This shows the strong relationship between traditional *gomango* governance system and agriculture as 96 respondent said 'yes'. This is because many of the poor tribals used to work in the field of *gomangos*. But 58 respondents of the same category said cannot say and 4 people said 'no'. Out of 72 non-agriculture-practicing respondents, 47 said 'yes', one 'no', 24 can't say. This shows a positive trend regarding the traditional *gomango* governance system. However, it reflected that the traditional *gomango* governance system was beneficial for the system. But it is not much clear as tribals are living in a transitional period to clarify how and why it was beneficial. The level of distinguishing between good and bad, yes and no is difficult for them. 'The Saoras always find it hard to generalise. They can say that so and so is a bad man; they do not find it easy to draw a general picture of 'badness' they are rather inclined to estimate someone by a single trait...' (Elwin, 1955:561).

Table 4.2 Traditional Governance System was Essential for the Sustenance of the Society

Variables	*Age*								*Religion*						*Occupation*					
Response	*Young*		*Middle*		*Old*		*Total*		*Hindu*		*Non-Hindu*		*Total*		*Agriculture*		*Non-Agriculture*		*Total*	
	F	%	F	%	F	%	F	%	F	%	F	%	F	%	F	%	F	%	F	%
Yes	66	49	50	79.7	27	84	143	62	72	66	71	59	143	62	96	61	47	65	143	62
No	1	0.7	4	6.3	0	0	5	2	1	0.9	4	3.3	5	2	4	2.5	1	1.4	5	2
Can't say	68	50.3	9	14	5	16	82	36	36	33	46	38	82	36	58	37	24	33	82	36
Total	135	100	63	100	32	100	230	100	109	100	121	100	230	100	158	100	72	100	230	100

British Period

After the advent of British the prestige of *gomangos, buyyas* etc. got enhanced. When the governor's agent toured these parts of area and when Saoras called them for important functions, these two officers, i.e., Buyya and *Gomango* were honored. They were given red turban to *gomango* and silver bangles to *Buyya* by which they will work as the agent of British Raj. In this connection a question was asked to find out whether there is any difference in the style of governance after British came to *Saora* land.

In Table 4.3 it has been given that, out of 135 young respondents, 66 said that there is a difference, 5 said no and 64 can not say. Among 63 middle aged group respondents 31 said 'yes', 7 no and 25 cannot say. These two groups do not have much idea about this, as their political socialisation has not been done properly which is also evident from Table 4.1 and Table 4.2. But in old category we have 19 affirmative response, one 'no' and 12 cannot say. This shows there was some difference in *gomango* style of governance. When we see the total responses in age category, 116 respondents said yes 50.43 per cent whereas 13, (5.65 per cent) 'no' and 101 (44.91 per cent) responses were in the category of cannot say. This shows the change but the result in 50 per cent cases specially among young tribals those who have less knowledge regarding the British colonisation. Elwin states that 'the *Gomangos* and *Buyyas* are not only the most wealthy, but they are recognised by government, and in the old days used to receive an official turban which was greatly prized. The *Gomango,* the Chief, is of great importance, for he is the intermediary between Government and the people; it is by his orders the villagers go to work for officials or the *Bissoyis;* his presence is essential at all village functions; in Koraput he is the arbiter in matrimonial disputes; and in practice everywhere he has the final say in the allocation for land.' (1955:50)

Likewise when religion was taken into consideration out of 109 responses of Hindus, 56 were yes (51.4 per cent), 9 were no (8.26 per cent) and 44 responses were cannot say (40.4 per cent). Same way out of non-Hindus, 121,60 said 'yes' (49.6 per cent), 4 no (3.31 per cent) and 57 cannot say. In both the categories cannot say or no response was dominant. From religious point of view also there was a change in governance system.

When occupation was taken into consideration out of 158 tribals engaged in agriculture 77, (48.7 per cent) said yes 12, (7.59 per cent) 'no' and 69, (43.7 per cent) cannot say. Likewise out of 72 respondents who

Table 4.3 Difference Between Traditional and British Period

Variables	Age								Religion						Occupation					
Response	Young		Middle		Old		Total		Hindu		Non-Hindu		Total		Agricul-ture		Non-Agriculture		Total	
	F	%	F	%	F	%	F	%	F	%	F	%	F	%	F	%	F	%	F	%
Yes	66	49.3	31	49	19	59	116	50	56	51.7	60	50	116	50	77	49	39	54	116	50
No	5	3.7	7	11	1	3.1	13	6	9	8.3	4	3.3	13	6	12	7.6	1	1.4	13	6
Can't say	64	47	25	40	12	38	101	44	44	40	57	47	101	44	69	44	32	44	101	44
Total	135	100	63	100	32	100	230	100	109	100	121	100	230	100	158	100	72	100	230	100

were engaged in other than agriculture 39 said yes, (54 per cent), one said 'no' (1.4 per cent) and 32, (44.4 per cent) cannot say. Both these categories said 'yes' to change and 50 per cent cannot say which also clearly reflect that there was a change. When further enquired, it has been said that there was a system of service, and *chowkidary* which has emerged in this period. Earlier revenue used to be paid to the King, but in the British period the *gomango* use to collect the revenue and pay to the officer staying at Gunupur. Changes in administrative set-up, political organisation and developmental administration have exposed them to external influence "The *Saora* rose in revolt in what are called "Fituris", but the British authorities stamped out the uprisings with an iron hand and maintained law and order through stern administrative measures" (Singh, 1984 :25).

Customary Law and Punishment

More or less the prevalent of legal system was as it is even after the British colonisation. Punishment for various types of offences consists of lavy of fines in the form of liqueur, fowl and goat which are offered to the village deities and a feast is prepared in which all village people takes part. Elwin states that 'Fines are inflicted on those who make the wrong sort of marriage or infringe tribal custom in other ways' (1955:570). The exact quantity, wherever depend on the gravity of the offence. The punishment in connection with murder of women is consider more offence and the fine was 8 buffalo, and as for man only seven buffalo has to be given as fine. At any time, if a thief is caught red handed, he could even be killed then and their. Whatever be the offence the practice of having village feast on a fine show that the entire population of the village live as a single family, and this concept which had been in vogue from the ancient times are still surviving. Payment of compensation, offerings to gods, etc. are some of the things, which every offender has to do. Therefore the person wronged, his relations and friends would pacify when their offerings are made and latter distributed and eaten by all the villagers. As a result of this, peace and tranquility once again prevail in the village. The community feasts serves the purpose of preserving village solidarity, providing the *Saora* an occasion for having a good meal and satisfying the hunger of their deities. Evans Pritchard in his Nuer study narrate the same as the *Saora* do, 'within the tribal territory, disputes were supposed to be settled by compensation'.

After Independence

After India became free, welfare measures initiated by the state and central government resulted in exposing the *Saora* more and more to outside contact and pressures ever advancing powerful social, economic and political forces. The impact of political forces the elective system; adult frenzies and local self-government have triggered off various political processes and generated new leadership. This has been done after the panchayat raj system was introduced in the country with the emergence of various political parties. Under its influence the traditional political system underwent several transformation and its dominance on the village community gradually diminished. Due to spread of education and exposure to outside world a kind of new leadership has emerged in *Saora* village. The traditional panchayat has now lost its importance. In every village new leaders such as ward members, sarpanch with their affiliation to certain political parties are actively at work and tackling the problems of the village quite effectively. To know the changing governance system, a question was asked to tribals, that 'if anything happens to them what they do and whom they approach'. 100 per cent tribal said that they approach the ward member first, then to sarpanch etc. and in a question to 'what is the system of governance today', there was 100 per cent positive answer, that is, 'the panchayat system which govern today's society'. For detail information an opinion was sought regarding the panchayat members activity. In Table 4.4 it is mentioned that out of 135 young respondent, 40 were 'satisfied', 28 were 'less satisfied', whereas 65 were 'not satisfied' and 2 did not say anything. Here, out of 135 respondents, 68 tribals were more or less satisfied but 67 tribals were not at all satisfied which shows not equal distribution of power and facilities among the tribals. In the same manner from 63 middle-aged tribals 14 were 'satisfied', 20 'less satisfied', 28 'not satisfied' and one did not respond. This also shows the result of unevenness in the context of dissatisfaction among the tribals. Among 32 old age group respondents, 7 'satisfied', 11 'less satisfied', 13 'not satisfied' and one remain silent. When we look at the agewise classification only 61, (26.52 per cent) tribal were 'satisfied' and 59, (26.45 per cent) were 'average satisfied' where 106, (46 per cent) tribals 'not satisfied'. This statistics shows that only those who are upper strata of the tribal hierarchy, they are happy with this, where the deprived among the tribals are still deprived which shows around 50 per cent. When data has been considered from religion point of view, out of 109 respondents, (27.25 per cent) were 'satisfied', 33 (30 per cent) 'average', 47, (43 per cent) 'not satisfied', and two cannot say (1.7 per cent). Among non-Hindus 34 were 'satisfied', 26 'less satisfied' 59 'not satisfied' and 2 cannot say. If we see both the Hindu and the non-Hindu categories, 50 per cent of the respondents were satisfied with the activities of the panchayat members whereas 50 per cent respondents were either not satisfied or did not want to comment. The 50 per cent who were satisfied have got some benefit from the panchayat members.

From occupational point of view total out of the 158 tribals engaged in agricultural occupation, 38 said 'satisfied' (24 per cent), 45 'less satisfied' (28 per cent), 73 'not satisfied'. Among tribals engaged in other activities 23 said 'satisfied' (32 per cent), 14 'less satisfied' (19 per cent), 33 'not satisfied' (46 per cent). This shows the trend of middle order satisfaction and dissatisfaction. Singh in this context says that due to panchayat system 'the associated aspects of political participation and specialisation which have been emerging as manifestations of change' (1984:26). T.R. Naik in his study of Bhils stated that, "soon after independence, Panchayats were introduced and the set up was brought into force in these areas also which then merged together to form the Madhya Bharat State. The traditional and singular supremacy of the Tadvi (Village chief) was challenged by the small council, which now began to be formed at the village level. (Naik,1969:173). The result of dissatisfaction and disenchantment is because of many reasons as the researcher observed in the *Saora* area. Mostly the elected members make a difference between them and common tribals. Since the office bearers of the panchayat are in touch with government officials, all the benefits in the name of tribals, are taken away by them. But simple, uneducated tribals never understand the complex government procedure for justice or help. As many of the tribals complained regarding roads, wells and schools which have not been sanctioned to their villages. This will be clear when we look into the statistics (Table 4.5) of economic benefits given by the panchayat for their development

Table 4.5 shows that out of 135 young respondents, 13, (9.6 per cent) have 'substantial' effect on their economy, 65 (48 per cent) 'average' and 56 (41 per cent) tribals have 'no' economical benefits from the panchayat. In the middle age group category out of 63 only 6 (9.5 per cent) 'substantial', 30 (48 per cent) 'average', 25 (40 per cent) 'no' benefits, and 2 cannot say. In old category, only one 'satisfied' 23 (72 per cent) 'average' and 8 (25 per cent) tribals no help. In total 230, only 20 tribals (8.70 per cent) got 'substantial' help 118, (51.30 per cent) 'average' help, 89, (39 per cent) have 'not' got any financial benefits from the panchayat. This shows that tribals are more or less benefited economically by the panchayat.

Table 4.4 Opinion Regarding Panchayat Members Activities

Variables	*Age*								*Religion*						*Occupation*					
Response	*Young*		*Middle*		*Old*		*Total*		*Hindu*		*Non-Hindu*		*Total*		*Agriculture*		*Non-Agriculture*		*Total*	
	F	%	F	%	F	%	F	%	F	%	F	%	F	%	F	%	F	%	F	%
Satisfactory	40	30	14	22	7	22	61	26.5	27	25	34	28	61	27	38	24	23	32	61	27
Average	28	21	20	32	11	34	59	26.4	33	30	26	21	59	26	45	28	14	19	59	26
Not Satisfactory	65	48	28	44	13	41	106	46	47	43	59	49	106	46	73	46	33	46	106	46
Can't say	2	1.5	1	1.6	1	3.1	4	2	2	1.8	2	1.7	4	2	2	1.3	2	2.8	4	2
Total	135	100	63	100	32	100	230	100	109	100	121	100	230	100	158	100	72	100	230	100

Table 4.5 Panchayat's Effect on Tribal Economy

Variables	*Age*								*Religion*						*Occupation*					
Response	*Young*		*Middle*		*Old*		*Total*		*Hindu*		*Non-Hindu*		*Total*		*Agriculture*		*Non-Agriculture*		*Total*	
	F	%	F	%	F	%	F	%	F	%	F	%	F	%	F	%	F	%	F	%
Substantial	13	99.6	6	9.5	1	3.1	20	9	3	2.8	17	14	20	9	11	7	9	13	20	9
Average	65	48	30	48	23	72	118	51	69	63	49	40	118	51	87	55	31	43	118	51
No. effects	56	41	25	40	8	25	89	39	36	33	53	44	89	39	58	37	31	43	89	39
Can't say	1	0.7	2	3.2	0	0	3	1	1	0.9	2	1.7	3	1	2	1.3	1	1.4	3	1
Total	135	100	63	100	32	100	230	100	109	100	121	100	230	100	158	100	72	100	230	100

From religion point of view out of 109 Hindus only 3 (2.8 per cent) got 'substantial' help, 69 (63 per cent) average help, 36 (33 per cent) 'no' help. It means 33 per cent Hindu tribals are not economically benefited. Likewise out of 121 non-Hindu respondents, 17 (14 per cent) got 'substantial' help, 49 (40 per cent) 'average' help, and 53 (44 per cent) 'no' help. This shows that 45 per cent Christians are deprived of economic benefits. It has the same trend as the trend in age. When occupation was taken into consideration out of 158 tribals engaged in agriculture practice, 11 (7 per cent) got 'substantial' help, 87 (55 per cent) got 'average' help, 58 (37 per cent) 'no' help. Among non-agriculture group nine got substantial help, 31 'average' help and 31 got 'no' help. After knowing all this regarding panchayat system; how it is helpful for today's tribal society and their economy; now we must see how these panchayat members are trying to preserve the natural resources and forest.

Panchayat and Forest Resources

As the traditional governance system more or less used to look after the forest but what happened to this natural resources after the independence? Apart from the government initiative to reserve and all that, what the tribals have at the local level today. To find out the relation between the panchayat governance system and forest a question has asked regarding'panchayat members activities to protect forest'.

The Table 4.6 shows that out of 135 young category tribals 6 (4.4 per cent) said that panchayat take steps to protect the forest whereas 122 (90 per cent) said 'no' step was taken by the panchayat member, and only 7 (5.2 per cent) said cannot say. Likewise out of 63 middle-aged tribals only 7 said 'positive' and 53 (84 per cent) said 'negative' and 3 (4.8 per cent) cannot say. Here the result shows maximum 'negative'. In the same manner 32 old tribals were asked the same question and one said 'positive', 25 (78 per cent) 'negative', 6 cannot say. This shows clear 'negative' aspect of the panchayat people to preserve forest and natural resources. When we see the total of 230 only 14 (6.1 per cent) said 'positive', 200 (87 per cent) 'negative', 16 (7 per cent) cannot say. This is very clear that today's panchayat activities are always confined to carry out the developmental plans without thinking about the ecology and environment. In this same way when we consider the religious perspective, out of 109 Hindu respondents, 10 (9 per cent) say 'positive' , 92 (84.6 per cent) 'negative' and 7, (6 per cent) 'cannot say'. Here is negative trend by maximum tribals. In the same way according to non-Hindus 4 said 'positive', 108 (89

Table 4.6 Panchayat Members Activites to Protect Forest

Variables	*Age*								*Religion*						*Occupation*					
Response	*Young*		*Middle*		*Old*		*Total*		*Hindu*		*Non-Hindu*		*Total*		*Agriculture*		*Non-Agriculture*		*Total*	
	F	%	F	%	F	%	F	%	F	%	F	%	F	%	F	%	F	%	F	%
Positive	6	4.4	7	11	1	3.1	14	6.1	10	9	4	3.3	14	6.1	7	4.4	7	9.7	14	6.1
Negative	122	90	53	84	25	78	200	87	92	84.6	108	89	200	87	139	88	61	85	200	87
Can't say	7	5.2	3	4.8	6	19	16	7	7	6	9	7.4	16	7	12	7.6	4	5.6	16	7
Total	135	100	63	100	32	100	230	100	109	100	121	100	230	100	158	100	72	100	230	100

per cent) said 'negative' and 9 (74 per cent) cannot say. From religious point of view panchayat members are having no attention to preserve the forest and ecology. Likewise the occupational category also respond in the same way. Among 158 agriculture group only 7 (4.4 per cent) said 'positive', 139 (88 per cent) said 'negative' and 12 (7.6 per cent) did not say anything. This is a negative trend. Among 72 non-agricultural group 7 said 'positive' 61 said 'negative' and 4 cannot say. This was also a negative trend.

From all these analysis it is proved that there is not much relation between governmental development policy and forest or natural resources. Although after independence we had given lot of importance to panchayati raj system and decentralisation. But this shows the fault of governmental planning not to make the panchayat members to understand the importance to preserve the natural resources. This is also one of the important reason for which all the government policies related to forest is failed.

Table 4.7 contains the suggestions and expectations of the tribals from the panchayat member regarding protecting the ecology and improving the condition of the tribals. Out of 135 young tribal respondents 71 (53 per cent) suggested for 'plantation' as important means to protect the ecology, 21 (16 per cent) suggested for 'creating awareness', 25 (19 per cent) 'did not feel' the need to protect the forest, 8 (5.9 per cent) suggested for the need of 'both' plantation and awareness to protect the ecology. However, the pertinent fact is that 25 tribals were opposed to any kind of forest protection, because they felt that, such kind of protection would collapse their economy. In same way out of 63 middle aged group, 27 (43 per cent) suggested 'plantation', 4 (6.3 per cent) for 'awareness' 16 tribals suggested 'not to protect', 85 (79 per cent) suggested for 'both' plantation and awareness and only 11 were in the category of cannot say. Likewise out of 32 old tribals 11 suggested 'plantation', 3 'awareness', 6 'not to protect', 11 cannot say. Out of total 230, 109 (47 per cent) suggested 'plantation' 28 (12 per cent) 'awareness', 47 (20 per cent) 'no need to protect', 14 (6.1 per cent) both 'plantation and awareness' 32 cannot say. Here mostly around 146 tribals suggested to protect the forest which is important for both their livelihood and for the preservence of ecology. It shows the level of understanding to preserve or protect forest. This also shows how tribals are interested to protect the forest but 47 per cent tribals suggested not to protect, as they do not understand the importance of forest or they may be solely depending on forest for minor forest produces and agriculture, or it might also be possible that the tribals may

Table 4.7 Suggestion to Safeguard Forest by Panchayat

Variables	*Age*								*Religion*						*Occupation*					
Response	*Young*		*Middle*		*Old*		*Total*		*Hindu*		*Non-Hindu*		*Total*		*Agriculture*		*Non-Agriculture*		*Total*	
	F	%	F	%	F	%	F	%	F	%	F	%	F	%	F	%	F	%	F	%
(a) Plantation	71	53	27	43	11	34	109	47	55	50	57	47	109	47	75	47	34	47	109	47
(b) Awareness	21	16	4	6.3	3	9.4	28	12	8	7.3	18	15	28	12	15	9.5	11	15	28	12
(c) No need to protect	25	19	16	25	6	19	47	20	29	27	25	21	47	20	43	27	10	14	47	20
(d) Both a & b	8	5.9	5	7.9	1	3.1	14	6.1	4	3.7	8	6.6	14	6.1	3	1.9	8	11	14	6.1
(e) Can't say	10	7.4	11	17	11	34	32	14	13	12	13	11	32	14	22	14	9	13	32	14
Total	135	100	63	100	32	100	230	100	109	100	121	100	230	100	158	100	72	100	230	100

have faced serviour harassment by the governmental officials by which they have suggested against the preservation of forest. When it was seen from the religion point of view, out of 109 Hindu tribals were interviewed, 55 said 'plantation' (50 per cent), 8 said 'awareness' (7.3 per cent), 29 said 'no need to protect' the forest (27 per cent), 4 for 'both' plantation and awareness (3.7 per cent) and 13 cannot say (12 per cent). Among 121 Non Hindu respondents, 57 said 'plantation' (47 per cent), 18 'awareness' (15 per cent), 25 'no need to protect' (21 per cent), 8 for 'both' plantation and awareness (6.6 per cent) and 13 cannot say (11 per cent). This shows the trend that panchayat must go for plantation and protect the plants and ecology. Likewise in the occupational category, out of 158 respondents who practice agricultural 75 said 'plantation' (47 per cent), 15 for 'awareness' (9.5 per cent), 43 (27 per cent) responses were against the protection, 3 for both plantation and awareness (1.9 per cent) and 22 (14 per cent) did not respond. Among 72 non-agricultural respondents 34 said plantation (47 per cent), 11 awareness (15 per cent), 10 no need to protect, (14 per cent), 8 for both plantation (11 per cent) and awareness and 9 cannot say (13 per cent). This shows the trend we need to go for more plantations and the duty must be given to panchayat.

As most of the tribals were in favour of plantation; they were asked about the kinds of plantation. Most of the people were preferred the plants like, mango, jack fruits, *kaju* etc. which are all cash crop. It shows that tribals do not show much interest in protecting the ecology or environment but they need the economic benefit out of it. But here we are not discussing it, here the important is panchayat must be largely involved in plantation and awareness by which the social ecology of the *Saora* tribe can be protected. So here it is the government intervention which is solely responsible for destruction of ecology and forest. However, the government is also responsible for trying to bring the tribals to the mainstream.

Change and Contradictions

The introductions of panchayati raj have seriously undermined the status and power of the village head. At present the important persons in *Saora* villages are the ward-members and Sarpanchas. While there is one Sarpanch for many *Saora* villages, at least each *Saora* village of an average size has a ward-member. The ward-member, being an elected member, has considered much more powerful than the traditional head. He is the link between the villagers and external authorities. Further, he plays an important role in distributing governmental benefits among the villagers. Moreover, being the most important vote bank of the village he has some leverage vis-a-vis the leaders of upper layers like MLA, Block Chairman and the Sarpanch. This linkage factor has made the ward-member influential at the cost of the village head.

In this connection a question was asked to know whether due to the emergence of panchayat the traditional role of *Gomango* has declined or not. In their response (Table 4.8) 131 (97 per cent) out of 135 young tribals felt that the status and role of traditional leader has 'declined' 2 says no, and 2 did not say anything. In the middle age category also 61 said 'yes' (97 per cent), 2 'no', and among 32 old category 30 said 'yes' (94 per cent), 1 'no' and 1 cannot say. In total 230, 222, (97 per cent) were of the view that status and role of *gomango* has 'declined'. This shows the clear trend of change in *Saora* leadership. Likewise in religion category among 109 Hindu respondent 104 (95 per cent) said 'yes', 4 'no' and 1 cannot say. Out of 121 non-Hindu respondents, 118 (98 per cent) responses were 'yes', 1 'no' and 2 cannot say. Here it also shows the trend of change. Among the occupational group, out of 158, 154 (97 per cent) agricultural group felt the decline of the *gomango* leadership, and out of 72 non-agricultural group 68 (94 per cent) said yes. This is a clear indication that the status and role of traditional *gomango* system has changed. The trend is so clear that the traditional leadership mechanisms are dyeing completely. As the mechanisms are dyeing, the natural resources are also dyeing. Because the village heads are not there to protect the big trees and other sacred trees for the benefit of the tribal community. Today's Sarpanch and ward members, are largely in connivance with the government officials, trying to cut the tree and sale, which is against the people's interests. This decline of traditional leadership only fulfills the interest of the state and capitalists.

This high trend of change is because of increased exposure of Saoras to the forces of modernisation like education and communication. It has brought a significant change in the attitude and values of Saoras. Their blind beliefs are yet to disappear. But it is evident that they have been able to give up at least a few of their tradition. Their attitudes towards authorities have similarly undergone some change. Some of them have either given up drinking (wine) altogether or are taking less wine than they were drinking in the past. In, fifties and sixties family planning was unheard of in the *Saora* society. However, with the passage of time, their suspicion and inhibition about it are slowly melting away.

Table 4.8 Decline of Traditional Governance System

Variables	*Age*								*Religion*						*Occupation*					
Response	*Young*		*Middle*		*Old*		*Total*		*Hindu*		*Non-Hindu*		*Total*		*Agriculture*		*Non-Agriculture*		*Total*	
	F	%	F	%	F	%	F	%	F	%	F	%	F	%	F	%	F	%	F	%
Yes	131	97	61	97	30	94	222	97	104	95	118	98	222	97	154	97	68	94	222	97
No	2	1.5	2	3.2	1	3.1	5	2	4	3.7	1	0.8	5	2	2	1.3	3	4.2	5	2
Can't say	2	1.5	0	0	1	3.1	3	1	1	0.9	2	1.7	3	1	2	1.3	1	1.4	3	1
Total	135	100	63	100	32	100	230	100	109	100	121	100	230	100	158	100	72	100	230	100

To know the attitude of the people today after the change of leadership a question was asked 'whether they like this change'. It has become evident from Table 4.9 that out of 135 young tribals, 110 respondents like the change of leadership (81 per cent), 11 did not like (8 per cent), 14 did not respond. Among 63 middle age-group, 54 like the change, (86 per cent), 6 (9.5 per cent) did not like and 3 cannot say. Likewise out of 32 old category respondents, 16 liked (50 per cent), 9 did not like, 7 cannot say. In total 230, 180 said 'yes', (78 per cent), 26 did not like (11 per cent) and 24 cannot say (10 per cent). This shows the positive trend of changing leadership. Among this community only few are tradition loving. But most of the tribals accept this changing trend of leadership. Among 109 Hindu respondents, 78, (12 per cent), people were in favour of changing status of traditional governing system, whereas 21, (19 per cent), did not like and 10 people remain silent. 102, (84 per cent) out of 121 Christian respondent said 'yes', 5, (4.1 per cent) no and 14 can not say. Majority respondents were for the change in the traditional governing system. From occupational point of view, out of 158 tribal engaged in non-agricultural occupation 122 were in favour of change (77 per cent), 17 no and 19 cannot say. Among non -agriculture group, 58 were in favour (81 per cent), 9 no and 5 cannot say. Here it is clear from this entire category that all section of this people liked or adapted to this change of traditional age-old practice.

In the past, age was an important variable of *Saora* leadership. The village leaders were invariably elderly persons whose voices carried weight. However, with the passage of time, age has lost much of its traditional importance in determining *Saora* leadership. Many Sarpanchs and Ward-members today are either young or middle-aged persons. Further, education and external exposure are increasingly becoming salient features of *Saora* leadership today. T.B. Naik in his study of *Bhils* also observed the same trend as "a further shift in this occurred with the participation of the younger people in the affairs of the Jati Panchayat. With a little spreading of education and with a growth of consciousness about the functional responsibilities of the council, the younger members of the village community, which had hitherto considered these matters as old men's affairs started taking active interest in its proceedings and actions." (Naik, 1969: 173)

Conclusion

There is no society where rules are obeyed automatically. The function of political and legal system is to defend society against its won

Table 4.9 Liking to the Changing Status of Traditional Governance System

Variables	Age								Religion						Occupation					
Response	Young		Middle		Old		Total		Hindu		Non-Hindu		Total		Agriculture		Non-Agriculture		Total	
	F	%	F	%	F	%	F	%	F	%	F	%	F	%	F	%	F	%	F	%
Yes	110	81	54	86	16	50	180	78	78	72	102	84	180	78	122	77	58	81	180	78
No	11	8.1	6	9.5	9	28	26	11	21	19	5	4.1	26	11	17	11	9	13	26	11
Can't say	14	15	3	4.8	7	22	24	10	10	9.2	14	12	24	10	19	12	5	6.9	24	10
Total	135	100	63	100	32	100	230	100	109	100	121	100	230	100	158	100	72	100	230	100

weakness, to keep it in good order and to adopt itself to the changes that are not in conflict with its basic principles. This has been done through the leadership. Mostly all tribals have some tradition of leadership. This has been categorized to institutional leadership, situational leadership, dictatorial and creative leadership. Traditional *Saora* leadership can be categorized as institutional whereas the modern leadership may be called as creative leadership.

Many of Orissa tribals have the institutional leadership. This picture has not completely change even today. The *Bhuyan* tribe as of their headman known as *sardar,* the *Saora* headman known as *gomango,* the *Kandha* call their headman *samanth* or *majhi,* Koyias as *pedda, goantia* or *naik.* The headman has not lost the importance even today. Prior to British rule the local self-government, governed *Saora* village. Each village was a separate kingdom by itself. The people in a particular village had their loyalty to the village head. The village head is known as *gomango.* He is the secular headman followed by the *Buyya, the Dalabehera, Karji* and *Badarahit.* This study has revealed that 57 tribal said that the *gomango* system of governance is good and 62 per cent said it was essential for the sustenance of the system (society).

After the British come into rule it certainly had certain difference in the style of functioning of the village leaders. As our result shows, 50 per cent said that the change and difference occurred at that time. Saoras were having their traditional customary law of imposing fine. There was no change in it during British rule. After Independence due to advent of political freedom and development plans, new leadership has governed the tribal life. This process has been further improved because of education and exposure to outside world. This study finds that though panchayat system has the importance but people are not satisfied with this kind of leadership and their way of functioning, as 46 per cent tribal said the performance is not satisfactory.

In the same way forest resources have not been protected, as 87 per cent tribals said this. This is an important deviation from the traditional leadership to modern one. The *Saora* tribals suggested to safeguard forest through plantation. The result shows that, 20 per cent tribals are not in favour of protection of forest as it denied them the access to it. This is due to imposition and corrupt rules and rituals of government officials. Changes are coming in the life styles of *Saoras* and also in their leadership structure. The power and prestige of traditional leaders are decreasing, while for modern leaders it is increasing, though it is not strictly a zero-sum game. The new power structures that have emerged at different levels after Independence, are not fully controlled and managed by *Saoras*. Clean caste people dominate many of these. It is only a few *Saora* elite like M.L.A. or a few Panchayat Samiti chairmen who exercises some powers. Most of other modern *Saora* leaders at the Grama Panchayat and village levels have powers more in name than in practice. They are generally content with their official designation and marginal benefits. The ignorance, poverty and long-existing fear from outsiders greatly inhabit the common *Saora* from asserting themselves. However, their diffidence would tend to be overcome by education, higher post and long tenure of office. Education, enables a *Saora* leader to be familiar with rules and regulations and to communicate himself better and in long run it will give him confidence to assert. A higher elective post provides a *Saora* leader with ample powers to assert himself vis-à-vis Government officials and clean caste leaders. Educated *Saoras* are slowly being attracted towards politics although their number, to date, is very small.

The *Saora* leaders are aware of the poverty and backwardness of *Saoras*. But development to them mostly means getting Government loan for buying bullocks and goats, to start small business or to reclaim land. They possess little knowledge of perspective, objectives and strategy of tribal development. Though they are aware of large-scale pilferage of developmental funds by Government officials, they in general, lack courage and articulation to protest against this. On the other hand, some of them have shown the tendency of themselves pocketing a part of this money in league with these officials. Having realised that in Indian democracy number matters in power-game, they have started challenging the traditional monopoly of clean caste leaders in local power structures. But they are yet to develop the required consciousness, motivation and courage to make serious efforts for the removal of poverty, ignorance and exploitation of *Saoras*.

References

Bailey, F.G., 1959, *Politics and Social Change: Orissa,* Oxford University Press.

Cohen, Abner,1969, 'Political Anthropology: The Analysis of the Symbolism of Power Relation', *Man,* No.4, pp. 215-235.

Cheater, A.P., *Social Anthropology*, Not available.

Dyson-Hudson, 1966, *Karimojong Politics,* Oxford, Clarendon Press.

Evans-Pritchand, E.E, 1940a, *The Nuer,* Oxford, Clarendon Press.

Evans-Pritchard, E.E, 1940b, *The Political System of the Anuak of the Anglo-Egyptian Sudan,* London, Lund Humphries.

Fortes, M., 1945, *The Dynamics of Clanship among the Tallensi,* London, Oxford University Press.

Frith, R., 1939, *Primitive Polynesian Economy,* London.

Goody, J.R., 1969, *Comparative Studies in Kinship,* London, Routlledge and Kegan Paul.

Gluckman, M., 1968, 'The Utility of the Equilibrium Mode 31 in the Study of Social Change', *Ameriacan Anthropologist,* pp.1-70.

Mishra, R.N., 'Tribal Politics in Orissa', *Encyclopedia of India and Her State* Vol. 7, pp. 646-659.

Mair, L.P., 1962, Premitive Goernment, Not available.

Naik, T.B., I969, *Impact of Education of the Bhils: Cultural Change in the Tribal Life of Madhypradesh,* New Delhi, Planning Commission.

Patnaik, Nitynanda, 1989, *The Saora,* Bhubaneswar, THRT. Publication.

Rao, V. V., 1976, *A Century of Tribal Politics in North East India (1874-1974),* New Delhi, S. Chand & Co.

Radchiffe-Brown, A.R., 1940, 'On Social Structure', *The Journal of the Royal Anthropological Institute of Great Britain and Irland,* Part-I.

Sinha, S.K., 1972, 'Tribal Solidarity Movements in India: A Review', in K.S. Singh (ed.) *Tribal Situation in India,* IAS, Simla, pp.410-22).

Singh, B., 1984. *The Saora Highlander: Leadership and Development,* Bombay: Somaya Publications.

Tyle, E.B., 1942, *Premitive Culture,* (7th ed.), 2 Vols,0 New York, Brentano's.

Weber, M., 1958. *The Religion of India,* Glencoe. Free Press.

5

Religion and Belief System

Religion is a very important aspect of social life particularly in simple societies. Social, economic, political and psychological life is intricately intertwined with the religious system, i.e., the ritual and belief system. Social anthropologists have often identified religion as a basic unit of structural analysis. In the case of *Saora* society and culture, religion too has a pervasive and dominant impact. It would be a difficult and fruitless to study the social structure and life styles of *Saora* without understanding their religious system. Therefore, in this chapter an attempt has been made to describe the religious structure of *Saora* society and its impact on various aspects of their life. To understand the religious activities of the tribals a comprehensive exploration of the life cycle is essential. Life cycle involves from cradle to grave, which shows the absolute dependency on religious believes and practices. However, it would be relevant to define religion before going into the dynamics of lifestyles. Here we have incorporated some of noted definitions of religion to give our understanding a theoretical base.

According to Herbet Spencer, "Religion is the recognition that all things are manifestation of a power which transcends our knowledge." For J.G. Frazer "religion is a propitiation or conciliation of powers superior to man which are believed to direct and control the course of Nature and of human life." Matthew Arnold believes "religion is ethics heightened, enkindled, lit up by feeling". Friedrich Schleimacher defined religion as "feeling of absolute dependence" — absolute as contrasted to other, relative feelings of dependence. Since that time there have been others who have sought to escape formalistic doctrinal definitions and to include the experiential, emotive, and intuitive factors, as well as valuation and ethical factors. These factors, what religion is like from the inside, include what William James called "the enthusiastic temper of espousal." These definitions appear to be more universally applicable to primitive and Asian religions than belief oriented ones.

Religion: Some Theoretical Reflections

Malinowski has argued convincingly that primitive man distinguishes between naturalistic techniques of hunting, fishing, and husbandry and the super naturalistic acts, which he also performs as indispensable accompaniments to these activities. The primitive gardener has at his command sound "scientific" knowledge of plant husbandry which he uses hand in hand with supernaturalism. Malinowski states, "but no person lays crop failure to super naturalistic cause when it may be attributed to poor husbandry" (Norbeau, 1961:128). Malinowski appears to be sound, however, in stating that much of the importance of religion applies to factors beyond the understanding and the control of man which may affect the outcome of his efforts. Given the most faithful performance of all known practical techniques of horticulture, for example, crops might still fail. Between acts of husbandry and end results lies an area of uncertainty and it is here where religion steps in (*Ibid.*, 129).

Most studies have stressed the function of ritual and belief in supporting social structure and institutionalized customs the family and other social units, the scheme of social stratification, moral or ethical codes, institutions such as marriage, and social relationships and placing upon them a stamp of sacred approval, ritual and belief are held to fortify the individual element expressed and also the whole. But religious rites are held to be particularly effective because of the formal real sanctification, which they give to the cultural norms they express. As Radcliff-Brown has discussed about, 'Religion and Society' in *Structure and Function in Primitive Society* (1952) that society depends for its existence upon common social sentiments, and ritual acts are symbolic expressions of these sentiments which reaffirm them and maintain their intensity.

E.E. Evans-Pritchard's succinct *Theories of Primitive Religion* (1965), for example, enumerates earlier, now-rejected studies on the stages of man's religious impulse, proposed in different combinations and sequences by successive evolutionist scholars. In these studies, besides monotheism we find fetishism, manism; nature-mythism, animism, totemism, dynamism, magism, polytheism and certain psychological explanations (1965:104). In 1962 Claude Levi-Strauss published a critique of the history of abstracting between social divisions and categories of the natural surrondings. Since then anthropologists have continued re-examining many analysis produced in the vain pursuit of origins.

With the rise of the sociological and anthropological disciplines, another factor has been projected into definition making—the social, economic, historical, and cultural contexts in which religion comes to expression. Sociologists and anthropologists rightly argue that religion is never an abstract set of ideas, values, or experiences developed apart from the total cultural matrix and that meant religious beliefs, customs, and rituals can only be understood in reference to this matrix. Indeed some proponents of these disciplines imply or suggest that analysis of religious structure will totally account for religion. Emile Durkheim, a pioneer in this societal interpretation, asserted in *The Elementary Forms of the Religious Life* (1962) that "a society has all that is necessary to arouse the sensation of the divine in minds, merely by the power that it has over them" (*Ibid.*, 207). Thus the gods are nothing more than society in disguise. Since Durkheim's time, sociologists have refined their methods of analysis, but some still maintain the essential Durkheimian view.

However, Sudhir Kakar (1982), for example, has compared Muslim and Hindu curative, *shamanic,* and Tantric techniques to psychotherapeutic devices; he likens demonological constructions to Freudian idioms yet stipulates that India does not share the West's tradition of introspection. Contextualized investigations of parallels between Western and Asian psychodynamics include works by Gananath Obeyesekere and Bruce Kepferer on Sri Lanka, by Robert A. on Nepal and Tibet, and by Sherry Ortner on Nepal. Ideas of Freud, Jung, and other luminaries such as Gregory Bateson, Ruth Benedict (1946), and Paul Radin remain pertinent in analysing styles of therapeutic narrative and ritual interaction coordinated with worldviews of disease and its cure.

Characteristic Structure of Religious Life

Despite the fact that none of the definitions specifies a set of characteristics which is present when and only when we have a religion, or gives us a unique essence, it does seem that they contribute to our understanding of the nature of religion. It appears that the presence of any of the features stressed by these definitions will help to make something a 'religion'. We might call such features, listed below, religion-making characteristics or characterstic structure of religious life. And a social group is bound together by these features.

1. Belief in supernatural beings (gods).
2. A distinction between sacred and profane objects.
3. Ritual acts focused on sacred objects.
4. A moral code believed to be sanctioned by the gods.

5. Characteristically religious feelings (awe, sense of mystery, sense of guilt, adoration), which tend to be aroused in the presence of sacred object and during the practice of ritual and which are connected in idea with the gods.
6. Prayers and other forms of communication with gods.
7. A worldview or a general picture of the world as a whole and the place of the individual therein. This picture contains some specification of an over-all purpose or point of the world and an indication of how the individual fits into it.
8. A more or less total organization of one's life based on the worldview.

As previously suggested religion adopt their tangible historical forms as matrices of cultural and social elements about the depth-centres of culture. Hence the beliefs, patterns of observance, organization structures, and types of religious experience are as varied as the matrices that give them birth, and that they in turn help form and reform. Even in the midst of this variety, however, we may distinguish certain characteristic elements and categories of structure as distinctively religious.

Traditionalism—All attempts to find a primitive religion embodying the primordial form of all subsequent religions have encountered two insurmountable problems. The first is the sheer arbitrariness of seeking the origin of all types of religion in a single form. The second is that wherever religion is recognized, if one uses the above definition of religion as a depth dimensional structure, one also encounters an existent tradition comprising stylized actions related to the pursuit of cultural goals, however meager it is, closely geared to survival needs. Present modes of religious activity always seem to look backward for origin, precedents, and standards. As cultures become more complex and literate, these traditions of ancient thought and practice become more elaborate and stylized.

Myth and Symbol—Religious traditions are full of myth and replete with symbol. Myth in most contemporary use simply means "false"; myths are the fanciful tales of primitives spun out as explanations of beginnings. Hence created myths are rationalizations of what prescientific cultures cannot understand through other means. Though this explanatory function of myth has been important, and even more basic function that of symbolic source apparently, even the writers of myths recognized the impossibility of expressing the fundamentally indescribable nature of absolute beginnings and ultimate realities. Hence poetry and symbol were their métier. In the way, religious myths have become modes of action, mankind's way of relating to physical and environmental realities. Thus, does religious man seek to grasp the actionable significance of the world and relate to it emotionally? In passing, it should be noted that all disciplines of thought and life have their mythology of guiding images and unproven assumptions. Symbol is the language of myth. When the crulically important but mysterious nature of ultimate reality—the basic concern of religious man can only be seen through a glass darkly, how else can one of it except in symbolic forms? Ordinary language will not serve for the fullness of either the question or the answer here. Therefore religious language is rich in analogies, metaphors, poetry, stylized actions (ritual), and even silence ("Be still and know that I am God"). For the symbol stands for something other and more than itself, it is only a finger pointing at the moon of reality.

Sacred places and objects—One of the striking features of historically observable religions is the presence of special religious areas and structures set apart from ordinary space by physical, ritual, and psychological barriers. Precincts, churches, mosques, synagogues, and shrines are the highly visible manifestations of religious discontinuity with the surrounding world. Various physical actions are often required of those who enter sacred areas to indicate this separation: ablutions, removal of footwear, prayers and incantations, bowing and kneeling, silence, preparatory fasting, special garb, and preliminary inward acts of contrition.

Sacred actions (rituals)—Just as it is impossible to think of living religions without their sacred places, so is it impossible to conceive of a religion without its rituals, whether simple or elaborate. The forms of ritual are familiar, involving the stylized saying of chanting of certain words, bowing or kneeling, offerings of various kinds including animal sacrifices, dancing and music making.

The sacred community—Every religion has some communal sense and structure. Ritual is essentially a group exercise, except for magico-religious rituals geared to personal desires. Hence ritual nearly always involves professional ritualistic and a group bound together by its experience. But the communal bonds vary greatly in nature and extent.

The sacred experience—The question of whether all depth experiences, experiences of transcendence, or unusual mind-body states should bc considered on at par with religious experiences, or are intrinsically religious themselves, has already been discussed. Here are considered only those experiences that occur within a declared religious context and are therefore doubly set apart, both as designatedly religious and as of special clarity and intensity even within that context.

With this theoratical underpininings it is pertinent that religion plays a vital role in every community's life. The *Saora* tribe of Orissa is no exception to this. Let us examine the religious life of the *Saora* tribe. The discussion and analysis has three aspects: traditional, modern and the changes and contradiction; which has affected the religious out look of the *Saoras.*

Traditional Saora Religion

Life cycle

In simplest primitive societies, every adult has some religious functions and the elders have most; as their capacity to hunt or garden wanes, their priest like role comes into ever greater prominence; women tend to receive more recognition and scope as religious functionaries than in the developed societies. There is some tendency towards religious specialisation in such societies, based on a variety of attributes, such as knowledge of herbalist lore, skill in witchcraft, the capacity to enter a state of trance or dissociation, and some times physical handicap that compels a man or woman to find an alternative means of support to subsistence activities. However, religious act and peformances though not in a specialised waytouches every individual.

Among the Saoras the religious process starts practically tribe immediately after the individual's birth. After the childbirth the umbilical cord is cut by means of a sharp edged arrow. The placenta is then buried in one corner of the courtyard of the house. Then the mother and the newly born baby are given bath in tapid water. From the day of delivery, the baby is given bath twice daily, once in the morning and again in the evening. The child is given bath twice a day because *Saora* believes in this way the child can be protected from cold, cough and fever. This is the way they take care of the child. After fith day chid can be taken by her mother to outside or even to the field. After 12 or 15 days the religious ritual takes place. First they shave the head of the child, then they go for naming ceremony. Mostly they mix the hair with the earth and make the plaster of the house. By this way the hair is saved for life long. During this time the child has been given a name. The *Saora* prefers the name of one of the ancestors for naming the child.

After one year, if it is a male issue then the stream god will be worshipped. If they will not offer the puja to the stream god the child might get some infection and elephantised. To worship the stream god, there will be a buffalo sacrifice. After this puja they also worship the *suryadevata.* To offer the puja to the *suryadevata,* they put an earthen pot inside the house. In that earthen pot, they put rice, any cropped vegetable (if the child eats that). This earthen pot will be preserved for several years. After five years this earthen pot will be thrown and a new pot will be kept in the name of *suryadevata.* At that time there will be a wall painting in the name of *suryadevata* In this wall painting, the picture of ancestors, earth god, village deity, jungle god, is drawn (see picture-1). At that time a goat sacrifice is done. The *kudanboi* do the puja in presence of other senior members of the *Birinda.* The *suryadevata* comes through the *kudanboi* and says that 'this is my child and I will protect him from all difficulties'.

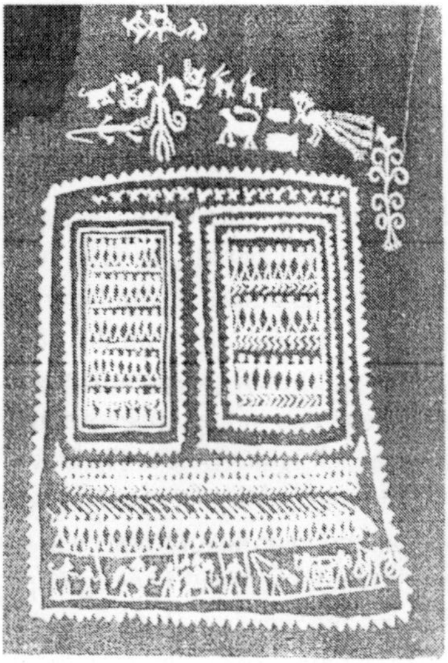

Picture-1: Saora icon: The reflections of religious philosophy and world-view and the abode of ancestral spirits

Upto 12 years, the parents take care of the child. During these years they also offer, puja to many other gods and goddesses. After 12 years, the child becomes marriageable. During this time there is a ritual called *Ananganpur.* Marriage is a simple affair for the *Saoras.*

After this the *Saora* life goes on. But around 20 years, if there is a fever, they go for a ritual named *galabipur.* After 30 year, if there is joint pain, they worship *Etainga.* Around 40, if the eyesight becomes weak, they worship *Ayamaya.*Formally there is no any otherr rituals after this period of life. The last ritual and rites performed after the death.

Incase death of *Saora* usually burn the dead body. The person who does the burning activities is called *siga.* He is a tribal. When a person dies all the *Birinda* people comes with paddy and rice. They keep all these in the deceased house. After that the dead body with rice and paddy is taken to the burning *ghat.* The *siga* puts on the fire. Few *Birinda* members with the *Siga* wait and watch there, upto the end. At the last, *Siga* will put all the rice and paddy to the fire and declare that this is over. In the next day the entire *Birinda* group with music goes to the burial ground to get back the ash. For female their brother use to come and collect the bone and ash and put it in their own burial ground. On the third day, the soul will come through the *kudanboai.* The *Birinda* group brings rice and paddy for the ceremony. Through *kudanboi,* the spirit will say everything detected about his/her life, how she died and who created problem for her when he or she was alive.

Peacock dance

On the third or fourth day, there will be a peacock dance. This is mostly practised by the rich tribals, as it involves lots of financial expenditure even though this is one of the belief system among *Saora* tribe. This starts with the process where all the *birinda* members go for peacock hunting. After hunting the peacock they will be back. Then they take this peacock to the end part of the village where there is a place called *Garmar,* where this peacock is sacrificed. There it will be cooked. From there all the tribals will be back to the deceased house with all the traditional music. In the evening a second group of tribals will come and they sing the folk song related to peacock sacrifice. These groups approach the family members through singing and dancing. Both the group will have interaction with each other and they will narrate why they did the peacock sacrifice and other matter related to this will be questioned by one group and answered by another group. These groups take the name of all the ancestral *birinda* during the process.

After ten days they go for *Guar* ceremony which is done to send off the spirit of the deceased into the unseen world for its salvation. This ceremony is also very expensive and makes a family insolvent. It is obligatory for his heirs to discharge this sacred duty among the *birinda* members, friends and relatives by offering a number of animal sacrifices like buffalo, goat, hen etc. This ceremony ensures the *Saoas* that now the spirit achieved the status of an ancestor. This religious practice shows their cultural identity. After this death ceremony, in the end of the year, there will be a ritual called *karja*

In this context Elwin in his book *The Religion of an Indian Tribe* (1955) cites many examples which can be traced to explore the life cycle of *Saoras*. He explains the case of two brothers who lived together with their father, until his death, when each set up a separate establishment. Shortly after one of the brothers had built his new house, he becomes very ill. He summoned a diviner-*shaman*, (*shaman* performing her religious act in picture-1) who ascribes his illness to the affliction of three gods. These gods had been regularly worshipped by his father, and his brother had painted an icon (i.e., a sacred drawing, on an inner house-wall, dedicated to gods and spirits, (see picture-1) in their honour. The *shaman*, impersonating the three gods, declared to the sick man that 'this man's father used to worship us, and so did his brother. So long as he lived with them he joined in the worship, but now he got separated from them, he neglects us. If he whishes to recover he must honour us in his house also'. The patient begged the *shaman* to paint an icon to the gods, sacrificed a goat before them, and we are told that he recovered from his illness.

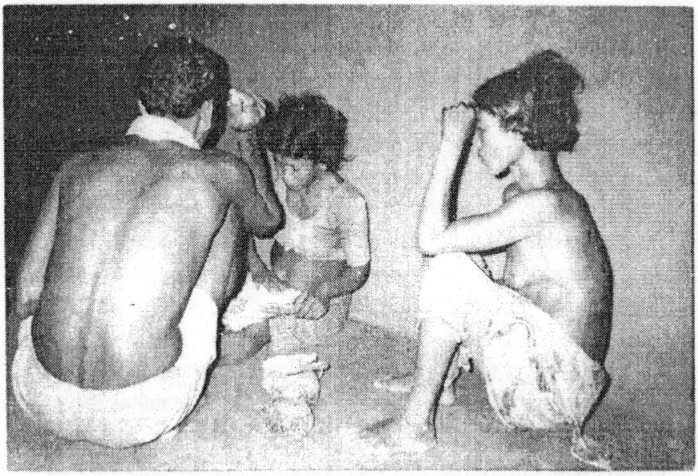

Picture-2: Appeasing the Angry Sonnums (ancestral spirits): A Shamanin performing a ritual to cure a patient with possession of ancestral spirits

The second example is in relation to affinal relationships. Although the matrilineal basis of *Saora* society is an important factor, once a man's wife died and a year after a girl came 'of her own accord' to live with the widower. She fell ill, and her illness was attributed by a diviner-*shamanin* (see picture 2) to the first wife's spirit. It would seem, although Elwin does not mention this, that the husband had married the girl before she became ill. The *shamanin,* reputedly possessed by the spirit, declared to her, 'What are you doing in the house I made? I was there first, and you have entered it of your own accord, and have never given me a thing.' On the *shamanin's* advice the husband instituted a ceremony of friendship (*gadding*) to bring his two wives— the living and the dead, together. Another *shamanin* acted as officiate, and said to the husband speaking as the spirit, 'When did you bring this woman into my house?' I had a little sister; she was the girl you should have married. She would have looked after me properly. The husband replied, 'But that was the very girl I wanted to marry. I went to ner father's house for her. But the old man made such a fuss that we quarreled. Then this girl came. She works well; you ought to be pleased with her. The *shamanin*, acting in the character of the dead wife, agreed to make friends with the new wife, and gave the latter a cloth and bracelets (supplied by the husband) in token of ritual friendship.

These examples state very well that how ritual and beliefs are part and parcel of *Saora* tribes in their life cycle. Without this, life of *Saora* is quite impossible. Apart from their life cycle and rituals, there is a concept of god, which needs a mention and comprehensive discussion.

Concept of God

The concept of a supreme god is almost non-existence among the *Saoras*. According to Verrior Elwin, "the *Saora* eschatology is confused and its doctrines vary from place to place, but it is possible to define certain broad principles that are generally accepted." It is true that in different parts different gods are considered 'supreme'. Even the Earthworm, *Lobosum* is given highest order in certain areas. The *Saora* gods are different from one another in composition, function, character and nature. Some are benevolent, some are neutral and some others malevolent. All these gods and spirits have constant demand on the living beings. If their demands are not met they can cause havoc. The malevolent spirits and gods are cared more than their benevolent counterparts as they can bring misery. When their depredations become unbearable the benevolent gods are approached. They are not so narrow- minded and bestow their blessings irrespective of how they are treated lavishly or austerely.

Therefore, Elwin, states that 'the whole structure of *Saora* theology and mythology may be regarded as an attempt to make the mystery and horror of the unseen more bearable'. The burden of 'wholly other' was too great for them to bear, and so they produced ghosts, who were related to them, deities who had the same desires and passions as themselves. Such ghosts and gods might still be alarming and dangerous, but they are not overwhelming; rationalization, of however simple a sort, had drawn their sting (Turner: 181).

Sonnumr or *Sunnam* is the general name for the *Saora* deities and spirits. The deities are called in different names such as *Labosum, Rudesum* and *Karunisum*, etc. The word *Sonnum* is used in a general sense when applied to a particular order of deities and spirits. Sitapati has recorded the following order of deities. (cited from N., Patanaik, 1989: 42-3)

1. *Sonnumanji*: (This is an important order which contains maximum number of deities)
2. *Bonadanji*: (This order includes deities like *Sonnum Bonad, Regan Bonad, Jhonad* and many others)
3. *Jnodanji*: (This is an order of spirits, which includes *Gusta Jnod, Kusath Jnod* and *Panosi Jnod*, etc.)
4. *Marnniji* and *Sunninji*: (This order includes a large number of deities and spirits who reside in the hills and these deities are very docile benevolent)
5. *Badongaji*: (Deities of this order also reside on the high hills)
6. *Kittunganji*: (This order includes a number of demigods in human forms)

Besides, there are some other orders of the deities such as *Deijenji*; (Super human beings), *Rajanji* (Kings and Dharam rajas), *Patranji, Kuaranji, Adanganji, Mallanji, Bullenji, Jalbanji, Bulkenji, Radobanji, Raganji, Joienji* and *Kulbanji* which include a large number of deities and spirits (*Ibid.*, 43).

Shamanism

In view of the widespread belief in tribal societies that spirits and gods frequently afflict the living with illness and misfortune to punish them, whether for quarrelling openly with their kin or for harboring malignant wishes against them, it seems feasible in this instance that the *shaman*, using the idiom of mystical affliction, was in fact redressing a breach of the customary norms governing behaviour between seminal brothers. It is believed that, the gods actively intervene to punish breaches between living kin and to maintain the continuity of Patrilineal ties. The *shaman* mediates between gods and men and makes the whishes of gods known to men (Turner: 184). The *shaman* may well have no structural links to either of the parties in a dispute. It is also possible that he has the permanent status of an 'outsider' or 'stranger' who has little stake as an individual in any of the ordered arrangements of secular society. He appears to mediate between persons or groups as well as between gods and ancestors, on the one hand, and the living, on the other. And as he mediates he mends not only the idiosyncratic tie that has been broken, but also adjusts a far wider set of relationships that have been disturbed by the quarrel.

Change and Contradictions

As we know change is inevitable for all social and cultural aspects of human life. In the same way *Saora* religion has changed and influenced to a great extent over the ages, because of development initiative by the government and Christian missionaries. This researcher observes that their culture and religion are in the verge of transition, which will be clear from the following discussions.

As it is clear by now that *Saoras* are more religious and their daily activities are defined in connection with religion. So to note the changes this researcher asked a question, 'why they believe in god'. As Table 5.1 shows 38 per cent of young *Saoras* say they believe in religion because of their belief and an equal per cent of respondents say they believe in religion due to self-interest and satisfaction. A minority of young 24 per cent says they believe in religion due to tradition. This depicts the mind of the young *Saora* where their beliefs largely rest upon belief and self-interest. The middle aged *Saoras*, a majority of them about 43 per cent believe in religion due to tradition. A minority about 25 per cent believes on god due to self-interest and satisfaction. Overall, majorities of the *Saoras* about 36 per cent believe in religion due to belief and 30 per cent says they do so due to tradition and a 32 per cent say they do so due to self-interest and satisfaction. The evidence of change lies in 32 per cent where it is reflected that tribal does believe in religion for their own self-interest and satisfaction.

When this is seen from religion point of view, 53 per cent Hindus say that they believe in religion due to tradition, validating the fact that Hinduism has been the traditional religion of *Saoras*. 15 per cent of Hindus say they believe in religion due to self-interest and satisfaction. A majority 48 per cent of the Christians say they believe in their religion due to self-

Table 5.1 Why Tribals Belive in Religion

Variables	*Age*								*Religion*						*Occupation*					
Response	*Young*		*Middle*		*Old*		*Total*		*Hindu*		*Non-Hindu*		*Total*		*Agriculture*		*Non-Agriculture*		*Total*	
	F	%	F	%	F	%	F	%	F	%	F	%	F	%	F	%	F	%	F	%
Tradition	32	24	27	43	11	34	70	30	58	53	12	9.92	70	30	51	32	19	26	70	30
Belief	51	38	21	33	11	34	83	36	33	30	50	41.3	83	36	50	32	33	46	83	36
Self interest & satisfaction	51	38	15	24	8	25	74	32	16	15	58	47.9	74	32	55	35	19	26	74	32
Can't say	1	0.7	0	0	2	6.3	3	1	2	1.8	1	0.83	3	1	2	1.3	1	1.4	3	1
Total	135	100	63	100	32	100	230	100	109	100	121	100	230	100	158	100	72	100	230	100

interest and satisfaction. It is pertinent from here that *Saora* tribe is witnessing a change in the mindset of their tribesmen; because the traditional system is in the verge of being replaced by a keen self-interest in religion.

From occupational point of view, 35 per cent of agricultural *Saora* seem to believe in religion due to self-interest and satisfaction, however 46 per cent non-agriculturist believe in religion due to interest and satisfaction. However 45.8 per cent non-agricultural belief in religion due to their own beliefs. Turner puts it as 'this interpretion would have to reckon with the fact that religious beliefs are customs, collective representations, social stereotypes, not private fantasies' (1967:193). To find out how religious activities are useful for practical purpose, a question was asked in this context whether the tribals offer or perform Puja/Prayer before going to forest. Here we are more interested in exploring the change in this vital link of tribals and ecology. This would also help us in judging the perception of the tribals about forest resources after government intervention. Table 5.2 shows that as regards prayer before going to forest 64.4 per cent of the younger *Saoras* say 'yes' while 34.87 per cent say 'no'. The middle aged *Saoras* seems to be more inclined towards offering prayer before going to forest as 78 per cent saying 'yes' but even here 22 per cent do say 'no'. These 22 per cent are some who don't offer prayers. The older generation of *Saora* tribes seems to be rather more inclined to offer prayers with a whopping majority of 87.5 per cent saying 'yes'. There are 12.5 per cent of the old *Saora* who do not offer prayer.

Among the youth the traditional practice to offer puja is still present in majority, the same case with the middle and old age group. But the variation shows that the large number of old, than middle age groups do religious practice where less number of youth practice it. It shows that the young tribals are not rigid to practice the tradition. It means there is a clear evidence of attitudinal change among the younger generation towards religion. In religion category Hindus are more likely to stick to the practice of offering puja before going to the forest with 80 per cent saying 'yes' and a 64 per cent saying 'yes' in Christianity category. It shows that irrespective of religious belief tribals offer prayers before going to forest. Though the Christian converted from Hindu do their age old practice which may be dominant even after accepting a different religion. While a majority of 73 per cent agriculturist and 68 per cent non-agricultural group have indicated 'yes' towards offering puja/prayer before going to the forest; however a larger percentage of agriculturists say 'yes', in

Table 5.2 Puja/Prayer Before Going to Forest

Variables	*Age*								*Religion*						*Occupation*					
Response	*Young*		*Middle*		*Old*		*Total*		*Hindu*		*Non-Hindu*		*Total*		*Agriculture*		*Non-Agriculture*		*Total*	
	F	%	F	%	F	%	F	%	F	%	F	%	F	%	F	%	F	%	F	%
Yes	87	64.4	49	78	28	87.5	164	71	87	80	77	63.6	164	71	115	73	49	68	164	71
No	47	34.8	14	22	4	12.5	65	28	22	20	43	35.5	65	28	43	27	22	31	65	28
Can't say	1	0.7	0	0	0	0.0	1	0	0	0	1	0.83	1	0	0	0	1	1.4	1	0
Total	135	100	63	100	32	100	230	100	109	100	121	100	230	100	158	100	72	100	230	100

comparison to non-agriculturalist, indicating the practice to be more prevalent amongst agriculturists. The basic reasons for this shift in attitude from a traditional society — who absolutely believes and respect the forest—to one where only 28 per cent saying 'no' towards offering puja and prayer before going to the forest today. This shows a great change in the attitude, as they no more fear the *Bana devata*. However, it can be said that the respect is also declined of *Saora* towards nature and forest.

This result is not a unique phenomenon of *Saoras* only. This seems to apply across the religious spectrum to magic prayer-rituals of the primitive, the *Voodoo* dance, sacrificial rituals, repetition of the Pure Land *Nembutsu*, Tibetan mantirc *Mandala* rituals, and the Roman Catholic Euchasrist (*Encyclopedia of Religion*, 1986:290). Campbell in his book *The Hero with a Thousand Faces* (1949), for example has stressed the continuity of certain themes both cross-culturally and temporally. These themes (like praying, offering puja) have been interpreted as expressions of transpersonal constancies in unconscious mental functioning which are at the same time expressions of fundamental cosmic realities.

From Table 5.2, it is evident that large number of tribals offer puja before going to forest. Now the question arises that 'why they offer puja/prayer'. This has been stated in Table 5.3. Here 60 per cent of tribals stating 'protection' as the reason for keeping up with this practice. The rest are divided between due to 'belief 13 per cent and 'to get more forest product' 12 per cent and 'not applicable' 15 per cent. Here it is clear that fear is one important aspect for which the tribals offer puja before going to jungle. Agewise classification shows that 56 per cent of younger generation relate it to 'protection', while 15 per cent say 'to get more forest produce; 65 per cent middle aged *Saoras* and 66 per cent of older generation gives 'protection' as the reason to offer puja before going to the jungle. What comes out as a highlighting fact that 15 per cent of young, 6.3 per cent of middle aged and 12.5 per cent of old age *Saoras* gives 'more forest produce' as the reason. Here it lies the real evidence of change.

From religious point of view 65 per cent of Hindus and 55 per cent of Christians feel 'protection' is the reason for offering puja/prayers while going to forest. Only 13 per cent and 13 per cent of Hindus and Christians respectively offer prayer due to belief. The majority of *Saoras* also do fear to go to the forest. The fear exists more as a respect towards the forest but this seems to be changing and even religion is no more acts as a barrier. In occupational category 60 per cent of agriculturalist and the equal number

Table 5.3 Reason of Offering Puja or Prayer

Variables	*Age*								*Religion*						*Occupation*					
Response	*Young*		*Middle*		*Old*		*Total*		*Hindu*		*Non-Hindu*		*Total*		*Agriculture*		*Non-Agriculture*		*Total*	
	F	%	F	%	F	%	F	%	F	%	F	%	F	%	F	%	F	%	F	%
Protection	76	56	41	65	21	66	138	60	71	65	67	55.4	138	60	95	60	43	60	138	60
Belief	16	12	7	11	6	19	29	13	17	16	12	9.92	29	13	21	13	8	11	29	13
More forest products	20	15	4	6.3	4	13	28	12	15	14	13	10.7	28	12	10	6.3	18	25	28	12
Not applicable	23	17	11	17	1	3.1	35	15	6	5.5	29	24	35	15	32	20	3	4.2	35	15
Total	135	100	63	100	32	100	230	100	109	100	121	100	230	100	158	100	72	100	230	100

25 per cent of non-agriculturists say they offer prayers to 'get more forest produce'. This is evident from the above fact that non-agriculturists are also still dependent on forest for their livelihood.

This result can be seen by the Confidence theories of religion. It can be begin with the notion of man's inward sense of weakness, and especially of his fears—of disease, of death, of ill fortune of all kinds—and these theorists see religious practices as designed to quiet such fears, either by explaining them away, as in doctrines of the after life, or by claiming to link the individual to external sources of strength, as in prayer. The best known Confidence theory was that set forth by Malinowski. He regarded magic as enabling man to pursue uncertain but essential endeavors by assuring him of their ultimate success. (Cited from Encyclopedia of Social Sciences, 1968:401)

Rituals: Why?

In each and every religion ritual plays very important role. Ritual is the action part of the religion. Stemming originally from Durkheim's *The Elementary Forms of the Religious Life* (1962) and Robertson-Smith's *Lectures on the Religion of the Semities* (1956), the sociological approach emphasizes the manner in which belief and particularly ritual reinforce the traditional societal ties between individuals; it stresses the way in which the social structure of a group is strengthened and perpetuated through the ritualistic or mythic symbolization of the underlying social values upon which it rests. The social psychological approach, of which Frazer and Tyler were perhaps the pioneers but which found its clearest statement in Malinowski's classic *Magic, Science and Religion*, emphasizes what religion does for the individual—how it satisfies both his cognitive and affective demands for a stable, comprehensible, and coercible world, and how it enables him to maintain an inner security in the face of natural contingency. Together these two approaches have given us an increasingly detailed understanding of the social and psychological functions of religion in a wide range of societies. Whatever is important in social life will receive ritual attention or that ceremonial represents symbolic expression of the beliefs and behaviour patterns arising from social interaction, which are cherished the most highly. By ritual expression these folkways or values become sanctified and are made to appear important and inviolable. Now here we will explore the ritual practices of Saoras and the changes in it.

Crisis Rites

Outstanding among crisis rites are ceremonials connected with the important, critical, but normally expectable events in the life cycle of the individuals, the biological crises of life, birth, sexual maturity, reproduction, and death. Rituals performed on these occasions have been called 'rites of passage' because they involve transition from one social status to another, and this expression has also included observances that mark the initiation of individuals into warrior societies, formal age-graded groups, and other associations not directly connected with the biological crises of the life span.

Crisis rites are markers of special events in the life of an individual and thus differs from recurrent ritual events such as planting and harvesting ceremonies, which have essentially equal meaning for many people. The significance of rituals to the individual, associate with the biological crises of life was first hypothesized by Arnold Van Gennep, who observed that 'individuals are eased through the difficulties of transition from one social role to another'. He contended that all these ceremonials are divided into three consecutive elements, called in French *separation, merge and aggregation*, which we may translate as separation, adjustment or transition, and reintegration (Norbeck, 1961: 141).

Birth Rites and Rituals

Birth is an important bio-social event in every society. While bringing out change in the status of married couple, it increases the number of societal members. In Table 5.4 it is evident that out of 230 tribals 141, i.e., 61 per cent go for prayer or puja and 75, i.e., 33 per cent go for naming ceremony. It means more than 91 per cent believe to perform ritual at a newborn baby's arrival. This is evident from all variables.

Now it is pertinent to make a sociological exploration why tribals practice the rituals. It may be naming ceremony or prayer or puja but for what? In Table 5.5 out of 230 respondents 51 per cent says that it is (rituals) that helps for better growth of the baby. 31 per cent says that by performing rituals we express our gratitude and thanks to god. 9 per cent says to do away with the evil spirit. In the age variables the growth of baby is more lauded. But in the variable of religion the data is bit different as 52 per cent Hindus says it is essential for all round development of the baby, whereas 49.6 per cent Christians said this. 15 per cent Hindus say to thank god while it is 45.5 per cent among the Christians. 17 per cent among the Hindus to get rid of evil spirits and only 2.48 per cent among Christians.

Table 5.4 Rituals on Birth

Variables	Age								Religion						Occupation					
Response	Young		Middle		Old		Total		Hindu		Non-Hindu		Total		Agriculture		Non-Agriculture		Total	
	F	%	F	%	F	%	F	%	F	%	F	%	F	%	F	%	F	%	F	%
Prayer/ Puja	88	65	35	56	18	56	141	61	45	41	96	79.3	141	61	97	61	44	61	141	61
Naming ceremony	43	32	20	32	12	38	75	33	54	50	21	17.4	75	33	52	33	23	32	75	33
Any other	2	1.5	4	6.3	2	6.3	8	3	6	5.5	2	1.65	8	3	5	3.2	3	4.2	8	3
No	2	1.5	4	6.3	0	0	6	3	4	3.7	2	1.65	6	3	4	2.5	2	2.8	6	3
Total	135	100	63	100	32	100	230	100	109	100	121	100	230	100	158	100	72	100	230	100

Table 5.5 Why Rituals on New Born Baby?

Variables	*Age*								*Religion*						*Occupation*					
Response	*Young*		*Middle*		*Old*		*Total*		*Hindu*		*Non-Hindu*		*Total*		*Agriculture*		*Non-Agriculture*		*Total*	
	F	%	F	%	F	%	F	%	F	%	F	%	F	%	F	%	F	%	F	%
Growth of Baby	68	50	35	56	14	44	117	51	57	52	60	49.6	117	51	85	54	32	44	117	51
Thanking god	53	39	10	16	8	25	71	31	16	15	55	45.5	71	31	55	35	16	50	71	31
Evil spirit	4	3	10	16	7	22	21	9	18	17	3	2.48	21	9	14	8.9	7	9.7	21	9
Can't say	10	7.4	8	13	3	9.4	21	9	18	17	3	2.48	21	9	4	2.5	17	24	21	9
Total	135	100	63	100	32	100	230	100	109	100	121	100	230	100	158	100	72	100	230	100

It shows that Hindu believers are orthodox and believe in ritual without any reason. So those who believe in Christianity they do not believe in evil spirit.

Likewise those who practice agriculture, 54 per cent says for betterment of the baby, and 35 per cent to thank god. Whereas 50 per cent non-agriculturist says to thank god, 8.9 per cent agriculturists say to do away with the evil spirits, among non-agriculturist it is 9.7 per cent. In B.C. Ray's book *The Changing Socio-economic Profile* (1989), Behura and Mishra writes that 'among Hunduised tribes Gond, Savar, Khond, Bhuyan etc. simulation of the Brahmanical concepts of purity and pollution are found to a considerable extent. Temporarily segregated persons are reintegratec into their society after the birth rites and the newly born child is also admitted to the society of its parents. Name-giving ceremony mostly goes along with this rite' (1989: 41). All elements of Van Gennep's scheme of rites of passage may be found in old Japanese practices surrounding child birth, customs which continue to be observed with waning faith and intensity in some modern rural communities of Japan (Norbeck, 1961: 142).

Marriage Rituals

Marriage is a remarkable event in the life of every individual, whether primitive or advanced. Marriage rites are an elaborate one, which begins with the attempts for bride acquisition to her affiliation with her affinal kin group and sexual consummation. In this study 28 per cent said ritual at marriage is to lead 'happy married life', 10 per cent because of 'tradition', 31 per cent for 'social recognition' and 30 per cent can not say. (Table 5.6) Among the age variables happy married life is prominent followed by social recognition. In religion category, Christians pronounced 'happy married' life about 43.8 per cent in compare to 11. 1 per cent Hindus. But more Hindus, 35 per cent says 'social recognition', it is 28 per cent among Christians. This reflects ideological difference between these two religions. Occupationally, 29 per cent agriculturist says happy married life in comparison to 26 per cent non agriculturist. 12 agriculturist says tradition in comparison to only 6.9 per cent non agriculturist, 33 per cent agriculturist says 'social recognition' as against 28 per cent non-agriculturist. It is prominent that the tribals do the feast and other rituals that legalise the marriage and the blessings of elders for a better life. Sociologically, this two are quite important. 'Marriage in tribal society is governed by strong social sanction, hence all forms of conjugal unions are legitimized by follow up marriage ceremonies. Social recognition is accorded to the union

Table 5.6 Why Rituals at Marriage?

Variables	*Age*								*Religion*						*Occupation*					
Response	*Young*		*Middle*		*Old*		*Total*		*Hindu*		*Non-Hindu*		*Total*		*Agriculture*		*Non-Agriculture*		*Total*	
	F	%	F	%	F	%	F	%	F	%	F	%	F	%	F	%	F	%	F	%
Happy marriage	39	29	18	29	8	25	65	28	12	11	53	43.8	65	28	46	29	19	26	65	28
Tradition	12	8.9	2	3.2	10	31	24	10	10	9.2	14	11.6	24	10	19	12	5	6.9	24	10
Social Recognition	49	36	17	53	6	19	72	31	38	35	34	28.1	72	31	52	33	20	28	72	31
Can't say	35	26	26	41	8	25	69	30	49	45	20	16.5	69	30	41	26	28	39	69	30
Total	135	100	63	100	32	100	230	100	109	100	121	100	230	100	158	100	72	100	230	100

only when this ritual is gone through and it takes place when all problems relating to the union are sorted out. Among the tribes of Orissa marriage ceremonies are simplest of all rites connected with the events in the life cycle of the individual (Roy: *Ibid.*: 43). Audrey Richards' account of the series of rites called the *Chsungu* of the Bema tribe of Northern Rhodesia describes it as a female initiation ceremony. Traditionally preceding marriage, the *Chsungu* is an integral part of series of observances by which a bridegroom is united with the family group of the bride. It consists of a long elaborate succession of ceremonies, which include singing, dancing, miming and much use of sacred paraphernalia. (Norbeck, 1961: 154).

Funeral Rites

Classic features of rites of crisis are often most clearly evident in obsequies. The bereaved refrain from many normal acts; they perform various rites of mourning for the prescribed period which varies from tribe to tribe and finally the funeral rite is performed, which marks the end of final formal mourning and after this the kins of the deceased are brought back to normal social relationships. This has been cent per cent proved by the study that 99.6 per cent tirbals do rituals at the time of dealth (Table 5.7). In Table 5.8 it is described 'why tribals perform funeral rites'. As the result shows 28 per cent said 'to mix with the *pitrulok'*, 11 per cent said 'not to be affected by the evil forces', 45 per cent said because of rituals 'the soul rest in peace', and 16 per cent said it is a 'law and practice'. Among the youth 50 per cent says about the 'sole rest in peace' followed by 'to mix with the *pitrulok*'. In religion category 35 per cent Hindus says 'to mix with the *pitrulok*' in comparison to 22.3 per cent of the Christians. 'Not to be affected by the evil forces' is responded by 18 per cent Hindus in comparison to 4.13 per cent of the Christians. 23 per cent Hindus say in comparison to 64.5 per cent Christians about 'the soul rest in the peace'. 'Law and practice' is also more among the Hindus 24 per cent in comparison to 9.09 per cent of Christians.

Occupationally it is also evident that 27 per cent says 'to mix with the *pitrulok*' in comparison to 32 per cent non-agriculturist. 'May the soul rest in peace' is more or less equal among agriculturist and non- agriculturist, i.e. 44 per cent and 47 per cent respectively. 'Law and practice' is more among agriculturist 30 per cent in comparison 22 per cent non-agriculturist. It is evident from the above discussion that though tribals are changing their believe towards rituals, the concept of soul still persists. 'The general belief is that the soul of the deceased does not leave their home environment until the final funeral rites are over.' 'A widow continues to be her deceased

Table 5.7 Rituals at the Time of Death

Variables	*Age*								*Religion*						*Occupation*					
Response	*Young*		*Middle*		*Old*		*Total*		*Hindu*		*Non-Hindu*		*Total*		*Agriculture*		*Non-Agriculture*		*Total*	
	F	%	F	%	F	%	F	%	F	%	F	%	F	%	F	%	F	%	F	%
Yes	135	100	62	98	32	100	229	99.6	108	99	121	100	229	99.6	157	99	72	100	229	99.6
No	0	0	1	1.6	0	0	1	0.4	1	0.9	0	0	1	0.4	1	0.6	0	0	1	0.4
Can't say	0	0	0	0	0	0	0	0.0	0	0	0	0	0	0.0	0	0	0	0	0	0.0
Total	135	100	63	100	32	100	230	100	109	100	121	100	230	100	158	100	72	100	230	100

Table 5.8 Why Rituals After Death?

Variables	*Age*								*Religion*						*Occupation*					
Response	*Young*		*Middle*		*Old*		*Total*		*Hindu*		*Non-Hindu*		*Total*		*Agriculture*		*Non-Agriculture*		*Total*	
	F	%	F	%	F	%	F	%	F	%	F	%	F	%	F	%	F	%	F	%
To mix with the *pitrulok*	44	33	12	19	9	28	65	28	38	35	27	22.3	65	28	42	27	23	32	65	28
Not to affect by the evil force	6	4.4	11	17	8	25	25	11	20	18	5	4.13	25	11	17	11	8	11	25	11
Soul rest in the peace	68	50	28	44	7	22	103	45	25	23	78	64.5	103	45	69	44	34	47	103	45
Law & Practices	17	13	12	19	8	25	37	16	26	24	11	9.09	37	16	30	19	7	22	37	16
Total	135	100	63	100	32	100	230	100	109	100	121	100	230	100	158	100	72	100	230	100

husband's wife until this second ceremony, and if she becomes pregnant in the interval between funerals, the child is his and shares in his property' (Roy. 1989:45).

Agricultural rite

In the same manner question has been repeated about the economic activities of the tribals. In Table 5.9 it is evident that 61 per cent of tribals say of practising ritual before cultivation and 37 per cent says 'no'. Among Hindus it is 71 per cent 'yes' in comparison 52.1 per cent of Christians. 47.1 per cent Christian says 'no' to this. In occupational category also 64 per cent says 'yes' among agriculturist in comparison to 54 per cent non-agriculture. 35 per cent and 43 per cent respectively says 'no' to this practice.

Importance of Priest Today

Now it is pertinent from the above discussion that religion is a very important institution for the tribals in general and *Saoras* in particular. Though in due course of time it has changed but the question arises that whether the dependency on priest, *shaman* or pastro has changed or not. Anthropologists who are less concerned than Weber with the genesis of religions and with internal developments in complex societies or their impact on the "primitive" world are inclined to contrast priest not with prophet but with *shaman* or spirit medium and to examine the relationship between these statuses as part of the normal working of the religious system in the simpler societies. In their excellently representative *Reader in Comparative Religion* (1958), the editors W.A. Lessa and E.Z. Vogt devote a whole section to this distinction.

Often, where there is a priest the *shaman* is absent, and vice versa, although both these roles may be found in the same religion, as among the plain Indians. According to Lowie (1954) a plain Indian *shaman* is a ritual practitioner whose status is acquired through a personal communication from a supernatural being, whereas a priest does not necessarily have a face-to-face relationship with the spirit world but must have competence in conducting ritual. In this pretext *Saoras* have been asked about 'the help of priest/priestess in rituals', which is shown in Table 5.10, where 96 per cent said 'yes', 3 per cent said 'no'. Agewise distribution shows that the younger *Saoras* seems to be more dependant on priest/priestess for offering rituals with 99 per cent saying so. 92 per cent of middle age and 93.75 per cent of old age *Saoras* seems to be dependant on priest/priestess for offering puja or rituals throughout their lifecycle. From religion point of

Table 5.9 Rituals at the Beginning of Cultivation

Variables	*Age*								*Religion*						*Occupation*					
Response	*Young*		*Middle*		*Old*		*Total*		*Hindu*		*Non-Hindu*		*Total*		*Agriculture*		*Non-Agriculture*		*Total*	
	F	%	F	%	F	%	F	%	F	%	F	%	F	%	F	%	F	%	F	%
Yes	70	52	43	68	27	84	140	61	77	71	63	52.1	140	61	101	64	39	54	140	61
No	64	47	17	27	5	16	86	37	29	27	57	47.1	86	37	55	35	31	43	86	37
Can't Say	1	0.7	3	4.8	0	0	4	2	3	2.8	1	0.83	4	2	2	1.3	2	2.8	4	2
Total	135	100	63	100	32	100	230	100	109	100	121	100	230	100	158	100	72	100	230	100

Table 5.10 Usefulness of Priest in Puja

Variables	*Age*								*Religion*						*Occupation*					
Response	*Young*		*Middle*		*Old*		*Total*		*Hindu*		*Non-Hindu*		*Total*		*Agriculture*		*Non-Agriculture*		*Total*	
	F	%	F	%	F	%	F	%	F	%	F	%	F	%	F	%	F	%	F	%
Yes	133	99	58	92	30	94	221	96	102	94	119	98.3	221	96	151	96	70	97	221	96
No	2	1.5	3	4.8	2	6.3	7	3	6	5.5	1	0.86	7	3	5	3.2	2	2.8	7	3
Can't Say	0	0	2	3.2	0	0	2	1	1	0.9	1	0.83	2	1	2	1.3	0	0	2	1
Total	135	100	63	100	32	100	230	100	109	100	121	100	230	100	158	100	72	100	230	100

view, the Christians due to their religious practices 98 per cent of them a larger majority—seems to be dependant on the pastro while 94 per cent of the Hindus feel so. 5.5 per cent of the Hindus say that they are not dependant on priest for religious practices.

From occupational point of view, 96 per cent of agriculturists and a greater majority 97 per cent of non-agriculturist says 'yes' for taking help of priest. This above argument can be seen that in the study of Raymond Firth (1964: 638) regards *shamanism* as itself "that particular form of spirit medium ship in which a specialist (the *shaman*) normally himself a medium, is deemed to exercise developed techniques of control over spirits, sometimes including mastery of spirits believed to be possessing another medium." This definition like that of Howells (1948) stresses the control exercised over spirits. Howells describes the *shaman* as "bullyragging" gods or spirits and emphasizes his intellectual qualities as a leader. This element of mastery makes the *shaman* a distinctive type of spirit medium, one who is believed to be possessed by a spirit (or closely controlled by a spirit) [and who] can serve as a means of communication between other human beings and the spirit world" (Firth 1964: 689). The spirit medium *per se* need not exert mastery; he is rather the vehicle of the 'transhuman' entity. That is because irrespective of age, religion and occupation *Saoras* do believe to take the help of priest, *shaman.*

In order to go deeper into the 'reasons for taking the help of priest, pastro and *shaman*' (Table 5.11) the result is pertinent and interesting. A majority of *Saoras* 66 per cent of the sample size feels 'priest is empowered' while 27.39 per cent says it is a 'religious prescription'. Only a low 5.65 per cent are unable to give a reason for taking the help from priest or pastor. Agewise 24.4 per cent of younger *Saoras* believe 'religious prescription' is the reason for taking the help of priest. The older generation however a good number 53.1 per cent cite 'religious prescription' is the reason for taking help of priest. Only 37.5 per cent of *Saoras* feel the 'priest is empowered'. It seems the older generation is dis-enchanted with the powers of priest. Religionwise break up shows that 61 per cent of Hindus and 69 per cent of Christians say their 'priest is empowered' and 27.3 per cent of Christians say that it is a 'religious practices' because of Baptism, confession etc. Occupationwise break up shows that the help of priest is of equal importance to agriculturists and non-agriculturists with 67.1 per cent and 63 per cent respectively. Higher percentage of agriculturists feels the priest is empowered.

On a question about the 'changing role of priest' (Table 5.12) 73 per cent of *Saoras* says 'yes' and 15 per cent 'no'. So a majority of the *Saoras* do feel that the role of priest has definitely changed over the ages. Agewise break up shows that the middle aged *Saoras* feel very strongly about the role of priest with 87 per cent saying 'yes'. 78 per cent of the older generation feeling so whereas 65 per cent young says 'yes'. Religionswise a majority of 87 per cent Hindus say the role of priest has changed. There is a definite change in the attitude of Hindus towards the role of priest. Occupationwise 75 per cent non-agriculturists say 'yes' that the role of priest has changed. A 72 per cent agriculturist says 'yes' .

We further tried to go deeper into the 'causes of changing role of priest' (Table 5.13). The important reasons cited by the *Saoras* are 'because of Christianity' and 'lack of good priests'. Overall, 50 per cent cite Christianity as the reason for 'changing role of priest'. 16.09 per cent of the sample say because of 'lack of good priest'. Agewise break up shows the younger generation seems to be confused as the real reason for changing role of priest. While a 38 per cent of the young says 'because of Christianity', 19 per cent say due to lack of good priest and 22 per cent are unable to give any reasons for this. The reasons for such confusion can be seen in the earlier fact wherein 98.5 per cent of *Saoras* take the help of priest in performing their religious duties. However, among in the middle aged *Saoras* 65 per cent said Christianity is the reason for change 66 per cent older generation says Christianity as the reason for change. So it is clear that the traditional role of priest has undergone a sea change due to the advent of Christianity. Among the religious group, Christian *Saoras* (43.8 per cent) say Christianity is the cause of changing role of the priest. Among Hindu *Saoras* 56 per cent say the role of priest has changed. Occupationally, 57 per cent of non-agriculturists and 46 per cent agriculturists says Christianity has changed the role of priest.

Change in Festivity

From the above discussion it is clear that the religious institution of the *Saoras* has changed to a great extent. Now a proposition has developed by the researcher that to know whether the 'festival celebration has declined or not' among the *Saoras*. (Table 5.14) Overall 72 per cent said 'yes' and 22 per cent said 'no' and 6 per cent 'can not say.' Age wise, the younger generation feels the same way with a 67 per cent saying 'yes' and a 30 per cent saying 'no'. Of the middle aged *Saoras* 81 per cent said 'yes' and 11 per cent 'no'. Of the older *Saoras* 75 per cent said 'yes'. The Religious and

Table 5.11 Reason for Taking the Help of Priest etc.

Variables	*Age*								*Religion*						*Occupation*					
Response	*Young*		*Middle*		*Old*		*Total*		*Hindu*		*Non-Hindu*		*Total*		*Agriculture*		*Non-Agriculture*		*Total*	
	F	%	F	%	F	%	F	%	F	%	F	%	F	%	F	%	F	%	F	%
Religious Prescription	33	24	13	21	17	53	63	27	30	28	33	27.3	63	27	38	24	25	35	63	27
Priest empowerment	96	71	43	68	12	38	151	66	67	61	84	69.4	151	66	106	67	45	63	151	66
Can't Say	4	3	6	9.5	3	9.4	13	6	9	8.3	4	3.31	13	6	11	7	2	2.8	13	6
No	2	1.5	1	1.6	0	0	3	1	3	2.8	0	0	3	1	3	1.9	0	0	3	1
Total	135	100	63	100	32	100	230	100	109	100	121	100	230	100	158	100	72	100	230	100

Table 5.12 Change in the Role of Priest

Variables	*Age*								*Religion*						*Occupation*					
Response	*Young*		*Middle*		*Old*		*Total*		*Hindu*		*Non-Hindu*		*Total*		*Agriculture*		*Non-Agriculture*		*Total*	
	F	%	F	%	F	%	F	%	F	%	F	%	F	%	F	%	F	%	F	%
Yes	88	65	55	87	25	78	168	73	95	87	73	60.3	168	73	114	72	54	75	168	73
No	24	18	5	7.9	6	19	35	15	10	9.2	25	20.7	35	15	21	13	14	19	35	15
Can't Say	23	17	3	4.8	1	3.1	27	12	4	3.7	23	19	27	12	23	15	4	5.6	27	12
Total	135	100	63	100	32	100	230	100	109	100	121	100	230	100	158	100	72	100	230	100

Table 5.13 Causes of Changing Role of Priest

Variables	*Age*								*Religion*						*Occupation*					
Response	*Young*		*Middle*		*Old*		*Total*		*Hindu*		*Non-Hindu*		*Total*		*Agriculture*		*Non-Agriculture*		*Total*	
	F	%	F	%	F	%	F	%	F	%	F	%	F	%	F	%	F	%	F	%
Because Chr-istianity	51	38	42	67	21	66	114	50	61	56	53	43.8	114	50	73	46	41	57	114	50
Lack good priest	25	19	7	11	5	16	37	16	28	26	9	7.44	37	16	27	17	10	14	37	16
Can't Say	29	14	12	19	1	3.1	42	18	10	9.2	32	26.4	42	18	31	20	11	15	42	18
Not app.	30	22	2	3.2	5	16	37	16	10	9.2	27	22.3	37	16	29	17	10	14	37	16
Total	135	100	63	100	32	100	230	100	109	100	121	100	230	100	158	100	72	100	230	100

Table 5.14 Decline of Festival Celebration

Variables	*Age*								*Religion*						*Occupation*					
Response	*Young*		*Middle*		*Old*		*Total*		*Hindu*		*Non-Hindu*		*Total*		*Agriculture*		*Non-Agriculture*		*Total*	
	F	%	F	%	F	%	F	%	F	%	F	%	F	%	F	%	F	%	F	%
Yes	90	67	51	81	24	75	165	72	93	85	72	59.5	165	72	121	77	44	61	165	72
No	41	30	7	11	3	9.4	51	22	10	9.2	41	33.9	51	22	27	17	24	33	51	22
Can't Say	4	3	5	7.9	5	16	14	6	6	5.5	8	6.64	14	6	10	6.3	4	5.6	14	6
Total	135	100	63	100	32	100	230	100	109	100	121	100	230	100	158	100	72	100	230	100

Table 5.15 Effects of Decline Forest Resources on Festival Celebration

Variables	*Age*								*Religion*						*Occupation*					
Response	*Young*		*Middle*		*Old*		*Total*		*Hindu*		*Non-Hindu*		*Total*		*Agriculture*		*Non-Agriculture*		*Total*	
	F	%	F	%	F	%	F	%	F	%	F	%	F	%	F	%	F	%	F	%
Yes	65	48	23	36.5	15	46	103	45	68	62	35	29	103	45	77	49	26	36	103	45
No	61	45	23	36.5	13	41	97	42	28	26	69	57	97	42	58	37	39	54	97	42
Can't Say	9	6.7	17	26.98	4	13	30	13	13	12	17	14	30	13	23	14	7	9.7	30	13
Total	135	100	63	100	32	100	230	100	109	100	121	100	230	100	158	100	72	100	230	100

occupation category has also the same trend of decline in festival celebration.

In the next question the researcher hsa tried to find out that 'is it true that decline in forest resources has the effect on tribal festival celebration'. In table no.5.15 it has been stated that 45 per cent of tribals says 'yes' whereas 42 per cent 'no' and 13 per cent can not say. The most important point is that among the young respondents the respons is very prominent i.e. 48 per cent said due to decline in forest resources their is a steady decline in the festival celebrations. Like wise old category also has 47 per cent but the middle aged group responses is poor only 37 per cent. In comparison between Hindus and non-Hindus 62 per cent and 29 per cent respectively has said 'yes'. Occupationally also 49 per cent agriculturists say 'yes' and 36 per cent non-agriculturist. Here the overall trend is that decline of forest resources has direct effect on festival celebration.

Conclusion

Religion as understood by anthropologist, is not an abstract set of ideas, values or beliefs, rather it is the matrix of social whole. Many studies have stressed the function of ritual and belief in supposing to social structure and institutionalized customs. This is very much found among the *Saora* tribe as their life cycle starts with rituals and end not even after the death. This stands with birth by cutting the umbilical cord. This continue up to 12 to 15 days followed by many other rituals and worship. Traditionally *Saora* religion involves lots of sacrifice of buffalo, hens on many occasions. Throughout the *Saora* life when even they fall ill they offer some puja and sacrifices. At the time of death rituals, important ritual called 'peacock dance' is performed, which enables the tribals to have 'dialogues with the dead'. This enables the tribal to know about the life of the deceased person.

Among *Saora* the concept of god is very much existence. But there is many gods for each and every aspect of the life. Among them some are benevolent, neutral and malevolent. Most of the gods have constant demand on the living being. When their demands are more, this is settled through the *shaman.* The *shaman* known as *kudanbai* among the *Saora.* This plays very important role in *Saora* life.

This picture has changed to a great extent. The *Saora* beliefs on god or supernatural being are due to tradition, beliefs, self-interest and satisfaction. Most of the tribals, even today believe in puja / prayer before starting any activities of their lives. This is due to fear psychosis and tribal wants 'protection'. That is why they believe in supernatural power, by which they are protected. *Saora* practices, crisis rites, birth rites, marriage rituals, funeral ritual, and rituals at the beginning of the cultivation. Ritual on newborn baby is due to growth of baby. The result in connection with causes of marriage rituals is variational with many differences. This reflects the changes and contradictions in relation to *Saora* practices. The result of the cause of death rituals is not prominent, 45 per cent tribals refer to "the sole rest in peace" is the main cause. This is due to domination of Christianity in the area.

The importance of religious officials in *Saora* land is very high 96 per cent. It shows how *Saora's* are dependent on religious officials or priests. That is because the priest is empowered to offer the puja. In other words, we can say that the priest is the mediator between the god/spirit and *Saoras.* The another important cause is of fearness of *Saora* to their ancestors. The contradictory result is, 75 per cent tribals opine that the role of priest has changed because of mainly Christianity. This result seems to be contradictory but in practice it is not. The maximum Christian also seeks the help of Pastro for the rituals. So the result is not dicey.

In the view of festival celebration 72 per cent tribals opine that there is a decline in festival celebration. This is due to many reasons. The 45 per cent tribals say because of 'decline in forest resources', whereas 42 per cent said not due to this. This change can be attributed to the changing socio-economic situation in the tribal area. Since people are busy to earn their livelihood and adapted to Christianity, so definitely they don't want to celebrate the cumbersome festivities with pump and gay.

References

Benedict, Ruth, 1946, *Patterns of Culture*, Baltimare, Penguin.

Campbell, J., 1949, *The Hero with a Thousand Faces,* Pantheon, New York.

Durkheim, Emile, 1962, *The Elementary Forms of the Religious Life,* London, Allen and Unwin.

Evans-Pritchard, E. E., 1965, *Theories of Primitive.Religion.* London, Oxford University Press.

Elwin, V., 1955, *The Religion of an Indian Tribe,* Oxford University Press.

Eliade, M.(*ed.*), 1986, *Encyclopedia of Religion,* Vol. 1, New York, Macmillan Publishing, pp. 308-315.

Firth, Raymond, 1964, 'Shaman'. Julius Gould and William L. Kolb (*ed.*), *A Dictionary of the Social Sciences,* Free Press. pp. 638-639.

Frazer, J.G., 1945, *The Goldent Bough,* abridged edition, London.

Freud, Sigmund, 1949, *An Outline of Psychoanalysis,* New York, Norton.

Freud, Sigmund, 1960, *Totem and Taboo,* London, Routledge and Kegan Paul.

Geertz, C., 1973, *The Interpretation of Culture: Selected Essays,* New York, Basic Books, Inc. Publisher.

Howells, W. W., 1948, *The Heathens: Primitive Man and His Religions,* New York, Garden city.

Kakar, Sudhir, 1982, *Shamans, Mystics and Doctors: A Psychological Inquiry into India and Its Healing Traditions,* New York.

Lessa ,W.A. and E.Z. Vogt, (*ed.*) 1958, *Reader in Comparative Religion: An Anthropological Approach,* Harper, New York.

Malinowski, B., 1948, *Science, Magic and Religion and other Essay,* Glencoe.

Norbeck, E., 1961, *Religion in Primitive Society,* New York, Harper and Row.

Pattnaik, N., 1989, *The Saora,* Bhubaneswar, THRT.

Radcliffe-Brown, A.R., 1952, 'Religion and Society' *Structure and Function in Primitive Society,* London, Cohen & West.

Ray, B.C., 1989, The Changing Socio-economic Profile, Not available.

Spencer, Herbert, 1896, *Prinicles of Sociology,* Vol. III, London.

Smith, W. Robertson, 1956, *Lectures on the Religion of the Semities,* New York, Meridian Library.

Tylor, E.B., 1871, *Primitive Culture,* Vol.2, New York, Brentano's.

Turner, V.W., 1967, *The Forest of Symbol: Aspects of Dembu Ritual,* London, Carlen University Press.

Van Genep, A., 1960, *The Rights of Passage,* London, Routledge and Kejen Paul.

6

Culture Leisure and Communication

Culture, a uniquely human attribute, is something which man interposes between himself and his environment in order to ensure his security and survival. Malinowski, points out that, the social heritage may be said to consist of a material part and a non-material, intangible, imponderable part, or, to put it in other words, culture is a total way of life and the instruments, mental, social and material, of which this way is constituted. On the one hand we have social culture and on the other material culture. Herskovits, American anthropologists, in his book, *Man and His Work* (1956: 17), has defined culture as the man-made part of environment. According to him, environment is of two types: (i) Natural environment, and (ii) Social environment. The total social environment of man is his culture, because it is made by man himself. The natural things, which are shaped into different forms, represent the work of the man. Thus, all material and non-material things made man represent culture.

Culture is said in Sanskrit as *Sanskriti.* This means how we live and what is our *sanskar*—socialisation and tradition. Here the *sanskar* or tradition of *Saora* tribe has been explored. Their nature of believes value and taboos has been discussed. The concept like *ukka* and *ersi* also defined. *Ukka* is a code of conduct with the inhabitant of other world like ancestor and god. Ersi shows how to behave with them. There are the codes of conduct to maintain the society in smooth order.

Due to various reasons our culture changes. Change in individual items can be explained as selections and rejections consistent with the cultural patterns. But the patterns themselves are also subject to change. There is a cultural orthogenesis, in which "the direction of at least some culture change is more predetermined by earlier forms of the culture than used by environmental press and individual variability". In the case of *Saora* tribe this has also happened. Their traditional believes values, activities, leisure and communication all are changing. Here it is not completely wiped out but coexistence of both the typical traditional and today's simple modern culture. For example *Saora* tribals are very keen about their own songs and because they understand the language and song but in the context of dress habits, they prefer the modern one. Here change has been evident in certain aspect but not in all the aspect.

The Soar tribes' relation with forest is also clearly evident from their material and non-material culture. The symbiotic relation is no more as the large scale of jungle have been depleted. The taboo in relation to forest and cutting trees has also been changed. It shows the loosing old and traditional value is one and important reason for deforestation. In this context the government interventions are also seen. This has resulted into contradiction and conflict in tribal society. Few tribals like to join the main-stream and leaving back their tradition and culture. But half of the tribals try to retain their culture. Here exclusively it has been discussed about *Saora's* mythological origin, values like *ersi* and *ukka*, their village pattern, folk songs, jokes and riddles to explore the traditional perspective of their culture. In today's context their daily social activities, leisure time, liking traditional and old ornaments and garments, music, etc. has been very carefully discussed.

The Concept of Culture

"Culture or civilization, taken in its wide ethnographic sense, is that complex whole which includes knowledge, belief, art, morals, law, custom, and any other capabilities and habits acquired by man as a member of society"(Tylor, 1871, 1958,Vol.I: I). What is emphasized in this definition is that culture is a social heritage; it is the gift of society to an individual. Bronislaw, Malinowski wrote the article on 'Culture' for the *Encyclopedia of the Social Sciences* (1933), placing emphasis on culture as a functioning, active, efficient well organized unity, which must be analyzed into component institutions in relation to one another, in relation to the needs of the human organism, and in relation to the environment, man made as well as natural. This concept of culture became the "common sense" of an entire American generation of anthropologists in the 1930s and 1940s.

The totality of human culture contains an element of patterning that provides the general framework for individual cultures and represents a historical summation of those cultures, which have segregated themselves as crystallized historical configurations of culture. The "universal pattern" of human history, in either sense, is not yet known but can only be gradually discovered through comparative-historical studies of the systemic, secondary, and configurationally patterns in all cultures, primitive and civilized (Kroeber & Kluckhohn, 1963)

. In both the primitive and civilised societies culture patterns tend to persist as organised bodies of custom in spite of changes in items of culture content. Changes in individual items can be explained as selections and rejections consistent with the cultural patterns. But the patterns themselves are also subject to change. There is a cultural orthogenesis, in which "the direction of at least some culture change is more predetermined by earlier forms of the culture than caused by environmental press and individual variability". Sapir called this "cultural drift", "Whenever the human mind has worked collectively and unconsciously, it has striven for and often attained unique form. The important point is that the evolution of form has a drift in one direction, that it seeks poise, and that it rests, relatively speaking, when it has found this poise". (quoted in *Ibid.*: 182)

The relevance of "cultural drift" to studies of cultural continuity and change is obvious. Eggan (1963) has recently applied it to an analysis of cultural changes in the Philippines, and Redfield have suggested ways in which the role of cities in cultural change may be interpreted as the product of "orthogenetic" and "heterogeneity" processes. (See the article by Redfield & Singer in Redfield 1962; also see Singer 1959).

Unlike cultural drift analysis pattern theory assumes that culture is created by individuals and groups and interacts with them as well as with the environment. However, these interactions of biology, psychology, and geography are the given conditions and starting points for cultural growth but not its determinants. Such a theory views the process of cultural growth as a historical process, as Boas emphasized, a "growing together" of elements of culture content from different sources, which have become associated in a historical configuration. The end result of this historical process, at any given time, is an associated set of patterns, a precipitate of the history of a particular group, of its past choices, conscious and unconscious. Culture is this precipitate "present in persons, shaping their perceptions of events, other persons, and the environing situation in ways not wholly determined by biology and environmental press". Culture is an intervening variable between human 'organism' and 'environment'. It is "an abstract description of trends toward uniformity in the words, acts, and artifacts of human groups" (Krober & Kluckhohn 1963: 182). Leslie A. White (1949:360), for example, speaks of culture as a specific and concrete mechanism employed by a particular animal organism in adjusting to its environment". In the same way Ralph Piddington (1952:219) states that "culture is essentially an adaptive mechanism, making possible the satisfaction of human needs, both biological and social."

The ecologist Angus Woodbury (1954: 412) recognized that social life is an adaptation for efficient use of time and space upon the earth. The existence of a social life, he thought, was forced upon members of a group by their need to cooperate in order to succeed in the struggle for existence. The zoologist William Etkin (1954: 134) wrote of the essential role played by social behaviour in an animal's adaptation to its environment and stated that various forms of group behaviour were as necessary to survival as any of an animal's physiological or structural characteristics. In their joint work, J. Arthur Thomson and Patrick Geddes (*Life Outlines of General Biology*, 1931, Vol. I, :120-126) listed seven advantages of social life, and in Lee R.Dice (*Natural Communities*, 1952:285-287) enumerated nine such advantages.

Social organization, generally is the way in which the individuals of a group within all animal species coordinate their behaviour in adapting to the exigencies of life. Human social organization is simply the way in which human beings, through cultural means, do the same thing. As White has observed: "Human beings have to be related to each other in an effective manner in order to carry on the business of life successfully. Social, political, ethical, artistic, ecclesiastical, and educational systems operate to accomplish this purpose. They are means of coordinating, integrating, regulating, and directing human endeavor towards the goal of all life: a secure and agreeable existence" (1949:183).

Suttles (1960: 304), however, writing of the potlatch among the Coast Salish, concludes that, "the drive to attain high status is clearly not the explanation of the potlatch. Nor is the production of surplus. Not the cooperation achieved by the potlatching community. The potlatch is a part of a larger socio-economic system that enables the whole social network, consisting of a number of communities, to maintain a high level of food production and to equalize its food consumption both within and among communities. The system is thus adaptive in an environment characterized by the features indicated before—spatial and temporal variation and fluctuation in the availability of resources."

Acknowledging all aspects of this, culture may contribute to ecological adjustment of a society, let us examine the process of cultural adaptation more closely. Basically, societies adapt to their environment by three means: technological, organizational, and ideational. Technology, which may be taken to include tools, machines, utensils, and weapons, along with the techniques associated with their use, is the most directly adaptive facet of culture. Man's occupancy of every corner of the earth could not have come about without the implements necessary to cope with the peculiar problems posed by each habitat. This is especially well illustrated by harsh environments. For example to survive in their Arctic habitat the Eskimo must rely on such sophisticated and specialized traits as the igloo, the kayak, the seal-oil lamp, the dog sled, the harpoon with bladder float, and snow goggles.

The second aspect of culture is organizational. To explain this White mentions that "social systems are social means of operating technological systems" (l949:182-183). It is certainly true that cooperation in human societies, especially for the purpose of procuring food, providing shelter and meeting the demands of offense and defense. Accordingly, all forms of social organisation involved in achieving these ends must be regarded as adoptive.

The ideational aspect of culture also serves to adopt a society to the prevailing conditions of existence. For example, it has been noted of nomadic peoples like the Eskimo, Tehuelche, and Lengua that even when the food supply is unusually plentiful, after a band has spent more than a few days or weeks in one spot, everyone becomes restless and anxious to be on the move. Ecological necessity has developed in them a psychology of nomadism. By being mentally adapted to normal ecological conditions, the individuals in a culture are always ready, and even eager, to make what is ordinarily the most appropriate response. The matter may be put in this way: a socio-cultural system works best when it makes people want to do what they have to do.

However it is pertinent from the above discussion that culture has two aspects: natural and social. The natural aspect has been molded by the people to have a social interpretation of it. This interpretation is called culture. In this nature-culture interpretation ecology palys a very important role. People's perception, adoptablility, eating habits, dress pattern etc. all reflects the culture as well as the ecology. Therefore, it is the ecology which defines the culture. With this theoratical understanding let us examin the *Saora* culture, leisure and communication.

Traditional Saora Culture

Traditional *Saoras* and especially the *Lombo Lanjia Saoras* which is the subject of this study, are fragment of a great tribe, with certainty we can say that they have lost their language and have been assimilated in culture and religion to their neighbours, evidence of which we will see when we further explore their culture and beliefs through our analysis. The basic common cultural traits of the hill *Saoras* are: they live in long streets, in which they build little shrines; they erect memoirs and sacrifice buffaloes for their dead, their religious needs are served by male and female *Shamans*, they engage in both terraced and shifting cultivation; their men put on a long brightly coloured loin cloth and their women wear a hand woven brown bordered skirt and do not usually wear anything else; they retain their own language and do not speak any other language.

Saora Mythology

Aitareya Berahmana describes the *Saoras* as descendants of the elder sons of *Viswamitra*, who were cursed by their father for an act of disobedience and this epitomizes the general attitude of Hindu classical writers towards the 'aboriginal'. (V. Elwin, *The Religion of an Indian Tribe*, 1955: 12) This race has traditionally maintained their individuality very strongly in ancient India. Not all ancient reference to the hill *Saoras* is pessimistic. G.Ramdas in his book *Aboriginal Names in the Ramayana* has identified the *vanars* of the epic Ramayana with our hill *Saoras*. Both *vanars* and *Saoras* are afraid of strangers; both love alcoholic refreshment; both enjoys a younger brother to marry an elder brother's widow; both drink from leaf-cups. More convincing is the point that while *vanar* men had tails, women apparently did not have 'this appendage'. This suggests the 'monkey-hosts' of *Sugriva* were non-than the *Arsi* (monkey) *Saoras* with their long-tailed loin cloth. To this we may add the very high place which 'Ramma' has in *Saora* mythology. (Cited from 1955:22-3).

Saora Village

A *Saora* village is a matter of streets; long rows of houses along each built on to its neighbor house with a common veranda running right along, are arranged in a very conceivable relation to each other. In some places it is found houses arranged in a round square. *Saoras* love to build their houses on mountain slopes. So their houses and streets run along the terracing principle. All round a *Saora* villages are little gardens where tobacco, maize and some time ginger are grown. The boundary of a *Saora* village has a shrine of a god or ancestor or may have an *Arsi* shrine to ward off evil spirits.

The village is shaded with sago and date palms. Since *Saoras* practice shifting cultivation the *Saora* villages are as small as only three or four houses. The *Saora* has an eye for beauty. The interiors are kept as beautiful and spotlessly clean, everything is neatly arranged for convenience. The whole village is sometimes demarcated and fenced with bamboo.

Saora House

The houses built by *Saoras* are of bored nature. They are raised above the ground to protect from wild insects and animals. The house from the inside is divided into two sections. Veranda may be in the front and may also beat the back only when there is a back door and are usually raised six feet above the ground and are reached by a flight of stone steps. The walls of the *Saora* house are built up of stone or rubble or of thick mud plaster. The roof is thatched and is supported by tower of poles plastered to the wall with mud. The *Saora* house witnesses a series of sacrifice throughout the life cycles of its inhabitants, as all sacrifices are alone indoors. The *Saoras* believe in *Dakosungboi* deity presides over welfare of building.

In the layout of *Saora* house it has been observed that the following material from forest is used. Palm thatch, wooden pillars used to signify gods. Wooden mortar which is made from sago or *sal* trees, pieces of wood again from sago or *sal* trees mixed with plaster of mud. Apart from this there is the use of baskets, gourds, pots all built out of forest produce.

Non-material Culture

The non-material culture of the *Saora* has two fundamental concepts namely—*Ukka,* i.e., custom and *Ersi,* i.e., taboo. Most of the taboos govern tribal behaviour in relation to the spirits. *Saoras* are confused to generalize the principles of conduct. For example, they are unable to point out so and so person is a thief but they found it difficult what constitute theft. The most universally condemned character is the proud man. Indeed pride not only divides the community but it also destroys good fellowship of drinking parties beneath the palms, it threatens a sudden dramatic explosion that will bring tragedy to a village. So a proud man is referred to as *duaiymaran* or *adaibobmaran*. There are various cases of heavy drinking men and proud men in the tribe. Villagers stay away from such men and do not even sit with him. As per the *Saora* beliefs a thief is condemned. The *Saora* believe that a thief has his own punishment as a thief is always hungry and wealth does not stay in his house and his harvests are poor.

The *Saora* also believe in work before food. Every person demanding his share of food must work. Any person who eats alone is also considered a thief. This feeling brings social solidarity. This brings- out the gregariousness among the *Saoras*. The belief of sharing and being together is the highlight of this tribal life style. A person who deceives is compared to a fox. They teach their children to be truthful, as they believe *Sat* (truth) to be an abstract power dwelling in the tribe. (1955:564). According to a *Saora* tribal legend a drunken, quarrelsome man, one day repented of his behaviour. He took an egg in his hand and called *Uyungsum* and *Darammasum* as witness, and say, 'I swear on this egg that I will drink no wine for three years. He touched his forehead with the egg, and broke it by throwing it the ground. But it is said that he could not keep his promise and went blind in both the eyes. (1955:565).

'Ukka' and 'Ersi' : Their Custom and Taboos

The life and behaviour of the *Saoras* is guided by two principles namely 'Ukka' and 'Ersi'. Let us examin in details how these two concepts of non-material culture of *Saoras* operates in real social, political, economic and cultural life.

Ukka is traditional behaviour and conduct, fidelity to tribal rules. In general terms it is akin to good conduct which is guided by tribal opinion. It has nothing to do with the spirits or supernatural sanctions. For example, if a person departs from *ukka* by offending his neighbour but this will not have anything to do with any god. It controls tribal dress code, the ornament they wear the decoration and built of the house. In short it is a general moral behaviour. Ersi relate to the tribal's conduct as seen by the spirits.

Table 6.1 Ukka and Ersi Differentiation

Behaviour / Action	*Ukka*	*Ersi*
Relates to	Fellow Men	Spirits / God
Tell lies	Yes	No
Steal or Murder	Yes	No
Steal a Lizard set free by Shaman	No	Yes
Tell lies to Spirits	No	Yes
Steal food offered as Sacrifice to god	No	Yes
Ordinary men commits adultery in marriage	Yes	No
Priest / Shaman commits adultery	No	Yes
Breach leads to	Modifiable punishment	Automatic fixed punishment

The difference and the meaning of *ukka* and *ersi* becomes closely evident (see Table 6.1). *Ersi* always towards the spirits, god and supernatural forces of the *Saora*. The interesting point is the *Saora* tribals consider theft as bad code of conduct whereas theft occurs from a sacrifice to god or sprits it becomes *ersi* which calls for automatic punishment. The breach of *ersi* is considered as a serious offence so much so that only a sacrifice in the form of a religious fine can aver one from the wrath of the sprits. Another aspect of *ersi* is that the punishment is to a large extent meted out to the sins by the sprits in the form of illness or other such troubles. However, the *Saora* tribals fail to put forth a time period after which the sprits against which offence is done may strike to punish. The tribals believe that if they do not behave in a certain fashion then the sprits might punish them for '*ersi*' for breach of manners. In fact '*ersi*' and *ukka* are differentiated on the following grounds.

Ersi—Code of conduct with the inhabitants of other world.

Ukka—Code of conduct with the inhabitants of the tribe.

Incest is however the greatest of *ersi* crime which includes all relationships between person of same blood. The most remarkable thing that the researcher found- amongst this race is that when a *Saora* commits an *ersi* or an *ukka* crime he/she immediately takes corrective action against it. When a person does not realise it is a belief amongst the *Saoras* that he will realise it by himself: as he/she is sure to fall ill or suffer great loss as an effect. So from this discussion it becomes clear that certain acts became *ersi* for *shamans* and priest whereas it is a common act of *ukka* for others.

Other Taboos

Apart from *ukka* and *ersi* other taboos which also mark the belief and behaviour of *Saora* tribes. It is a taboo to throw babies hair on the ground or elsewhere, some one might urinate on it. A woman is not allowed to touch a tree, which exudes a blood-red gum resin, as it is believed by the *Saoras* that it might lead *Menorrhagia* (*Ibid.*: 526). Drinking of milk and eating of beef are a taboo in the *Saora* tribe. The Saoras do not have any totemic taboos. Apart from these taboos *Saoras* have few more taboos, which has given below.

1. **Offending Mountain Spirit :** This taboo is very easily broken as every hill or mountain is supposed to have its deities and hence expect tribute. The common cause of offence to such a deity could be to clear a forest without offering apology and sacrifice (*Ibid.*: 514).

2. **Cutting Sacred Trees:** There is a taboo for cutting trees. The banyan is regarded as shrine of gods and is also drawn in their wall paintings. It is taboo to cut it (*Ibid.*: 515).
3. **Touching Trees:** It is taboo to touch the wood tree struck by lighting, for to do so may attract lighting to ones owns house. It is a taboo for a woman to touch *Pterocarpus marsupium* tree (*Ibid.*: 526).
4. **Building With Certain Materials:** It is a taboo to build a house with bricks and tiles as they believe it would attract excessive spirits. They believe tamarind wood is a taboo or tigers prowl round the house. The use of banyan pipal and cashew wood is also taboo (*Ibid.*: 529).

The taboos show the clear relationship between tribal and forest. Therefore it is the natural environment, i.e., forest that defines the non-material culture of Saoras. It is certain that the tribals have a great regard and attachment for their forest resources and it has been proven in a resettlement exercise with Birhores. The tribals have an immense resistance to change and to leave their forest resources. In case of Birhores they could not adjust to the new constructed houses and farming for one week and returned back to their own traditional natural set-up.

In contrast Saoras, over the years accepted shifting agricultural practice. Mostly female are burdened lots amongst the tribal. The men comparatively take less part in agricul tural activities, mostly they go to forest to hunting or for minor forest product, or drinking wine or roaming around.

Now the pertinent question before us is to find out what are the changes has come up in *Saora* culture due to alteration of environment. Before going to analyze that it would better to see the folk song and riddles to explore the close proximity of *Saoras* with forest. However, in sociological and anthropological literature there is an extensive study, analysis and interpretation of folk life. There is a specialised fied of folklore and folklife studies. It would better to explore these anthropoliogical literature briefly to sketch the relationship between folk society, envirnoment and culture.

The Fields of Folklore and Folklife Studies

The matters that occupy the student of folklore and folklife studies may be placed under four large groupings. One of these sectors is oral literature, sometimes called verbal art or expressive literature. Under this rubric fall spoken, sung, and voiced forms of traditional utterance that show repetitive patterns. One large subdivision is folk narrative, which in turn has its own manifold distinctions. Another major subdivision is folksong or folk poetry, with its own family of related species. Traditional tales and songs correspond to the written production of Novelists and poets, but they circulate by word of mouth and without known authorship. They may be short anecdotes and rhythms or elaborate romances and epics. Certain brief genres of oral expression are classed as proverbs and riddles. Oral literature can and frequently does enter into written literature. (Dorson, 1972:2).

In direct contrast to this oral folklore is physical folklife, generally called material culture. This deal with the visible rather than the aural aspects to folk behaviour that existed prior to and continue alongside mechanized industry. Material culture responds to techniques, skill, recipes, and formulas transmitted across the generations and subject to the same forces of conservative tradition and individual variation as verbal art. How men and women in tradition-oriented societies build their homes, make their clothes, prepare their food, farm and fish, process the earth' bounty, fashion their tools and implements, and design their furniture and utensils are questions that concern the student of material culture. In a tribal society all processes are traditional and products hand made, although of course innovation occurs. (*Ibid.*: 2-3).

In between oral literate and material culture lies areas of traditional life facing in both directions. One such area we may call social folk custom. Here the emphasis is on group interaction rather than on individual skills and performances. English antiquaries lumped under "custom and usage" a great many community and family observances connected with villages, manors, landmarks, households, churches, holidays, and such rites de passage as birth, initiation, marriage, and death. Customs of this sort include "telling the bees" of death in the family by draping the hives in black, or nailing up a horseshoe on the front door to avert witchcraft, or making a wish before tasting the first fruits of the season. These customs are often closely bound up with deeply held folk beliefs, which in themselves constitute a folklore genre. General and special customs usually involve a physical action (giving the food), a shared belief (the premonitory dream), and a material object (the penny loaf). Customs that have acquired considerable magical and sacred potency are known as rituals (*Ibid.*).

The participation of large social units in public performances and entertainment leads to another kind of social folk custom to which the terms festival and celebration generally apply. Music, dance, costume, floats, and processions may all enter into festivals, which are based on both religious and secular traditions. Certain games and recreations, or sports and pastimes as Joseph Strutt called them in his pioneering work on the subject are learned through tradition rather than by codified rules and regulations. The difference is between base ball and what may have been a precursor, a game such as one a cat still played by boys; a short stick is tilted against a stone and then knocked in the air and struck with a larger stick (*Ibid.*).

The study of folk culture and oral tradition in India is basically the study of Indian traditions. The study of Indian traditions, as emphasized by D.P. Mukerji, Ramkrishna Mukerjee and many others, is of vital importance. The reality, according to Ramkrishna Mukerjee, is a concomitant understanding of the past and the present. And in order to draw effective generalizations on social change, going into the past is very essential; without it we cannot draw generalizations. However, emphasizing the value of folk music R. C. Mehta observes: 'We are waging a war against poverty—a much harder war but a more real one. In this war against poverty and in our task of the building up of our nation, the great energy lying in our folksongs and within our reach, should be harnessed... Our governments—Central and State—should very extensively employ the music and folksongs as an important tool for making the task of nation building more acceptable and cheerful to our millions of men and women.' (in Sankar Sen Gupta, 1964: 50-1). Therefore, it is pertinent here to deal with the concepts associated with 'folk' analysis and studies.

Folk culture : Redfield has used concept of 'folk culture' first for the 'type of society which he encountered in Tepoztlan and subsequently as an ideal type in opposition to city life. Other anthropologists use the terms 'folk culture' and 'folk society' uncritically in the sense of non-primitive but relatively simple cultural types which are coming in contact with modern industrial civilization. The definition of 'folk culture and society' in terms of ideal polar type (urban and non urban) groups all non-urban people together are against of urban group. If we use these concepts in this sense the analysis of folk culture in the city is not possible. But anthropologists, using the concepts of folk culture and folk society, thought that these concepts may afford a useful framework for empirical research and the exploration of more general theories of culture. This shows that neither folk society is whole society, nor folk culture is a whole culture. Instead, they are a part of a larger social unit. The folk component of this larger unit is also a part of the pre-industrial urban centres. In this sense folk and urban are not polar concepts; rather, they are both integral parts of the definition of a certain type of socio-cultural unit in which the pre-industrial city also exists. But the primitive peoples are not included in folk category because they are complete in themselves, and their culture is a whole culture in itself.

However, the use of the concept of folk culture in latter sense explains that a folk stratum is a part of a pre-industrial society, and is coterminous with the entire community in the rural setting, whereas in the urban setting it is merely a part of the community. This point of view distinguishes the use of the term folk culture from the concept of folk society, which Redfield uses more or less indiscriminately. Thus while distinguishing the concept of folk culture from the concept of 'folk society' we may say in the words of George M. Foster that a folk culture 'may be thought of as common way of life which characterizes some or all of the people of many village, towns and cities within a given area', and a folk society 'may be thought of as an organized group of individuals characterized by a folk culture' (1953:70). Many elements of folk culture may occur in social aggregates, which are not basically folk societies, but folk societies cannot exist apart from folk culture.

Folktale : Folktales are all those prose narratives, which are simple, entertaining, with or without moral, less systematic, less specialized, easy to understand and memorize with some scope of addition, subtraction and modification by almost all the members of a folk-groups. Folktales, while dealing with situations familiar to listeners, are not usually based on historical facts; but are mostly of fictitious nature and have predominance of fanciful ideas of the folk. Telling of folktales includes, not only the texts but also the fanciful expression, gesture, acting, repetition and other recurrent patterns of the story-tellers. Like folksongs, folktales also have no known originator and are transmitted spontaneously by oral tradition from person or from generation to generation (Bascom, 1956, *The Forms of Folklore: Prose Narratives*: 4).

Folksong: A folksong is a lyrical, short, simple, less artistic, rhythmic song of a folk community. It generally reflects the social heritage, the environment and the life of the folk living in a particular territory. It is usually created by the folk for their own entertainment, enjoyment, or emotional outlet. It is easily sung, understood and learnt on occasions—like birth, first hair cutting ceremony (*Mundana*), sacred thread wearing ceremony, marriage, festivals, special days during special period of the year, while engaged in household or agricultural work or in other activities—by almost all the members of a folk-group with no distinction of singer and listener. It requires no prior setting and no professional skill. It has the capacity of free addition, subtraction, and modification and has no known originator or processor. It is transmitted, circulated and perpetuated spontaneously through oral tradition from person to person or from generation to generation (A.H. Krappe, *The Science of Folklore*: 153).

Indigenous folk songs all share the following characteristic feature, i.e., poetical devices. They are (1) formal and (2) semantic (or substantial). The poetical devices are the product of a tradition which is a living and variable organism. According to the changes the culture undergoes, the tradition may be gradually enlarged by new elements, of elements may fall into oblivion and decay due to rapid processes of acculturation. Some of the innovative processes occurring in Indian folksong in general and in sad, folksongs in particular, are historically traceable and may be attributed to the influx of the ideas promulgated by *Bhakti* movements, revivalist movements, and also Christian missionary work, to mention only three of the possible sources of influence. Together with the newly introduced ideas we mostly observe a change in the formal pattern of the songs stemming from non-indigenous movements: the vocabulary and the stylistic make-up are often enlarged or at any rate somehow modified (for which cf. Thief-Horstmann, 1975).

To sum up, the criteria by which a song can be determined as an indigenous traditional folksong are (*Ibid.*: 221) (1) that it relies on a tradition owned by the whole group, (2) that it is the common property of the group (or a sub-group of it), whereas the individual authorship is of at best secondary importance, (3) that it is linked up with various modes of performances; "link up" here means that it is often developed during performance and that it is not desk-work product. With this categorical analysis further an attempt has been made to explore and analyse the *Saora* folksongs. This analysis will make us to understand their life, culture and nature. Morever, this kind of analysis is more scientific and accurate.

Folk Songs of Saora

The researcher had the opportunity to hear the folk songs of the *Saora* tribe. The researcher found a close link of the tribal and the forest. Folksongs (and consequently music) are the main cultural achievement in the sphere of arts of the *Saora* tribe. Therefore, it seems interesting to see how the rich original tradition harmonizes or clashes with the relatively recently implanted heterogeneous situation brought about by missionary efforts and how they are linked up with tradition.

Nature, Culture and Gender: A Synoptic View

First girl says to second girl: I have not yet put any garland on my head

Second girl says: I am making a garland of Jasmine flower,

First girl says: Now I am making a *mahul* flower garland,

Second girl says: Now I am making a mango flower garland,

First girl says: I am making a *charkoli* flower garland now,

Second girl says: I am now making a *amala* flower garland, other girls sing: *In chorus* lets make *Sal* flower garland or lets make *Kangu* flower garland or *Piasal* flower garland.

Then they say in chorus: lets go to the *Dunger* in a line and then to another place by washing away forest and making another *Dunger*.

Interpretation

The folk song not only shows how deeply the women enjoy flowers of different variety but also the joy they get out of using the forest resources. Flowers are a symbol of joy in every culture and society. But what is most remarkable is that the *Saora* women make garlands and enjoy contemplating and thinking about the flowers of different varieties such as mango flower even *amala* flower and flower of trees which are used in making of their houses and firewood. The varied use of flower has come over the generations and now they enjoy using them and thinking about them. Many of the trees mentioned in their folk songs are almost on the verge of extinction inspite of government intervention on such a long period of time. The last part of the folk song does definitely reflect the cultivating aspect of the *Saora* tribes, i.e., shifting cultivation. The girls find the process they follow for *Dungar* cultivation, by cutting the parts of forest and preparing them for cultivation.

Work, Nature and Leisure

A male sings: Bring *Tangia* and *Barsi* and lets cut jungle and let's get wood from the jungle and then let's go to a particular *Dungar* which looks like the lizard and see the crop how it has grown. As a monkey goes around with joy even we would jump around the *Dungar* looking and dancing around. As a peacock digs the mud (earth) even we would dig up mud and plant some trees there.

Interpretation

This seems like a remarkable folk song that talks about the attitude and work culture of the male *Saora*. It is not males but females who mostly go for farming; so the male are generally left around the village for going to the jungle and hunting, and drinking wine. Another fact comes out is that the tribal definitely do cut trees for firewood, building of houses, and for shifting cultivation. In order to point out the fact, that the tribals are not really concerned of ecological imbalance due to their ecological set up of mind and their traditional way of life. Here it also reflected the material culture as of *tangia, barsi* the implenents they use for cutting trees.

A classification to which Michael R. Done point out in his book *Jungle in Nature and Culture* in the reference to Zimmermans use of the word *'Jangale'* and *'Jangala'*. *Jangala*: A devėlopment wild area where forest was cleared earlier may be more or less than five years ago. It definitely has trees and shrubs, whereas jungle only where forest has not been cleared. Our analogy as it proceeds and our effort to understand the key difference between *Jangala* and *Jangale* is that the tribals do cut trees but only from *jungala* and not vehemently from the *jangale*. As a *Dungar* is left in the wildness it develops into a *jungala* and this is once again cut by them to be used for cultivation. The folksong also points out to the practice amongst the tribal to plant trees, which is evidence to protect the nature.

Religion

In this song tribal says- when we will go to rope the paddy, rope the *kendula*?

First we will start from the east,

We will do that by taking the name of god.

We will do the work happily and back home happily.

Interpretation

This reflects that religious notion are attached with work. The religion also guides that work would be started from the east. If all the work will be started by taking the name god things will be end in well and will help to lead a happy life.

Socialisation and Nature

An old man waking up and the children are asked,

Have you prepared the *daa*,

Is it perfect? (Sharp and Strong),
Because for *podu* cultivation we will go to cut the jungle,
Have you made every thing ready? (1)
We have to go to deep into the jungle by kneeling, bending and crouching,
It will be long, arduous and painful
Take it easy do not brood,
Keep your arsenal sharp and shining.(2)
Did you get the axe sharpened from the blacksmith?
Can you go to the forest unless you keep these implements ready? (3)
In deep forest the thrones and leaves are intertwined,
If you are not carrying sharpened implements how will you cut it? (4)
Only *kuradhi, tangia* will not do,
With this *katuri* and *daa* etc have to be taken (5)
If you intend to go to another forest,
Then make a prior observation of this soil,
And find out which crop will flourish,
Are you sure that we will reap,
Does lizard face like *kangu* and peacock eyes like *kandul* will be better? (6)
If the earth is favorable, then we will cut the *shal*, *piashal*, *gambari*, and mango trees and starts the shifting cultivation,
If not then all this labour will go waste (7)
But we will not cut the *mahula* tree, only the branches will be cut, because from this we get *mahula, tula*.
Because with the help of *mahula* we will do the puja,
New married couple will collect it happily,
So our culture won't be destroyed. (8)
While collecting the *mahula* it will be strong sun,
Even though the new couple will collect it happily.(9)
In the month of May *Dunger* cultivation will come,
So do not be lazy (10)
First we will put the paddy in pestle (*dhinki*-rice making wooden) to get the upper layer of the paddy to make rice,
Do not be lazy,
See the peacock, hen has started calling,

If you are not getting up you will be in trouble. (11)
Now see the crow has also called,
The sun has also risen in a round shape,
When you will go to work?
If you sleep like *telunipoka* near the hearth (by getting the heat),
Then when you will go to work?
Then people will also say to you. (12)
The ground nut *koda* which looks like (*Bankulibadi*),
The implements of agriculture which looks like rabbit head and other instruments,
I have kept ready,
Now you take all this
And go to field (13)
You are not listening,
The hen has given the call,
The small insects (*mimir*) who lives in the house,
They have also given the call,
What, are not you able to listen this!,
Please wake up, pigs have also given the call. (14)
We have framed the *juhali* from neem, *gambhari* wood,
If you sleep it will not be right,
Get up and go to field because we have to cultivate the land,
The dew has come like rain,
Please wake up and go to the field.
Flood has come in the river,
It will destroy everything,
Please go and do the work,
When you will do?
Be hurry up! (15)
You have to carry the watered rice (*peja bhat*),
You have to make the salt and chilly powder,
If you sleep when you will do all this. (16)
Hai daughter,
When you will wake up,

Putting hand on eye and yawning,
The bird likes *Kapta*,
Who sleeps early, get up early and also get up late,
Do not be like *Kapta* bird.(17)
Wash your face,
And do not sleep now near the hearth. (18)
Call your friends and relatives,
The rock is zic-zac,
We have to go,
Be ideal by calling your friends,
It would not do if you will be late. (19)
We have to go early,
Because the rocks are quite zic-zac,
If you walk slowly, it will not do,
Do not walk like proud hero,
Be calm and sober to go. (20)
When you will back you have to bring the toothbrush,
Leaves to eat food,
Fire wood,
Then you have to cook the food and feed your children,
If you have to say to the children to bring,
Do not scold them,
This should be said in love and affection. (21)
Daughters,
It is not right always to hold the combs,
And sit in front of the mirror,
This work and that work will be done,
Only when you wake up early (22)
If you will not why show the style?,
How it will work,
It will be only grass if you will not clean it.(23)
When you will go to work,
Do not go with bare body,

Carry these things,
Smoking leaves, fire pot,
If you feel cold please smoke,
By which the mosquito will also go,
Take the clothes also. (24).

Interpretation

Society exists because of the handing down of the tradition and civilization to the new comer. This is done through the process of socialisation. Here in this song it reflects many thing of Soar tribe. Firstly, it reflects how the elder people are concerned about their children. By songs they convey the massage to younger ones how to take life and in which way. Secondly, it also reflects what kind of occupation they do. Here it has been referred to shifting cultivation, which they do. The reference to go to jungle and cut the jungle is also evident.

Thirdly, what the material culture they have—which they use for their daily needs. Here it is referred to *daa*, *katuri*, *tangia* etc. Here the natures of ecological bent of any of the elders have also been expressed, by talking of thorny forest. For this what kind of implements is required and how sharpen it should. All this reflect the ecological mind set of the *Saora* tribe. Fourthly, the very important aspect of human life is its relation with nature. As it is widely known that crow, hen always calls early in the morning. Here it is also evident that peacock, crow, hen, pig, mimir (small insects at home) always give the signal that the day has come. The relation of man and species quite evident, which is neglected in many sociological studies. The symbiotic interdependence of man and animal in relation to the nature and culture is pertinent. Here the example of a bird has given who has both aspects. The example of *Kapta* who sleeps early and get up early and at time does not. Here the elder people, meant to say that, oh my child! we know that you wake up in time but at times you become lazy. Here it has been compared with a bird. The dire consequence of laziness has been also reflecting. If you will be lazy, you will not have the basic thing to survive. You will be ill- treated by your friends. Which reflect that how individuals are subjected to social criticism.

Fifthly, it is also evident what kind of food they eat. They carry the *peza* and *bhat* with salt and chilly powder to the jungle where they do all the activities and eat the food there only. It is also reflected that how elder should behave with the children for work.

Saora Jokes and Riddles

A riddle is an ambiguous and concisely formed metaphorical question, which is difficult to answer, or which if apparently interpreted gives a different meaning than what it actually incorporates. It is also learnt and transmitted spontaneously through oral from person to person (cited from Srivastav, *op.cit.*, : 12).

Joke: When a bamboo is in the mother's house it wears clothes when it goes to the mother-in-law's house it becomes nude.

The *Saora* man use this joke to display a loss of prestige and ego by transfer of a young man from mother's house to mother-in-law's house after marriage. The practice of giving bamboo on marriage is also depicted here. However, the remarkable link is once again depicted between the *Saora* culture and forest resource through bamboo.

Riddle: Name a child whose nose always sinks. Answer: *khajur*. The wine tribal drinks. Once again the definite link between tribal life and forest resources. Here the date or palm fruit become evident.

Riddle: Name a man whose nose is always in noose? Answer: *salap* tree in which they put a string around to get wine. Once again the definite link between the tribal culture and forest is clearly evident. The salap tree from where *Saoras* used to get country made wine for their consumption.

Riddle: Name a mountain that is always wearing a garland? Answer : date palms tree, the fruit is always hanging like garland. The palm trees, from where they used to get wine, being glorified as a mountain with garland.

Riddle: Name an old lady who is cleaning? Answer: broom. The broom is made of date plam tree leafs, thatched leaves and jocularly refers as an old lady.

Riddle: Name a person who is always eating black grass? Answer : scissors. Here the adoption of a modern instrument into the tribal life and culture is being brought out. Tribals have a way to refer things of daily use in a humorous way.

Material Culture of Saora

Man made culture is widely defined as material culture. This includes dwelling houses, farms, agricultural instruments, musical instrument, household assets etc. *Lanjia Saora* has a rich man made culture based on forest resources (See picture 3). Altman and Chemans in his book

Picture-3: Fuel and Fodder: Stock for the daily need of man and animals by the Saoras during lean season

Culture and Environment has made the classification of physical environment into man made and natural. Natural culture consist of natural resources, i.e., forest, mountains, oceans, etc.

For this study we have taken only one aspect of natural resources forest. However it is an attempt to find the effects of man made culture on forest and the effects of external sources like government intervention on tribal life and ecology. In R.M. Sarkar's language 'human culture is subjected to modification in response to changes in environment'. 'Change in culture', he adds, 'creates profound alteration in a population's biology.'

When we talk about ecology we are largely considering the ways in which all living organisms interact within the environment. In order to study the material culture along the ecological perspective we must at the outset determine "What constitutes material culture. In this case *Saoras* are not a nomadic tribe rather settled and practicing shifting cultivation. So the subject of our study comprises Homo sapiens with sedentary habits.

The Dress and Ornament

The real clothing of *Saoras* is 'the eternally dressed nakedness of the brown skin', which adorns them with beauty and dignity. There is a rule, founded in the mythology, that they should not wear too much: there is a common tradition that they originally dressed in leaves. The traditional cloth for both sexes is woven for them by *Doms*, from yarn handspun by the *Saoras* themselves; it is generally woven very well and artistically is most attractive (Elwin, 1955:42).

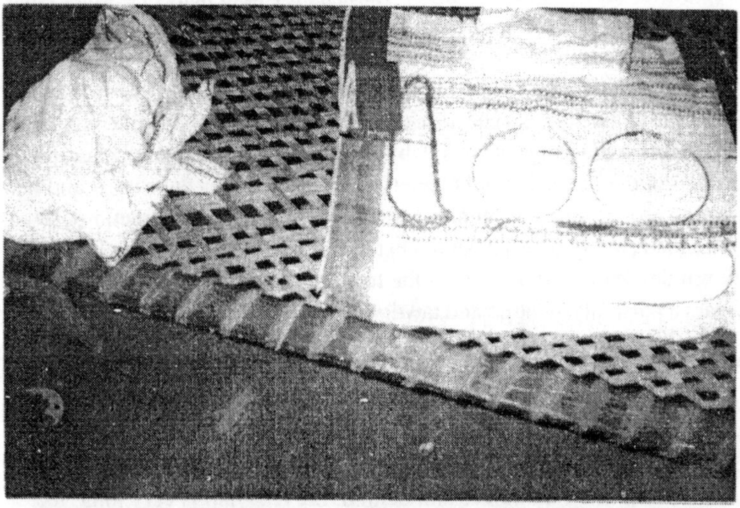

Picture-4: Ornaments of Socio-cultural importance displayed on a traditional cloth

Women's Wear

The *Saora* women wear a simple skirt with a brown border top and bottom; it is round the waist and tucked in at the front. In the chill of the early morning, they cover themselves with miscellaneous wraps—many of them the cast-off cloths of ancestors or tutelaries but later in the day they discard these and work in nothing but the skirt. Women have to bear a painful operation of discomfort which lasts almost a decade of her lifecycle is the ear. In adolescence their holes are pierced in the lobes of their ear and they are gradually enlarged by bits of straw and reed being forced into the pierced hole and then after some time when it gradually gets bigger with wooden plugs of tamarind wood or sago palm. Once a year this plug gets larger and larger until it becomes almost around three inches in diameter causing the skin around the ear lobe to look like a strip of brown leather. When the plugs are removed they are immediately filled with varied ornaments and decorations in both the ears. Women were seen buying ornaments for their ears from the local markets, brass springs and wooden petal ear rings. After the ear women pay their attention to hair and throat. A *Saora* woman combs her hair carefully, collects it into a bun and wraps it into a ball and puts a brass hairpin. *Saora* women wear brass chains and brass flowers around the hair and even a brass spike. Although these are traditional ornaments the new *Saora* women are definitely take interest to newer ornaments which are almost like their own ornament. *Saora* women throat is aptly decorated with a number of necklaces. In other tribes where women are topless like Bondas or Marias, they wear heavy necklaces that almost suffice the purpose of a blouse, but our *Saora* women wears only a few necklaces. The most interesting point to note is that women now a days are not inclined to making their own beads but buy them as they are available in the market. The nose of *Saora* women adorned with three little rings. One of the rings is thick, while others are thin and the thicker one is shaped like a heart. Brass bracelets are used to cover their wrist and her fingers are covered by numerous rings in each hand, sometimes even more than twenty on each hand. On the legs *Saora* women wear bronze or aluminum anklets and rings on the toes; in some places the Chief's wife wears a particularly large and tawdry anklet too (*Ibid.*).

Men's Style

The traditional dress of men is the loin-cloth, which may be a plain white strip or it may be gay with coloured patterns and tassels of red cotton. It is passed between legs, cover the genitals in a sort of bag, and hangs down in a flap before and behind; the rear flap is very long, like a tail. Headmen have special coloured turbans in view of their exalted status. Nowadays *Saora* only wears a turban when he is dancing or when going out of village. Some men were also seen wearing brass necklaces. A young man often sticks a feather or a few flowers in his hair.

Picture-5: Gathering needs: An old Saora with his collected material resources for house building and fuel

Another most important aspect of the tribal culture of the *Saoras* is tattoo. A tattoo is the line down the middle of the forehead. Women have a lot of tattoos whereas men have less of it. Women also have dots on either side of the line on their cheeks and chin. The usual reason for the tattoo marks is either that we do it because it looks nice' or that 'our parents had these marks on their foreheads, and unless we had the same they would not recognise us when we will went to the under world' (*Ibid.*, 45).

The Concept of Work, Leisure and Communication

Leisure is generally considered as free time—time not spent doing something for utilitarian purposes, such as working. The definition of leisure must therefore include more than simply freedom from work. It must also include freedom from other social forms of obligations, such as visiting relatives or travelling back and forth to work. In sociological literature and research the followings are included in leisure studies. (a) Children's game and athletics; (b) art and literature; (c) popular culture; (d) the mass media; (e) voluntary associations; or (f) professional recreational issues such as leisure counselling, recreation programme development, recreation training, and so on. The salient of these topics to the sociologist of leisure is obvious, but each emerged as a topic of study in its own right and deserves separate treatment.

The concept in the sense of Lundberg, leisure being 'the time we are free from the more obvious and formal duties which a paid job or other obligatory occupation imposes upon us' (1943:2). Leisure, as against work, is normally assumed to be task-free. However, one may use leisure, the compulsions associated with work are absent. It is assumed that one at leisure is free to choose his activities or to change them, and he need not be concerned about goals. One's leisure activity need not be firm or precise, regular or measured, in the sense that work must be.

Leisure, then, seems to afford more freedom of choice in activities, and people differ widely in their choices. Thus choices may be different as between the sexes or according to age groups. Differences may be seen as between persons of different educational level. But cutting across all these differences are those associated with social class. At one time certain leisure pastimes were the monopoly of the high and well born and were considered to be more cultured than the pastimes of the poor, attitudes which still survive. However, Dumazedier's definition, 'Leisure is activity to which the individual may, freely devote himself outside the needs and obligations of his occupation, his family and society, for his relaxation, diversion and personal development. These three functions; *delassement*, and developement, are not always distinguishable. All three may be present in a single activity, as when a secretary, who is also an amateur artist, uses a leisure hour to sketch the outline of a landscape. People can be asked to report how they budget their time during a given day their various activities can then be sorted into predetermined categories.

Robinson (1977:90) divided the day into hours of obligatory activity and hours of free time. Obligatory activities included work, housekeeping, chidcare, catering to personal needs, and necessary travel. Robinson subdivided free time into organisational activities (such as participation in voluntary associations), attending to the mass media (e.g., movie attendance) and socialization and recreation ("including mainly visiting and conversations, but also sports and hobbies, relaxation, and organised forms of social entertainment"). Free time, like almost every other scarce resource, is distributed unequally among the population. Those under thirty have more free time, apparently because they spend less time on housework and shopping. Being married diminished free time for both partners, children further reduce a couple's free time, albeit loose for the woman than for the man. Getting a job naturally increases obligations; the unemployed, students, and the retired have, by Robinson's definitions, more free time. The rich seem to have no more free time than the poor, but free time does increase with years of schooling, probably because better educated people budget their time more efficiently. What is more, and far more importantly, free time depends on the totality of social conditions, which continues to hold people under its spell..(Adorno, 1991: 162).

For example, only one quarter of the American population regularly engages in outdoor, active leisure. This probably represents a decline over the last fifty years (Check & Burch 1976:17). Furthermore, the average American has narrowed the range of his leisure-time pursuits, "spending noticeably less time sleeping, eating, reading, frequenting places of entertainment (especially movies), playing sports, listening to the radio, motoring, playing cards, dancing and going to church services" (Robinson & Voncerse 1972:79). We need not look far for the leisure pursuit that has replaced these more active pastimes. About 1.5 of our daily 4 hours of free time is spent watching television. Furthermore, listening to the radio or watching television is our most popular "secondary activity" —one we engage in while also doing something else (Robinson 1977: 100). Robinson (1977:97), for example, considered time spent in religious activities to be free time rather than obliged time. To many sociologists, however, the distinguishing characteristic of religious behaviour is in fact a sense of obligation. This is no trivial caveat. According to Robinson's data, about one-half of an women's and one-third of all men's non-work hours involve religious activities.

An interpretive sociology of leisure exists only in scattered (through often brilliant) examples (Polsky 1967). A classification of leisure activities into meaning clusters would make the leisure variable easier to use and possibly more significant. Several strategies 298 have been used to seek these clusters. Havighurst (1957) used interviewer ratings, Bihsop (1970) used factor analysis and Csikszentimihalyi (1975) based his classification on the speculations of Caillois (1961). Duncan (1978) adopts a different strategy for discovering meaning clusters. Most studies of leisure hypothesize relationships between individuals and their various leisure activities. Duncan, however, suggests that activities should be clustered according to the types of participants they attract. The five resulting "leisure types," Duncan claims, more clearly indicate clusters of meaning in leisure. This approach also takes into account the fact that some people never participate in leisure activities—a fact likely to be overlooked if people are described in terms of activity factors. Which of these alternative methods of clustering makes the relation between leisure and other social roles intelligible remains to be seen.

Development of the personality, or personal development, is a wider concept than 'self improvement', as many use that term, and is not so loaded with moral compulsion. In the process of personal development the individual acquires self-discipline and poise, understanding, perhaps social orientation. It means more than merely using leisure to get ahead. As the function of personal development is realized in one's life it means that he is developing into a more companionable human being in his social relations, a good sport in the highest sense of the word when he plays a game, and the sort of person another enjoys working with. It means developing those qualities of citizenship which identify one as a good neighbour, friend, family member, and without presuming to be the symbol of the good and right. It can also include work and study during leisure to advance oneself through education and training.

The sociology of leisure, broadly conceived, has grown in recent years, especially in sub-fields such as sport and popular culture. The research conducted by sociologists of leisure is marked by increasing methodological sophistication, especially in the area of survey research and quantitative data analysis. Sociologists with an interest in leisure no longer bear the stigma of the curious notion that one cannot seriously study unserious social behaviour. However, there is a close link between leisure and culture. It depends upon the culture of the society; what kind of leisure it permits. Therefore, it is pertinent here to look into the theoratical construction of leisure and culture.

With the appearance of the discipline of anthropology in the late nineteenth century, the classical conception gave way to various anthropological conceptions of culture. Here are two such conceptions, what called the descriptive conception and the symbolic conception (Thompson, 1990:123). The descriptive conception of culture refers to the varied array of values, beliefs, customs, conventions, habits and practices characteristic of a particular society or historical period. The symbolic conception shifts the focus to a concern with symbolism: cultural phenomena, according to this conception are symbolic phenomena, and the study of culture is essentially concerned with the interpretation of symbols and symbolic action. The symbolic conception is a study starting point for the development of a constructive approach to the study of cultural phenomena. But the weakness of this conception in the form that it appears, for instance, in the writing of Geertz is that it gives insufficient attention to the structured social relations within which symbols and symbolic actions are always embedded. Hence it can be called the structural conception of culture. Cultural phenomena, according to this conception may be understood as symbolic forms in structured contexts; and cultural analysis may be construed as the study of the meaningful constitution and social contexualization of symbolic forms.

By viewing symbolic forms in relation to the structured social contexts within which they are produced and received, the structural conception of culture provides a basis upon which we can being to think about what is involved in the emergence and development of mass communication. As far as mass communication is concerned,it is in certain ways and by virtue of certain means, with the production and transmission of symbolic forms. Mass communication is certainly a matter of technology, of powerful mechanisms of production and transmission; but it is also a matter of symbolic forms, of meaningful expressions of various kinds, which are produced, transmission and received by means of the technologies deployed by the media industries.

Thus Malinowski, writing in the 1930s and 1940s, espoused a 'scientific theory of culture' and endorsed a qualified evolutionary perspective; but his main concern was to develop a functionalist approach in term of the satisfaction of human needs. Clifford Geertz in his magisterial work, *The Interpretation of Culture*, represents an attempt to draw out the implications of this conception for the nature of anthropological inquiry. Geertz describes his concept of culture as 'semiotic' rather than 'symbolic', but this difference in terminology is not significant here. For Geertz's overriding concern is with questions of meaning, symbolism and interpretation. 'Believing with Max Weber, that man is an animal suspended in webs of significance he himself has spun, I take culture to be those webs, and the analysis of it to be therefore not an experimental science in search of law but an interpretive one in search of meaning'. Culture is a 'stratified hierarchy of meaningful structures'; it consists of actions, symbols and signs, of 'twitches, winks, fake-winks, parodies' as well as utterances, conversation and soliloquies. In analysing culture we are engaged in unraveling layers of meaning, describing and re-describing actions and expressions which are already meaningful for the very individuals who are producing, perceiving and interpreting these actions and expressions in the course of their every day lives.

Geertz's interpretative approach to the study of culture is of great interest, representing a development within anthropology, which converges in certain respects with developments elsewhere in the social sciences and humanities. Underlying this approach is a conception of culture which have been described here as, 'culture is the pattern of meanings embodied in symbolic forms, including actions, utterances and meaningful objects of various kinds, by virtue of which individuals communicate with one another and share their experiences, conceptions and beliefs.' (*Ibid.*: 132).

Work, Leisure and Communication Among the Saora

The daily activities of the *Saoras* are different from their general notion of social activities. As it is understood that tribals are never free, it means they do have always work and while doing so they also relaxed and enjoy. They always do some sorts of work may be collecting minor forest produces, making agricultural instruments or doing cultivation etc.Table 6.2 shows that tribals do not able to understand the concept of social activities. So we have 39 per cent 'no' and 10 per cent 'can not say'. But it is stated that 13 per cent tribes do 'political' activities where as 38 per cent think about the 'development of the village' or they try to discuss the village problems. The religion and occupational categories does not have much significant results as 14 per cent and 13 per cent Hindu and non Hindu respectively do 'political activities' and 33 per cent and 42 per cent 'awareness and developmental' work. Here this results are not significant, what exactly tribals do in the social activities

Now the important aspect of tribal is spending their 'leisure time' (Table 6.3). Only 7 per cent tribes say they spend their leisure time by 'drinking wine'. 8.9 per cent young, 3.2 per cent middle and 7 per cent old responded said tha they 'drink wine' in their leisure time. In the same way 8.3 per cent among Hindus and 6.6 per cent among non-Hindus says spending leisure time by taking wine. This is 11 per cent and 0 per cent respectively among agriculture and non-agriculture worker. It shows the significant decline of 'taking wine'. The main cause is Christianity. Because many tribals told to this researcher that, if they drink wine they will not be allowed to go to the church and the person will be out of Mandal. Among Hindus it is the demonstration effects of the Christians, not to take wine and wine is consider as bad or profane by the Hindus. But in the age category the old age group has still more who prefers to take wine in the leisure time.

The other responses are doing 'house hold activities' 33 per cent, and 59 per cent responses 'always busy' and no time for leisure. This is the trend among the Hindus and non-Hindus. Non-Hindus are more busy as 64 per cent in comparison to 53 per cent Hindus. The response of agriculture and non-agriculture group is 'always busy' 58 per cent and 60 per cent respectively. This does not show the significant difference. Here it is a clear trend that today tribes are 'always busy'. The traditional festival and merry making has gone. *Saora* tribes always try to keep them busy to work hard and get more and more for better life.

When we go by various definitions given by sociologist in the perspective of work and leisure for, *Saoras* compulsions associated with their ecogical settings and ecological bent of mind. As the tribals have seen from their childhood that, never their forefather spend time by sitting ideal and by doing something or other or by going to forest or collecting the fruits or hunting etc. So it is the ecology which is solely, responsible for not having the leisure time among the *Saora*.

Secondly, the concept of leisure is an urban and industrialized phenomena. Leisure is as Duncan claims that, some people never participate in leisure activities— a fact likely to be overlooked if people are described in terms of activity factors. Most recent studies have assumed either that work spills over into leisure or that a person seeks compensation in leisure for the debilitating effects of work.

This is very much widely known that *Saoras* are fond of radios. Even it is a normal practice that they carry the radio with them always wherever they go. In this connection the frequency of listening radio has been sought, which shows their interest to have a modern means of communication. This reflects their leisure or awareness about the daily happening. It can be considered as non-material culture of the *Saoras*. Here out of 135 young 36 per cent listing to radio 'daily', 30 per cent 'occasionally' and 34 per cent 'do not listen'. Among the middle group 24

Table 6.2 Daily Social Activities

Variables	*Age*								*Religion*						*Occupation*					
Response	*Young*		*Middle*		*Old*		*Total*		*Hindu*		*Non-Hindu*		*Total*		*Agriculture*		*Non-Agriculture*		*Total*	
	F	%	F	%	F	%	F	%	F	%	F	%	F	%	F	%	F	%	F	%
Politics	18	13	8	13	5	16	31	13	15	14	16	13	31	13	21	13	10	14	31	13
Awareness/ Village development	63	47	18	29	6	19	87	38	36	33	51	42	87	38	59	37	28	39	87	38
No	49	36	28	44	13	41	90	39	48	44	42	35	90	39	65	41	25	35	90	39
Can't say	5	3.7	9	14	8	25	22	10	10	9.2	12	9.9	22	10	13	8.2	9	13	22	10
Total	135	100	63	100	32	100	230	100	109	100	121	100	230	100	158	100	72	100	230	100

Table 6.3 Spending Leisure Time

Variables	*Age*								*Religion*						*Occupation*					
Response	*Young*		*Middle*		*Old*		*Total*		*Hindu*		*Non-Hindu*		*Total*		*Agriculture*		*Non-Agriculture*		*Total*	
	F	%	F	%	F	%	F	%	F	%	F	%	F	%	F	%	F	%	F	%
Drinking wine	12	8.9	2	3.2	3	9.4	17	7	9	8.3	8	6.6	17	7	17	11	0	0	17	7
Household work	40	30	25	40	11	34	76	33	40	37	36	30	76	33	47	30	29	40	76	33
Always busy	83	61	36	57	16	50	135	59	58	53	77	64	135	59	92	58	43	60	135	59
Can't say	0	0	0	0	2	6.3	2	1	2	1.8	0	0	2	1	1	1.3	0	0	2	1
Total	135	100	63	100	32	100	230	100	109	100	121	100	230	100	158	100	72	100	230	100

Table 6.4 Frequency of Listening Radio

Variables	*Age*								*Religion*						*Occupation*					
Response	*Young*		*Middle*		*Old*		*Total*		*Hindu*		*Non-Hindu*		*Total*		*Agriculture*		*Non-Agriculture*		*Total*	
	F	%	F	%	F	%	F	%	F	%	F	%	F	%	F	%	F	%	F	%
Daily	48	36	15	24	11	34	74	32	35	32	39	32	74	32	45	28	29	40	74	32
Occastio-nally	41	30	19	30	10	31	70	30	27	25	43	36	70	30	49	31	21	29	70	30
Don't listen	46	34	29	46	11	34	86	37	47	43	39	32	86	37	64	41	22	31	86	37
Total	135	100	63	100	32	100	230	100	109	100	121	100	230	100	158	100	72	100	230	100

per cent 'daily', 30 per cent 'occasionally' and 46 per cent 'do not listen'. Among old 34 per cent 'daily', 31 per cent occasionally and 34 per cent 'do not listen'.

In the same manner among Hindu and non-Hindu frequency of 'daily' is 32 per cent each, 'occasionally' 25 per cent and 36 per cent respectively. In the same way among agriculture and non-agriculture it is 28 per cent and 40 per cent 'daily' respectively and the frequency of 'occasionally' is 31 per cent and 29 per cent respectively.

Now the overall trend is 'daily' 32 per cent; 'occasionally' 31 per cent- and do not listen 37 per cent. It reflects 63 per cent tribal is aware about the radio and they listen to it, which is significant, as they belong to preliterate society. It also shows tribes considered radio as a means of communication and leisure. This is one of their material culture which they posses it and shows their modern practices. Here radio as a means of mass communication, and a medium of transmission of symbolic forms. Singh also in his study of *Saora* leadership found that "radio listening had positive impact on both the sections of leaders". (1984:128).

Music

As we know music gives pleasure, entertainment and brings mental peace. Tribles in traditional days always having their festival, where they drink wine and sing their traditional folk songs. Due to the influence of modern forces the tribal society is no more , secluded, it has been influenced by exterme force to a great extent.

It has been reflect from Table 6.5 that tribes now not only have their own folk music but also listen to the other songs like Oriya, Telgu and Hindi. But when asked to differentiate between all these songs, they say Saora folk song is far better. They say their song is beteer because they clearly understand it. The figure is 58 per cent among youth, 71 per cent among middle and 75 per cent among the old age group. The figure shows how in difference of age improve the frequency of listening to their own music, which they like. In the second category that is modern music is more musical, so they listen to it. The figure is 40 per cent young, 21 per cent middle and 13 per cent old. In this figure the young has more likeness towards modern music. Among Hindu and non-Hindu 69 per cent and 60 per cent prefers the first one. Only 28 per cent and 57 per cent , prefers the second one. The important factor here is non-Hindu prefer modern music more; which shows the Christians are better exposed and for them language is not a problem. Further it seems adoption of Christianity helps them to understand other languages.

Table 6.5 Difference Between Tribal Music & Modern Music

Variables	*Age*								*Religion*						*Occupation*					
Response	*Young*		*Middle*		*Old*		*Total*		*Hindu*		*Non-Hindu*		*Total*		*Agriculture*		*Non-Agriculture*		*Total*	
	F	%	F	%	F	%	F	%	F	%	F	%	F	%	F	%	F	%	F	%
Tribal music is easy to understand	78	58	45	71	24	75	147	64	75	69	72	59.5	147	64	103	65	44	61	147	64
Modern music is more musical	54	40	13	21	4	13	71	31	30	28	41	56.9	71	31	48	30	23	32	71	31
Can't say	3	2.2	5	7.9	4	13	12	5	4	3.7	8	11.1	12	5	7	4.4	5	6.9	12	5
Total	135	100	63	100	32	100	230	100	109	100	121	100	230	100	158	100	72	100	230	100

Occupationwise break up shows 65 per cent agriculturist and 61 per cent non-agriculturist prefer the first one whereas 30 per cent and 32 per cent to the second. It shows the attachment to their own language is more and that entertains them better. The overall trend is 64 per cent prefers the tribal music and 30 per cent about the modern music. It means 30 per cent change in tribal music, culture and way of life.

Garments

In this same way it has been explored that which garment is more preferable and for what. Here we have two choice in Table 6.6. The first is traditional garment is good, strong, durable and Hinduis which has been said by 32 per cent tribal. The second is modern garment is good, decent and influential it is 65 per cent. The age wise figure shows 22 per cent young, 35 per cent middle and 69 per cent old prefer the traditional one. Secondly 76 per cent young, 59 per cent middle and 31 per cent old prefers the second and modern garment. Here the result is high among young where in traditional dress pattern the old *Saoras* figure is high. It is obvious that young people are more prone to like the modern garments as they are product of modern epoch. The religion break ups shows 43 per cent and 22 per cent Hindu and non-Hindu respectively prefers the first one. But 56 per cent and 73 per cent Hindu and non-Hindus prefers the modern one. The trend to adopt modern garment among the Christians is more. Occupationally 36 per cent agriculturist and 24 per cent non-agriculturist prefers the first and traditional one. 61 per cent agriculture and 72 per cent non-agriculture group prefers the second and modern one.

Here the tendency is more towards modern garments. This is more among young Hindu, non-Hindu, agriculturist and non-agriculturist. G. Mohapatra in his study found that "the younger generations are more sensitive to the fashionable. dress and houses with two rooms than the older generations"(1983:35). But it is quite contradictory when we compare with the choice of music. In music the important is language, which is understandable or not. But in the matter of garments, it is nothing like that, so the result is high. In first choice we have a point called Hinduised, it is understood that all the traditional garments, have a close link with religion. It means tribals are discarding the Hinduised practices which makes them traditional and reflects their identity of beings backward. So they do not want to see or identify themselves with a difference. Therefore it is a clear trend to accept modernity. However, to assestion whether the tribals are considered themselves being influenced by various external and modern

Table 6.6 Difference Between Tribal and Modern Garments

Variables	*Age*								*Religion*						*Occupation*					
Response	*Young*		*Middle*		*Old*		*Total*		*Hindu*		*Non-Hindu*		*Total*		*Agriculture*		*Non-Agriculture*		*Total*	
	F	%	F	%	F	%	F	%	F	%	F	%	F	%	F	%	F	%	F	%
A	30	22.22	22	34.92	22	68.75	74	32.17	47	43.12	27	22.31	74	32.17	57	36.08	17	23.61	74	32.17
B	102	75.56	37	58.73	10	31.25	149	64.78	61	55.96	88	72.73	149	64.78	97	61.39	52	72.22	149	64.78
C	3	2.22	4	6.35	0	0	7	3.04	1	0.92	6	4.96	7	3.04	4	2.53	3	4.17	7	3.04
Total	135	100	63	100	32	100	230	100	109	100	121	100	230	100	158	100	72	100	230	100

A. Traditional Garment is Good, Strong, Durable and Hinduised
B. Modern Garment is Different, Decent and Influential
C. Can't say

Table 6.7 Influenced to Adopt the Modern Garments and Music

Variables	*Age*								*Religion*						*Occupation*					
Response	*Young*		*Middle*		*Old*		*Total*		*Hindu*		*Non-Hindu*		*Total*		*Agriculture*		*Non-Agriculture*		*Total*	
	F	%	F	%	F	%	F	%	F	%	F	%	F	%	F	%	F	%	F	%
Yes	116	86	42	67	15	47	173	75	72	66	101	83	173	75	117	74	56	78	173	75
No	17	13	18	29	14	44	49	21	35	32	14	12	49	21	36	23	13	18	49	21
Can't say	2	1.5	3	4.8	3	9.4	8	4	2	1.8	6	5	8	4	5	3.2	3	4.2	8	4
Total	135	100	63	100	32	100	230	100	109	100	121	100	230	100	158	100	72	100	230	100

factors to adopt modern garments or not; a clear qustion has been has asked. From Table 6.7 it is clear that they are influenced by the material and social factors to accept the modern music and garments. The result is 75 per cent 'yes' and 21 per cent 'no'. It means the external forces have greatly helpful to change or influence their material and non-material culture.

As it is evident from the above discussion that culture is a holistic concept and due to various factors there is a great change taking place in *Saora* life, and culture. However, by considering the cultural traits of *Saoras* in their daily activities, leisure and communication; it is reflected that due to external forces a crisis, contradiction and change is taking place. Let us examin what crisis, contradiction and change is all about and how sociologist and anthropologist understood it. With this orientation we will also see the crisis, contradiction and change among the Saora.

Crisis, Contradiction and Change

Culture change is the conceptual formulation that refers to the many ways in which societies change their pattern of culture: Internal factors such as new inventions may lead to an increased food supply and populations growth, or external factors such as conquest by another society may bring about culture change. We know from the records of prehistory and history that the patterns of culture of every human society are constantly changing. The rate and type of change may be slow and gradual, as it was during the Paleolithic, or fast and drastic, as it has been in contemporary societies.

Factors Influencing Culture Change

The data on change do not yet permit any easy generalizations concerning the relative primacy of various factors that way generate significant shifts in rates and types of culture change. Some anthropologists favour a basically Marxist, or New-Marxist, interpretation and give primacy in their theories to such factors as " the amount of energy harnessed per capita per year" (White 1949). Some, such as Steward (l955) place emphasis upon ecology and stress the "adaptation of a culture to its environment" as the primary factor. Other scholars emphasize the importance of "religious ideology" (Weber 1922), cultural "themes" (Opler 1945), and "cultural focus" (Herskovits 1955) or, like Geertz (1957), point to inherent incongruities and tensions in social and cultural systems that generate constant pressure for change. Still others have developed more specialized theories, such as Murdock (1949 p.199), who concludes that ...... social organization is a semi-independent system comparable in many respects to language, and similarly characterized by an internal dynamics of its own" or Hallowell (1955) and Wallce (1961) who stress the psychological aspects of culture change.

Any change in the ecological niche occupied by a society influences culture change. Such a change may occur as a result of either (a) natural environmental changes, or (b) the migration of a society from one ecological niche to another. New cultural adaptations are always required for survival in the case of such shifts in ecological niche. Any contact between two societies with different cultural patterns influences change in both societies. The diffusion, or borrowing, of cultural elements that occurs has made these exchanges important in culture change throughout history. More profound and sustained cultural contact, usually called "acculturation" generated even more significant shifts in the rates and types of change in the two cultures.

Any evolutionary change occurring within a society is obviously a factor of critical importance. Following Murdock (1949, p.184), "evolution" is used here simply to designate "processes of orderly adaptive change". For example, when a society with a food-gathering economy has domesticated its plants and animals and has thereby increased its food surplus potential, the requirements of the new food-producing technology and the ensuing population growth pose critical problems. The need for division and specialization of labour, social controls, and distribution of the surplus leads to adaptive changes in the cultural patterns. Or if a society (for whatever reasons) shifts from matrilocal to patrilocal residence, then again there are adaptive changes in a whole range of cultural patterns, as Murdock (1949) has demonstrated. However, there are various models which have been developed and used to expalin cultural changes. These models are considered as the tools to explain social and cultural change.

Models for the Study of Culture Change

Macroscopic models. The most inclusive models, with respect to both cultural coverage and time span, are those utilized by White (1949) and Childe (1951) for the study of cultural evolution. Both deal with trends and stages in the culture of mankind as a whole. White's most significant proposition is that technological development expressed in terms of man's control over energy underlies social changes and cultural achievements (1949, pp. 363-396). Childe is especially noted for his formulation of the important shift from food gathering to food-producing societies in early human history. These model so dealing with what Steward (1955) has called "universal evolution", advance propositions about world culture as a whole but cannot explain particular features of particular cultures. An attempt to solve this conceptual and methodological difficulty has more recently been proposed by Sahlins and Service (1960), who differentiate between "general" and "specific" cultural evolution. In his model, Steward proposes a different methodological solution described as "multilinear evolution," in which "regularities in culture change" are studied by comparing sequences of change in a series of particular cultures. His classic paper (1955, pp.178-209) utilizing this model is his comparison of the development of "irrigation civilizations" in five arid or semi-arid areas of the world; Peru, Mesoamerica, Mesopotamia, Egypt, and China. Although more recent empirical evidence has not supported his generalizations concerning irrigation works as the crucial factor in all these areas, the comparative framework be proposes is a fruitful one that can be utilized on other ranges of culture change data.

Another model that involves social and cultural changes over relatively long time spans is that of Redfield, whose classic study (1941) of the shift from "folk" to "urban" society has stimulated many further studies of culture change, including the present interest in the emergence of and changes in "peasant society". Drawing upon the earlier ideas of Durkheim, Maine, Morgan, and Tonnies, Redfield designed a fields study that compared four communities in Yucatan: a tribal village, a peasant village, a town, and a city. Using degree of isolation and degree of homogeneity in culture patterns as the independent variables, he shows how three types of culture change accompany lessening isolation and homogeneity: disorganization of the culture, secularization, and individualization.

Microscopic models. Among the many models that are less extensive in scope, but still focused upon changing social and cultural systems, are those of Murdock (1949) and Leach (1954). Murdock (1949, pp. 201-221) is mainly concerned with changes in social organization, and he singles out the "rule of residence" as the aspect of social structure that acts as a filter, capable of responding to a variety of quite diverse external stimuli but in only a limited number of ways. He proposes that change in a social system regularly begin with a modification of the rule of residence, and other changes in kinship structure and terminology follow in predictable order. Leach, on the other hand, utilizes what might be called an "oscillation model in his description of Kachin society, where there is a regular oscillation between two polar types of political value systems to which the people can appeal and still be considered members of the society.

Cultural Contradictions Among the Saora

Since there is a debate that the government always try to bring the tribals into mainstream; few people agree with this and few other differ in this context. To find out this critical position *Saora's* opinion has been sought. In Table 6.8, it has stated whether government protects the culture of tribals or not. The result is 43.04 per cent says 'yes' and 43.48 per cent 'no'. So the result is halfway. Since this is the result now we must see how government has protected their culture. (See Table 6.9) 32.6 per cent tribals say inviting for radio programme is the way our culture is protected. It means government is interested to keep up our traditional culture so, they are inviting to perform the stage by which their culture will not die. Here 13.9 per cent have the strong radical and negative view which reflects that tribals no more interested to seen as tribals. So they are saying 'no need to protect our' culture. This radical figure is 18 per cent , 9.52 per cent, 6.25 per cent among the young, middle and old category respondents respectively. It seems the traditional culture is repressive and the sign of backwardness. On this basis people also make the distinction and considered the tribals as inferior.

In religion break up 40.37 per cent Hindus and 25.62 per cent non Hindus prefer radio programme where as 12.84 per cent and14.88 per cent having the radical view, 'not to protect the culture', that is because it discriminate them from others. Occupational break up shows 24. 68 per cent and 50 per cent prefers radio program and 17.72 per cent and 5.56 per cent gives the radical view. This radical view shows the 'cultural crisis' among the tribes. Here it is a mix result of keeping up their culture and also giving it up. This is very significant sociologically as it shows the crisis, contradiction and change.

In this connection it has been further tried that 'does tribal wants that government should protect their culture'. (See Table 6.10). Here 45.22 per cent says 'yes', 11.74 per cent 'no'. Among the young, middle and old it is 43 per cent, 47.6 per cent and 50 per cent said 'yes' respectively where as 'no' for 8.1 per cent, 15.9 per cent and 18.7 per cent respectively. Likewise Hindu and non-Hindu it is 41.28 per cent and 48.76 per cent says 'yes'. 11.57 per cent and 11.93 per cent said 'no'. Occupational break up shows 50.63 per cent and 33.3 per cent yes in comparison to 10.76 per cent and 13.9 per cent no.

So this result is quite confusing as few, 45 per cent tribal wants that their culture should be protected whereas 50 per cent have the negative view. But what this researcher found, this is because of the changing

Table 6.8 Does Government Protect Your Culture?

Variables	*Age*								*Religion*						*Occupation*					
Response	*Young*		*Middle*		*Old*		*Total*		*Hindu*		*Non-Hindu*		*Total*		*Agriculture*		*Non-Agriculture*		*Total*	
	F	%	F	%	F	%	F	%	F	%	F	%	F	%	F	%	F	%	F	%
Yes	63	47	24	38	12	38	99	43	50	46	49	40.5	99	43	61	39	38	53	99	43
No	57	42	28	44	15	47	100	43	40	37	60	49.59	100	43	77	49	23	32	100	43
Can't say	15	11	11	17	5	16	31	13	19	17	12	9.917	31	13	20	13	11	15	31	13
Total	135	100	63	100	32	100	230	100	109	100	121	100	230	100	158	100	72	100	230	100

Table 6.9 How does Government Protect Your Culture?

Variables	*Age*								*Religion*						*Occupation*					
Response	*Young*		*Middle*		*Old*		*Total*		*Hindu*		*Non-Hindu*		*Total*		*Agriculture*		*Non-Agriculture*		*Total*	
	F	%	F	%	F	%	F	%	F	%	F	%	F	%	F	%	F	%	F	%
Radio Programme	41	30.37	21	33.33	13	40.63	75	32.61	44	40.37	31	25.62	75	32.61	39	24.68	36	50.00	75	32.62
Radical View	24	17.78	6	9.52	2	6.25	32	13.91	14	12.84	18	14.88	32	13.91	28	17.72	4	5.56	32	13.91
Can't say	17	12.59	13	20.63	7	21.38	37	16.09	16	14.68	21	17.36	37	16.09	28	17.72	9	12.50	37	16.09
Not Applicable	53	39.26	23	36.51	10	31.25	86	37.39	35	32.11	51	42.15	86	37.39	63	39.87	23	31.94	86	37.39
Total	135	100	63	100	32	100	230	100	109	100	121	100	230	100	158	100	72	100	230	100

Table 6.10 Do Tribals Want That Government Should Pròtect Their Culture

Variables	*Age*								*Religion*						*Occupation*					
Response	*Young*		*Middle*		*Old*		*Total*		*Hindu*		*Non-Hindu*		*Total*		*Agriculture*		*Non-Agriculture*		*Total*	
	F	%	F	%	F	%	F	%	F	%	F	%	F	%	F	%	F	%	F	%
Yes	59	43.7	30	47.6	16	50	105	45.65	45	41.4	59	48.76	104	45.21	80	50.63	24	33.3	104	45.22
No	12	8.12	10	15.9	06	18.7	28	12.17	13	11.75	14	11.93	27	11.74	17	10.76	10	13.9	27	11.74
Can't say	64	47.4	23	36.5	10	31.25	97	42.17	51	46.75	48	39.66	99	43.05	61	38.6	38	52.77	99	43.04
Total	135	100	63	100	32	100	230	100	109	100	121	100	230	100	158	100	72	100	230	100

attitude of the tribals. This may be called as identity crisis of the *Saoar* tribe. They do not want to recognised as forest dweller or living in the remote terrain areas. They want to be merg with the mainstream society which few of our planners suggested. This is evident that their culture is in the stage of crisis where contradiction and change is dominantly figured.

Conclusion

Culture as it has been explored in the above discussion is considered from both material and non-material perspective. In many of our discussion it has been referred to as common sense. This common sense drifted from generation to generation through oral, conditional, socialization and learning. This can be referred in the context of time and space. The ecological aspect may be discussed in three points, adoption, technology and ideational. The technology is always referred as material culture and the adoption and ideational referred to our feelings and adopting the changes in due course of time. This is reflected through ecological set up. The discussion on traditional *Saora* culture shows that the *Saora* group legendary have the relation with *Ramayana,* the tribals considered their geneology from monkeys and believe that they are the son of *Vishwamitra.* In this legendary sense we can also say that their reference to lion-cloth, means tale or *Lanjia Saora* is correct. The traditional village setup, and the house are arranged in a row and having the close relation with each other. They do have some kitchen garden. The house is made of many forest resources.

Traditionally their non-material culture is referred as *Ukka* and *Ersi;* these are taboos, which govern their behaviour with themselves and with the god. The proud activity of the *Saoras* is condemned by themselves. The taboos show a great relation of *Saoras* with forest as they do not even touch and cut the trees. This shows their ecologically govern and socially accepted mind set. Folk culture, folk tradition, folk songs, and folklore all are part of tribal culture. The concept is here used very loosely as it shows the total picture of the *Saora* tribe. So the *Saora* society can be referred as folk society, where folk culture, folk tradition and folk songs are essential part of it. The *Saora* folk songs have been classified here; this has a relation with nature, forest, culture, gender, work and leisure. So this is evident, as these are part of folk society. Here the reference is made about a material and physical aspect of culture which is intertwined with values, beliefs, faith and religion. This is evident from the jokes and riddles of *Saora.* The careful analysis of riddles reveals that it is based on the forest ecology. We can give an example of one riddles which shows that how people joke at a person with reference to 'bamboo' when he goes from mother's house to mother-in-law house. In the context of material culture related to traditional dress and ornaments of male and female has been discussed. The man wears loincloth and women wear the blouse and scot. Apart from this women wear various ornaments in their nose, ear and throat.

With this above traditional *Saora* culture the change can be traced in many aspect of their life. There are various factors, which influences changes. This is of internal and external sources. The internal changes occur when invention will lead to an increase in food supply and population growth. External factors are related to other society as in case of *Saoras,* they have been access to outside traders, officials and school teachers. The models to study cultural changes is discussed in the context of macroscopic model, which explains that due to progress and advancement of society culture changes. This change occur in each and every aspect of the society. The other model is of shift from 'folk' to 'urban', advocated by Redfield. To analyze the changes here in *Saora* tribals the microscopic model is more useful as there is change in each and every aspect of the tribals. This is clear by seeing the leisure activity of the tribals. Leisure as it defines the free time from the formal duties. But in this context it is found that they do not have leisure time, as they are always busy. So it can be said that leisure activities is profane for them, as they categorised this like laziness. This can be said in different way as they take all their activities so lightly, that they enjoy the work. Here the classification of Robinson of free time can be fit. A free time *Saora* use it for organisational activities, but the number is very less. The second is of attending mass media, where it is perceived many *Saoras* use their time by listening radio and visiting movies. Among the old generation is found to spend their leisure activities to do the socialization activities.

Culture in anthropological literature have two components, one is descriptive conception and another is the symbolic conception. The descriptive is related to our values and beliefs, where symbolic is related to symbols. On the basis of symbolic forms in relation to the structural context the development of communication takes place. Mass communication is a matter of technology, which significantly uses the symbol to express meaningfully. In this study it is found that most of the *Saora* tribals are influenced by the symbolic expression of the technologically advance communication system. So here it is pertinent to say that the *Saora* culture is influenced by the modern transmission system. This can be explained by seeing the difference between tribal music and modern music. Maximum tribals have access to radio, T. V. and music system, but they prefer the music of *Saora* language, which they claim that, they can easily understand it. This is the finding that the culture of *Saora* is changing because of the modern means of communication. Not only this but also their traditional dress pattern, 75 per cent people opine that they are induced by modern garment. This has the main attributes, as few said the traditional dress and ornaments are Hinduised, where the modern one is not Hinduised. It reflects that the tribals do not want to be referred as tribals due to the use of the traditional garments and ornaments. This is the contradiction. Another contradiction is that, few tribals are in favour of government to protect their culture, but 50 per cent says that no need to be protected it, in both instances, the tribal identities are understood as inferior and must be discarded. Therefore, it can be concluded by saying that *Saora* culture is no more secluded, it is on the verge of changing. The work, leisure activities are also changing due to modernisation and practice of modern means of communication.

References

Altman. I and Chemans, 1984, *Culture and Enviornment,* Cambridge Univeristy Press.

Bosserman, P. and Kutcher, L., 1974, 'Leisure and the Coming of Post-industrial Society', *Current Research* in *Sociology,* The Hague: Mouton, pp. 109-46.

Boas, F., 1938, *The Mind of Primitive Man,* New York.

Check, N. and Burch,W., 1976, *The Social Organisation of Leisure in Human Society,* New York, Harper & Row.

Dorson, R.M., (ed), 1972, *Folklore and Folk Life: An Introduction,* London, The Univ. of Chicago Press,.

Dumazedier, J., 1974, *Sociology of Leisure,* Amsterdam, Elsevier.

Elwin,V, 1955, *The Religion of an Indian Tribe,* Bombay. Oxford Univ. Press.

Eggan, F., 1963, 'Some Aspects of Culture Change in Northern Phillpines', *American Anthropologist,* Vol. 43.

Gupta, Sankar Sen, (ed.), 1964, *Studies in Indian Folk Culture,* Indian Publications.

Geertz, Clifford, 1973, *The Interpretation of Culture,* New York, Basic Books.

Hersokovits, 1956, *Man and His Work,* New York, Knopf.

Krappe, A.H., *The Science of Folklore,* London.

Kando,T., and Summers. W., 1971, 'The Impact of Work on Leisure: Towards a Paradigm and Research Strategy', *Pac. Sociol. Rev. 14,* pp. 310-27.

Kelly, J. 1976, 'Leisure as a Compensation for Work Restrain', *Soc. Leisure.,* pp.73-82 .

Kroeben, A.L., and C., Kluckhohn, 1963, *Culture : A Critical Review of Concept and Definations, New York*, Vintage.

Murdock, G.P., 1949, *Social Structure*, Macmillan, New York.

Malinowski, B., 1944, *A Scientific Theory of Culture and Other Essays*, Chapel Hill, University of N. Carolina Press.

Malinowski, B., 1933, 'Culture' in *Encyclopaedia of the Social Science*, New York.

Parker, S. and Smith, M., 1976, 'Work and Leisure', *Hand Book of Work Organisation and Society*, (ed.), R. Dubin, Chicago, Rand Mc Nally, pp. 37-64.

Robinson, J., 1977, *How Americans Use Their Time: A Social- Psychological Analysis of Every day Behavior*, New York, Praeger.

Redfield, Robert, 1930, 'The Regional Aspect of Culture' *American Sociological Society : Papers and Proceedings*, Vol. XXIV, pp. 30-41

Redfiled, Robert, 1941, *Folk Culture of Ukotan*, Chicago, University of Chicago Press.

Steward, J.H.,1955, *The Theory of Cultural Change: The Methodology of Multilinear Evolution*, Urbana Univ. Press.

Singer, Milton (ed.), 1959, *Traditional India: Structure and Change*, Philadelphia, American Folklore Society.

Singh, B., 1984, *The Saora Highlander: Leadership and Development*, Bombay, Somaya Publication.

Thief-Horstmann, M., 1975, *Encyclopedia of Indian Tribes: Tribal Culture, Customs and Affinities*, pp. 217-18.

Tylor, E.B., (1871) 1958, *Primitive Culture: Researches into the Development of Mythology, Philosophy, Religion, Art and Custom.* 2 vols. Gloucester, Mass.

Thomson, J. Arthur and Patrick Geddes, 1931, Life Outlines of General Biology, Vol. I.

White, Leslie A., 1949, *The Science of Culture: A Study of Man and Civilization*, Farran New York.

White, L., 1949, *The Science of Culture: A Study of Man and Civilisation*, Farrar, New York.

Wilensky, H., 1960, 'Work, Careers and Social Integration', *Inter- Social Sci. J.* 12, No.4, pp.543-60.

7
Economy Ecology and Development

Radcliffe-Brown defines "Social structure," as a network or system of social relations including persistent social groups and differentiated social classes and social roles. It is assumed that each structural system is a functional unity in which all the component parts contribute in a harmonious way to its existence and continuity. To test this all kinds of social phenomena—morals, law, etiquette, religion, government, economics, education, language—need to be studied "not in abstraction or isolation, but in their direct and indirect relations to social structure, i.e., with reference to the way in which they depend upon, or affect the social relations between persons and groups of persons. (Radcliffe-Brown 1952: 195). This interrelated aspects of the economic structure of *Saora* tribe has been discussed here with reference to other aspects of their life, that is of ecology and development. There are two aspects to the relationship of primitive society to nature: the objective economic and the subjective ideological. The important expression is the community's ownership of a definite territory (its source of existence) and the economic development of that territory.

In *Economy and Society* Weber (1978:64) stresses that "all 'economic' processes and objects are characterized as such entirely by the meaning they have for human action." And in *General Economic History* (1981) Weber exemplifies this approach by observing that: "There is great difference between the fact that a Chinese or Japanese "peasant is hungry and knows that, while the Deity is unfavorable to him or the spirits are disturbed and consequently nature does give rain or sunshine at the right crisis, even to the fact the social order itself may be held responsible for the crisis, even to the poorest labourer. In the first case, men turn to religion; in the second, the work of men is held at fault and the labouring man draws the conclusion that it must be changed" (1981 :292). In *Economy and Society* Weber (1978) says that the notion of economic power is "indispensable" to economic sociology (the exact term Weber uses is *Verfugungsgewlt* or "powers of control and disposal"). According to Weber, a number of important economic phenomena—such as profit-making, consumer behaviour, and so on—can only be understood if the role of economic power is logical observations on economic behaviour in different civilizations (mainly China, India, and Europe), on different types of economic ethics (e.g., "internal ethics" versus "external ethics"), and on different types of economic roles (e.g., "the alien trader" versus "the resident trader"). It should finally also be mentioned that both works contain a sophisticated attempt to develop sociology of markets (1978:68).

In this chapter economic activities of the tribals in general and *Saora* in particular has been carefully examined. *Saora* tribes' economic activities are primarily forest based. Traditional economic activities of the *Saora* tribes were evolved around minor forest produces and slash and burn cultivation. It has been focused here the economic activities of *Saora*, their traditional aspects, and the changes after independence. The development initiatives undertaken by government agencies have a significant dent in tribal life and social structure. Further it has been explored here how the changes have been perceived by the *Saoras* and to what extent the government initiative have had impact on tribal economy, forest and ecology. However, before going into the tribal economic activities, the economic anthropoligical literature needs to be reviewed to give a theoatical shape to the analysis.

Economic Anthropology

The organised effort to systematically explore economic anthropology was made with study of the *Kula* transactions in the Trobriand Island by Malinowski in the nineteen-twenties. Though Malinowski did not regard the *Kula* as an example of economic activity, he nevertheless set forth fundamental principles of economic anthropology or economic sociology. It allowed to break away from the study of structure and function and distinguished an important aspect what we agree to define as 'economic' activity. It is in fact a part of the totality of social life; and while it is necessary, for purposes of understanding, to dissect it out of that totality, it is equally necessary to put it back: that is, to view it in all its functional relationships to the rest of the society. This has in fact set the tone of later writing. According to Firth *(Elements of Social Organisation,* 1951): The choice, the behaviour, the values of any one person is conditioned by other people.... The less any individual acts in isolation, the more he must be responsive to choices, or the expectation of choices, by others. Economic organisation is set in social framework. However, G. Dalton and Karl Polanyi, in their writings which have aroused wide interest hold a substantially different view. For Polanyi, "the term economic is a compound of two meanings that have independent roots. We will call them the substantive and the formal meaning". The substantive meaning of economic derives from man's dependence for his living upon nature and his fellows. It reforms to the interchange with his natural and social environment, it so far as this results in supplying him with the means of material want satisfaction. The formal meaning of economic derives from the logical character of the means-end relationship, as apparent in such words as 'economical' or 'economizing'. It refers to a definite situation of choice, namely, between the different uses of means induced by an insufficiency of those means. If we call the rules governing choice of means the logic of rational action, then we must denote this variant of logic, with an improvised term, as formal economics. However, the two root meanings of economic, the substantive and the formal, have nothing in common.

Polanyi writes that 'formal' economics has relevance only to the industrial West; only here, he believes, is to be found what Dalton call's the 'market principle'. By that he means a pervading market system, such that potential sellers and buyers are in virtually perfect contact, and are able to command virtually complete relevant information, and where the various sectors of the market are integrated, so that prices made there determine the supply of factors of production. According to Polanyi and his followers, it is only in such a context that 'formal economics', as an explanation of observed events, can make sense.

In 'primitive and archaic' societies, on the other hand, Polanyi asserts that different 'patterns of integration' of the economic system are to be seen. These he calls reciprocity and redistribution. Reciprocity occurs where there are movements of goods between social units (tribes, households or the like) which are on the same structural level that is, they are not subordinated to one another. It refers to movements of goods into a structurally superior center (capital city, ruler's court) and the corresponding diffusion of goods from such a centre into structurally subordinate parts of the society: programmes of tribute-gathering and of doles or rations.

In relying exclusively on natural products, herdsmen and hunters have been regarded as enslaved by their environment. Montesquieu (1748/

1949) was perhaps the first to popularise deterministic explanations of economic activity. He regarded production as depending on the climate, the fertility of the soil and topography, and population density as being affected by the labour requirements of the different productive activities so determined. Environmental determinism has found its way into school geography textbooks, with their emphasis on the way Eskimo and Bedouin lifestyles are constrained by and adapted to the exigencies of the Arctic tundra and the Arabian desert. But productive activities are themselves cultural, and in the same environments we find very different economics. While the Eskimo of the North American taiga and tundra were hunters, gatherers and fishermen, drawing a very clear distinction between their summer and winter activities, today in Alaska they are the recipients of windfall oil revenues that have drawn some of them into industrial employment and others into the alcoholism of boredom. The Lapps of the Russian and Scandinavian taiga-tundra in contrast, used to follow and live off reindeer herds. Today, in the USSR (former USSR), herding has been collectivised, while in Scandinavian countries a substantial proportion of former herders have been reduced to living off welfare rather than animals. The Bedouin of Saudi Arabia today drive Cadillacs as well as keeping camels and practicing falconry, thanks to their oil revenues. As yet the Somali of the Ogaden desert have not been affected by the energy industry. They continue to herd their camels, sheep and goats in quite different units to those of their immediate Ogaden neighbours, the Boran Galla, even though their physical environments are practically identical. So even under the same environmental circumstances, different societies produce and organize their production differently Culture counts even in the exploitation of nature: the adaptation of men to their environments is not passive, even where land is merely the subject of labour.

The inventions that have enabled men progressively to shape and control, rather than merely respond to their environments, Bronowski (1973 :20) calls a 'brilliant sequence of cultural peaks', or *The Ascent of Man.* This model of ascent, of movement upward towards a 'better' system, summarises and informs the evolutionists attitude to those who have been left behind by progress, those whom Sahlins (1974: 8) described as the 'Paleolithic disenfranchised'. Even fishermen, with their factory ships that enable modern fleets to remain at sea for up to six month without putting into part, have retained something of the stigma that attaches to nomadic herdsmen and hunters The margins of production, as well as to the margins of society, by their sedentary fellow-humans. 'Developing' the mobile is usually envisaged as finding them an alternative, settled occupation.

Spencer conceived the military and industrial types of society as an abstract conceptual apparatus to account for the broad evolutionary as sweep of human history. He also saw two types of society in his book *The Principles of Sociology* (1897:484) as opposed in principle: "By as much as cooperation ceases to be compulsory, by so much does it become voluntary; for if men act together they must do it either willingly or unwillingly." In the industrial society, the principle of integration is the principle of freedom; men interact by forming contractual agreements. Political intervention should be minimized, for it upsets the voluntarily coordinated activities of free individuals. Thus, in the end Spencer viewed his industrial society much as Adam Smith did his competitive economy. Power is so differentiated and dispersed—and free men are so motivated—that integration is effected by balancing individual interests in a vast system of voluntary interchanges. Active social integration in the industrial society thus becomes unnecessary for Spencer, just as active political regulation becomes unnecessary for Smith.

Durkheim maintained that the only viable principle of integration permitted in Spencer's industrial society is the principle of contract of free exchange. No independent integrative action, above and beyond negative controls to prevent persons from hurting one another, is necessary. Durkheim doubted the possibility of stability in such a society, which would hang together only on the basis of momentary contacts among individuals. In contrast to Spencer, he maintained that powerful forms of integration operate in differentiated societies. Durkheim found this type of integration—which he termed "organic solidarity"—primarily in restitutive laws, which contain rules governing the conditions under which contractual relations can be considered valid. Other forms of organic solidarity above and beyond the law are customs, trade conventions, and implicit understandings among economic agents. Dukheim's difference with Spencer, then, is that he gave independent analytic significance to the problem of integration in complex societies. Weber also stressed the political legal regulation of money and exchange. Above all, rational capitalism cannot flourish unless the political authority guarantees the existence of a money supply with relatively stable values. As to the type of medium of exchange, Weber saw the advantage of the institutionalization of generalized money currency (as opposed to payments in kind, which are limited to specific transactions), since currency allows for expansion of the market and creation of credit. Finally, Weber, like Durkheim, stressed the importance of a legal framework to guarantee the validity of contracts, and advocated a functioning administrative and judicial system to enforce these legal regulations.

Malinowski also stressed the integrative significance of magic for economic activities. The constriction of a canoe, is accompanied at every stage by magical rituals. Malinowski interpreted this magic as a kind of supplementary force to well-exercised craftsmanship, supplying "the psychological influence, which keeps people confident about the success of their labour, and provides them with as sort of natural leader." (*Argonauts of Western Pacific,* 1922: 116) The impingement of non-economic variables appears even more clearly in the realm of exchange. Malinowski identified forms such as the pure gift, which usually involves presents (without expectation of return) between husband and wife, and between parents and children. Even forms of exchange that involve payment for services rendered are strictly regulated by custom. In still rather cases material goods are traded for non economic items such as privileges and titles (*Ibid.*, 177-186). As Malinowski repeatedly pointed out, conventional supply and demand theory cannot account for such patterns of exchange.

A few years after the appearance of Malinowski's monograph, Marcel Mauss (1872-1950), Durkheim's student and collaborator, produced a small volume entitled *The Gift,* (1954) in which he surveyed a vast anthropological literature on ceremonial exchange patterns. In such exchange Mauss observed binding obligations— on the giver to give, on the receiver to receive, and on the receiver to reciprocate (though the timing and exact amount of the return gift is open to much variation). Mauss, like Malinowski, found it impossible to interpret the traditional exchanges in purely utilitarian or economic terms. Rather he emphasized the gift as a symbolic binding-together of a kinship unit or tribe (1954:70-71).

The work of Firth *Economics of the New Zealand Maori,* (1959) also deserves mention, largely because it represents a more profound effort to synthesize anthropological research and economic theory. Malinowski, whose attitude toward technical economics was more negatively critical, fell short of this synthesis. In his monograph on the *Maori of New Zealand* and *The Tikopia,* Firth organized his discussion around traditional economic categories of division of labor, income, capital, distribution and rational calculation; but he also showed how these activities were conditioned by the dynamics of chieftainship, kinship, magic, and prestige systems. In a more recent work on the economic structure of the Malay fishing industry, Firth demonstrates how certain spheres of economic activity, especially marketing and credit, lend themselves to technical economic analysis, whereas in an other spheres, such as production and labour supply, are strongly influenced by familial, religious, and other non-economic variables.

Contemporary Economic Anthropology

Major among the contributions that gave economic anthropology its name are those of Karl Polanyi, George Dalton and their students, who came to be known as the "substantivists", and those of Firth and those who followed his line and came to known as "formalists". The two groups have contributed a lot, each in its own way, to an understanding of the subject matter. All the time they confronted each other with attack on both theory and method. In many ways they reached a stagnant position and kept repeating their arguments over and over again. In the last few year two new approaches with their roots in the opposing groups started to gain influence in the field through advancing new alternatives for development. Barth leads these new groups on the one hand and a group of a young generation of Marxists, predominantly French, on the other. A number of review articles on the topic have been published, the most significant being those of Dalton (1969), Firth, and Meillassoux (1972). These articles serve to give a summary of the position of economic anthropology. Dalton's statement that "both fieldwork and synthesis in economic anthropology suffer from inadequate theory" (1969:63) has some truth in it. If the absence of such a theory, controversy persists as to the merits of various alternative frames of reference for the analytical treatment of "primitive" and peasant societies. "The main point of contention has aroused heated controversy: the extent to which anthropologists should adopt conventional economics as to analyze primitive and peasant economies" (Dalton 1969:64). Although the substantivist and the formalist "agree that knowledge of economics of... industrial capitalism should figure explicitly and importantly in economic anthropology." As Dalton puts it: "They disagree sharply... on the appropriate way to incorporate conventional economics and knowledge of our own economy" (1969:65). The substantivist group, in Dalton's words, "describe the salient characteristic of industrial capitalism and economic theory so as to provide a base of contrast with that sub-set of economies we call "primitive." (They)...then show how variants of reciprocity and redistribution act as integrating organizational principles of land and labour allocation, work organization, and produce disposition, ...and how external trade and money uses in such economies are derivative expressions of reciprocal and re-distributive modes of transaction (1969:65).

This group argues that to employ our own concepts of economic theory "to analyze the non-market sectors of primitive and peasant economies is as distorting as it would be to use the concepts of Christianity to analyze primitive religions" (Dalton 1969:65-66). Moreover they emphasize the distinctiveness of the different primitive economies and implicitly argue against the possibility of generalizations. Firth states that "economic relations can be understood only as part of a scheme of social relations....Economic anthropology deals primarily with the economic aspects of the social relations of persons" (Firth 1951: 137-138).

Cultural Ecology, Marxism and the Development

The traditional categories of anthropological functionalism, predicated upon the study of a single, integrated local culture (with widely shared norms and patterns of behaviour), could not easily be adapted to the study of all the varied groups and relations contained within a nation state. Steward therefore concluded that 'the greatest need of contemporary social anthropologists [was for] an adequate conceptualization of the phenomena of socio-cultural systems above the tribal level' and to meet that need he offered, in 1951, the concept of 'levels of socio-cultural integration'. 'Socio-cultural integration' was, however, more than a rehearsal approach, which allowed the separation of national society into sub-cultures and institutions at different levels of complexity. It was also a way of looking at the process through which modification occurred in any element of a subculture, or in the relationship of all elements, as 'simpler forms' gradually became ... specialized, dependent parts of new kinds of total configurations.' (Cited from Alcantara, 1984:71). Socio-cultural integration was also used by Steward to describe the static state of any subculture at any moment, as it had been shaped both by interaction with its physical environment and with the wider world. One might say, for example, that the kind of 'socio-cultural integration' of the Tarascans was different from that of the Lacandones, because the first group lived in temperate cornfields and had sustained long contact with Spanish and Mexican culture, while the latter lived virtually isolated in the jungle.

Folk Verses Peasant Economy

The concern of both Stewart and Wolf with changing forms of socio-cultural integration, characteristic of particular types of insertion into the wider system, must be considered part of a more general trend among

American anthropologists during the 1950s toward analysing the social mechanisms which increasingly seemed to link the inhabitants of rural communities with individuals and groups outside the confines of the village. Redfield, for example, found it necessary to ask himself (in a series of lectures delivered at Swarthmore College in 1955) what 'kinds of social relations... one comes to describe if one begins with some local... community and tries to do justice to the fact that many of its relations are with outsiders' (*Ibid.*: 78). A peasant community was, after all, not only a part-culture, but also a part-society (as in a series of lectures delivered at Swarthmore College in 1955); and in fact it might prove to be 'so incomplete a system that it [could] not well be described as a [self-contained] social structure,' any more than it could be pictured as a self-contained cultural system.

This shift in emphasis from the rural community as a part-culture (the social structure of which was presumed to be largely independent of the wider world) to a part-society, the members of which were intimately related to the outside world, required a change in terminology, for the prevailing usage of 'folk' implied a virtually exclusive cultural dependence. Therefore in the course of the 1950s the 'folk' became the 'peasantry,' and the earlier tend fell quickly into disuse. Not surprisingly, it was Steward who presaged the need for change by noting, in 1951, that Redfield's 'folk' really described a kind of integration rather than a particular culture content. Foster followed with a similar comment in 1953. And Wolf took the final step of insisting upon utilizing the 'term "peasant" (to indicate) a structural relationship, not a particular culture content,' in his analysis of types of Latin American peasantries of 1955. His suggestion was taken up by Redfield during the same year and made applicable to all those small cultivators, throughout history, who farmed for subsistence, not for profit, and who look [ed] to or (were) influenced by gentry or towns-people,' constituting (as Foster had also noted) 'the rural dimension of old [urban] civilization with the latter.

The unanimous agreement among structural functionalists, cultural ecologists, and Marxists that 'peasant' be substituted for 'folk' did not mean, however, that all understood the nature of interaction between rural villagers and the wider society in the same terms. Redfield and Foster were quick to admit that the peasantry must, by definition, be politically and culturally dependent upon the larger socio-cultural system; and they recognized a reciprocal dependence of urban society upon the agricultural goods provided to non-cultivators by the peasantry. Nevertheless, on balance, they consistently assumed the peasantry to be the more dependent of the 'two halves of the social system,' and therefore rejected any suggestion that a peasantry was likely over the long run to provide more to the larger system than it received in return.

Wolf, on the other hand, insisted that the peasantry was not so much dependent as exploited: it produced a volume of agricultural goods appropriated through the exercise of power by groups with superior claims over the means of production, or over the use of force. In return, it was true, the peasantry light receive protection or service of other kinds; but Wolf clearly did not consider these services a sufficient repayment for the value of goods delivered. The local village unit was in fact an inherently superior kind of survival system. Its peasant households could survive through self-provisioning if ties with the wider socio-economic system were broken, while the same could not be said of urban inhabitants or gently. Therefore the latter were in the last analysis most dependent upon the former, and illustrated their dependence in the process of exploitation.

At the heart of this difference between Redfield and Foster, on the one hand, and Wolf on the other, lay basically incompatible suppositions of the structural-functionalist and Marxist paradigms. As Alvin Gouldner has pointed out in his lucid essay on 'Reciprocity and autonomy in functional theory, 'functionalism was—and is—premised upon the 'operation of a 'principal of functional reciprocity,' "through which all interaction among groups and individuals within a given system was assumed to involve the exchange of equally valued goods or services. The very persistence of the system was taken as proof of the operation of a basically 'balanced' reciprocity, and exploitation was therefore definitionally impossible. Marxism, in contrast, suppposed that an extremely 'unbalanced' reciprocity could be upheld over long periods of time through utilization of the compensatory mechanism of force.

The element which seemed most clearly to serve as a 'balancing' mechanism within the structural-functionalist evaluation of the relationship between peasantry and non-peasantry was the value placed upon the cultural contribution made by urban elites to the quality of rural life. Redfield said in 1955, "It will not do to describe these relations only as relations of ruler and ruled or of exploiter and exploited, although these elements are likely to be present....The cultural relations between the two halves are to be emphasized. Sjoberg puts it well: '...the elite exhibits to the highly valued achievements... and provides the peasant's social system with a sophisticated justification for its existence and survival.' Thus in return for peasant's goods, the elite provided cultural standards, and in the process cancelled out the debt.

The city was always the repository of the 'great tradition', and therefore an adequate social framework for the elite within the structural-functionalist paradigm. The peasantry existed in relation to the city, as the entire folk-urban continuum made patent. But if one looked at the question from the point of view of Marxism, the key element in maintaining the relationship between peasants and non-peasants of higher status was power, and power was exercised not by a city, but by a state. It is not surprising, therefore, that Wolf insisted upon defining the peasantry primarily as subjects of the state: .....it is only when a cultivator is integrated into a society with a state— that is, when the cultivator becomes subject to the demands and sanctions of power holders outside his social stratum— that we can appropriately speak of peasantry.' Any kind of assets (tools, land, etc.) are "capital", any transfers of goods including stealing and giving, are "exchanges" if not trade; any old man benefiting from collective work is converted into an entrepreneur and calculator of marginal returns; any kind of returns are "interest" whose rate are sometimes computed as being 100 per cent; such institutions as the potlatch are described in terms of wild stock-market speculation (Meillassoux 1972).

Strategy for Economic Development of Tribals

The Scheduled Tribes and the Scheduled Castes were granted constitutional safeguards by the Constituent Assembly on the ground that these sections of the society have long been sufferers of exploitation at the hands of the non-tribals and the then government. Another objective of the constitution in granting special protective treatment to these sections of the society was to create situations for a rapid economic and political integration of the groups Scheduled Tribes and Scheduled Castes in the mainstream of the nation life. The constitution allows a plurality of culture but at the same time makes it obligatory on the part of different ethnic groups to adhere to the nation's economic and political life. The economic and political idioms of systems of the nation state, therefore, constitute the mainstream of national life. The tribal groups like several other ethnic groups of the country are free to maintain their socio-cultural identity— their cultural sense of belongingness; the government, surely, has nothing to do with his freedom of cultural pluralism. But in the field of economic and political activities the government is largely concerned with providing opportunities to the scheduled groups so that they can be assimilated in the mainstream. Here, government's interference is obligatory.

When the government and for that matter any other agency comes out with a programme of political and economic development of the scheduled groups, the prime objective is to seek involvement and participation of the members of these group in economic and political development of the scheduled groups. The prime objective is to seek involvement and participation of the members of these groups in economic and political development programme. The tribal groups in the process of social change have to be integrated in the mainstream of national life they have to come at par with other advanced ethnic groups of the country. In the field of economic development they have to raise their standard of living and become active partners in the market and competitive economy that we have accepted as a part of our economic development programme.

The planner's insistence on the assumption of compact tribal villages has gone in favour of the non-tribals. The proposed sub-plan should, therefore, be viewed on the assumption that the tribals live in scattered villages. This will provide a proper perspective to our emphasis on sectoral allocations.

The second assumption of the planners as evident from the past record is that the tribal society is homogenous to them, there is no role of status, power, and wealth in this society. Lord Baden Powell who talked about the Indian Village Republics has also propounds such a view of tribal society. There is a definite and subtle social and economic differentiation in the tribal society. There are big landholders, uneconomic landholders and landless labourers among tribals.

The third assumption, which has remained with the planners all through the plan period, is that in the sub-plan area there area no geographical or ecological imbalances to them. The tribals are inhabited in a similar or identical native land. The reality is far removed from this assumption. The whole tribal area may be divided into hilly and plain region. The tribals living in the hilly region are known as palvi, i.e. living in the pal- hills. The tribals of pal do not have material relations with the non-pal tribals. The difference in the regions is, therefore, both ecological and socio-cultural. The problems and needs of the people of hilly and forest regions are different from the people living in plains. For instance, for the tribals of hilly and forest region the importance of transport facilities and aforestation is greater than the tribals of the plains. For the plains the canal irrigation is a priority whereas for the hilly region there is a greater need for individual wells. The priorities have to be sorted out and determined according to the nature of the problem, of a particular category of region.

This strategy has also adopted for *Saora* tribals. Because of these interventions, lots of changes have taken place in their economy, polity, culture, social structure and ecology.

Basic Economic Activities of Tribals

The tribes of India have got a heterogeneous cultural pattern largely depending on ecological settings and ethnic environment. Different scholars have suggested a three-fold to eight-fold classification of tribal economy. Broadly the basic economic activities of the tribals may be classified (Chaudhuri, 1982) under the following heads:

1. Food-gathering including hunting and fishing
2. Pastoral
3. Shifting hill cultivation.
4. Cultivation
5. Handicrafts
6. Trade and Commerce, and
7. Labour-work—agricultural and industrial.

Broadly speaking, the tribes of north-eastern India follow shifting hill cultivation, those of central and western zones are mostly engaged in cultivation and the economy of a number of tribes of southern regions is based on food-gathering. The most interesting aspect of tribal economy is that, they rarely follow one occupation exclusively and among the subsidiary occupations, handicrafts, gathering and labour-work are followed by many.

An analysis of tribal economy clearly demonstrates the dependence of the tribals on land forest. The agriculturists depend on land directly while the daily labourers indirectly. Similarly, the food-gatherers, hunters and even those groups practising handicrafts depend on forest indirectly. The forest-dwellers, mostly the different tribal communities depend primarily on the minor forest products for their subsistence, while the forest-based industries depend on the commercially valuable wood. Besides the forest-dwellers, to a vast majority of the tribal population, forest is one of the main sources of subsistence for them. They collect food from the forest, use the timber to construct their houses or make different types of implements, collect fuel wood for cooking and different other objects from the forests required by them for a variety of purposes.

Traditional Saora Economy

The economic activity of the tribal consists of a variety of activities, and includes gathering, collecting of edible items from the forest, hunting, fishing, and pastoralism, and shifting cultivation and plain land cultivation.

In the past their dependence on gathering, hunting and shifting cultivation was more, because the environment was bounteous and there was no restriction on their use of the forest even a few decades ago. With the shrinkage of vegetation cover, degradation of forests, depletion of forest resources and progressive imposition of restrictions on forest, the Lanjia *Saoras* are very much hard pressed like other tribal groups with regard to gathering, hunting and practice of shifting cultivation. Due to the lack of alternative resources forest dwelling communities are being impoverished.

The traditional economy of the Lanjia *Saora* is of no difference from the other tribes. The principles of social and moral life of the Lanjia *Saora* are partially derived from the geography and ecology of the agency terrain where they live in small terrain, which are mostly on hill slopes.

Basis of Subsistence

The mainstay of their life is Sweden cultivation *(Bagoda or Angwal)* and terrace cultivation. The Sweden occupies a significant place in Lanjia *Saora's* socio-economic life.

Lanjia *Saoras* primarily constitutes a pre-farming society in which their economic life is blended into their kinship structure. The economy of Lanjia *Saoras* is less productive. The modes of production and exchange systems are simple. They are confined to small farming and usually produce rice, maize, pulses etc., essentially for their consumption than for the market. Hence, the motive for production is to ensure the smooth continuation of household system. The labour involved in the process of production is basically from the household. The Lanjia *Saoras* are familiar with gardening, cultivating the swidden, terrain and plain lands and grazing the domestic animals. Therefore, the economic system could be viewed as a traditional alternative strategy for survival. From swiddens they harvest 16 or more types of crops like paddy, oilseeds, vegetables, pulses, green leaves and a variety of fibers for home-use and the surplus, if any, is exchanged. The types of crop and the cropping-pattern are so associated with their economic life that the principal meals for six months are obtained from this source. It is the place of spending their time with family and lineage members, of negotiating with betrothal and of worshipping gods and spirits for their well being of the individual and the community.

Terraced Land

The first and fundamental need for tribal survival and cultural viability is continued habitation in and use of the traditional land areas. The tribe's economic resource management, socio-political organization, and belief systems are tightly woven into the particular land areas inhabited and used to obtain and produce all necessities. The members of a tribe are intimately familiar with locations of different game animals and their habits, as well as the vegetation within the traditional range. Maintaining the traditional land-based patterns of environmental adaptation is essential to the perpetuation of most aspects of the tribal way of life.

Terraced land cultivation is practiced for growing paddy by the transplantation method but only in limited areas. Normally this type of land is owned individually and only a single crop is raised traditionally. From the month of June the cultivation begins with the preparation of the seedbed through ploughing and leveling. The traditional method of manuring the paddy field is accomplished with the cattle and goat dung and oil cakes. L.K. Mahapatra (1972) has observed that notwithstanding the fact that terrace cultivation ensures perennially irrigated and permanent land to be utilised for a more dependable means of food supply with perhaps greater carrying capacity per acre of land compared to shifting cultivation. It is curious that the Lanjia *Saora* should persist in shifting cultivation. He adds that there are other occupational specialization reported from other sections of the Lanjia *Saora.* In the context of the availability of the two known alternatives, i.e., terrace cultivation and fruit orchardry practiced by the Lanjia *Saora* for some generations, he proposed a study of the underline physiographic, technological, economic and social factors to help understand the forces which have led to the perpetuation of shifting cultivation.

There is no denying the fact that the cereals, pulses and millers, which they grow on the hill-slopes, are not suitable for wet cultivation. The problem of changing from shifting to settled cultivation is intertwined with the problem of changing their food habits. Commenting on *Bagoda* (shifting cultivation), N. Patnaik observes that the *Saora,* like other tribal communities, are not entirely guided by rituals and superstition, nor are they wholly "pre-logical" and "irrational". Within the traditional world of their culture, there is the conservative mind, deeply interested in ceremonials in order to keep themselves in touch with the supernatural reality, which helps them to maintain the traditional ethical system. This is also to be found that the empirical and rational knowledge about land, soil, wind, animals, etc. are based on keen observation and experience. Both the domains, though structurally and functionally distinguishable, are integrated parts of their culture. It is the rough recognition of both beliefs and experience which makes their life meaningful and which appears to be fundamental in preparing programs designed for their economic and cultural development.

Table 7.1 Area Under Shifting Cultivation in Orissa and the Tribes Involved

District	*Area (Sq. Kms)*	*Tribles Involved*	*Poulalation (apporx.)*
Dhenkanal	1,167.00	Khond	4,410
Ganjam	2,980.11	Lanjia *Saora*	79,000
Kalahandi	1,323.50	Khond	33,000
Keonjhar	2,527.73	Pauri Bhuyan Hill Junang Bhuyan	28,000
Koraput	11,528.07	Hill Bonda, Hill Didoyee, Koya, Khond, Khond Paraja Gadaba, Laljia *Saora* Kutia Khond, Dongaria Khond	3,40,000
Phulbani	8,435.20	Khond	1,95,000
Sambalpur	6,852.44	Khond	12,002
Sundergarh	2,270.08	Fauri Bhuyan	15,000
Total	370,884.13		7,06,412

Source: Govt. of Orissa 1983.

The agriculture of the Lanjia *Saora* is imbued with their knowledge of the crops suitable for cultivation on the hill-slopes, the geographical conditions of the locality and the importance of appropriate, hard work organized with team spirit. The operation of clearing and burning the shrub is finished shortly before the beginning of rains, so that the ashes get mixed with the soil and add to its fertility. Similarly, they have fixed timings for hoeing the field, planting the crops and weeding them. In all these, they are guided by a clear knowledge of weather and season, plants and pests, soil and resources. The environmental condition, resources and agricultural operations are fitted in a routine conforming to one another.

They have conviction in the reliability of this knowledge. The social arrangements for property relations and its inheritance in Lanjia Society put a strong brake against the economic individualism. All landed property jointly owned are termed as *matam.* The landed property like swiddens and terrace fields are inherited and distributed jointly. As such there are 'Kheja matam' (swiddens and terrace fields inherited by the lineage members), 'Jojul matam' (common inheritance from the lineage of great and great grandfathers), 'Salal matam' (swiddens and terrace, fields are created by joint labour), Sagu Chasha (joint claim over the income from matams). The group solidarity and social cohesion of the Lanjia *Saora* society is further expressed in holding the property of 'Garajang Andruku' (Village ownership). The members of different lineage and religious groups living in the village have the claim of joint ownership and inheritance of the property of 'Garajang Andruku'. As an agricultural community, the property relations in the Lanjia society are the major concerns and have been variously expressed in their social life of lineage identity and village unity. There are reasons for standing against the conclusion that the lineage members of Lanjia society remember and recognise the ancestors till 5 or 6 generations- after which the social principles of lineage or 'Kheja' exogamy, thin out. The amorphous character of Lanjia *Saora* society is assumed from the fact that the Lanjia *Saora* migrates very often from one locality to another terrain in search of fresh swiddens. But the property relations and the equip distribution of income from the matam sources among all the lineage members, however they live in distant places, cement the band of Kheja or *Birinda* continuum. The social solidarity of Lanjia *Saora* is in no way weaker than the tribal people having centralized political organisation for regulation of their cultural and social autonomy. In addition to wet or terraced cultivation the *Saoras* practice shifting cultivation quite extensively. The shifting cultivation is known by the term Bagada Chasa among the *Saoras* and each and every family has a few patches of swidddens either in the hill slopes or at the hill tops yielding mainly minor millets and pulses.

Every *Saora* village has a well-defined boundary and its inhabitants carry on shifting cultivation in the hills located within the village boundary. Some hills are close to the village and others at a distance. Traditionally the hills are distributed on the basis of *Birinda* or extended families. Members of a particular *Birinda* used to have swiddens exclusively in a hill and no outsider was allowed to share the hill for shifting cultivation. An individual who has been cultivating a particular plot continues to own it as long as he is capable of cultivating it. Thus individual ownership of swiddens on hereditary basis is in vogue among the *Saoras*. With the increase in population and out migration there has been some change noticed in the distribution of swiddens in a particular hill. Today cases of outsiders cultivating hills belonging to a *Birinda* other than their own are not unknown.

Shifting Cultivation

Shifting cultivation starts with the work of forest clearing, which begins in November and continues till the end of December. In this work women cut down the undergrowth's and low thickets with the help of sickles and men cut down the trees and creepers by axes. After the trees are felled the women chop them into small pieces and pile them with combustible matter in several heaps in the swidens. The *Saoras* do not cut the trees flush with the ground. Their practice is to cut the trees high above the ground. It is done so because the coppice growth from the stools give them tender leaves which they eat by mixing with ragi or rice gruel, their staple food. During forest clearing they spare the trees called *Barada, Aranadh* and *Karki,* which also provide edible leaves. They also cause no damage to the creeper plants called *Samatila,* which also gives them edible leaves. The felled trees and creepers are left for three months to dry and in the month of March men set them on fire. No sacred fire is used for this purpose. Either a matchstick or a lighted branch of twig serves the purpose.

The Lanjia *Saoras* practice shifting cultivation *(angwal)* extensively over the hill slopes as an easy means of production. This type of cultivation, they believe, is highly suitable to their topography and soil type because of non-availability of wet land and labour. The methods and technique involved in the cultivation differ from village to village owing to the size of land holding, texture of soil, vegetation contours and humidity. It is found that about six varieties of cereals, five categories of pulses, four type of root crops including one variety of oil seed and five types of edible green leaves are grown during the process of cultivation (Mohapatra, 1990:38). Here it is evident that the consumption of all these crops ensures a kind of balanced diet to the tribal. Normally two plots of land are cultivated simultaneously to avoid any risk against crop failure as well as for sufficient yield. The same plot is cultivated for two to three years and then abandoned for about five years or more depending on the level of its recuperation. Bell dwelt at some length on shifting cultivation, called *Podu* or *Dongar*

Chash cultivation in the district of Koraput. He observed that the most primitive tribes were the worst addicts of this practice, as they inhabited the remotest parts of the district, control of the practice is especially difficult.

Here this researcher feels that, in one respect, the ecology encourages functions of shifting from place to place. A balance is struck between the cultural resources, the possibilities that the habitat affords for their production and the length of time that areas of land can be exploited. This is particularly true of the horticultural lands since they can no longer be used after three years of cropping and it becomes necessary to move on. The result is that there is as low migration of resources areas, chiefly of horticultural areas across the tribal territory. The land in cultivation moves further and further from any given village until a point of suspension is reached at which the walking and working distance of the gardens is too far from the village for effective or efficient exploitation. At this point a village or part of a village must move. Moving the villages' involves decision-making with respect to time, new location; and so on. Plainly, moving a village involves a community decision. A community institution for handling the decision making is necessary. Technologically speaking, the moving itself is not a community task and does not involve supervision and direction. Therefore, one would not expect the institution of decision-making to be a directive one, but a consultative one.

As a solid social and economic unit, the extended family does not go on forever. When a man's sons start to raise families of their own, the extended family gradually begins to segment. When the family head becomes too old to visit the gardens, control over them passes to his eldest son, or in the immaturity of the son, to the head's younger brother. The old man and his wife will usually move out of their large house into a smaller one, and his successor takes over his house. By slow process , the family head is thus divested of former status and power.

Economy and Ritual

However, mixed with all these activities based on their knowledge, a number of rituals are performed in a rigorous sequence and order, their observances being considered as much indispensable for a good crop as the usual agricultural activities. But they believe that if they perform only the ritual ceremonies and carry out the physical work in a perfunctory manner, the crops would suffer. Their experience shows that if they do not clear the slope properly, they get a poor yield. In such cases, they do not resort to rituals but to hard work, guided by knowledge. Their experience has also led them to believe that despite their efforts and forethought they get bad results in certain years. This is attributed to bad luck and to invisible forces and agencies, which thwart strenuous efforts. To control them they take recourse to propitiation of deities and performance of rituals.

Religion is heavy drain on the *Saora* economy. The sacrifice of animals, e.g., buffalo, pig and fowl prescribed for appeasing the deities on the occasion of disease or death or other adversity followed by feasting with food and drink is expensive and the *Saora* is not usually in a position to defraty the expenses in cash. He has necessarily to go to the local *Dom* (Christianised untouchable Hindu) to buy the animal on the promise to pay in kind at the cheapest rate at the time of next harvest. As the *Saora* is in distress, the *Dom* is able to drive a hard bargain, which is to his own profit, resulting in indebtedness of the *Saora* from which it is hard for him to recover. The ceremonies also make serious inroads into the working-time of the family or families.

Several ceremonies are performed in connection with shifting cultivation. A ceremony is performed on the day of sowing. Before the seeds are mixed and sown broadcast the village priests known as *buyya* and *kudan* worship the hill gods by offering them liquor and by sacrificing fowl and goat They worship the goddess Laxmi by offering liquor and by sacrificing fowl. A small ritual, which involves the offering of either a fowl or a goat to the hill god called *Barusim*, is observed towards the end of August after the *kanju* is harvested. The next ceremony follows before the *jana* is threshed and *kandua* is harvested. On this occasion fowls are offered to the hill-gods. The *Saoras* believe that if these ceremonies are performed they will get good crop from the swiddens.

On the credit side, religion is an incentive to produce more in agriculture so that it's demands can be met. It strengthens and boosts the *Saora*'s morale. They upheld very high morale of economics that the economic advantage at the expense of his lineage of community members is against the social norms. Violations of such norms, progressively reduces the individuals social well being and consequently the individual cannot make capital for happy life out of it.

Economic Cycle

The *Saoras* start sowing in the month of April by dibbling *kandula* (cajanus cajon-red gram) in the holes made in rows by means of a dibble. After the red grams have sprouted a mixture of seeds such as *Kagnu* (Bari-minor millet), *Jana* (Kambur-sorghum vulgare), *Ganga* (Ganga-minor millet), *Ghantia* (Kurei-minor millet), Jhudunga (Kandran—a kind of bean) and *Burubudi* (Soraimai—a kind of bean) is sown and the swidden is hoed to cover the seeds under and to get the ashes mixed up with the soil. Both men and women do the hoeing by means of a hoe. Hoe is a forked piece of wood tipped with a pointed iron. Weeding begins in June and is done by women with the help of knife (*Kadati*) made of iron. From the month of August to January both men and women guard the crops grown in the swiddens is against the inroad of wild animals such as wild bear, Percupine and jungle fowl. For this purpose they erect temporary field huts in some convenient position on the swiddens and spend most of their time in these places watching the crops and scaring away the animals and birds by the beat of drums. At night one can see the hillside dotted with fires and hear the sweet music of the flutes and the thrum of the drums.

In August crops like *Kangu*, small *Ganga* is harvested. The Saoras harvest *Kangu* by removing the ears of the crop with a knife and carry them home where they thresh them , with their feet. But they cut the *Ganga* plants from above the ground and thresh them with the help of bullocks. In November crops like *Ganga*, *Ghantia*, *Butubudi* and *Jhudanga* are harvested. They remove the ears of *Ghantia* with the help of a knife and thresh them by beating the ears with a stick. *Burubudi* and *Jhudunga* are plucked by hand and then dried to take out the seeds by beating them with a stick. *Jana* and *Kandula* plants serve as stalks for the creeper plants of *Burubudi* and *Jhudunga*, *Jana* is harvested in the month of December. The *Saoras* dry them in the threshing floor and thresh them by beating with a stick. In January *kandula* is harvested by pulling the pods off the shrubs into baskets and threshed with sticks.

One of the important cash crops of the *Saoras* is turmeric and ginger which is grown in swiddens. It takes two years to be harvested and does not interfere with the growth of other crops. It grows well in the soil, which is sufficiently loosened by hoeing. A swidden is cultivated for two or three years after which it is left fallow for a period of 6 to 8 years. The *Saoras* do not grow a kind of crops in all these years. For example, they choose to grow *burubudi* and *Jhudunga* in preference to *ghantia* in the first year. Similarly they do not grow all crops in equal quantity in all the years. For instance *Jana* and *Kandula* are not grown in the same extent. It is the experience of the Saoras that both of them hinder each other's growth. That is why one is grown more extensively than the other in a year is and the extent of cultivation of these crops is reversed next year.

Storing Seeds

The *Saoras* follow different methods for storing different types of seeds. They store the seeds of *burubudi* and *jhudunga* in a new earthen vessel, whose mouth is tied with a piece of cloth tightly so that no insect does any harm to the seeds. But they store the seeds of *kangu*, *ganga*, *jana* and *kandula* in bamboo baskets, which are sealed with straw plastered with mud.

Methods of Irrigation

Saoras of Parlakhemundi sub-division in particular, are the best-terraced cultivators. Terraced fields in which water flows throughout the year are locally called as *Sarroba* and are exclusively meant for paddy cultivation. The upper terraces, which are dry, are locally called as *Jvanum* and used for cultivating *Ragi* (elusing corocana) *Biri* (Phaseolus mungo) and *Kulthi* (dolichos biflorus).

The terraces are built right up to the beds of the hill streams and extend many hundreds of feet from the depth of the valleys to the hill slopes and in some places rising up to the hilltops. The terraces are works of great engineering skill. The platform of each terrace is flat throughout and the fail of each terrace is stone packed. The construction of the terraces is so ingeniously and skillfully done that no soil is carried down with the water that flows from the higher terraces to the lower.

The water management is equally skilful. The flow of water from one terrace to the other is controlled by channels and waterways, which are provided in the ridges of the terraces. There is another way of facilitating flow of water from higher terraces to the lower ones. Two or three pits are packed with boulders. The water flows into these pits and from there through the boulder trickles to the terraces down below. The water management is so skillful that it avoids flooding of the terraced fields. In many places water trickles level to level through stone fencing and ultimately flows down into the lands in the plains. But in no case either the soil is carried over with water from the terraced fields or any damage is caused to the stone walls. All *Saora* families do not possess terraced land. Such terraced fields are privately owned and handed down from father to sons. They are valuable assets to the *Saora* and sometimes mortgaged to local moneylenders.

As water is available throughout the year paddy is the only crop grown in terraced fields. Two crops are harvested in a year. Two varieties of paddies are grown in the terraced field, the short duration variety called

Ambadhan during summer season and long duration variety called *Badadhan* during Kharif. The different varieties of paddy grown in the terraced fields are *Ranga dhan, Jaipa dhan, Sanagadh dhan, Katanoda dhan, Kandula dhan* and *Amba dhan* . Some progressive farmers among the *Saoras* have taken to cultivation of high yielding varieties of paddy such as *Jaya* and *Ratna* and also apply chemical fertilizers and pesticides, which are supplied to them by the developmental agencies. As all people do not have terraced fields, large-scale adoption of improved agricultural practices is not possible at present.

Paddy is grown by transplanting method. The agricultural operations connected with terraced fields start with the preparation of seed bed in June which is followed by preparation of the fields with the help of bullock-driven plough and leveler for transplantation in July, weeding in September and harvesting in November-December in case of long duration variety in kharif season.

Again they start ploughing after the harvesting is over in November-December. Thereafter they apply cow-dung manure and plough it and puddle the soil thoroughly and transplant the seeding in family and after sometime take up weeding and regulate flow of water through irrigated channels. Harvesting is the last activity of the series of agricultural operations carried out in the terraced fields. Threshing of paddy is done in the courtyard in front of one's own house. *Ragi* is cultivated in dry fields. No manure is applied in these fields. The transplantation of *ragi* starts after the first shower of rains and harvesting in the months of July and October respectively.

Division of Labour

As observed in the agricultural activities there is a division of labour based on sex. Among them women who seem to be more hard working are found busy continuously throughout the whole day. Apart from vital task of child rearing, women have to do all the household chores such as fetching water, cleaning the house and utensils, cooking and carrying the food for the male members working in the field. In addition to these works collection of minor forest produces is the main job of the women. In shifting cultivation, women do several items of work like debasing, dibbling, hoeing, weeding, watching the crops, harvesting, winnowing and storing while the men cut the big trees, fire the felled trees and watch the crops and occasionally assist women in other items of wofk. In wet cultivation both men and women drive plough. In addition to this, women carry on the important task of transplanting, weeding, reaping, harvesting and storing the produce from the terraced cultivation. In the disposal of agricultural and forest produce women play important role by carrying the products to the weekly markets for sale.

Domestic Animals

The *Saoras* domesticate cattle, buffalo, pig, poultry and duck. The cows, bullocks and buffaloes are used as draught-animal and in payment of bride price. On ritual occasions they serve as sacrificial animals. The Saoras of advanced section take milk and on festive occasion pigs, fowls and ducks are killed for meat.

The *Saoras* mostly perform agricultural activities on a cooperative basis. According to this system which is called *Ansir* the villagers works on one another's land on the basis of reciprocity and mutuality of obligation. No payment of wage is involved to the workers by the person on whose land they work. This is being replaced gradually by payment of wage in cash under the impact of monetized economy. A sense of possessiveness and acquisitiveness has developed in some farmers and in their hand wealth in the forms of land and money has accumulated. These affluent *Saoras* manage their agriculture by employing hired labour.

Minor Forest Produces

In areas covered with forest the Saoras collect minor forest produce of food, fodder and for subsidiary income. They collect different varieties of green leaves, roots, tubers, fruits and flowers for consumption, *karanja* and other seeds for extracting oil, fuel wood, small timbers and fibers for construction and repairing of houses and woods for fashioning agricultural implements and household articles. They carry on hunting and collect medicinal herbs during their leisure hours. But with the shrinkage and desiccation of forest, hunting and food gathering pursuits are not of as much importance as they were before.

Dependency on Market

They sell different varieties of agricultural and forest produces for cash in the local weekly markets and purchase daily necessities like salt, chilly, tobacco, dried fish, etc. from the visiting peddlers mainly through barter. In these transactions the *Saoras* are always loser. The local traders and merchants take advantage of the illiteracy and ignorance of the *Saoras* and exploit them in such economic transaction by weights and measures and paying them a low price for their goods. With the establishment of

LAMPS in many areas which procures the produce the *Saoras* from payment of a reasonable price and supply them with their daily necessities at a fair price the Saoras have got some relief. But the unfair practices of the itinerant traders and peddler are still continuing in the tribal areas.

Change and Contradictions

When a society with a food-gathering economy has domesticated its plants and animals and has thereby increased its food surplus potential, the requirements of the new food producing technology and the ensuing population growth pose critical problems. The need for division and specialization of labour, social controls, and distribution of the surplus leads to adaptive changes in the cultural patterns. Or if a society (for whatever reasons) shifts from matrilocal to patrilocal residence, then again there are adaptive changes in a whole range of cultural patterns, as Murdock (1949) has demonstrated. The *Saora* economic activity is consisting of variety of activities, and includes gathering, collecting of edible items from forest, hunting, fishing, pastorals, shifting cultivation and plain land cultivation. In the past their dependence on gathering, hunting and shifting cultivation was more, because the environment was bounteous and there was no restriction on their use of the forests, even few decades ago.

Tribal life has been evolving around the forest since ages. Though several waves of change have been experienced from time to time, forest continues to be the main source of life of the tribals. In Table 7.2 it is stated that, in the whole Rayagada district, Gunupur block has 7,077 hectares of forestland and many hectares cultivable land. The economic activities of the district can be seen from the Table 7.2 where it has mixed picture of both- agriculture and dependency on forest. To know about the dependency of forest of *Saora* tribes a question was asked that 'is forest their main source of living'. It has given in Table 7.3. In response to this 132 tribals out of 135 young, 61 out of 63 middle and 32 out of 32 old said 'yes'. This is 97.83 per cent.

Religion wise break up shows that 105 out of 109 Hindus and 120 out of 121 non-Hindus said 'yes'. This is 98 per cent. It is where as only 4 Hindus and 1 non-Hindus said no. It shows that forest is the principal source of living for the forest dwelling tribes like *Saora*. Further occupational break up also implies the similar trend as 155 out of 158 agricultural group and 70 out of 72 non-agricultural group said 'yes' whereas only 3 agricultural group and 2 non-agricultural group respondent

Table 7.2 Block Wise Land Utilisation Pattern of the District, Rayagada (Area in Hectares)

Sl. No	*Year/ Block*	*Forest Area*	*Miscellaneous tree crops and groves not included in net area shown*	*Permanent pasture and grazing lands*	*Culturable other waste*	*Land put to non-Agricultural uses*	*Barren and uncultivable land*	*Current fallows*	*Other fallows*	*Net area Shown*
1	2	3	4	5	6	7	8	9	10	11
	1992-93	1,15,911	3,221	7,275	10,649	24,937	1,60,463	44,618	19,730	1,15,187
	1993-94	1,23,017	2,809	8,745	8,397	26,203	1,40,031	44,434	18,920	1,29,433
	1994-95	1,00,218	3,898	8,963	11,912	25,140	1,74,740	42,307	15,150	1,20,745
	1994-95—									
1.	Rayagada	12169	243	1575	1491	2918	18763	3392	1821	13435
2.	Kasipur	2043	213	1188	692	4297	5501	10574	4650	20255
3.	Kalyansingpur	7669	383	646	659	2139	13224	2902	1253	12233
4.	Kolnara	5588	604	643	1833	2352	15300	2299	1110	12035
5.	Ramanguda	4973	574	753	2472	2139	9641	3851	2403	6366
6.	Gunupur	7077	742	493	233	3552	24208	3065	285	10490
7.	Padampur	8160	216	329	567	1135	15235	1521	488	7247
8.	Gudari	9428	370	423	1421	2036	8158	1899	1441	4990
9.	Muniguda	12233	263	962	1298	1840	25167	5680	688	15900
10.	Chandrapur	14715	188	1304	915	1201	12325	1740	256	6831
11.	Bisam-Cuttack	16163	199	647	341	1531	27218	5384	755	10963

Source : District Statistical Handbook, Rayagada, 1995

said 'no'. Hence it implies that not only agricultural workers but non-agricultural workers also consider forest as the main source of living. In the study of K. Sujatha mentioned that, 'more than 90 per cent of Scheduled Tribe workers are engaged in the primarily sector or sector of economy related to the exploitation of the natural resources' (2000: 3).

It has been pretty clear that forest is the main source of living of the tribals. Hence they are heavily dependent on forest. It is evident from this study that basically the tribal people use forest for two main reasons. First one being cultivation, i.e., shifting cultivation, tarraced land, swidden farming and the second is to use the minor forest produces for selling, besides using the forest produces for medicinal and other purposes. (see Table 7.4).

Agewise distribution shows that out of 135 young, 46 depending on forest because of 'shifting cultivation' 58 because of 'minor forest produces' 18 for 'both shifting cultivation and minor forest produces' where as only 13 depends on forest for 'any other' purposes. Out of 63 middle age responses 17,22,15 and 9 are respectively for 'shifting cultivation', minor forest produces, and for 'any other' uses as well. Similarly, out of 32 older people 7,4,21 and 0 are respectively for the above purposes. The above trend shows that less then 10 per cent of the total respondents are depending on forest for any other purposes as mentioned in Table 7.4. Religionwise distribution reflects that out of 109 Hindus , 34, 39, 26 and 10, and out of 121 non-Hindu 36, 45, 28 and 12 are respectively for 'cultivation', 'minor forest produces' both for 'shifting cultivation and minor forest produces' and 'any other' purposes. Therefore, it implies that it is not religion but the living condition, pattern and its socio-culture environment, which induces the tribals to depend on forest. Again occupational distribution highlights that out of 158 agriculture workers 60 depend on forest for 'minor forest produces' followed by 50 on 'shifting cultivation' and the similar trend is shown in the non-agriculture workers category where 24 depends on forest for 'minor forest produces' followed by 20 for 'shifting cultivation' out of 72 respondents.

Tribal lands include not only areas, which are obviously inhabited at a given time, but also others that may be used or occupied only intermittently in supra annual cycles. Hunter-gatherers—the Kalahari in Southern Africa and Australian Bushmen, for example, range over wide areas and exploit them systematically' (Maybury-Lewis, 1968). Pastoralists, such as the Masai in Kenya and Tanzania, the Fulani in Nigeria, the Bedouins of Cyrenaica in north-eastern Libya, the Shah Saran of Iran, and the Gujjars

Table 7.3 Forest as Main Source of Living

Variables	*Age*								*Religion*						*Occupation*					
Response	*Young*		*Middle*		*Old*		*Total*		*Hindu*		*Non-Hindu*		*Total*		*Agriculture*		*Non-Agriculture*		*Total*	
	F	%	F	%	F	%	F	%	F	%	F	%	F	%	F	%	F	%	F	%
Yes	132	97.78	61	96.83	32	100	225	98	105	96.33	120	99.17	225	98	155	98.1	70	97.22	225	98
No	3	2.222	2	3.175	0	0	5	2.2	4	3.67	1	0.826	5	2.0	3	1.899	2	2.778	5	2.2
Can't say	0	0	0	0	0	0	0	0	0	0	0	0	0	0	0	0	0	0	0	0
Total	135	100	63	100	32	100	230	100	109	100	121	100	230	100	158	100	72	100	230	100

Table 7.4 Cause of Dependency on Forest

Variables		*Age*								*Religion*						*Occupation*					
Response		*Young*		*Middle*		*Old*		*Total*		*Hindu*		*Non-Hindu*		*Total*		*Agriculture*		*Non-Agriculture*		*Total*	
		F	%	F	%	F	%	F	%	F	%	F	%	F	%	F	%	F	%	F	%
(a)	Shifting cultivation	46	34.07	17	26.98	7	21.88	70	30	34	26.61	36	33.06	70	30	50	31.65	20	27.78	70	30
(b)	Minor forest products	58	42.96	22	34.92	4	12.5	84	37	39	34.86	45	40.5	84	37	60	37.97	24	33.33	84	37
(c)	A & B both	18	13.33	15	23.81	21	65.63	54	23	26	26.61	28	12.4	54	23	32	20.25	22	30.56	54	23
(d)	Any other	13	9.63	9	14.29	0	0	22	10	10	11.93	12	14.05	22	10	16	10.13	6	8.333	22	10
Total		135	100	63	100	32	100	230	100	109	100	121	100	230	100	158	100	72	100	230	100

of north-western India, require large areas of land which may seem to the casual visitor to be unoccupied. Shifting agriculturists, like the Kalinga of the Philippines, also leave large fallow areas to recuperate before replanting.

To the extent that tribal groups inhabit marginal areas, much larger land areas may be required to support the population than would be the case in more fertile regions. When commons shifting-agriculture methods are used, new areas are needed for clearance every two to five years when weeds encroach and yield decline. This method of tropical forestland use does not damage the environment when practiced by and appropriate number of people, since exhausted soils have time to recuperate while other tracts are planted. The isolation and small size of the cleared areas avoid excessive erosion and acceleratere growth of forest. Tribal societies practicing such systems have traditionally developed population control, which enables the society to stay within the techno-environmental carrying capacity of the land. However, to establish a direct link between *Saora* economy and forest it has been further explored to find out 'how they use the forest produces'; whether they use it for personal consumption or sell it in the market or for both.

In Table 7.5 the age wise distribution about 'uses of forest produces' shows that 47.39 per cent for 'personal use' and 17.83 per cent 'for selling' the minor forest produces were as 34.78 per cent uses the products for both personal use and selling. Religion and occupational break up does not show any remarkable difference so far as the uses of the minor forest produces. Occupationwise break up shows out of 158 agriculture worker 74 goes for 'personal use', 30 'for selling' and 54 for 'both' selling and personal use. It shows that for *Saoras* forest is very-very important. Likewise out of 72 tribals involves in non-agricultural practices 35 for 'personal use', 11 'for selling', 27 for 'both'. The analysis suggest say that forest is important source of living the *Saora*.

From above tables it is pertinent that for *Saora* tribes forest is as essential as it was before. 'Finney, working in New Guinea, set out to discover the basis of indigenous motivation to enter cash cropping and "modern" commercial ventures. She concludes that differences in response in various parts of New Guinea are best explained by varying opportunity costs. Ward, similarly studying the effects on the response of indigenees to new opportunities presented by the construction of the Rigo Road into Port Moresby from the back country, details the larger than expected response by rural people to the new opportunities for commercial sale. (Cited from Kearney, 1975: 278).

Table 7.5 Use of Forest Products

Variables	*Age*								*Religion*						*Occupation*					
Response	*Young*		*Middle*		*Old*		*Total*		*Hindu*		*Non-Hindu*		*Total*		*Agriculture*		*Non-Agriculture*		*Total*	
	F	%	F	%	F	%	F	%	F	%	F	%	F	%	F	%	F	%	F	%
(a) Personal Use	51	37.78	33	52.88	25	78.13	109	47	54	49.54	55	45.45	109	47	74	46.84	35	48.61	109	47
(b) For selling	20	14.81	16	25.4	5	15.63	41	18	20	18.35	21	17.36	41	18	30	18.99	11	15.28	41	18
(c) Both A & B	64	47.41	14	22.22	2	6.25	80	35	35	32.11	45	37.19	80	35	54	34.18	26	36.11	80	35
(d) Can't say	0	0	0	0	0	0	0	0	0	0	0	0	0	0	0	0	0	0	0	0
Total	135	100	63	100	32	100	230	100	109	100	121	100	230	100	158	100	72	100	230	100

George Pfeffer and D.K. Behera in their study state that, 'a large number of tribals eke out through collection of non-timber forest produces like sal and kendu leaves: Mahua flowers, Sal seeds; fruits, resins, lac. Tassar cocoons, etc. In Bihar, Orissa, M.P. and Himachal Pradesh, it has been noted that more than 80 per cent of the forest dweller collect/get 25 per cent to 50 per cent of their food from forests. Collection of honey and other non-timber forest produces are important sources of income for the tribals. But they are always ill paid and the market is practically controlled by the businessmen' (1997:237).

Decrease Forest Resources

The tribal economy has undergone tremendous changes in due course of time. The changes were due to various measures undertaken by the government from time to time as a result of which the tribal society has lost its original substance to a great extent The changes occurred could be seen in different spheres of tribal life, be it social, political, economic, cultural and ecological as well. The cause of the changes could be subscribed to two important reasons. First, substantial reduction in forest covers and second, the tribal people's hesitation to pursue their traditional occupation. It is viewed that there is an immense decline of forest resources. To find out the decrease of forest resources a number of questions have been asked and analyzed below.

A question has asked, that 'are tribals getting the same amount of forest produces as of their ancestors'. In Table 7.6 it is shown that out of 135 young tribals 131 say 'yes', out of 63 middle-aged tribals 58 yes, 32 old tribal say yes. Likewise religion and occupation break up also shows the result of 95 per cent of depletion of forest resources. It is realized by almost all the tribal community that there is a danger of decrease of forest resources.

It is obvious to find out now why forest has decreased. This has been stated in Table 7.7 that reduction in the forest cover has been phenomenal during last 100 years. The tribals, however, attribute three important factors responsible for the shrinking forest cover. 'Population growth' has played a pivotal role closely followed by 'lack of rain' and 'deforestation'. In age distribution, out of 230, 88 for 'population growth' and 62 for 'lack of rain', 45 for 'deforestation'. It shows that the tribals have felt the pressure of population growth and the rainfall have not only been erratic but abysmally low. The cause of the scanty rainfall may be further subscribed to deforestation. The above response about the cause of deforestation is equally felt in religion and occupational break ups.

Table 7.6 Forest Resources have Decreased

Variables	*Age*								*Religion*						*Occupation*					
Response	*Young*		*Middle*		*Old*		*Total*		*Hindu*		*Non-Hindu*		*Total*		*Agriculture*		*Non-Agriculture*		*Total*	
	F	%	F	%	F	%	F	%	F	%	F	%	F	%	F	%	F	%	F	%
Yes	131	97.04	58	92.06	32	100	221	96.09	107	98.17	114	94.21	221	96.09	154	97.47	67	93.06	221	96.09
No	1	0.741	4	6.349	0	0	5	2.174	2	1.835	3	1.479	5	2.174	1	0.633	4	5.556	5	2.174
Can't say	3	2.222	1	1.587	0	0	4	1.739	0	0	4	3.306	4	1.739	3	1.899	1	1.389	4	1.739
Total	135	100	63	100	32	100	230	100	109	100	121	100	230	100	158	100	72	100	230	100

The Effects of Depletion of Forest on *Saoras*

It is very clear from the above-mentioned result that forest has depleted to a great extent. Population growth, deforestation and lack of rain are the main causes. Now it is pertinent and interesting to see how this has affected to tribals. Decline in forest cover is directly proportional with availability of forest produces. As the total forest cover reduces so also reduces the forest produces which have affected the tribals in one way or the other. The availability of forest produces is reduced to such a level that the response in every variables is more than 97 per cent (Table 7.8). Therefore, it is evident that irrespective of the different age groups, religions and occupations the answer is loud and clear that the tribals have been significantly affected by the reduction of the forest produces.

The shrinking forest cover and the resultant decrease in the forest produces push the tribals to work as labourers. Their traditional occupation or pattern of living as cultivation, patoralism, hunting etc. have decline steadily. The response to the question about 'the way tribals managing their life after the substantial reduction in forest produces'; is equivocal irrespective of age, religion and occupation. Around 65 per cent respondents have said to be engaged in 'labour work' and around 21 per cent are 'managing by adjustment'. A little less than 10 per cent have said to be 'taking loans' to manage themselves by pursuing small business (Table 7.9).

Since forest has depleted and people are managing with labour work or taking loan etc, this has caused migration. In this connection a question was asked to know 'how far deforestation is responsible for migration'. Table 7.10 shows that out of 135 young 91 say 'yes', 34 'no' and 10 can not say. Likewise out of 63 middle aged tribal 50 say 'yes' and out of 32 old 17 say 'yes' and 15 say 'no'. The conception of middle and old is lesser important than the young. Young result shows it is more because of forest depletion. But for old it may not be the cause rather young guys are much more interested to go and see new places. Likewise religion break up shows 77 Hindus say 'yes' (71 per cent0, 28 'no' (26 per cent) out of 109 Hindus. Among 121 non-Hindus 81 says 'yes', (61 per cent), 31 'no' (26 per cent) and 9 can not say. From above result the close relation between migration and deforestation is evident.

Among 158 agriculture worker 105, (66 per cent) say 'yes' and 43 'no' (27 per cent). Among non-agriculture worker 53 say 'yes' (74 per cent), 16 'no' (22 per cent). It is viewed that agriculture workers are more vulnerable as they principally depend on forest. However, migration is more because of deforestation. But it is not that pertinent among non-

Table 7.7 Why Forest has Decreased

Variables		Age								Religion						Occupation					
Response		Young		Middle		Old		Total		Hindu		Non-Hindu		Total		Agriculture		Non-Agriculture		Total	
		F	%	F	%	F	%	F	%	F	%	F	%	F	%	F	%	F	%	F	%
(a)	Deforest-ation	34	25	7	11	4	13	45	20	17	16	28	23	45	20	31	20	14	19	45	20
(b)	Population growth	51	38	21	33	16	50	88	38	50	46	38	31	88	38	64	41	24	33	88	38
(c)	Lack of rain	32	24	21	33	9	28	62	27	28	26	34	28	62	27	45	28	17	24	62	27
(d)	A & B both	10	7.4	9	14	1	3.1	20	8.7	8	7.3	12	9.9	20	8.7	9	5.7	11	15	20	8.7
(e)	A & C both	8	5.9	5	7.9	2	6.3	15	6.5	6	5.5	9	7.4	15	6.5	9	5.7	6	8.3	15	6.5
	Total	135	100	63	100	32	100	230	100	109	100	121	100	230	100	158	100	72	100	230	100

agricultural worker group. Since the above table shows migration is more significant as the cause may go beyond from deforestation The causes of migration of the tribals are manifold. However, principal among them is to obtain more wages as shown in Table 7.11. Age distribution shows that 107 out of 230 have said to get 'more wage', followed by 51 for 'regular work', 41 'to repay loan' and 31 for 'food problems'. Similarly, in religion break up 92 refers to 'more wage', 65 for 'regular work', 53 'to repay loan' and 20 for 'food problem' and a similar trend is clear in occupational structure also.

The above classification shows how the tribals were plagued by multiple problems to sustain their life. Simultaneously it also underlies the inadequate development measures taken by the government for the welfare of the forest dwelling communities.

Tribal Dependency on Forest Today

Considering the rate at which the forest covers is shrinking it may not be far away when there would be no forest cover at all. Tribal life and forest is knitted in such a way that without forest, life for the tribals become impossible. The response in this regard is loud and clear. The religion, age and occupational break up shows that more than 97 per cent said " no" to the question 'is life possible without forest' (Table 7.12). Hence forest appears to be indispensable for the survival of the tribals. As from Table 7.12 it is clear that 'life is just impossible' for tribals without forest. A categorical question was asked ' what will happen if jungles are destroyed'. Irrespective of age, religion and occupa.ion the overall respond is overwhelming. Only few tribels are not able to answer this question otherwise out of 135 young 45, 38 and 35 all say 'ecology', 'economy' or 'both' will vanish. Among 63 middle 15, 20 and 10 say this respectively. Same ways 109 Hindu break up shows 26, 42 and 21 'ecology', ;economy' and 'both will disturb. Among Christian 41, 33, and 24 are having the same opinion. Among agricultural and non-agricultural workers also the response is promising (Table 7.13). It is clear from this above result that apart from economy tribals also considered jungle from ecological point of view.

The Weekly Market

The weekly markets play an important part in the tribal economy because these tribal markets serve as the main channels through which the local products and the imported goods are distributed. The sociological importance of the tribal markets cannot be ignored because it shows "the relation between castes, elements of space and the scale of specific

Table 7.8 Decrease of Forest Products has Affected Tribals

Variables	*Age*								*Religion*						*Occupation*					
Response	*Young*		*Middle*		*Old*		*Total*		*Hindu*		*Non-Hindu*		*Total*		*Agriculture*		*Non-Agriculture*		*Total*	
	F	%	F	%	F	%	F	%	F	%	F	%	F	%	F	%	F	%	F	%
Yes	132	98	62	98	28	88	222	97	105	96	117	97	222	97	151	96	71	99	222	97
No	2	1.5	1	1.6	4	13	7	3	3	2.8	4	3.3	7	3	6	3.8	1	1.4	7	3
Can't Say	1	0.7	0	0	0	0	1	0.4	1	0.9	0	0	1	0.4	1	0.6	0	0	1	0.4
Total	135	100	63	100	32	100	230	100	109	100	121	100	230	100	158	100	72	100	230	100

Table 7.9 How Tribals Manage After the Substantial Depletion of Forest Resources

Variables	*Age*								*Religion*						*Occupation*					
Response	*Young*		*Middle*		*Old*		*Total*		*Hindu*		*Non-Hindu*		*Total*		*Agriculture*		*Non-Agriculture*		*Total*	
	F	%	F	%	F	%	F	%	F	%	F	%	F	%	F	%	F	%	F	%
Doing Labour Work	88	65.18	41	65.07	21	65.62	150	65.21	71	65.13	78	64.46	149	64.78	104	65.82	47	65.27	151	65.65
Managining by Adjustment	28	20.74	12	19.04	6	18.75	46	20	22	20.18	24	19.83	46	20	32	20.25	15	20.83	47	20.43
Taking Loan	14	10.37	07	11.11	3	9.37	24	10.43	11	10.09	12	9.91	23	10	15	9.49	6	8.33	21	20.43
Can't Say	05	3.70	03	4.76	2	6.25	10	4.34	05	4.58	7	5.78	12	5.21	07	4.43	4	5.5	11	4.78
Total	135	100	63	100	32	100	230	100	109	100	121	100	230	100	158	100	72	100	230	100

Table 7.10 Destruction of Forest is Causing Migration

Variables	Age								Religion						Occupation					
Response	Young		Middle		Old		Total		Hindu		Non-Hindu		Total		Agriculture		Non-Agriculture		Total	
	F	%	F	%	F	%	F	%	F	%	F	%	F	%	F	%	F	%	F	%
Yes	91	67	50	79	17	53	158	69	77	71	81	67	158	69	105	66	53	74	158	69
No	34	25	10	16	15	47	59	26	28	26	31	26	59	26	43	27	16	22	59	26
Can't Say	10	7.4	3	4.8	0	0	13	5.7	4	3.7	9	7.4	13	5.7	10	6.3	3	4.2	13	5.7
Total	135	100	63	100	32	100	230	100	109	100	121	100	230	100	158	100	72	100	230	100

Table 7.11 Cause of Migration

Variables	*Age*								*Religion*						*Occupation*					
Response	*Young*		*Middle*		*Old*		*Total*		*Hindu*		*Non-Hindu*		*Total*		*Agriculture*		*Non-Agriculture*		*Total*	
	F	%	F	%	F	%	F	%	F	%	F	%	F	%	F	%	F	%	F	%
Regular work	25	19	17	27	9	28	51	22	33	30	18	15	51	22	31	20	20	28	51	22
More wage	65	48	29	46	13	41	107	47	46	42	61	50	107	47	73	46	34	47	107	47
To repay loan	26	19	10	16	5	16	41	18	17	16	24	20	41	18	29	18	12	17	41	18
Food problem	19	14	7	11	5	16	21	13	13	12	18	15	31	13	25	16	6	8.3	31	13
Total	135	100	63	100	32	100	230	100	109	100	121	100	230	100	158	100	72	100	230	100

Table 7.12 Is Life Possible Without Forest ?

Variables	*Age*								*Religion*						*Occupation*					
Response	*Young*		*Middle*		*Old*		*Total*		*Hindu*		*Non-Hindu*		*Total*		*Agriculture*		*Non-Agriculture*		*Total*	
	F	%	F	%	F	%	F	%	F	%	F	%	F	%	F	%	F	%	F	%
Yes	2	1.5	3	4.8	0	0	5	2	5	4.6	0	0	5	2	3	1.9	2	2.8	5	2
No	132	98	58	92	32	100	222	97	101	93	121	100	222	97	154	97	68	94	222	97
Can't Say	1	0.7	2	3.2	0	0	3	1	3	2.8	0	0	3	1	1	0.6	2	2.8	3	1
Total	135	100	63	100	32	100	230	100	109	100	121	100	230	100	158	100	72	100	230	100

Table 7.13 What will Happen if Jungles are Completely Destroyed?

Variables		*Age*								*Religion*						*Occupation*					
Response		*Young*		*Middle*		*Old*		*Total*		*Hindu*		*Non-Hindu*		*Total*		*Agriculture*		*Non-Agriculture*		*Total*	
		F	%	F	%	F	%	F	%	F	%	F	%	F	%	F	%	F	%	F	%
(a)	Economy will be Disturbed	38	28.14	15	23.80	9	28.12	62	26.95	26	23.85	41	33.88	67	29.13	47	29.74	20	27.77	67	29.13
(b)	Ecology will be Disturbed	35	25.92	20	31.74	8	25	63	27.39	42	38.53	33	27.27	75	32.60	58	36.70	20	27.77	78	33.91
(c)	Both a and b	45	33.33	10	15.87	11	34.37	66	28.69	21	19.26	24	19.83	45	19.56	20	12.65	17	23.61	37	16.08
(d)	Can't Say	17	12.59	18	28.57	4	12.5	39	16.95	20	18.34	23	19	43	18.69	33	20.88	15	20.83	48	20.86
(d)	Total	135	100	63	100	32	100	230	100	109	100	121	100	230	100	158	100	72	100	230	100

commodities". Thus keeping in view of its sociological importance a weekly market of Puttasinghi, in *Saora* land was studied during the fieldwork. Besides this market, few other tribal markets like Jalatara and Gunupur (in Gunupur town) were also visited in order to have a fair idea about the tribal markets in general and to support the data.

The market site of Puttasinghi is near the Puttasinghi police station and high school and has been named after the village Putta that is the main market of this study area. It is connected in *katcha* road to various villages of this the region. Thus, in order to reach the market village of Putta from other villages one has to cover 10 to 15 km approximately. In this connection, it was observed that most of the buyers and sellers of Tarbel, Lade areas used to come to attend the Puttasinghi market by terrain of the hills. The weekly market in the Puttasinghi village is operated on every Monday; it start from about 6 a.m. and continues till 2 p.m. The areas of the Puttasinghi village market approximately a little less than acre in area. It was reported that this market was started 20 years back and since then it is being held regularly.

Table 7.14 Composition of the Market in Saora Land

Caste/ Tribe	*Commodities*	*No of Stall*	*No. of Seller*		*Total*
			Male	*Female*	
Kumuti	Cloths	8	8	—	8
Saora	Local Vegetables	23	6	17	23
Doms	Earthen pot	2	2	—	2
Saora	Baskets	3	3	—	3
Saora	Forest Produces	8	2	6	8
Kumuti	Tea Stall*	1	3	—	3
Brahmin	Pan Shop*	2	2	—	2
Saora	Tea Stall*	2	2	2	4
Dom	Saloon*	1	1	—	1
Saora	Iron etc	2	2	—	2
Saora	Ready made Garments	3	3	—	3
Sundhi	Medical Shop*	2	2	—	2
Kapu Reddy	Dry Fish	1	1	—	1
Kumuti	Almunium utensils	2	2	—	2
	Total	60	37	25	64

* Permanent Shops

In addition to the Puttsinghi market the other weekly markets are also visited, though less frequently, by the other villagers including *Saoras*, both as purchasers and sellers, On every Saturday a market is operated at Jalatara nearly at a distance of about six miles away from Puttasinghi and Sagada panchayat. A little away from the main settlement just below the crossroads leading to direction, the market is held in the open ground.

The market of Jalatara starts from 6 a. m. and gets over by 2 p.m. The area of Jalatara market is a little more than one acre, where 500 to 700 people are reported to assemble on the market day. Another market is also held at Gunupur, the tahsil headquarters, on every Thursday. The market at Gunupur starts from 8 a. m. the morning and get over by 3 o'clock or half past. Approximately 500 to 1000 people assemble on every market day in the market place.

On the basis of the visits made by this researcher to the Puttsinghi weekly market on different occasions, it may be stated that near market site approximately 600 persons assemble in the peak hours on the market day and the whole atmosphere is surcharged with din and gaiety. It is seen that the large groups of people wonder here and there while some examine the wares and inquire about their rates. Others sit together, engrossed in idle gossip or in some sort of heated discussion. Men, women and children of the different neighbouring tribes and castes attired in their traditional dress are seen coming towards market in long queue and more freely inside the market. In this connection it should be mentioned that most of the articles which the buyers purchase are essential commodities like kerosene oil, salts, edible oils, dry tobacco leaves. *Bidis, mandia,* millets, rice, etc., besides articles like cloth, earthenwares, aluminium wares, dry fish etc. Few constables are also posted there on every market day to look after the law and order in and around the market. The people assembled in Puttasinghi market may be classified in the following way:

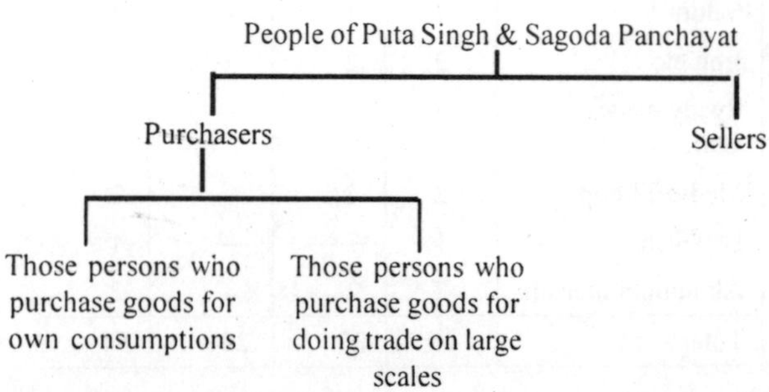

Thus we see that among the people of Puttasinghi and Sagada market there are main two groups, i.e., purchasers and sellers. But intensive enquiries reveal that there are two types of purchaser, i.e., those who purchase articles for personal consumption and the number of such, from the major group of people attending the market, and the second group of purchasers are those who purchase articles from the first group of purchasers for doing trade on large scale.

In the Gunupur or Puttasinghi market, goods available for sale and purchase may be broadly classified in two categories (a) the local products and (b) the imported commodities. The local products include the articles grown in the fields and *bari* lands such as rice paddy, pulses, oil-seeds, tobacco leaves, vegetables like the brinjals, tomatoes, chilies, garlic, onions and ginger particularly. The manufactured articles include earthen pot, bamboo baskets, winnowing fans, iron implements, etc. The imported articles include the mill-made cotton cloth and also ready made garments such as shirts, half pants, etc, as well as such articles for which there is a local demands such as salt, sugar, betel nuts, coconuts, bidis, match-box, kerosene oil, multi-coloured bead necklaces, toilet and washing soaps, cotton thread, lantern and its wicks, chimneys, aluminium ware etc. It was observed that the buyers would haggle with the sellers over the price of most of the imported articles and they seemed to be well informed about the prevailing prices.

Besides this, the rate of hair cutting was also recorded and it was observed that the rate of hair-cutting would differ from man to man or from child to adult. In the Puttasinghi market an adult hair-cutting rate was Rs.2 while for children it was only Rs. 1. Some time the style and shape of hair cutting also matters in determining the rate of hair cutting as reported. In this connection mention may also be made that in the Puttasinghi market the transactions for all the imported commodities and most of the local products are made always in cash. However, sometimes the cases of the barter transactions were also noticed but the cases were very few.

Relation Between Forest and Urbanisation

To assess the economic activities of tribals it can be seen in context of urbanisation and development to find out tribal's exposure to mainstream society. However, as a consequence of primitive man's regular action and intervention on the ecological system, the ecological equilibrium is sooner or latter disturbed and resulting into far-reaching changes, which we cannot foresee. This indicates that even at that early stage of social,

Table 7.15 Relation Between Forest and Urbanisation

Variables	*Age*								*Religion*						*Occupation*					
Response	*Young*		*Middle*		*Old*		*Total*		*Hindu*		*Non-Hindu*		*Total*		*Agriculture*		*Non-Agriculture*		*Total*	
	F	%	F	%	F	%	F	%	F	%	F	%	F	%	F	%	F	%	F	%
Yes	91	67	30	48	18	56	139	60	72	66	67	55	139	60	91	58	48	67	139	60
No	12	8.9	14	22	8	25	34	15	13	12	21	17	34	15	25	16	9	13	34	15
Can't Say	32	24	19	30	6	19	57	25	24	22	33	27	57	25	42	27	15	21	57	25
Total	135	100	63	100	32	100	230	100	109	100	121	100	230	100	158	100	72	100	230	100

Table 7.16 Suggestion to Protect Forest

Variables	*Age*								*Religion*						*Occupation*					
Response	*Young*		*Middle*		*Old*		*Total*		*Hindu*		*Non-Hindu*		*Total*		*Agriculture*		*Non-Agriculture*		*Total*	
	F	%	F	%	F	%	F	%	F	%	F	%	F	%	F	%	F	%	F	%
Plantation	68	50	33	52	22	69	123	53	53	49	70	58	123	53	87	55	36	50	123	53
To check Deforest-ation	22	16	15	24	5	16	42	19	26	24	16	13	42	18	30	19	12	17	42	18
Education/ Awareness	24	18	5	7.9	4	13	33	14	14	13	19	16	33	14	19	12	14	19	33	14
Economic Rehabi-liation	20	15	7	11	1	3.1	28	12	16	15	12	9.9	28	12	18	11	10	14	28	12
Can't Say	1	0.7	3	4.8	0	0	4	1.7	0	0	4	3.3	4	1.7	4	2.5	0	0	4	1.7
Total	135	100	63	100	32	100	230	100	109	100	121	100	230	100	158	100	72	100	230	100

economic and cultural development people not only adapt to the environment but also seek to influence it actively. And they do this not just by their presence as a part of the ecological system but frequently quite deliberately. In this context a question has been asked that, 'is their any relationship between forest and urbanisation'. In Table 7.15, out of 135 young responded 91 said 'yes', 30 out of 63 middle-aged responded 'yes' followed by 18 out of 32 old respondents. It shows that younger people are better informed about the mainstream and the development process whereas old and middle ages are of less knowledge on similar issue. Religionwise break up shows no variation unlike the occupational break up. The non-agricultural respondents are well aware of the out-side world than their agricultural counterparts. Overall trend shows that there is a relationship between forest and urbanisation.

Forest Safeguard Measures

With the above changes and developments *Saora* tribals have perceived the apparent possible threat of forest disappearance, which may endanger their very existence.

And therefore they have thought of protecting it by different methods. Plantation would certainly protect the forest from extinct. The opinion of thes triblas have been depicted in Table 7.16. More than 53 per cent have suggested for 'plantation' followed by 'to check deforestation' by 18 per cent. 'Economic rehabilitation' is also in the agenda of the tribals which accounts for 12 per cent and most importantly 'educational awareness' is of 14 per cent. In this pretext the outstanding feature is the awareness of the tribals in connection with the protection of the forest.

Conclusion

Economy of any nature is solely dependent on natural resources. Without natural resources no economy can flourish. Likewise, the *Saora* economy is mostly based on forest. Dalton and Polanyie very clearly mentioned that, economy has two meanings. One is substantative meaning, which is depending on nature for living or sustaining life. This may result into ecological imbalance if the dependent level is more. The Second is of formal meaning, which is based on choice and availability. The formal meaning of economy is not applied to this study. For tribal studies the 'integrated patterns' of economy is more important because it involves reciprocity and redistribution. This integrated approach of economy has followed by Durkheim and Malinoski. This integration can be considered general as the social mechanisms which increasingly link the inhabitants of rural communities with individuals and groups outside the boundary of their village.

The strategy of the development of Scheduled Tribes and Scheduled Castes is vested in the Constitution providing opportunities to scheduled groups so that they can be assimilated in the mainstream. In the field of economic development they had to rise their standard of living and become active in this marketing and competitive age. The planner has many ideas for the economic development of the tribals; but the problem is that the tribal economy is not only of one kind. It has been classified from food gathering including hunting and fishing, pastoral, shifting cultivation and then settled agriculture to business etc. So it is difficult to formulate a clear cut policy of economic development. However, most of the tribals in India for their economic activities depend on land and forest. The forest dwellers depend primarily on the minor forest products for their subsistence. The traditional *Saora* economy is totally based on forest. The principles of social and moral life of Lanjia *Saora* are practically derived from the geography and ecology of the agency terrain. The traditional economy of Lanjia *Saora* is less productive becomes they confined to small farming; this is because to ensure smooth continuation of household system.

The *Saoras* practice terraced land cultivation for growing paddy by the transplantation method. The social arrangement for property relations and its inheritance in *Saora* society is a big hurdle against the economy individualism. All landed property is jointly owned. Every *Saora* village has well defined boundary and its inhabitants do shifting cultivation in the hills located in the village boundary. The reason for shifting cultivation is ecology, because a balance is struck between the cultural resources with the possibilities that the habitat affords for their production and the length of time that area of land can be exploited. Apart from this *Saora* has cattle, buffalo, pig, poultry and duck as of their economic assets. They do lot of sacrifices of these animals in various time of their life. Many of the *Saora* traditionally depend on forest for minor forest products and sale these in the local markets.

Now, the *Saora* economy has partially changed, but the practice of shifting cultivation is still persisting among many tribals. 98 per cent *Saora* even said today that forest is their main source of living, because of shifting cultivation and minor forest produces both. The result is 90 per cent. The minor forest produce is used for personnel as well as for selling. This shows *Saora* also want little bit of money for their daily activities, so they sell the minor forest produces in the market. In response to this researchers quarry 96 per cent tribal said that the forest resources has decreased. This is due to; deforestation, population growth, lack of rain and etc. All these played a very distinctive role for decrease in forest resources. This decrease of forest resources has affected 97 per cent of the tribal population. Since 97 per cent tribal are affected, 69 per cent tribal said this is resulted into migration. Maximum tribals migrate because of more wage and regular work. This is evident that the forest-based economy of *Saora* is in the verge of changing. *Saoras* have asserted that their life is not at all possible without forest. This is indispensable for their survival.

In the context of tribal market today the researcher observed that in the *Saora* market, persons come to purchase and many comes here to purchase in cheap rate and sell it in the other market. The tribal market is full of local products and forest-based materials. The composition of the market is of various caste group like *Saora, Doms*, *Kumuti* and *Kapu* Reddy and etc. This can be seen in the context of an organisation. In this connection 60 per cent tribals said there is relation between forest and urbanization. This is due to the connection of *Saora* land with the Gunupur market. There is bus and trees communication in the whole day by which *Saoras* are well connected with the small town of Gunupur. This relation has brought many changes in the ideas, economy and social aspect of *Saoras*.

At the end of this chapter *Saoras* suggestions have been discussed. There are various ways to protect forest. The suggestions are plantation, check deforestation, educational awareness and economic rehabilitation. This will enable the *Saoras* from the suffering of deforestation and their dependency for economic activities can be protected without much damage to their culture, civilization and ecology.

References

Chaudhuri, B., and Chaudhuri S., 1982, 'On Some Tribal Problems' B.Choudhury (ed.), *Tribal Development in India*, New Delhi, Inter-India Publications.

Dalton,G., 1969, 'Theoretical Issues in Economic Anthropology' *Current Anthropology*, 10 (I), pp. 63-102.

Firth, Raymond, I95I, *Elements of Social Organisation*, London, Watts.

Firth, Raymond, 1959, *Economics of the New Zealand Maori*, New Zealand, Wellington, Owen.

Firth, Raymond, 1951, *We the Tikopia*, London, Gorg Alen.

Malinowski, B, 1922, *Argonauts of Western Pacific*, London, Routledge.

Mauss, Marcel, 1954, *The Gift*, Glencoe,Ill:The Free Press.

Meillassoux, 1972, 'From Reproduction to Production: a Marxist Approach to Economic Anthropology'. *Economy and Society* 1(1).

Mahapatra, L.K., 1972, 'Social Movement among Tribes of India', K.S. Singh, (ed.), *Tribal Situation in India*, Shimla, IIAS.

Murdock, G.P., 1949, *Social Structure*, New York, Macmillian.

Montesquieu, 1784, *The Spirit of the Laws*, Oxford, Oxford University Press.

Patnaik N., 1989, *Saora*, Bhubaneswar, THRT Publication.

Polanyi, K., 1944, *The Origins of Our Time*, London.

Radcliffe-Brown, A.R., 1952, *Structure and Function in Primitive Society: Essays and Addresses*, Cohen and West, London, Free Press.

Spencer,H., 1897, *The Principles of Sociology*. Vol. III, London, Williams & Norgate.

Sujatha, K., 2000, *Education Among Tribals*, New Delhi, NIEPA.

Weber, M., 1978, *Economy and Society: An Outline of Interpretive Sociology*, Berkeley:Univ. Calif Press.

Weber, M., 1981, *General Economic History*, New York, Transaction.

8

Social Ecology and Forest Resources

Since the inception of human civilisation forest have played a very important role in our life. As we all know that once upon a time the whole human civilisation was living in forest. And through the process of social evolution the human civilization has reached at this stage. In this chapter we have highlighted the importance of forest for human beings for both the purpose of using and preserving it for the future. At the outset it has been described here the ecological dimensions of human society with reference to ecological anthropology by tracing the history of few aboriginal communities across the world. Then a historical review of the role of forest in the Orissa's political and social history is illustrated. Secondly, an attempt has been made to capture the initiative taken by the Government to maintain a balance between the need to preserve the forest and the requirements of tribal life. It is crucial from the point of view that the dependence of tribals over natural resources particularly on forest is not seen only as a means for their subsistence living but also for the very survival of their culture and civilisation. At this juncture, we will also focus upon the changes that have taken place from the pre-British period to present day with special reference to forest and tribes of Orissa.

Social Ecology: An Anthropological Dimension

A convenient framework for indicating promising new directions in ecological inquiry and how these relate to a focus upon social and cultural aspects of community living is provided by consideration of criticisms that have been or can be made of past work in ecological anthropology. The approaches set forth in articles by Rappapot and Vayda (1969:112-19, and 1968:477-97). These are the approaches that critics have labeled "new ecology" (Murphy, 1970: 152- 71), "newer ecology"(Lesser, A., 1968: 92-96), and "new functionalism," "neo-functionalism," or "neo functional ecology" (Friedman, 1974:444-69). The label of "cultural ecology" is also sometimes applied, but Viyda and Rappaport and Flannery have rejected this as a designation for their chosen areas of inquiry and have applied it to other approaches including Steward's (1955) and Harris's (1968) which they have criticized.

The larger units of the study—populations, communities, and ecosystems are not only interlinked but also are interdependent particularly in the context of the ecological anthropology. Indeed, according to Orians (1973), "perhaps the greatest challenge" for ecologists is the "development of theories about the properties of communities on the basis of selection for the attributes of their component individuals" (Orians 1973: 1239). By focusing on how individual organisms respond to hazards and problems, biologists can hope to come closer toward meeting this challenge, insofar as the attributes of individuals favoured by selection must include the ability to survive the hazards of particular times and places. This can be further explained from the concrete examples based on field studies. In this chapter an attempt has been made to understand and explore Saora ecology. To discuss about *Saora*, forest and ecology, it is required to see that how there is a close line between nature and primitive society.

Nature and Primitive Society

The transition from the Palaeolithic to the Mesolithic age was accompanied by profound changes in the economy, way of life and social relations in many respects associated with the end of, mass hunting for large herbivorous animals. Man was compelled to seek new means of subsistence. The active search for new ways of mastering the ecological environment was frequently accompanied by attempts to create more favourable conditions of life and hunting. The aborigines of Tasmania, whom the Europeans found at a stage of development corresponding to the Upper Paleolithic age, and who died out by the end of the 19th century, regularly burned vegetation on large areas of the island. The ecological effect of those fires over thousands of years were very great and irreversible: the nature of vegetable growth and the top soil changed on large areas, moist forests were replaced by shrubland and savannas, and the climate changed. Fire removed impassable forest from whole regions, which was a boon for the Tasmanian hunters, but at the same time it destroyed the plant cover and enhanced soil erosion.

The aborigines of Australia, who in the 19th century were on the whole at a Mesolithic stage of development, while some tribes were in the Upper Palaeolithic not only wiped out the large marsupials of a whole continent, but, like the Tasmanians, regularly burned down shrubs and grasses on vast areas. In the view of some scientists, this resulted in the disappearance of forests and other unfavourable consequences. T. Mitchell, one of the first explorers of Australia, wrote that fire, grass, kangaroos and people in Australia, all depended upon one another, and if one disappeared the others could not exist.

Mitchell noted the existence of a kind of ecological equilibrium in which the primitive hunter was the active factor. A part of the ecological system, he was at the same time a force regulating the interactions of other parts in his interests. However, as a consequence of primitive man's regular action on the ecological system, the ecological equilibrium is sooner or later disturbed and far-reaching change, which we cannot foresee, occur in nature. This indicates that even at that early stage of social, economic and cultural development people not only adapt to the environment but also seek to influence it actively. And they do this not just by their presence as a part of the ecological system but frequently quite deliberately.

The prerequisites for a producer economy are: relative stability of the primitive social structure alongside with an inherent ability to develop; collective ownership of land, the basic means of production; economic links of the community with a specific territory; correct succession of economic activity according to the natural cycle. These and other fundamental properties of the hunter-gatherer society constitute the socio-economic base for the formation of producer economy. The main motive force of the transformation of food gathering to the producer economy is the system of socio-economic relations itself.

The dependence of a primitive hunter and gatherer society on cultural conditions is probably no greater than of a society based on a producer economy. Being technically inferior, it relies mainly on mechanisms of social adaptation evolved over thousands of years to oppose the pressure of the natural geographic environment. In the words of Karl Marx, the primitive community with its typical natural unity with objective, naturally formed conditions of production was the "first great productive force"(Marx & Engel's, *Works*,Vol.46, Part I, p. 485). The community itself mediates the relationship of primitive men to nature.

Anthropological research on agriculture began, perhaps necessarily, with the gross differentiation of types, the charting of their global distribution, and their association with evolutionary stages. For Morgan, cultivation was one of the key elements in the transition from savagery to barbarism, and its development was speculatively associated with concepts of property and with technology. Agriculture succeeded pastoralism according to the early evolutionists, and Ratzel (1869, *The History of Mankind*) regarded it as an improvement because it "forces on a man the wholesome habit of labour" and is followed by the accumulation of capital the development of trade, and a fuller organization of the social ranks. Generalizations based on limited ethnographic data or single factor explanations have the healthy effect of igniting scholarly debate and sending workers to the field with new research orientations. If the neglect of food production as an important area of study for cultural anthropology was to be remedied, questions of what people actually did for a living, when for how long, and with what results had to be answered by long-term observation and painfully slow collection of quantitative data. Moreover, a farmer's activities and choices could not be understood without a much more detailed knowledge of his local environment.

A fruitful concentration on shifting cultivation in Southeast Asia took from a series of reports on the Lamet of Indochina, the Iban of Sarawak and the Hanunoo of the Philippines, with the addition of general surveys by Pelzer, Gourou and Spencer, Conklin set high standards in his collection of rainfall and soil analysis data, his exhaustive step-by-step enumeration of stages in site selection, cutting, burning, cropping and following that make up the swidden cycle, and his attention to native categories of land usage, climate, soils, vegetation, and labour. A truly ecological understanding of any agricultural system requires not only the study of dynamic interrelations with the effective physical environment (soil, water, temperature, topography) but also quantitative consideration of energy transfers with the human organisms (Newman, 1962: 22-34).

There are two aspects to the relationship of primitive society to nature: the objective economic and the subjective ideological. The former finds expression in the community's ownership of a definite territory (its source of existence) and the economic development of that territory. The second aspect is a reflection of the economic attitude towards the land in ideological form. Thus, the subjective ideological attitude of the Australian aborigines to the land is expressed in the links of the tribe with totemic sanctuaries on the community's land.

At the same time, primitive man's attitude to nature also includes the epistemological sphere, the vast domain of man's cognition of the surrounding world, the earth and the Universe. This system of notions organizes social experience and brings order into the chaos of phenomena, thus helping the society to master the world in practice. Man began to accumulate systematic knowledge about the vegetable and animal world back in the Palaeolithic age: 15,000 years ago, if not earlier. Primitive man was familiar with the cyclic character of life in nature, he observed the phases of the Moon and knew how to record all this, having knowledge of the rudiments of writing and counting (A.Marshack, *The Roots of*

Table 8.1

Trees and Plants with Food Value Available in Orissa and Madhya Pradesh

	Botanical Name	*Local Name*	*Edible*
1.	Aegle marmalos	Bel	Pulp or fruit
2.	Agaricus Spps.	*Kumbhi*	Different types of Mushrooms grow wild in forest and are eaten.
3.	Agati gradiflora	August	Flowers as vegetables
4.	Agava sisilana	Sisal	Raw reduced stem
5.	Alipinia spps.	Banhardi	Rhizomes
6.	Amaranthus spps.	Chulai	Leaves and Seeds
7.	Amorphophallus prainii	Dhai	Corn
8.	Anona reticulata	Ramphal	Fruit
9.	Anona squamosaosum	Sitaphal	Fruit
10.	Arisaema tortuosum	Bankanda	Underground corn
11.	Artocarpus integri Folia	Khatal	Fruit
12.	A. lakoocha	*Barhal*	Fruit
13.	Aurum spps.	Kanda	Rhizomes
14.	Asparagus recemosus	Satmuli	Roots tubers
15.	Averrhoa carambola	Kamrakh	Fruit
16.	Bauhinia Variggata	Kachnar	Unmature pods
17.	Bssela alba and Rubra	Poisag	Leaves
18.	Bassia latifolia (Madhucaindical)	Mahua	Flower, also fermented into alcohol
19.	Bridelia retusa	Kasali	Fruit
20.	Buchanania muricatus	Achar	Fruit & Seed
21.	Bambosa spps.	Bans	Suckers
22.	Colonynetion muricatus	Ghatlai	Fruit
23.	Canvalia spps.	Nada sem	Pods
24.	Capparisaphila	Karil	Fruit
25.	Cariota urens	Tulphi	Sap. The sap of this plam is used as an alcoholic drink

	Botanical Name	*Local Name*	*Edible*
26.	Carum strictocarpum	Masala	Root & Seed
27.	Coccinia Indica	Kundru	Fruit
28.	Chenopodium spps.	Bathua	Leaves
29.	Chlorophytum tuberosum	Safed musli	Root tubers
30.	Chemetis similifolia	Agia	Root
31.	Cleome viscose	Hurhur	Leaves and seeds
32.	Colocasia antiquorum	Kanda	Rhizomes
33.	Corehorus capsularis	Chech	Leave
34.	Cordia myxa	Lasoda	Fruit
35.	Castur speceous	Keokanda	Rhizomes
36.	Cucumismelo var momordica	Kakri	Fruit
37.	Cucurbita pepp	Kumhra	Fruit. There are about 30 types of Kumhra
38.	Curcuma angustifolia	Tekhur	Rhizomes
39.	Cyperus Mugosus	Kaseru	Rhizomes
40.	Diosearea alata	Baichandi	Swollen root
41.	D. Pentaphylla	Suar Kanda	Swollen root
42.	D. bulbifira	Ratkanda	Aerial bulbs
43.	Diospyrus melanoxylon	Tendu	Fruit
44.	Dolichos bifforus	Kuthi	As pulses
45.	Emblica officinalis (phyllenthus officinalis)	Amla	Fruit
46.	Eugenia jambolana & spps.	Jamun	Fruit
47.	Feronia acida	Kabet, Kaith	Fruit
48.	Ficus bengalensis	Bar	Fruit
49.	F. glomerate	Gular, Umar	Fruit
50.	Flacoursia ramontehi		Fruit
51.	Gmelina arborea	Gambhari	Fruit

	Botanical Name	*Local Name*	*Edible*
52.	Guizotia alyssinica	Tamtil	For oil & roasted seed
53.	Hedychium spps.	Banadag	Rhizome
54.	Ipomea aquatica	Narisag	Leaves
55.	Lantana camara		Fruit
56.	Luffa spps	Taroi	Fruit
57.	Mangifera indica	Am	Fruit
58.	Manihot utilisima		Roots
59.	Mimosop hexandra	Khirni	Fruit
60.	Mamoridca cochin chinesis	Kheksi	Fruit
61.	Moringo oleifera	Senjna	Munga Fruit
62.	Morous alba	Tut	Catkin
63.	Mucuna prurens	Kimach	Unrip pods
64.	Nelumbium nucifera	Kamal	Seeds & roots
65.	Opunia dellenii	Nagphani	Fruit
66.	Phyllenthus distichus	Harphul	Fruit
67.	Partulaca spps.	Golsag	Leaves
68.	Ponamia Pinnata	Karanj	Seeds yield oil
69.	Psidium gujava	Behi	Fruit
70.	Randia uliginosa	Pandra	Fruit
71.	Rumex dentatus	Plan Bhagi	Leaves
72.	Schleichera trijuga	Kusum	Seed oil
73.	Semicarpus anacardium	Bhilwan	Thalamus
74.	Shorea robusta	Sal	Fruit after boiling
75.	Silax macrophylla	Ram datua	Roots
76.	Spondias mangifera	Amra	Fruit
77.	Tamarindus indics	Imli	Fruit & seed
78.	Terminalia spps.	Koa	Roasted fruit
79.	Trapa bispinosa	Sighara	Nuts

	Botanical Name	*Local Name*	*Edible*
80.	Ventilago calyculata	Keoti	Seed oil: the seed oil is said to be superior to pure ghee in Baster.
81.	Zizyphus jujuba	Ber	Fruit
82.	Z. rotundifolia	Jhadi Beri	Fruit
83.	Z. Oenoplia	Makoi	Fruit

Source : Fernandes, Menon et at 1988 pp. 151-153

Civilization, New York, 1972). Ethnography also testifies to primitive man's knowledge of certain laws of nature, as indicated in the foregoing discourse. Besides the epistemological understanding of social laws the primitive man too had developed a keen sense of identifying the natural habitat—the animal and plant categories, not just for curiosity but also for his own survival. It is the same case with the tribe under study and one can understand the systematic effort they have made to identify and use various plant and animal species. Table 8.1 containing the local names of various plants and their food values is given. For better understanding the botanical names of these plants are also given.

A Social History of Forest

As we have already discussed in Chapter II regarding the people, climate and forest of Orissa, it is clear that on 18 April 1891, Orissa was created as a new province out of Bengal Presidency. The total seven forest division of Bihar and Orissa, was under the charge of a Conservator of Forest. In 1928 Sambalpur division was divided into east, and west for it's better management. It was after 45 years when a separate province of Orissa was created on April 1, 1936, the state forest department, was looked after under a conservator of forest.

Forest of the Ex-princely States

The year 1948 witnessed the birth of the new state of Orissa when the then 25 princely states known as Gujarat region merged with the coastal belt known as the Mughalbandi region but the ex-princely state of Mayurbhanj merged with the rest of Orissa only on January 1, 1949. After the merger the state government created 22 territorial forest zones and two research and working plan divisions all under the direct control of the Chief Conservator of Forest.

Under the ex-princely states there existed '*Khesra* forests'. These were the *Sadharan* forest unreserved but demarcated, that were managed by the people. These forests were known as *gram jungle* in other parts of the state. Although the real management of the *Khesra* forest was taken over by the state forest department (FD) in 1958; these forests continued primarily to suffice the needs of the local people. These village forests were tracts of land containing vegetation thick or thin that were recorded as *Gramy Jungle* in the Orissa Survey and Settlements Acts, 1958. Although the ownership of these lands lies with the state government, people were usufructs subject to conformity of the forest laws of the state.

Ex–Zamindari Forests

By the year 1957 the then zamindari forests also had come under the state forest department after the merger of princely states. Prior to this the management of these forest was under the *Anchal Sasan*. The Orissa Preservation of Private Forest Act 1947 was enacted to control exploitation of forests by zamindars. On November 15,1957 these forests of 19, 891.2 sq. kms were transferred to the forest department of Orissa government.

With regard to the rights and concession enjoyed by the villagers in different classes of forests wide variations were experienced from region even within the ex-princely states. Nevertheless, there were similarities in the nature of rights and concessions in all the area of the state. No right existed for the people in matters of access to reserved forest 'A' except the concessions of free removal of certain minor forest produece (MFP) for domestic use. People of the princely states used to pay 'Nistar-cess' and enjoy certain rights in the reserved forests 'B' and the *Khesra* Forest. Such rights usually consisted of free removal of unreserved species; removal of reserved species on 1/4 or 1/2 royalty rates and free removal of MFP's. 'Nistar-cess' with its local expressions like '*Bankar*', '*Kantakar*' and '*Ranwa*' is a commutation of payments to be made by their tenants for free use or use at concessional rates of timber and other forest produce from *Khesra* forest and reserved forests 'B'. Those days when this tax was first levied the forests were in plenty and demands on the forest were small. No limit was fixed on the quantity of produce to be removed in lieu of the payment.

Prior to independence by and large all the forests of Orissa were managed under the Indian Forest Act (IFA), except in the districts of Ganjam, Koraput and a small segment of Phulbani where the Madras Forest Act was enforced. Reserved forests also existed in these regions of southern Orissa then governed by Madras Forest Act 1882. Reserved forest existed in the territory of Mughalbandi under IFA 1927 whereas in the ex-princely states these were of two different categories like reserved forest" 'A' and 'B'. During this period there also existed protected forests in the area under IFA 1927 and *Khesra* forests in the ex-princely states.

Causes of Deforestation

It would be pertinent here to mention the major causes of deforestation in Orissa. Fire, floods and cyclones are among the dominant natural causes of forest destruction in Orissa. But damages caused by natural hazards do not seem to be serious as seen in the annual report of the forest department for 1959-60, 1963-64 and 1971-72 to 1977-78. Fires by accidents, deliberate burning of jungle by smugglers, often in connivance with forest officials, illegal felling shifting cultivation, huge industrial projects, development infrastructure (like hydroelectricity projects, railways, roads, etc.) mining, irrigation, dams and resettlement projects (like in Dandakaranya) etc. have been the major causes of destruction of forests. During 1971-72 to 1981-82 Karanjia Division seems to have experienced the maximum extent of deforestation followed by Sundargarh and Jeypore Divisions, respectively. The total areas deforested during the same period are to the extent of 18,106.45 Hectares.

In the early sixties the total forest cover in the Orissa State was more, than 43 per cent (6.8 million hectare) of the total geographical area. By 1991, according to the Forest Survey of India, the forest cover has been reduced to 30.3 per cent (4.7 million hectares). Estimates of the degraded forest area vary from 12 million hectares to about 3 million hectares. Sal is one of the most important tree species in the State, with a coverage extending over about 1.7 million hectares.

Imbalanced Ecology: From Virgin Forest to Barren Land

Forest Today

After the unification of Orissa in 1948 the different forest laws came in force in various regions; classifying forests into very many classes were declared to be under IFA by the Indian Forest (Orissa Amendment) Act 1954. Keeping other classes of forests intact in the other two regions the 1954 Act paved the way for the merger of reserved forest 'A' and 'B' with the reserved forest under IFA and declared the earlier *Khesra* forest as protected forests in the ex-princely states.

Forest Administration

For administrative and management purposes, the forest in Orissa are divided into Reserve (A class and B class) Protected forest. Protected forests are of two types demarcated and undemoarcated, where the demarcated is under management of the Forest Department. As per the Forest Department records (1991-92) the total forest area consists of 47 per cent reserved forest (2.61 million hectares), 28 per cent demarcated forest (1.57) million hectares and 25 per cent undemarcated forests (1.42 million hectares).

Reserve Forests are fully under the control of the Forest Department and are managed under various silvicultural systems. All other forest areas are included within the village boundaries (Orissa Survey and Settlement Rules, 1962). According to the 1966 State Government order for reservation of lands for various purposes, 10 per cent of the effective village area is reserved as village forest area (*Gramya jungle*) for the exercise of rights and privilege by the villagers and for other development works.

In protected forests, only the forest crop (Trees) is managed by the Forest Department, the land is owned and controlled by the Revenue Department. These forest may be recorded in revenue records as reserve lands (Village Forest/*Gramya Jungle*) or cultivable or uncultivable wastelands, *patra jungle* (Scrub Forest), *jhati jungle* (Forest with minor crops), *pahad* (hill) and so on. Rights and privilege of the local community vary with the type of forest restricted in reserved forests and more liberals in protected forests.

Forest and Orissa Government

Although earlier the subject of forest and protection of wildlife was in the state list but since 1976 it has been transferred to the concurrent list of the Indian Constitution. Nevertheless, the state government has been the major player in the matter of forest administration. From organizational viewpoint the state administrative infrastructure inherited from the colonial rule proved to be grossly inadequate after independence as the fast changing socio-political scenario began to seriously undermine the bureaucratic authority rendering the forest laws unenforceable. Table 8.2 depicts the districtwise forest area in Orissa. As per the data Orissa has 155707 sq. km. geographical forest area. It has 26331.15 reserve forest, 15432.69 demarcated protected forest area, 14200.5 undemarcated protected forest area and unclassed 15.18 sq. kms. area of forest.

Though the resolution of 1988 and 1990 of Orissa government may be stepping stones in involving local communities to protect forest, these are weak measures since these offered the villagers only bona fide forest requirements like small timbers and fuel wood in lieu of forest protection responsibilities. Since the bona fide requirements are usually met from the forests legally or illegally, the villagers were in fact not offered any additional incentives by the orders of 1988 and 1990. Therefore, the new government order issued on July 3,1993 provided for 50 per cent share of any major harvest, in addition to all intermediate producers, to the protecting committees. The districtwise classification of forest areas has been given in Table 8.2. The nature of forest in the study area viz, Rayagada district is also figured in the Table 8.2.

Protection of Forest

Community based forest protection is not new to Orissa. Communities claim to have taken up protection as early as 1950's. Estimates of the area under protection and the number of communities involved range from 1,87,000 acres and 1,181 organisations (PCC 1990) to 1.5 million hectares and 6085 villages committees. There is, however, no consensus on these figures. Neera and Kundan Singh in their study estimate the number at around 1,50,000 to 2,00,000 hectares and 300 villages (1994).

In response to the forest denudation and ever depleting forest produce some villages in Orissa had undertaken active measures for protection and conservation of forests way back in the 1940s, 1950s and have been effectively and sustainably managing the forest patches since then. For example village Lapanga in Sambalpur district which has a strong tradition of forest protection. Over the years, faced with increasing depletion of forests, more and more rural communities in the states have come to protect forest. These efforts became widespread in the late 1970s and 1980s. At present for Orissa by a conservative estimate 3,000 villages are protecting over 2,00,000 hectares of forest The community action for forest management is present in almost all the districts of the state with higher concentration in Denkanal, Mayurbhan, Koraput, Sambalpur, Puri and Bolangir districts of Orissa. Thus, a large forest area in Orissa is now *de facto* a common property managed by communities though these are *de jure* a state property.

Table 8.2 Districtwise Classification of Forest Area in Orissa (As on 01/04/96)

Sl. No.	District	Forest Area (Area in Sq. km.)					
		Geographical Area	Reserve	Demarcated Protected	Undemarcated Protected	Unclassed	Total
1	2	3	4	5	6	7	8
1	Angul	6347	1742.59	334.56	1431.15	1.29	3509.59
2	Balasore	3705.8	202.68	3.68	57.37	0.19	263.92
3	Bargarh	5831.6	580.07	1159.43	181.29	0.16	1920.95
4	Bhadrak	2787.9	—	24.96	—	—	24.96
5	Balangir	6551.5	1080.83	25.63	540.89	0.14	1647.49
6	Boudh	3444.8	1015.14	42.68	57.94	1.02	1116.78
7	Cuttack	3915.2	517.55	134.46	107.03	0.45	759.49
8	Deogarh	2781.7	578.39	247.4	274.4	0.07	1100.26
9	Dhenkanal	4597.1	1141.02	14.78	672.84	0.04	1828.68
10	Gajapati	3016.8	416.89	108.15	1759.91	0.13	2285.08
11	Ganjam	8070.6	1472.26	1150.85	457.8	0.86	3081.77
12	Jagatsinghpur	1739.4	1.23	89.12	—	—	90.35
13	Jajpur	2884.9	6.34	397.05	18.14	0.01	421.54
14	Jharsuguda	2203.2	25.67	124.33	271.01	0.43	421.44
15	Kalahandi	8197.4	1449.03	869.57	1531.98	0.54	3851.12

(Contd.)

Sl. No.	District	Forst Area					
		Geographical Area	Reserve	Demarcated Protected	Undemarcated Protected	Unclassed	Total
1	2	3	4	5	6	7	8
16	Kendrapara	2565.6	14.49	184.9	—	—	199.39
17	Keonjhar	8303	1833.02	648.41	43.41	0.24	2525.08
18	Khurda	2887.5	294.37	266.93	607.52	0.68	1169.5
19	Koraput	8379.3	478.72	1030.9	369.26	0.3	1906.18
20	Malkangiri	6115.3	352.43	940.6	661.92	0.3	1955.25
21	Mayurbhanj	10418	3350.31	348.04	977.78	1.98	4678.11
22	Nawapara	3407.5	—	981.85	139.4	0.44	1121.69
23	Nayagarb	3954.2	1301.99	391.07	310.45	0.25	2003.76
24	Nowarangapur	5290.1	535.57	1041.51	7.09	0.12	1584.29
25	Phulbani	5464.9	2010.06	1755.91	689.82	1.99	4457.78
26	Puri	3054.8	15.66	—	85.88	0.51	102.15
27	Rayagada	7584.7	777.21	1796.88	1353.3	0.11	3927.5
28	Sambalpur	6704	2158.26	402.3	801.56	1.18	3363.3
29	Sonepur	2284.4	326.98	4.87	177.77	0.03	509.65
30	Sundargarh	9712	2652.39	911.87	666.59	1.72	4232.57
	Orissa	155707	26331.1 5	15432.69	14200.5	15.18	56059.52

Source : Govt. of Orissa, Forest Department.

Community initiatives for forests protection in most cases have been not merely in response to the severe forest destruction, degradation and its ecological effect but also in response to resultant scarcity in forest produces that form part of the communitiess' life supporting system. This engendered a desire to save forest patches for posterity and also an urge in the local communities to assert control over the forests, otherwise open to all. Generally, the villagers start protecting patches, which are considerably degraded but have the rootstock in fact as such patches regenerate rapidly once protected. Efforts for regenerating forests were initially limited to non-reserved forests, but now have spread to reserved forests also.

Village Community

In Orissa's villages community level organisatians have existed for long. These organizations provided a forum to discuss the changes in their life-support bases and to decide on collective actions. Since these villages organisations were already handling other common resources bases like ponds, temple lands etc. The village community also do other activities like resolving conflict, organising religious and cultural functions. Therefore, forest have been given to the community for its management.

Each district, even each cluster of villages have certain distinct management practices. The diversity of the local institutional arrangements is a result of their responsiveness to the fast changing local conditions.

Villages have informal, and at time formal, organizations to protect and manage forest patches in their vicinity. The informal organizations are often a group of village elders, or village protection committees, or village councils. The formal organizations are village level youth clubs, voluntary organization, which are in fact registered bodies. In some cases the motivating factor for forest protection has been the presence of some voluntary organizations in the area while in majority of other cases the dire necessity of maintaining the life support resources, i.e., forest produces, has led to formation of local level voluntary organisations.

Role of Forest Department

The role of the forest department in this matter came much later. Initially, in case where forest protection was being done in reserved forests, village forest protection committees (VFPCs) have been formed under the guidance of the forest department. Now the state department has gradually involved villagers to form VFPCs for the protection of no reserved forests also. Essentially these are formalization of forest protection efforts already undertaken by the villagers, i.e., by the youth clubs or the village committees. Thus there exist two types of VFPCs those formed with the guidance of the forest department and the other being, subcommittees of the village councils. In most cases although the VFPCs are in existence, the youth clubs play the dominant role as they take tough stand against offenders. Most of the committees are found to be struggling under financial constraints. In order to meet expenses incurred in protection of forests, funds are generated chiefly from the sale of forest materials to the villagers at a cheaper rate.

Government and Development

The rich forest resources of Koraput district is under constant pressure mainly due to practice of shifting cultivation by the tribals, increased demand of the people for timber and fire wood, encroachment into forest land by displaced persons during the implementation of different projects, and lastly due to the diversion of forest land for various developmental projects being executed in this district. Forestry is proposed to be given greater push along with wasteland development and steps to reduce fuel wood use. It has been proposed for preservation of the existing forest by complete ban on felling of green trees for a period of 10 years in the forest of this district. A scheme for rehabilitation of degraded forest is being implemented under Rural Landless Employment Guarantee Programme (R.L.E.G.P.) It has been proposed for fuel wood plantation in each of the 514 Gram Panchayats of the district.

Forest Policy

Regarding forest policy of 1988 a leading sociologist and thinker Prof. K. L. Sharma says that it is "a mechanical construction as the present policy becomes more of an imposition from the above rather than something emancipating from the base" (A comment on NFP resolution 1988). He further clarified by giving the exam,'e that tribals are a part and parcel of forests all over the world. Therefo, , .heir consciousness, what they think of forest and of their relationship with them in every day life must be the basis of ideation or policy formulation. What people feel, as their needs in relation to forests must be taken as the basic ingredient of the forest policy. Forest may not be looked upon as a source of revenue. They are a renewable natural resource and a national asset. But the reality is different as Prof. Sharma pronounces by giving the example of Bihar, Assam, Himachal Pradesh, Madhya Pradesh and some other states forests have become a source of revenue for the respective state governments. Forest is the life support system for the tribal folks. The government and intermediaries have not only been destroying these support systems for the tribals, but also re-channeling the natural wealth depriving the tribals even the minimal possible benefits. To substantiate these points the researcher has asked few questions to the tribals. It has been found that tribal's access to forest and forest produces has been minimised to a great extent through successive imposition of sanctions by the government from time to time. More than 50 per cent respondent has said to be affected by government imposition, more than 25 per cent claimed to have been seriously affected (Table 8.3). Tribals have been affected by forest laws; which is also reflected in their social economic, cultural in there social economic, culture and other spheres of their life. In this context, the study would recommend the government to make the imposition people-friendly to avoid making the lives of the people miserable.

So far as the restrictions by government on forest is concerned, 53 per cent of respondents voiced their protest against the impositions and a little over 32 per cent supported the government stand. Mixed reaction came from 11 per cent of the total respondents (Table 8.4). This shows , that the tribals are at a considerable discomfort at the government's imposition of restriction on forest. In this connection Fernandes, Menon and Viegas state that 'state control of forests is based on completely new concepts of ownership. It is a change over from the view of the forest as a life support system for the use of the tribal community to its understanding as a raw material subject to corporate ownership by the capitalist coming from outside the area'. There is a competition between the tribals and the state. (1988:245).

Within this context of competition for scare resources, tension is inevitable between groups representing different interests. In the eyes of the forest dwellers, the forest official represents the state and industry that are today competing for the resources on which the people have depended for centuries. This tension exists particularly between the weaker sections among the forest dwellers and the lowest rung of the forest department viz. the forest guards and foresters since these categories come in constant contact with each other. In the study they have stated that, tribals have different types of contacts which differ according to the

Table 8.3 How Tribals are Affected by Government Imposition?

Variables	*Age*								*Religion*						*Occupation*					
Response	*Young*		*Middle*		*Old*		*Total*		*Hindu*		*Non-Hindu*		*Total*		*Agriculture*		*Non-Agriculture*		*Total*	
	F	%	F	%	F	%	F	%	F	%	F	%	F	%	F	%	F	%	F	%
[illegible]	[illegible]	25	19	30	7	22	60	26	28	26	32	26	60	26	42	27	18	25	60	26
[illegible]	[illegible]	60	32	51	20	63	133	58	63	58	70	58	133	58	92	58	41	57	133	58
[illegible]	[illegible]	13	10	16	3	9.4	31	13	13	12	18	15	31	13	20	13	11	15	31	13
[illegible]	[illegible]	1.5	2	3.2	2	6.3	6	3	5	4.6	1	0.8	6	3	4	2.5	2	2.8	6	3
[illegible]	[illegible]	100	63	100	32	100	230	100	109	100	121	100	230	100	158	100	72	100	230	100

Table 8.4 Opinion on Govenment Restriction on Forest

Variables	*Age*								*Religion*						*Occupation*					
Response	*Young*		*Middle*		*Old*		*Total*		*Hindu*		*Non-Hindu*		*Total*		*Agriculture*		*Non-Agriculture*		*Total*	
	F	%	F	%	F	%	F	%	F	%	F	%	F	%	F	%	F	%	F	%
Good	48	36	15	24	11	34	74	32	36	33	38	31	74	32	45	28	29	40	74	32
Bad	72	53	37	59	12	38	121	53	51	47	70	58	121	53	88	56	33	46	121	53
Both good and bad	11	8.1	6	9.5	9	28	26	11	16	15	10	8.3	26	11	18	11	8	11	26	11
Can't Say	4	3	5	7.9	0	0	9	3.9	6	5.5	3	2.5	9	3.9	7	4.4	2	2.8	9	3.9
Total	135	100	63	100	32	100	230	100	109	100	121	100	230	100	158	100	72	100	230	100

Table 8.5 Relationship Between the Forest Dwellers and the Forest Officials

SEE	*Forest Guard*			*Forester*		
	1	2	3	1	2	3
LIC	38 (60.32)	4 -10.53	5 -8	29 -46.03	4 -13.79	5 -7.94
LC	25 -27.17	3 -12	-8.7 11	-23.91 30	-13.64 3	-5.43 11
MC	31 -33.33	4 -12.9	11 -11.83	30 -32.26	3 -9.1	11 -11.83
UMC	13 -59.09	4 -30.77	8 -36.36	12 -34.55	4 -33.33	8 -36.36
UC	1 -50	1 -100	1 -50	1 -50	1 -100	1 -50
	108 -39.34	16 -14.95	33 -12.13	94 -34.56	15 -15.96	30 -11.03

Source : Fernandes. Menon et. al. 1988 p. 245.

The higher class, on the contrary, are by and large, not approached by the officials but take the initiative in contacting them. They go mostly not with the cases of illegal felling, but to get permission to fell trees for domestic or commercial purposes. The lower class by and large have 'passive' contacts with the forest officials particularly forest guards, i.e., they are forced into these contacts either because the forest guards and other officials come to them with demands and threats or because they are forced to go to the forests to cut firewood, bamboo etc. for survival. The upper classes, on the contrary, have more frequent 'active' contacts with the officials, i.e., those in which they themselves take the initiative for their own gain.

Conclusion

By seeing the forest laws from pre-British period to today and government intervention for the development of the tribals, we may conclude that we are living in a transitional period. In one way the complexities of forest laws and restriction on forest has made the tribals life miserable and they are forced to cut the tree and destroy the existing forest and tree species. Secondly, the government has created the attitude to accept the modern trend to live a comfortable life which has affected the environment and ecology. For example, tribals were not accepting the *pucca* house, but by seeing it from the migrant official and others, they have started doing so. If every tribal household go to make *pucca* building and prepare the bricks for it, how many trees they have to cut? This will definitely lead to erase the forest completely as the greedy trends have been making the ground among the tribals.

As the social ecology is defined in sociology and social sciences, it is the inter-dependence of socio-cultural domain with biophysical aspect of the society. The very existence of society has been traced from the day of evolution of homo sapian, where the homo sapian were living in the jungle. Here this link has been developed in connection with the *Saora* tribal of Orissa.

The main thrust has been on the historical analysis of Orissa's forest. This has stated from the date of 1 April 1936 from the very day of Orissa . During that time there were only one Conservator of forest, who was looking after the forest of the area. In the year 1948 Orissa witnessed a birth of new state because of merger of twenty-five princely states. As a result twenty-two forest zones have been created. To save the forest from the exploitation of the zamindars Private Forest Act 1947 was enacted. In this enactment right and concession have given to the villagers. This was done in the context of division of forest as "A" and "B" forest. Forest "A" is not at all accessed to the people. Forest "B" was accessed to the people and they were paying "Nistar-Cess" for it. This was the situation upto independence. After independence the situation changed and 1948 different forest laws came into force in various region classifying forest into many classes. Here the forest "A" and "B" have been merged with reserved forest under Indian Forest Act.

Though law has taken its course, the depletion of forest has also come to exist by this time. The main cause of depletion was shifting cultivation and connivance of smugglers with the forest officials. Upto 1982 the total area deforested are to the extent of 18,106.45 hect. Due to better management and protect the forest from depletion, protected forest has been classified as demarcated and non-demarcated forest and managed by forest department.

At the outset the forest policy of 1988 has been discussed. This policy is a kind of imposition on tribals as nothing satisfactory has been suggested to make the grass-roots level participation more effective for the development of tribals. In this above perspective this study finds out that 50 per cent tribals are sufferer because of government intervention and 25 per cent tribals life have been affected seriously. In toto government intervention has created disenchantment among the tribals for their simple day to day needs. In the same line this study also finds out that 53 per cent tribal clearly said this government imposition and intervention is bad and against the tribal interest. But this has a contradictory result as 11 per cent tribals said both good and bad. This is due to the simple understanding of the tribals as they think the government intervention is in the interest of forest and the people. This result seems more contradictory when we see the analysis when maximum tribals suffer for the exploitation by the forest guard and other forest officials.

So it is evident here that the government intervention on forest for tribals is negatively correlated to the development and progress of the society.

References

Czech Conroy, Abha Mishra and Ajay Rai, *Learning from Self-initiated Community Forest Management Groups in Orissa: Practices, Prospects and Policy Implications* (Discussion Paper), NIR Project.

Friedman, J., 1974, 'Marxism, Structuralism and Vulgar Materialism', *Man* 9, pp. 444-69.

Fernandes, Walter, et. al., 1988, *Forest Environment and Tribal Economy: Deforestation, Impoverishment and Marginalisation in Orissa.* New Delhi, Indian Social Institute.

Government of Orissa, 1962, *Orissa Survey and Settlement Rules*, Govt. of Orissa.

Harris, 1968, *The Rise of Anthropological Theory.* New York: Grorwell.

Lesser, A., 1968, 'War and the State' in *War: The Anthropology of Armed Conflict and Aggression*, ed. M., Fried, M.Harris, R. Murphy, Garden City: Natural History Press, pp. 92-96.

Murphy, R.F., 1970, 'Basin Ethnography and Ecological Theory' *Language and Cultures of Western North America*, ed. E.H.Swanson Jr.,Pocatello:Idaho State Univ. Press, pp.152-71.

Marx and Engel, *Works*, Vol. 46, Part-I.

Morgan, L.H., 1907, *Ancient Society,* New York.

Marshack, A., 1972, The Roots of Civilizaton, New York.

Neera and Singh, 1994, *Forest, People and Protection: Case Studies of Voluntary Forest Protection by Communities in Orissa.*

Ratzel, 1869, *The History of Mankind,* not available.

Rappapot and Vayda, 1968, 'Ecology: Cultural and Non-Cultural', *Introduction to Cultural Anthropology*, ed. J., A. Clifton, Bostone: Houghton Mifflin, pp. 477-97.

Sharma, K L, 1988, *A Comment on National Forest Policy Resolution.* Unpublished Paper.

Vayda, A.P., 1969, 'An Ecological Approach', *Cultural Anthropology*, Bucknell Rev. 17 (1), pp. 112-19.

9

Change and Development

In the development paradigm, the role of education is critically acclaimed and in most of the developing countries education is regarded as an article of faith. It is believed that this powerful instrument will lead them to the path of progress and modernisation. It is now being realised that development planning must incorporate socio-cultural realities for its success. Geographical isolation, regional differentiation, political situation, social stratification, economic opportunities and infrastructural arrangements determines the degree and directions of development. Therefore, it is imperative to take note of these factors in planning for socio-economic development.

Education is a dynamic and powerful tool for social and economic development but its effectiveness largely depends on its spread and utilization. Despite many decades of effort, a vast majority of population in India has remained outside the education system. Apart from lack of access and quality expansion of education it also suffered from the lack of social opportunities. The presence of acute social hierarchy, gender and group discrimination has affected the progress of education at the social level. The spread of education has largely been confined to urban and developed rural territories. Structural barriers like difficult terrain; inaccessible locations and sparsely populated areas continue to deprive many people from the benefit of education. In other words, geographical or spatial constraints and socio-economic and cultural pattern of the population prove to be the major hurdle in their path towards educational achievements. The vast tribal population in India is a classic example of such problem. The tribal, population suffers from double disadvantage of spatial and socio-economic constraints with regard to overall development as well as education.

At the outset, the chapter discusses how the government agencies worked for educational upliftment for the Lanjia *Saora* tribe. How far government educational plans brings change and development in the area. In this perspective what are the causes of educational backwardness of the Lanjia *Saora* tribe has been discussed. The main focus is on the dependency on forest, and how it has been affected by education or vice versa. Before going to discuss all this it is necessary to focus how education, development, and change are important for tribal studies.

Education and Development: A Socio-Anthropological Perspective

By education we mean the process by which the cultural heritage is transmitted. Cultural heritages as Malinoski states are "... skills, ideas, reaction patterns, moral values, social attitudes and the beliefs, which constitute citizenship and personality" . Durkheim considers education as a social institution that functionally promotes consensus and social integration in new generation through convention of these personal qualities that can further be considered as a social process. Education is a potent agent not only for the social and psychological charming but it may influence productivity and economic development also and that's the reason why, for the last few years in the literature of development there has been much talk about the relationship between education and economic development and about education as investment (V.K.R. V. Rao, *Education & Human Resource Development*, Allied Publishers, New Delhi 1966) Apart from the physical capital investment, non-physical factors such as health, research, knowledge, organisation and administration etc. play an important role in change and development. (Gunnar Myrdal: *Asian Drama. An Enquiry into the Poverty of Nations*, Vol. II London, 1968, p. 1541). Education helps in the socialization of the child and the development of human personality, social mobility, occupational change and the rise of professionalism: it may increase productivity and economic development, as pointed out by Strumilin, Young, Schultz and Denison.

In the past education was one of the main considerations for hierarchical classification in Hindu society. Lack of it is largely responsible for the exploitation and pitiable plight of the tribals. For the tribals, education is the pivot on which their success depends. Education disseminates knowledge. Knowledge gives inner strength, which is very essential for the tribals for attaining freedom from exploitation and poverty. Due to ignorance and illiteracy, the tribals have not been able to take advantage of new economic opportunities. Disposition of tribal area to the developmental process have brought in juxtaposition two distinct value systems one based on tradition, ignorance and the other on technology and innovations. Harmonious synchronization of the two systems is essential for development of tribal people. In this process, education assumes a key role. The most important aspect of education in the tribal areas is that of informing the community of the new innovations in science and technology as well as the developments in the economic and political fields. Education must be meaningful to the people.

The tribal areas are rich in natural resources. A number of projects, both major and medium viz. irrigation, energy generation and industrial set up, have been set up in the tribal area. The tribals, due to lack of education and requisite skills are not able to take advantage of the new economic opportunities which have been grabbed by the outsider migrated to the tribal areas. It not only deprive them of the opportunity in the new ventures but also alienates them from their resource base, i.e., the land, forest and subjects them to exploitation by the middlemen and contractors in forest operations and also by the moneylenders.

Tribal Education: Indian Context

India has the single largest tribal population in the world compared to any other country with a population of 67.75 millions (1991 census). They constitute 8.1 per cent to the total population of the country. They are one of the most disadvantaged group in terms of educational development. Individual tribal groups have diverse socio-cultural life and are at various levels of social, economic and educational development. They have different degree of exposure to modernity and social change. The Scheduled Tribes constitute the most deprived and marginalised sections of Indian society. In this context, a host of welfare and developmental measures have been initiated for their social and economic development. The approaches and policies for their development have undergone changes and improvisation from time to time. In order to understand the educational development of tribes it is imperative to have a brief analysis of various trends in the policies and programmes of tribal development in general and education in particular.

The approaches and policies for tribal development in India can be broadly divided into four phases. The first phase covers the pre-independence period, during which the British adopted a policy of isolation and maintained a laissez faire. The second phase from 1947 to 1952 was more of a transition period for development of both general population and as well as for tribes since the administrative system witnessed structural changes during this period. From the year 1952 to 1975 the formulation of Five-Year Plans and systematic approach for planned development was adopted. During this period community development approach followed by formulation of Multipurpose Tribal Development Blocks was in vogue. This period constitutes the third phase. However, for the first time a comprehensive policy for tribal education was incorporated in the National Policy of Education 1986 followed by a programme of action with detailed strategies for implementation of the policies. This provides a new perspective for tribal education for quantitative and qualitative improvement. Further, the revised policy of 1992 and programme action strengthen the special policy and programmes for tribal education.

As a result of various programmes and policies we can visualise the result of a long run effort of tribal development and education. This can be measured only through the indicators of educational development. Factors like high literacy rate, low drop out rate and higher learning achievement could be described as development indicators. Literacy is an important and primary index of educational development. A glimpse of this data will provide the actual position of literacy among the tribals in relation to the decadal growth of tribal literacy, the gap between the tribal and non-tribal population in term of literacy, and inter-tribal variation etc.

The data in Table 9.1 present the rate of literacy since 1971-91. It has been found that literacy rate has gone up from a low of 11.30 in 1971 to 29.50 in 1991 for Scheduled Tribes. But the increase in the percentage of literacy does not express the over all growth of educational standard. In fact in terms of absolute number the number of illiterates have increased over the years. In comparison to general population the deprived groups have fared pretty badly and the gap between them is quite big. It is clear that, scheduled tribes have lagged behind the other disadvantaged group, i.e., scheduled castes in their educational progress. The degree and level of educational spread has not been same.

At the state level, among various segments of population and among various groups the progress had been uneven. The data indicates that some of the states with higher tribal concentration in relation to their total population have done exceedingly well in terms of higher literacy rate. States in the north-eastern region of India like Mizoram, Nagaland and Meghalaya fall in this category. While in the states like Madhya Pradesh, Orissa, Rajasthan, Andhra Pradesh tribal literacy is very low although these states are inhabited by much larger number of tribals than the northeastern states. The Table 9.2 also reveals that the states where the

Table 9.1 Literacy Rate 1971, 1981 and 1991

Census Year	Literacy Rate			Gap Between Rest of the Population	
	Scheduled Tribe	Scheduled Caste	Rest of the Population	Scheduled Tribe	Scheduled Caste
1971	11.3	14.67	33.8	22.5	19.13
1981	16.35	21.38	41.22	14.87	19.84
1981	29.6	37.41	62.65	33.05	25.24

Source : Census of India, 1971, 1981, 1991

literacy among tribes is lower than the national averages also lag behind the national general literacy rate. This can be further emphasized in the context of Orissa and its tribal district like Koraput.

Tribal Education in Orissa

During post-independence period, facilities in various forms have been provided in accordance with the principles of state policy under Article 46 of the Constitution for educational interest of Scheduled Tribes as a special responsibility of the central and state governments . Generally, the facilities have been extended by providing special residential and non-residential schools, school buildings, free studentship, scholarship and stipend, free dress, reading and writing materials and mid-day meals etc, The overall literacy rate of Orissa in 1991 was 49.1 per cent with 36.78 per cent for the Scheduled Castes and 22.31 per cent for the Scheduled Tribes in comparison to the national average of 52.1 per cent, 37.4 per cent and 29.60 per cent respectively. It might be instructive and illuminating to compare and see how the incidence of literacy among the tribal people of the state has increased during the last three decades in comparison with that of the general population. Table 9.3 indicates the districtwise percentage of literacy among the tribals and general population during the census, 1981.

It is seen that the percentage of literacy among the Scheduled Tribes was 13.96 as against 34.12 per cent in the total population. In all districts the literacy status of the tribal population is far behind that of the general population. It is interesting to note that the literacy status of tribal's males (23.27 per cent) is more or less equivalent to that of the females (21. 11 per cent) in the general population. It is also seen that in all districts the percentage of literacy for the total population, males and females among

Table 9.2 Literacy Rate of Scheduled Tribe (1971, 1981 and 1991)

State/Union Territory	1971			1981			1991		
	Male	Female	Persons	Male	Female	Persons	Male	Female	Persons
INDIA	17.6	4.85	11.3	24.5	8.05	16.35	40.7	18.19	29.6
Andhar Pradesh	8.33	2.13	5.34	12	3.48	7.82	25.3	8.68	17.16
Arunachal Pradesh	8.72	1.7	5.2	20.8	7.31	14.04	44	24.94	31.45
Assam	34.6	17.16	26.03	—	—	—	58.9	38.98	49.16
Bihar	18.5	1.85	11.46	26.2	7.76	16.99	38.4	14.75	26.78
Gujarat	21.8	6.15	14.12	30.4	11.64	21.14	48.3	24.2	36.45
Himachal Pradesh	26.3	5.53	15.89	38.8	12.82	25.93	62.7	31.18	47.09
Karanataka	21.7	7.67	14.85	30	10.03	20.14	48	23.57	36.01
Kerala	32	19.4	26.72	37.5	26.02	31.79	63.4	51.07	57.22
Madhya Pradesh	13.5	2.18	7.62	17.7	3.6	10.68	32.2	10.73	21.54
Maharashtra	19.1	4.21	11.74	32.4	11.94	22.29	49.1	24.03	36.79
Manipur	38.6	18.87	28.71	48.9	30.38	39.74	62.4	44.48	53.63
Meghalay	30.1	22.79	24.49	34.2	28.91	31.55	49.8	43.63	46.71
Mizoram	60.2	46.88	53.49	64.1	55.12	59.63	86.7	78.74	82.73
Nagaland	30.2	17.68	24.01	47.3	32.99	40.32	66.3	54.51	60.59

(Cont.)

State/Union Territory	*1971*			*1981*			*1991*		
	Male	*Female*	*Persons*	*Male*	*Female*	*Persons*	*Male*	*Female*	*Persons*
Orissa	16.4	2.58	9.46	23.3	4.76	13.69	34.4	10.21	22.31
Rajasthan	12	0.49	6.47	18.9	1.2	10.27	33.3	4.42	19.44
Sikkim	25.4	8.9	17.7	43.1	22.37	33.13	66.8	50.37	59.01
Tamil Nadu	13.3	4.48	9.02	26.7	14	20.46	35.3	20.23	27.89
Tripura	23.6	5.76	15.03	33.5	12.27	23.07	52.9	27.34	40.37
Uttar Pradesh	22.5	15.58	14.59	31.2	8.69	20.46	50	19.86	35.7
WestBengal	14.5	3.09	8.92	21.2	5.01	13.21	40.1	14.98	27.78
A & N Islands	24.1	11.1	17.85	38.4	23.24	31.11	61.2	48.74	56.62
Daman & Diu	20.3	5.08	12.73	33.7	18.89	26.43	63.6	41.49	52.91

Source : Census of India, 1971, 1981, 1991

Table 9.3 District-wise Percentage of Literacy among Scheduled Tribe and Total Populaltion 1981

District	Percentage of literacy among total Population			Percentage of literacy among the Scheduled Tribe		
	Total	Male	Female	Total	Male	Female
1	2	3	4	5	6	7
Sambalpur	40.02	47.98	19.67	19.98	32.65	7.16
Sundargarh	36.17	47.34	24.12	22.7	32.88	12.52
Keonjhor	29.89	42.61	16.95	15.26	25.78	4.86
Mayurbhanj	25.47	37.01	13.82	14.5	24.59	4.52
Balasore	41.84	45.07	28.32	11.21	19.36	2.9
Cuttack	45.33	58	32.3	10.78	18.45	2.93
Dhenkanal	36.7	51.4	21.39	14.65	25.18	4.02
Phulbani	26.61	41.96	11.26	18.59	32.98	4.74
Balangir	25.78	39.92	11.54	15.3	27.39	3.5
Kalahandi	19.35	31.18	7.65	11.54	21.25	2.14
Koraput	**15.83**	**23.17**	**8.44**	**6.31**	**11.05**	**1.65**
Ganjam	30.78	45.15	16.87	10.82	18.29	3.67
Puri	45.71	49.48	39.38	19.32	32.71	5.81
Orissa State	**34.12**	**46.9**	**21.11**	**13.96**	**23.27**	**4.76**

Source : Census of India 1981.

the Schedule Tribes is far behind as compared to the general population. The percentage of literacy among tribal females is 4,76 per cent against 21.11 per cent for their counterparts in the general population.

Education being the most important thrust area for socio-economic development of S.T. and S.C., the state government have undertaken various measures and programmes to improve the educational standard of these communities. Therefore, by the end of 1995-96, 202 High Schools including 51 for girls (Table 9.6), 109 Ashram Schools and 34 Kanyashrama (Table 9.5), 121 Residential Sevashrams, 951 Sevashram (Table 9.4), 8 special adivasi hostels and 1548 primary school hostels were functioning in the state. Moreover, up- gradation have been made in case of 3 Ashram school to High schools, one Kanyashram to girls high school, 20 Sevashrams to Ashram School, one Sevashram to Kanyashrama, 11 Sevashrama have been converted to residential Sevashram during 1995-96. Pre-Matric Scholarships have been awarded to 170680 S.T and 2,49,515 S.C. students

Table 9.4 Enrolment in Sevashrama and Residential Sevashrams

Year	Sevashrama				Residential Sevashrams			
	No.	Number of students on Roll			No.	Number of students on Roll		
		SC	ST	Total		SC	ST	Total
1	2	3	4	5	6	7	8	9
1990-91	1048	21292	51742	103650	79	1546	5558	8450
1991-92	1030	22662	53649	105355	94	1690	6660	9844
1992-93	1015	20415	54681	105664	105	1940	7136	10707
1993-94	1004	22655	55281	110334	113	1959	8473	12077
1994-95	983	21495	56363	107180	112	2065	9711	13529
1995-96	951	23192	58031	111028	121	1546	11762	16640

Source : Welfare Department, Govt. of Orisa.

Table 9.5 Number of Ashrams and Kanyashrams and Students on Rolls.

Year	Number of Schools			Number of Students on Roll			
	Ashram	*Kanyashram*	*Total.*	*S.C*	*ST.*	*Others*	*Total*
1	2	3	4	5	6	7	8
1990-91	68	30	98	2593	6942	1450	10985
1991-92	71	29	100	2594	7544	1520	11658
1992-93	73	29	102	2584	7630	1513	11727
1993-94	73	31	104	2433	8300	1617	12350
1994-95	89	33	122	2713	10867	2265	15845
1995-96	109	34	143	2766	11334	2575	16675

Source : Welfare Department, Government of Orissa.

Table 9.6 Number of High School and Students on Roll

Year	*Number of Schools*			*Number of Students on Roll*			
	Boys	*Girls*	*Total.*	*S.C*	*ST.*	*Others*	*Total*
1	*2*	*3*	*4*	*5*	*6*	*7*	*8*
1990-91	128	35	163	7175	21116	6803	35094
1991-92	130	38	168	7169	21154	6761	35084
1992-93	134	40	174	7524	22456	6759	36739
1993-94	138	42	180	7375	24388	6995	38758
1994-95	143	46	189	7489	26513	7481	41483
1995-96	151	51	202	8026	28112	7745	43883

Source : Welfare Department, Government of Orissa.

Table 9.7 Category wise Literacy Rate by Sex in Different Block/Urban Areas of Rayagada Distrcit 1991 Census

Sl. No.	Name of the Block/ Urban	All Class			S.C.			S.T.		
		Persons	Male	Female	Persons	Male	Female	Persons	Male	Female
1	2	3	4	5	6	7	8	9	10	11
1	Rayagada	15.9	23.75	8.37	17.81	27.5	8.18	8.23	14.2	2.56
2	Kashipur	13.2	22.04	4.47	16.08	27.5	4.64	6.51	12.1	1.13
3	Kolanara	26.03	37.69	14.62	28.26	43.2	14.02	13.6	22.8	4.87
4	K. Singpur	18.89	28.78	9.41	21.41	34.5	9.07	8.83	15.1	2.99
5	Gunupur	23.16	33.18	13.42	29.33	41.5	17.5	11.14	18.4	4.22
6	Gedari	19.27	29.29	9.3	26.51	41.7	11.46	11.22	19	3.53
7	B. Cuttack	21.01	31.47	11.19	19.22	32.4	6.45	8.61	15.6	2.19
8	Chandrapur	16.4	25.46	7.05	20.92	33.7	7.65	9.06	15.4	2.51
9	Muniguda	21.47	31.61	11.44	13.96	22.6	5.42	8.77	14.7	3.15
10	Ramanguda	28.34	40.95	15.7	24.08	36.8	11.31	15.54	26	5.27
11	Padmapur	34.51	48.97	19.93	25.83	40.8	10.95	17.28	28.6	6.48
URBAN										
1.	Rayagada (M.)	61.89	72.36	50.7	34.23	47.1	21.03	20.98	32.3	10.22
2.	Gunupur (N.A.C.)	57.95	69.9	45.89	32.29	47.2	18.53	18.75	26.9	10.85
3.	Gudari (N.A.C.)	60.76	72.56	48.84	25.41	38.5	13.66	22.94	32.1	14.18
4.	Chandili (C.T.)	63.6	75.43	50.9	37.02	53.7	20.27	13.52	20.4	7.37
	DISTRICT	26.01	36.53	15.63	21.46	33.6	9.49	10.39	17.7	3.4
	RURAL	20.79	31.01	10.79	19.64	31.5	7.95	10.12	17.4	3.21
	URBAN	61.3	72.43	49.57	33.26	47.4	19.37	19.77	29.9	10.17

Source : Welfare Department, Government of Orissa.

Table 9.8 Number of Primary School, Middle School and Secondary Schools

	Year / Block / U.L.B.	*Number of Primary*	*Number of Middle*	*Number of Secondary*
	1992-93	1,333	147	53
	1993-94	1,346	147	56
	1994-95	1,360	147	59
1	Rayagada	304	13	8
2	Kashipur	283	20	4
3	Kolanara	298	11	4
4	K. Singpur	229	13	4
5	Gunupur	332	15	8
6	Gudari	244	9	1
7	Bissam Cuttack	235	16	6
8	Chandrapur	83	7	2
9	Muniguda	140	11	4
10	Ramanguda	170	8	4
11	Padmapur	232	15	6
	URBAN			
1	Rayagada (M)	98	5	4
2	Gunupur (N.A.C.)	83	3	3
3	Gudari (N.A.C.)	40	1	1

Source : District Statistical Hnadbook 1995 pp 49-50.

and Post-Matric Scholarship to 17,191 S.T. and 27,989 S.C. students during this year. Following table (Table 9.4, 9.5, 9.6) gives a clear picture of the initiative taken by the state government for educational development of Scheduled Tribes.

Educational Development in Rayagada District

The literacy rate in the district as per 1991 census is 26.01 per cent against the state average of 49. 1 per cent. The S.C. literacy rate is 21.46 per cent in comparison to total literacy rate 36.78 of the state and district literacy rate of S.T. is 10.39 per cent in comparison to 22.31 per cent of the state. This picture shows a very poor performance of Scheduled Tribes education of the district. In the Table 9.7 it is clear that Padampur block has

Table 9.9 Number of Colleges for General Education, Teachers and Students in Different Blocks and Urban Areas of Rayagada District

	Year / Block / U.L.B.	*Number of College*	*Number of Teacher*	*Number of Students*	*SC*	*ST*
	1992-93	9	148	3,864	409	255
	1993-94	10	159	3,996	429	269
	1994-95	10	175	4,154	401	286
	1994-95					
1	Bissan-Cuttack	1	5	172	25	14
2	Padmapur	1	19	91	9	1
3	Kalyansingpur	1	6	28	7	1
4	Ramanguda	1	11	209	16	15
5	Muniguda	1	12	225	33	25
6	Kasipur	1	5	89	10	10
	URBAN					
1	Gunupur (N.A.C.)	1	42	1,234	125	116
2	Giudari (N.A.C.)	1	10	173	17	12
3	Rayagada (M)	2	65	1,933	159	92

Source : District Statistical Handbook 1995 pp 49-50.

the highest ST literacy rate of 17.28 per cent followed by 15.54 per cent of Ramanguda block. This also reflects very low literacy performance in spite of many suitable steps taken by the state government.

As on 1995 the district has 1,360 primary schools, 147 middle schools and 59 secondary schools. Highest number of primary school exist in our study block Gunupur, i.e., 332 followed by 304 of Rayagada block. The number of middle school is 20 (highest in Kasipur block) followed by 16 in Bissam Cuttack, 15 in Gunupur block. This is a notable fact that the number of middle school is very less in comparison to primary school of the district (See Table 9.8). Likewise there are total 10 colleges for general education in the district of which only one is womens' college. There are 175 teachers in those 10 general educational colleges and 4154 total number of students in the year 1995. Among them 401 and 286 students are of S.C. and ST resepctively. (See Table 9.9). This also shows a very poor aptitude for

Table 9.10 Literacy Rate in Gunupur Block

Category	Male	Female	Total
General	33.18	13.42	23.16
Scheduled Caste	41.45	17.5	29.33
Scheduled Tribe	18.38	4.22	11.14

Source : District Statistical Handbook 1995.

Table 9.11 Number of Primary, Middle, Secondary School & Collages, Teachers and Students in Gunupur Block

School/College	*No. of School*	*No. of Teacher*	*No. of Students*			
			Total	*SC*	*ST*	*Per cent*
Primary School	332	332	7025	798	4112	58.534
Middle School	15	74	14393	296	304	20.362
Secondary School	8	57	1166	193	433	37.136
College	1	42	1234	125	116	9.4003

Source : District Statistical Handbook 1995.

higher education among the tribals of the district. The reasons for this poor result has been discussed the educational level of *Saora* land.

Educational Profile of Gunupur Block

As it has been already discussed that Gunupur is our study area and it is under the administrative district of Rayagada, therefore it is pertinent to focus the literacy of the *Saora* land to derive the standard of education among the tribals.

Literacy Rate in Gunupur Area

The Table 9.10 shows the level of literacy among the people of Gunupur block. In this block the tribal literacy is 11.14 which is very less in comparison to the total literacy of the block of 23.16. Among the tribal male education is 18.38 comparison to the block level literacy of 33.18, but female literacy is 4.22 among the tribals in comparison to the total female literacy of the are a 13.42. It shows the female literacy among the tribals is quite neglected. In all these processes the level of education among the *Saora* tribals is very less.

The Table 9.11 show that in the Gunupur block there are 332 primary schools and it has total 7,025 students out of which 4,112 are scheduled tribe students, 798 Scheduled Caste students, and 2115 remaining are general students. Since this area is tribal inhabited area the number of students admitted into school education is more as evident from the above in Table 9.11. After primary schools there is 15 middle schools in this area where the total students is 1,493 whereas the Scheduled Tribes students are only 304. This clearly indicates the level of education among the *Saora* tribe. Though for primary 4,112 students admitted, for middle school only 20.36 per cent students continue. This clearly states the high drop out among the scheduled tribe students. For secondary level there are eight schools where the total student is 1,166 but the tribal representation 433, i.e.37.13 per cent. This also shows neglecting aspect of the tribal education. Here the number of tribal students varies from middle 304, secondary 433 because at this level tribal students from other area they join the local schools. When we see the college level the total students 1,234 and the scheduled tribe students are 116 which is 9.40 per cent . This trend also shows the poor level of higher education among the scheduled tribe in this area.

Saora Attitude Towards Education

By the general observation of the researcher, it is found that tribal's attitudes towards education is very poor. One of the notable problems of education for the tribals especially in the rural areas where about 80 per cent per cent of the total population lives, is that education operates under the Law of Diminishing Demand. This is because the majority of the parents are illiterate and think that there is no demand for education to cater their environmental needs which reflects their ecological mindset. The economic condition is such that the parents are indifferent to education; they are neither against sending their children to school nor do they take interest in sending them to school. If at all they prevent the children from going to school, it is mainly due to economic reasons. The researcher had the occasion to talk with some parents in *Saora* villages about their indifference to education. Some of them categorically stated that they were not very much in favour of sending their children to schools because they would be required to look after their cultivable lands when the parents grow old. They did not mind sending them up to certain level to enable them to read and write. They would rather encourage their children to go to schools if education was given by considering their need and their environment. Perhaps the migration of educated children to outside discourage some of the parents from sending their children to schools.

The tribal people, being mostly cultivators, are engaged in the fields from early dawn to dusk. There is a greater demand for additional hands. Hence the parents withdraw their children from schools and put them on to work in the fields; minding the cattle or primary level is mind-boggling. The socio-economic conditions, the house-hold environment and the school atmosphere are some of the factors that lead to excessive dropout rate. The majority of the teachers at the primary level are neither trained nor qualified—ignorant of child psychology, they punish the children for childish behaviour or for poor learning ability.

Tribals are not against education even for women. When the missionaries first started to teach them how to read and write, the womenfolk were advised by the elders that it was not good for them. This did not deter the women folk. This is because tribal society has never kept the women in seclusion (*purdah*); they share life with men shoulder to shoulder. Women are held in higher esteem in the tribal culture than in some surrounding cultures. Higher education for them however was not very much valued. The educated tribals offer a great contrast to their illiterate brethren in their attitude to education. As opposed to the latter, they have very high aspiration for education. They prefer to send their children to schools and would do everything to give them education. The villagers hold teachers in high esteem. They respect the teachers and look to them as their leaders in village affairs. This gives a hope of eradicating the tribals' indifferent attitude to education but it needs on a concerted and an organised effort.

Broadly, the attitude and aspiration of the tribals have three stages. The first is the passive stage where they showed apathy. The second is the stage of indifference which, as pointed out earlier, is due to ignorance. The third is the stage of positive attitude and aspiration. Indifference is the major prevailing attitude in the rural areas where about 80 per cent of the tribal population resides. This can be proved when we see the responses of a question as to 'whether tribals think that education will change and enhance the standard of living of the Lanjia *Saora*'. In response to this out of total sample of 230, 135 young from which 124 responed said 'yes' (92 per cent) and 10 'no', (7.4 per cent) one 'can not say". Among the middle and old age group it is 100 per cent. When this has been further classified on religion basis, it show that 105 Hindus say (96 per cent) 'yes'

Table 9.12 Does Education Enhance Standard of Living ?

Variables	*Age*								*Religion*						*Occupation*					
Response	*Young*		*Middle*		*Old*		*Total*		*Hindu*		*Non-Hindu*		*Total*		*Agriculture*		*Non-Agriculture*		*Total*	
	F	%	F	%	F	%	F	%	F	%	F	%	F	%	F	%	F	%	F	%
Yes	124	92	63	100	32	100	219	95	105	96	114	94.2	219	95	150	95	69	96	219	95
No	10	7.4	0	0	0	0	10	4.3	3	2.8	7	5.79	10	4.3	8	5.1	2	2.8	10	4.3
Can't Say	1	0.7	0	0	0	0	1	0.4	1	0.9	0	0	1	0.4	0	0	1	1.4	1	0.4
Total	135	100	63	100	32	100	230	100	109	100	121	100	230	100	158	100	72	100	230	100

3 Hindu 'no' and one 'can not say'. Non-Hindu 114 says 'yes' and 7 'no'. In occupational point of view it has the responses like out of 158 total agricultural group 150 'yes' (95 per cent), 8 'no' and out of 72 non-agriculture group, 69, (96 per cent) 'yes', 2 'no' and one 'can not say'. Out of total 230, 219, (95 per cent) 'yes', 10, (4.3 per cent) 'no' and one 'can not say'. This statistics show that maximum tribal opine in the affirmative tune. From the point of view of age, religion occupational it is 'yes' for education. So from this it is clear that education is a powerful agent for tribal development and change. After finding out the strong willingness for education, it is important to see the level of education of this tribe, which will clear and show the relationship between the expectation and reality.

Level of Education Among Saora Tribe

The education of *Saora* tribe was quite neglected before independence. In 1866 AD (Three years after the coming of British) there was not a single school in the undivided district of Koraput (Gazetteer: 359) After ten years a school was opened at Gunupur area and in Koraput district. Here it may be mentioned that the Christian missionaries rendered valuable services and did a considerable amount of spadework for spread of education (Gazetteer: 309). They earnestly took up the work of educating children and adults. The Schlesoring Holstein Evangelical Lutheran Mission Society of Germany (SHELM) and its worthy child, the Jeypore Evangelical Lutheran Church (JELC), maintained for some time about 25 per cent of Higher Elementary and about 12 per cent of Lower Elementary schools in the district. Towards 1895-96, there were 120 schools in the Agency under the charge of the Assistant Agents at Koraput and Parvatipuram with 2,551 pupils. (Gazetter:359).

Considering the population of the district, the progress was indeed inspiring. But it was inevitable under the circumstances. The bulk of the population is composed of aboriginal tribes. Although complete apathy to education among the hill tribes was not found, though the general attitude in the villages was one of complete indifference. Besides, the schools were opened for obvious reasons of policy in the larger villages where the best attendance could be expected. But the hill tribes live in small settlements. Lastly, the unhealthy climate coupled with the existence of vast areas of inaccessible forest belts kept this district out of the light of modern civilisation for a long time.

In 1931 only 15 persons in every one thousand could be classed as literate. Muslims were the best-educated community, with 150 per thousand literates, followed by the Christians with 10 per thousand. Among the subdivisions Gunupur has always been the most advanced, and in 1931 it was found that there were 32 per thousand literate.

Sagada and Puttasingi Panchayat

In the Sagada panchayat where this study was conducted the tribal literacy is 34 per cent. There are only seven schools and anganbadi in this area. The Lanjia *Saora* Development Agency provided 17 non-formal education centre for the tribals. This shows the standard and level of education among the tribals in this two panchayats. But when we go by the statistics of the whole block of Gunupur where mostly Lanjia *Saora* resides their educational level is very less. Since education is less, their understanding to protect forest is also very less as there is a direct link between education and ecology. In this connection a question was asked to assess 'how government has helped for educational development for the tribals' in this area. In Table 9.13, where it has stated that 93, (40 per cent) said 'beneficial' and 128, (56 per cent) 'not very beneficial'. So it is clear from above statistics that government intervention has a minimum impact on the level of education.

Causes of Educational Backwardness

There are several factors responsible for slow progress in educational development among the tribe. These factors can be broadly be classified under two broad groups, i.e., (1) Institutional and administrative factors and (2) Socio economic factor, under the first category following observations have been made.

Early authorities (Elwin 1963, Srivastava, 1967) have observed that inadequacy of educational institutions in the tribal areas is a major impediment in the progress of education among the tribes. Although special yardstick has been prescribed to have a primary school in tribal areas, there are still many sparsely populated tribal village/basti having no school. According to Universal Bench Mark Survey conducted in 118 Blocks of the Sub-Plan area of Orissa in 1979 about 50 per cent of the hamlets/ villages have no primary schools within their habitations, further, 27.85 per cent still depend on primary school in other habitations located at a distance of below one Km., and 13.00 per cent between 1 to 3 Kms. Sometimes multiple approach to the system of education created confusion among the tribal students. There are traditional schools and special schools

Table 9.13 Benefits of Govt. Measures for Education

Variables	*Age*								*Religion*						*Occupation*					
Response	*Young*		*Middle*		*Old*		*Total*		*Hindu*		*Non-Hindu*		*Total*		*Agriculture*		*Non-Agriculture*		*Total*	
	F	%	F	%	F	%	F	%	F	%	F	%	F	%	F	%	F	%	F	%
Beneficial	49	36	33	52	11	34	93	40	39	36	54	45	93	40	57	36	36	50	93	40
Not very Beneficial	83	61	26	41	19	59	128	56	66	61	62	51	128	56	94	59	34	47	128	56
Can't Say	3	2.2	4	6.3	2	6.3	9	3.9	4	3.7	5	4.1	9	3.9	7	4.4	2	2.8	9	3.9
Total	135	100	63	100	32	100	230	100	109	100	121	100	230	100	158	100	72	100	230	100

besides several other types with different curriculum and sets of facilities provided by the management. The special schools meant for the tribals indicate discrimination and discourages the tribal students seeking admission.

Studies conducted by T.H.R.T.I. and other agencies and the findings of the Dhebar Commission (1960) and Commissioner for Scheduled Castes and Scheduled Tribes have revealed that inadequacy or non-availability of suitable infrastructure facilities like school building, hostel, teacher's quarters, equipment, water supply, etc. are responsible for slow progress of education among the tribal people. Absenteeism of teachers and non-availability of right type of teachers who are familiar with tribal language, customs and modes of life are also stated to be the reasons for slow progress. Curricula and methods of teaching and the textbooks prescribed which are not familiar to them do not encourage tribal students. Lack of supervision and inspection at regular interval and if at all any inspection is done, silent over taking appropriate and prompt actions for removal of bottlenecks is responsible for slow progress in the advancement of education in tribal areas. As regards socio-economic and its allied factors hindering progress of education, following facts may be mentioned.

Language is said to be one of the major impediments for the spread of education. Medium of instruction in Oriya is not easily intelligible to the tribal students speaking their own dialect. Most of the teachers appointed also do not understand the language of the students. This causes communication gap between teacher and pupil. Imparting education through books in tribal language is also difficult as many tribal languages have no script and cannot be prepared properly in some other languages. In order to eradicate this hindrance some States have adopted tribal languages, which have script as medium of instruction at primary level. Lack of motivation, enthusiasm and knowledge of the utility of education among the tribal parent's stand as barrier in educational advance.

Because of economic hardship, they have a subsistence economy in which all members of a house, irrespective of age and sex, have to work according to the capacity for earning their livelihood. As a result of this, tribal parents engage their children in some household work instead of sending them to school. Moreover, lack of congenial environment of institutions do not attract the tribal children. Unsuitable atmosphere like space and light or reading, lack of parental care and guidance at their homes and villages for reading do not help tribal children to devote time at home in their studies. Celebration of religious festivals and socio-religious

Table 9.14 Reasons for Educational Backwardness

Variables	Age								Religion						Occupation					
Response	Young		Middle		Old		Total		Hindu		Non-Hindu		Total		Agriculture		Non-Agriculture		Total	
	F	%	F	%	F	%	F	%	F	%	F	%	F	%	F	%	F	%	F	%
Lack of Infra-structure	11	8.1	7	11	4	13	22	9.6	12	11	10	8.3	22	9.6	16	10	6	8.3	22	9.6
Financial Problems	51	38	22	35	21	66	94	41	42	39	52	43	94	41	68	43	26	36	94	41
Parent's Backwardness	40	30	16	25	5	16	61	27	29	27	32	26	61	27	39	25	22	31	61	27
More work oriented	6	4.4	5	7.9	0	0	11	4.8	6	5.5	5	4.1	11	4.8	7	4.4	4	5.6	11	4.8
All the above	27	20	13	21	2	6.3	42	18	20	18	22	18	79	18	28	18	14	19	79	18
Total	135	100	63	100	32	100	230	100	109	100	121	100	230	100	158	100	72	100	230	100

ceremonies, like marriage and death rites divert the attention of the tribal children.

Evil design and intention of the neighbouring non-tribal people and traders and moneylenders do not encourage the tribals to send their children to school, so that the tribal will remain where they are. In this context a question have been asked to the *Saora* tribal to find out the 'cause of educational backwardness'. In table.9.14 it has been stated that 'lack of infrastructure' 22, (9.6 per cent), 'financial problem' 94, (41 per cent), 'parents backwardness' 61, (27 per cent) 'more work oriented' 11, (4.8 per cent), and all the above reasons are responsible for educational backwardness. So with all the above mentioned categorical problems all other problems are still persist which this researcher found in the study area. Interplay of these factors have resulted in alarming rate of wastage and stagnating in the educational development among the tribal people. In this context, wastage may be defined as dropping out of students before completion of a given course and stagnating means both low rate of enrolment in comparison to total strength in the school-going age-groups and also students already enrolled, when taking several more years to complete a given course. As per the Universal Benchmark Survey in the Tribal Sub-plan area of Orissa in 1979 only 10.35 per cent in the age group of 0-6 years were going to school. Similarly in the age group of 6-11 years and 11-16 years, only 31.31 per cent and 15.63 per cent were attending schools, respectively. Enrolment of tribal students at Primary School and High School levels during 1988-89 as mentioned in the booklet entitled, "Education in Orissa" of the Directorate of Elementary Education (Statistics Cell) gives a similar picture. The strength of student 437 at M.E. School level is roughly one-fifth of the Primary level and at High School level it is about one-tenth.

Education and Forest

While discussing the drawbacks of educational development of tribals we have discussed contents of education, where it has been clearly stated that their environmental needs and culture has not been taken up in the school, college educational curriculum. The general contents of education have been extended to the tribal areas, which in many cases are not relevant, particularly at the level of primary education.

Secondly, today education makes the people and tribals more greedy and consumeristic. The increase interaction of tribals with the development agencies and exposable to market economy has helped them to understand

Table 9.15 How More Education will Preserve Forest?

Variables	*Age*								*Religion*						*Occupation*					
Response	*Young*		*Middle*		*Old*		*Total*		*Hindu*		*Non-Hindu*		*Total*		*Agriculture*		*Non-Agriculture*		*Total*	
	F	%	F	%	F	%	F	%	F	%	F	%	F	%	F	%	F	%	F	%
Understanding the value of forest	79	59	36	57	22	69	137	60	71	65	66	54.5	137	60	97	61	40	56	137	60
Less dependency on forest economy	18	13	4	6.3	4	13	26	11	10	9.2	16	13.2	26	11	26	10	10	14	26	11
Education brings awareness	7	5.2	12	19	0	0	19	8.3	5	4.6	14	11.6	19	8.3	15	9.5	4	5.6	19	8.3
Impossible because we depend on forest	23	17	6	9.5	4	13	33	14	17	16	16	13.2	33	14	20	13	13	18	33	14
Can't say	8	5.9	5	7.9	2	6.3	15	6.5	6	5.5	9	7.44	15	6.5	10	6.3	5	6.9	15	6.5
Total	135	100	63	100	32	100	230	100	109	100	121	100	230	100	158	100	72	100	230	100

their limitations in terms of bargaining with the outsiders (Sujatha , 2000:50). When we have been educated and looking for higher standard of living and the opportunity, it is a general tendency among the human species to exploit the natural resources to a get profit and seek pleasure. That is the same case of tribals.

But the true sense of education can be the only solution to this. As tribals opine that more education will help to preserve forest by 'understanding the importance and value of forest', 'less dependency on forest' and 'education brings awareness'. The crucial response in this regard is that out of 230 tribals only 33, (14 per cent) said that it is impossible that more education will preserve forests, as they solely depend on it. Otherwise our response in respect of age, religion and occupation is loud and overwhelming as 137, (60 per cent) say 'education will help to understand the importance of forest', 26, (13 per cent) say 'less dependency on forest economy' and 19, (8.3 per cent) says 'education will bring awareness'.

But today the situation is grim as tribals are forced to cut the jungle since they do not have any alternative. After the panchayati raj and other developmental programmes have started the small leaders to cheat the people and have connivance with the government official to cut the tree and sell in the local area to get the profit. Here it is the educated person those who have a high rank in the society, they use to do all this by which there is a large scale forest depletion. And as a result the poor man suffers to construct his material and cultural aspects of its livelihood. This was clearly substantiated when we saw (Chapter VIII) where the forest guard and ranger use to ask for money to the innocent tribals if they cut the tree for a genuine reason. There are many tribals who have told this to the researcher. It is solely the education and opening of the tribal society responsible for the degradation of social ecology of the whole area.

Conclusion

During the past few years, tribal education has witnessed a rapid transformation particularly in the area of access, pedagogic reform and community participation. It is always accepted that education is a dynamic and powerful tool for socio-economic development and changes, in each and every society. This is also applicable to tribals in general and *Saora* tribes in particular. Through education the cultural heritage is transmitted from one generation to another and functionally promotes consensus and social integration among new generation. The tribal population is 8.1 per cent of total population of our country. Due to various welfare measure, there is a progress in it. It has been found that since 1971-91 the literacy rate has increased from 11.3 0 to 29.50. Likewise in Orissa by 1991, it is 22.31 per cent. There is increase in the number of sevashram, residential sevashram, and kanyashram, which helped for the educational upliftment of the tribals. At the district level literacy rate is 10.39 per cent and at the block level (Gunupur) it is 11.14 per cent. There is an increase in the number of primary and secondary school in the area.

The general observation of this researcher is that *Saora's* attitude towards education is very poor and it operates in the law of diminishing return. This is due to illiteracy and ignorance of parents followed by non-conducive atmosphere of education. Their economic life is also not in favour of education as they put the child to work. But with contradiction to this one of our analysis shows that 95 per cent tribals said education could enhance the standard of living. Likewise the intervention of government for educational development is below the satisfaction level and not very beneficial. There are many causes for educational backwardness of the tribal, to which language or medium of teaching is more acute. The other causes are financial problem, parents backwardness, lack of infrastructure etc.

In this above finding the forest resources and education is also evident that the educational backwardness of *Saora* is because of not teaching the immediate tribal needs. In the whole educational process nothing has been taught about their own cultures and forest. But even though 60 per cent *Saora* said that education can bring change in the values to understand the importance of forest. Therefore, it can be very clearly set out that through educational development change can be possible and the protection of natural resources also.

References

Durkheim, E., 1956, Education and Society, D. Fox (Trans.) Glencoe, Ill, Free Press.

Gunnar Myrdal, 1968, *Asian Drama : An Enquiry into the Poverty of Nations*, London, Vol. III.

Government of Orissa, 1980, *District Gazateer, Koraput*. Cuttack, Govt. Press.

Government of Orissa, 1988-89 *Education in Orissa*, Directorate of Elementary Education (Statistic cell) Govt. of Orissa.

Government of Orissa, 1989, *Scheduled Tribes and Scheduled Castes of Orissa*, Bhubaneshwar, Harijan and Tribal Welfare Department.

Malinowski, B., 1943, 'The Pan–African Problem of Culture Contact', *American Journal of Sociology*, Vol. XLVIII, No. 6, pp. 649-665.

Patnaik, N., 1972, *Tribes and Their Development: A Study of Two Tribal Development Blocks in Orissa*, Hydrabad, NICD.

Pati, R.N., and Jena, B., (ed), *Tribal Development in India*, New Delhi, Ashish Publication.

Rao, V.K.R.V., 1966, *Education and Human Resource Development*, New Delhi, Allied Publishers.

Rath, S.N., 1981, 'A Note on Tribal Education', L.P. Vidyarthi (ed.) *Tribal Development and its Administration*, New Delhi, Concept Publishing Company.

Sujatha, K. 2000, *Education Among Tribals*, New Delhi, NIEPA.

Srivastav, O., 1978, 'Continuing Education and Tribal Development: The Role of College near Tribal Areas, *Indian Journal of Adult Education*, 39:4.

10

Conclusion

An attempt has been made in this study to explore the inter-linkages and interdependency of various institutions developed by *Saora* tribals on forests. How far the symbiotic dependency of these institutions has disturbed in due course of time has been systematically explored. Many studies have been reviewed in the beginning of the study to arrive at a theoretical base to this study.

With this background of theoretical analysis and studies on man and nature, a relationship has been traced between the *Saora* tribe of Koraput district of Orissa and their forest resources. It has been discussed at three levels—Orissa, Koraput district and *Saora*-inhabited region. The Koraput area occupies the hilly and southern forest region of Orissa. A great socio-economic and cultural similarity exists between Orissa on the one hand and Koraput and *Saora* tribe on the other. The Koraput region is mostly dominated by Scheduled Castes and Scheduled Tribes. Therefore, there are differences in the language and festivals prevalent across Orissa and those in the Koraput region. Further the Koraput people speak their own dialect 'Koraputia'and *Saora* speak their 'Saora' dialect. Tribal festivals are a bit different than the pan-Orissan festivals.

The discussion has started with social structure of *Saora* tribe. To draw insight from existing literature, the contribution of anthropologists like H. Spencer, Radcliffe Brown, R. Firth, B.Malinowski has been discussed. On the basis of the writings of these anthropologists, we can say that social structure evolves from an interaction between tribes and their forests or their ecosystem. The *Saora* tribe has its own distinct patterns of living and social interaction. The social structure of this tribe is based on their family, marriage and kinship, with strong roots in their local ecosystem.

Traditionally, the *Birinda* lineage had more importance and the people of one *Birinda* were considered as a single family. On this basis their marriage and kinship was governed. By this rule, *Saoras* cannot marry in their own *Birinda.* For death, marriage and other ceremonials the whole *Birinda* takes a collective initiative. Among the *Birinda* families the important ones are *Gamangos, Naik, Karji, Dalbehera, Bad-Rahit,* etc. The *Saora* village coexists with these *Birinda* groups or families. Traditionally *Gamango Birinda*s with the help of others like *Naiks* and *Dalabehera* used to decide the village affairs and the decision of the *Gamango* head arrived from of consensus was supposed to be the final. The *Birinda*-based social structure was not only sensitive about society but also about nature and forest. In traditional times, cutting of big trees by tribals was punished and fined.

In the course of time, this system has changed. The family, marriage and kinship rules are no more rigid. Tribes of *Saora Birinda* are marrying within their own *Birinda*, unlike their predecessors. The importance of forest is not the concern of *Gamangos*, as the *Gamango* has lost his importance in the tribal area. There is a change in the family size and structure. Due to their economic needs, the tribals earlier used to marry more than one wife by which their economic status could increase. The shifting cultivation requires lot of labour so they used to marry more than one wife to put them to work. All this has changed under the impact of education and Christianity. Compound family is being replaced by nuclear family.

As the *Birinda* system underwent change, it had a definite impact on the traditional political structure of *Saora.* Their traditional political life was dependent on family bonds. In traditional political life the *Gamango* was given the highest position followed by *Dalabebra, Bad rahit.* These people maintained the system and a fine was imposed on anybody deviating from the established practice. This system has completely disappeared now.

Nowadays, the traditional *Gomango* governance system has been completely taken over by the Panchayata raj system. Tribals elect their Panchayat members like Sarapanch, and ward member. For any kind of help or justice, the tribals approach the ward members first, then Sarpanch. The activities of panchayat members are not that effective in comparison to *Gomango* system, though many tribals accept the change and like it. But the modern Panchayat leaders are not taking any initiative to safeguard the forests resulting in disruption in social institutions, which were traditionally dependent on ecosystem. This can be attributed to the government intervention. In this context tribals have suggested that

Panchayat member must take initiative for plantation, social awareness and economic rehabilitation by which forest can be protected, thereby nurturing the ecology, economy, culture and religion of the *Saoras*.

After the political system, this study has tried to understand the religion and belief system of *Saoras*. The traditional *Saora* religion has two important aspects: (a) Shaman (religious official), (b) The concept of many goods. There are a number of gods in *Saora* religion. The rites and rituals govern the whole life of *Saora*. Lot of sacrifice is involved in their traditional Hindu religion. The impact of Christianity is also being noticed. The tribals cite economic exploitation as the cause for leaving Hindu religion. The traditional religion of *Saora* has changed to a considerable extent. It seems to the researcher that only ten percent tribals now believe in their traditional religion in toto. Though 90 percent tribals have not converted to Christianity, yet they do not practice the age-old rules, rites and rituals. With this, the traditional festivals and religious functions have changed. *Saoras* are celebrating X-mas with more pomp and gay. There is a declining trend of *Saora* traditional festivals mainly due to decline of forest resources. This related factor of forest and festival celebration makes it explicit as to how the social ecology is important for sociologists and social ecologists both. This clearly corroborates the proposition as to how forest has defined the economy, religion and culture of *Saoras*.

In the cultural context, the material and non-material culture of the *Saora* have been traced. The concept of *Ukka* and *Ersi* is existing to a negligible per cent. The material culture is mostly forest-based even today with the co-existence of modern things like TV, Radio, and Tape recorder. Thus, modernity and tradition are found to co-exist in material culture while in the context of non-material culture, beliefs, values all have changed significantly.

The folk songs and folk culture reflect the forest, tribe relation. *Saoras* can be considered as folk society, where folk culture, folk tradition and folk songs are essential part of the total culture of the *Saora* community. In the context of the dress and ornament, *Saoras* have adopted the modern dress and ornaments leaving the traditional dress and ornaments. The tribes categorise their traditional dress and ornament as 'Hinduised', and hence inferiors. In the perspective of tribal music *Saoras* are fond of their own music, as they can understand it. Their frequency of listening to radio, and other recreational activities has been discussed in this study where it was found that, they are moving away from their traditional songs and recreational activities. The microscopic model of change can explain it better as it involves changes in each and every aspect of society. On the cultural front *Saora* society has changed in all aspects. Few *Saora* take up social activities in their free time, some go to watch movies and others listen to radio. The old-age people are busy socialising and teach the traditional way of life to the younger generation.

The communication system has also been responsible for change in *Saora* society. It can be understood in the context of descriptive and symbolic conception. The descriptive aspect of culture is related to beliefs, values and attitudes. This has changed due to various reasons, which created and recreated new symbols. This has been because of the use of new technology, which expresses the symbols meaningfully. This is evident by seeing the TV, radio, music systems, etc. However, there is contradiction, as it is found that tribals prefer the music in their own language, because they cannot understand other languages. In dress and ornaments, they prefer the modern one because of two reasons: (a) the traditional dress is related to Hinduism, (b) it also reflect and shows that they are 'tribal'. Because of these two reasons they discard their traditional dress to change their identity as tribals.

Like *Saora* culture, *Saora* economy is also fully based on forest. It is important at two levels for *Saora*: (a) substantive (b) formal. The forest is mostly the base of the economy of the *Saora*, on which they depend for their subsistence. On the formal context, it is based on choice and availability. *Saora* don't have any alternative or choice. So it is the substantive basis of *Saora* economy. It can also be called substantive nature of their economy. The *Saora* economy can be seen in an 'integrated patterns' as it involves reciprocity and redistribution. The peasant community is discussed in this study as folk peasantry, as it reflects the whole notion of economy and culture. A reference has also been made here to various developmental strategies provided by the Constitution to bring the tribals into the mainstream. A coercive economic planning is difficult as the tribals adhere to a different kind of economy. The *Saoras* are considered as settled tribals. Because of the practice of shifting cultivation the nomadic nature is very less. The social arrangement of property relation is a hurdle for better economic growth of the tribals.

Today, the *Saora* practise shifting cultivation and also depend on forest for minor forest produces. The quality of forest produces has deteriorated due to deforestation, population growth and fluctuating climatic conditions. Due to lack of rain and depleting forest resources the *Saora* tribals are migrating, for higher wages and regular work. This reflects the change in forest ecology. The picture of tribal market is also reflected: many outsiders came to local market to buy the local products at cheap price and sell it in other markets. This study also brings out the linkages of forest and urbanization. This linkage reflects considerable exploitation of forest resources, as there is a constant link of *Saora* land with the block level market Gunupur. This has brought change in the ideas, economy and other social aspects of *Saora*.

It is evident that the forest-based economy of *Saora* has changed and tribals have suggested plantation, check on deforestation, educational awareness and economic rehabilitation as means to bring desired change in their economy, culture, social structure, religion, etc.

For this, various forest policies have been traced. Much before the independence Orissa had only one Conservator of forest. When Orissa merged with twenty-five princely states twenty-two forest zones were created. To save the forest from the exploitation of zamidar, Private Forest Act 1947 was enacted. This has divided the forests into Forest "A" and Forest "B" where the public can only use the "B" forest, for which they have to pay 'Nistar-Cess'.

This situation underwent change after Independence in 1948. Forest "A" and "B" have been merged with the provision of reserve forests under Indian Forest Act. In spite of this, the depletion of forest has increased, mainly because of two reasons; (a) Shifting cultivation, (b) Connivance of smugglers with forest officials. The total area of deforestation by 1982 is upto the extent of 18, 106.45 hectare. After this 1988 New Forest Policy has come into existence. In this context, Prof. K.L. Sharma observes that this policy came "from the top". Many *Saora* opine that government interaction has created the disenchantment among the tribals and it is bad for the tribal interest. It is found that the government intervention is not people oriented as it only fulfils the interest of state and not of the people.

To make the forest more people oriented, what can be done? In this perspective tribal education has been examined. Many *Saoras* said that education could bring change in their life and ecology. Due to various government plans there is a change in the literacy rate among the tribals. There are many constraints which have been observed by this researcher—for example, as of medium of teaching, parent's backwardness, and lack of infrastructure are the various important causes of educational backwardness. The new Education System also misses the link of local needs in its teaching, which delinks forest and ecology from social institutions. But education can bring change in the forest ecology and tribal life only through "proper education", which must be based on the local needs.

Findings

1. The forest is no more available for tribal needs. By which, the survival strategy is in danger leading to change in the social structure, religious activities, culture and economic activities.
2. The forest eco-system has completely altered and adversely affecting the rainfall in the region. It is pertinent to note here that deforestation has created shortage of rainfalls leading to further depletion of forest resources. Since forest ecology is disturbed and rainfall is less, the water level and watershed properties automatically have gone down.
3. Due to opening of tribal areas to outsiders and modern means of transportation and communication, people from different parts have come and exploited the tribals in many ways resulting in the migration of the *Saora* to other areas. The modern market clearly shows how people from other areas come to buy the local products at cheap rate and sell them in outside markets at higher prices.
4. The constitutional safeguards are not fully known to the *Saoras* and the positive discrimination policy has not worked in constructive way for the development of tribals. The local traditional power structure has been replaced completely, as also the forest ecology. The modern heads (Sarpanch) do not have the sense of the importance of forest and the need to safeguard it.
5. The forest policies have created tensions at local level and compel the locals to bribe the forest guard and officials for any minor dependence on forest. The tribals are not at all responsible for depletion of forests. It is the faulty forest policy and greedy officials who misuse their power to put the tribals in trouble.
6. The depletion and deforestation have affected the tribals. Their autonomy has been snatched by the developmental plans. For their socio-economic and cultural needs *Saoras* are depending on the urban areas, and are also migrating for regular work and higher wages. Therefore, their autonomy is no more. This also shows the change.
7. The dependency of *Saora* on forest has decreased, because the forest is no more available in plenty to them. Whatever forest is available to them even today is not possible to use because of various

government rules and regulations. Therefore, the dependency on forest has decreased.

8. The perception of *Saora* has changed because of the establishment of school, Lanjia *Saora* Development Agency, and regular bus and jeep connection of the *Saora* land to the Gunupur market. This has made the *Saora* to be in touch with the outside. So, these changes have brought transformation in their perception about forests. They no more considered forest as sacred.

9. The depletion of forest has changed the socio-cultural set-up of *Saoras* as their compound family is changing and they area accepting nuclear family, *Birinda* based tradition is replaced by individualism, *Gamango* system of governance is taken over by panchayat members, their traditional religion is taken over by Christianity, culture is adapted to modern music, dress, beliefs and values. Their perception of nature as traditionally reflected in their folk songs is missing now. This has a negative impact on their economy, as migration and dependency on urban area have increased. Thus, due to depletion of forest resources and unavailability of forest materials, their socio-cultural set-up has changed.

It is evident by the above discussion that there is a great change in forest ecology which in turn has brought about changes in each and every aspects of *Saora* life.

Appendix

Interview Schedule

Name of the respondent:

Address:

Family And Kinship

Name of head of the household.

Types of family Joint / Nuclear / Compound / Extended.

Number of family members.

Name of the Birinda (Extended family descended from common ancestors.)

How long have your generation been living in Birinda.

Family Details:

Name	*Age*	*Sex*	*Relationship*	*Occupation*	*Religion*	*Edn.*

Political and Legal System

What was the system of governance in tradition, society ?

What do you think about the system of governance in traditional society?

How far that was beneficial for the sustenance of the system?

Do you think that the prevalence of the customary laws and convention help your society? Do you think that the British, period was different than the traditional society?

If yes please mentioned how?

What is the system of governance today?

Do the panchayat members work effectively?

Are they playing any constructive role about the protection of forest resources?

What is the impact of the panchayat activities upon your economic life? Did the Panchayat ever punish against the illegal forest destroyer? if so please mention the mode of action against them?

In your opinion what are the urgent issues about safeguarding forest resources has to be taken-up by the panchayat?

Do you think that the Panchayat has any effect on you and your family?

If yes what are these?

Do you find any decline in the role and status of *Gamangos* or Buyyas?

if yes how?

Do you like the changing status of the *gomangos* or *Buyyas*?

Religion, Belief System and Culture

What is your religion?

Why you believe in religion?

Do you offer puja/prayers before going to forest for hunting?

If yes, Why?

Do you take the help of Priest /shaman for puja? Yes/No.

If yes why?

De you think that it was changed over the years of its existence?

If yes why?

Did your fore-fathers worship trees, if yes, why?

How was the traditional belief system?

Whether the festival celeberation has declined?

How was it related to nature, forest and river?

How the decline of forest resources has affected your celebrations?

What kind of rituals you perform at the time of newborn baby?

Why?

Do you perform any ritual at the time of marriage?

Please explain why?

What kind of rituals you perform at the time of death?

Why?

Do you believe in performing any rituals at the beginning of the cultivation of your land?

Do you perform any other rituals at any points of life cycle?

If so, what are these?

Tell something about your *puja bidhi* and the material you use?

Why you use that?

Do you aware of any other religion/ faith? Yes/ No

If, yes what are those?

How do you difieienriate between your practice with, others?

Do you like it? Yes/ No

If yes why, If no why not?

What's your daily social activity?

How do you spend your leisure time?

How often you listen to Radio?

Which programme you like most?

Why?

How your music is different from the music coming up in radio?

How your garments are different from modern garments?

Do you, think that you are influenced to use modern garments?

If yes, why?

Do you think it is better?

Economy, Law & Forest

Do you think that forest is your main source of living?

If yes how?

Do you use the forest produces for your personal requirement ?

Do you think that your ancestors were also depending upon the forest for the same way as you do?

Do you opine that forest produce was sufficient for their sustenance?

What are the things your forefathers were getting from forest.

a) Green leaves & roots b) Tuber, c) Fruits & flowers, d) Karanja & other seed for extracting oil e) Fuelwoods f) Any other (specify).

Are you getting all these forest products today?

Do you think that the quantity your forefathers were getting is same or it has decreased?

If yes why?

Do you think that you are affected by decreasing forest produces?

If yes how do you manage?
Do you think that destruction of forest is the cause of migration of the tribals?

What are the other causes of migration?

Where do they migrate?

Have you lever thought what will happened if jungles are destroyed?

Do you think that you can live without forest?

How are you affected by restrictions imposed by the Government on forest?

Do you think that imposition by govt. is favourable / bad?

If yes why?

If so how?

What measures do you suggest further to preserve the forest?

Do you think that the forest and urbanization is correlated? If so how?

What is the impact of urbanization, upon forest?

Have it ever affected you? If so how?

Institution for Development by Government

Do you know what are the development measures taken by government for your upliftment?

Do you think that it helped you to solve your problem?

Do the government protect your culture?

If Yes, How?

If No, Do you want that your culture should be protected?

Do you think that the different development programs are enough to meet the requirement?

What you suggest the government to do for the betterment of the tribals?

Education

Do you think that education will enhance you standard of living?

What are the reasons for educational backwardness?

How far the govt. measures helped for education?

What are the drawbacks of govt. measures of education?

Do you think that more education will lead to preserve the forest, if so how?

Bibliography

Journals

Banerjee, Biswanath, 1968, 'Relation Between Environment and Culture among Some Indian Primitive Communities Living in the Hills', *Bulletin of the Cultural Research Institute,* 7:l-2,pp.56-61.

Bebarta, P.C., 1959, 'Concepts of Disease and Therapeutic Practices Among the Hill Souras of Orissa,' *Vanyajati, 7:2,* April, pp, 44-48

Bhattacharya, A.D., 1952. 'Dead Rites, Funeral Ceremonies and Idea of Life after Death Among the Hill Saora of Orissa,' *Bulletin of the Dept. of Anthropology,* 1:2, July, pp. 1-16.

Biligiri, H.S., 1965. "The Sora Verb: A Restricted Study', *Lingua,* 15,pp. 231-50.

Butel, F.H., 1986, 'Sociology and Environment: The Widening Road Towards Human Ecology,'*International Social Science Journal,* No. 109, pp.337-56.

Caffon W.R. and R.E. Dunlap, 1980. 'A New Ecological Paradigm for Exuberant Sociology,' *American Behavioral Scientist,* Vol. 24,.No.1, pp. 15-45.

Chattopadhaya, K, 1990. 'Social Ecology of Forest Delta', *Man in India,* Vol. 70 pp. 253-265.

Chakravarti, Bhabsh, 1976. 'Relationship Between Ecology and Economy: A Case Study on the Birhars', *Bulletin of the Cultural Research Institute,* 12:1-2, pp. 88-101.

Choudhury, B.,1964. 'Doripur — A Magico Religious Ceremony for Curring Fever Among the Hill-Saoras,' *Adibasi,* No.3, Bhubaneswar, pp. 64-68.

Das, Haris Chandra, 1966, 'Changing Economy of a Soara Community' *Historical Journal,* 13:4, Jan,pp.39-42.

Das, N., 1995, 'A Note on the Markets in the Saora Land in Orisssa' *Vanyajati,* 7:3, July, pp.98-I03.

Das, Nityanada and B. Choudhury, 1959, 'Economy of a Saora Ceremony' *Vanyajati,* 7:3, July pp. 17-24.

Dmitry, Gorbenko Ghemamov, 1991, 'Man and Nature: Partners in Survival' *Folklore,* 32 (4), pp.53-56.

Elwin, Verrier, 1945, 'Soara Fituris' *Man in India,* Vol. XXV, Ranchi, pp. 64-68.

Elwin Verrier, 1952, 'The Saora Priests, *Bulletin of the Dept. of Anthropology,* Jan., pp.59-85.

Fernandes, Walter, 1990, 'Forest Policy: A Solution to Tribal Deprivation?' *Indian Journal of Social Work,* 51(1), pp.35-36.

Gill, G.S., 1977, 'Problems of Land Alienation in Gunnpur Block,' *Administrator,* 22:1 Spring, pp. 195-200.

Gooch, P., 1994, 'Domadic Van-yujjars, Fight to Maintain the Life in the Forest,' *Indigenous Affairs,* No.3, IWGIA, Copenliagen.

Guha, *R.,* 1994, 'Forestry Debate and Draft Forest Act: Who Wins, Who Loses?', *Economic and Political Weekly,* 20 August

Gupta, Anil, 1985 , ' Socio-ecological Paradigm for Analysing Problems of Poor in Dry Regions', *Ecodevelopment News,* No.32-33, March, 1985 pp. 68-74.

Gupta, V.K., M. V.M. Desai, and A.K. Ganguly, 1981. 'Fuel Forest and Desert, *Science and Culture,* 47. N 11, November, pp. 379-389.

Imam, Balu, 1990, 'Ecological Background of Chhotanagpur–Its Imbalance and Tribal Communities,' *Man in India.* Vol. pp. 266-277.

Jahagirdar, M.P., 1994, 'System of Forest Villages and Changing Scenario,' *Man In India,* Vol. 74, pp. 141-151.

Jain, S., 1984, 'Women and People's Ecological Movement: A Case Study of Women's Role in the Chipko Movement in UP', *EPW,* XIX, pp.41.

Josi, Gopa, 1981, 'Forest Policy and Tribal Development: Problem of Implementation, Ecology and Exploitation,' *Social Action,* Vol.31.

Khiewtam, R.S. and P.S. Ramkrisnan, 1989, ' Soeio- cultural Studies of the Sacred Grove at Cherapunji and Adjoining Areas in North- Eastern India,' *Man in India,* Vol. 69, pp. 64-71

Kulkarni, Shard, 1982, ' Encroachment of Forests: Govt. versus People', *Economic and Political Weekly,* Vol. XVII.

Laura, Rival, 1993, 'The Growth of Family Trees: Understading Huaorani Perceptions of Forest', *Man,* Vol. 28, pp. 635-652.

Mahapatra, L.K., 1962, 'The Dophla and the Miji Society: A Preliminary Ecological Analysis', *Sociologous Newseries,* Vol., No.2, pp. 158-167.

Mahapatra, K., and K.K. Devi, 1973. 'Shifting Cultivation in Orissa' *Adibasi,* Bhubanesewar, XIV. N 4, pp. 11-28.

Panda, P., and Others, 1990, 'ICDS in Tribal Orissa: A Case Study', *Indian Journal of Social Work,* 51 (4), pp. 583-594.

Patnaik, U.N., 1963-64, 'The Saora of the Ganjam Hills', *Adibasi,* Bhubaneswar, pp 6-13.

Patnaik, N.K., 1970, 'Changing Community's Culture', *Man In India,* Vol. 1, No.2, April -June, pp. 189-196.

Paul, Shankman, 1991, 'Culture Contact, Cultural Ecology and Dany Warfare;' *Man,* Vol. 26, pp.229-321.

Pradhan, Prasanna K., 1978, 'The Economics of Land Utilisation: An Ecological Perspective'*Administrator,* 23:1, Spring, pp. 159-66.

Prasad, Saileswar, 1970, 'Maler of Rajmahal Hills: Ecology, Economy and Social Organisation', *Vanyajati,* 18:3, July, pp. 121-30.

Ratha, S. N., and D.K. Behera, 1990, 'Rethinking Totemism: Man-Nature Relationship in Maintaining the Ecological Balance,' *Man in India,* Vol. 70, pp. 245-252.

Ray, H.M., 1990, 'Impact of Ecology on Savara Way of Life', *Man in India, Vol* 70, pp. 329-335.

Rav, Sachin, 1953, 'Aspects of the Culture of the Soaras', *Man in India,* 6.2 November, December pp. 34-6

Reddy, B. Krishna, 1991 'Forests and Sugalis in Andhrapradesh: Historical and Anthropological Perspective' *Man in India,* Vol.71,pp.611-19.

Rodgers, W.A., 1994, 'The Sacred Groves of Meghalaya' *Man in India,* Vol.74, pp. 339-48.

Roy Burman, B.K., 1990,'Shifting Cultivation: An Aspect of Tribal Exploitation', *Indian Journal of Social Work,* 51 (1), pp.57-74.

Sarkar, R.M.,1990, 'Eco-cultural Perspective of Sedentarization of the Nomadic Birhors', *Man in India,* Vol.70, pp.288-304.

Singh, G.S,1997, 'Sacred Groves in Western Himalaya: A Eco-cultural Imperatives', *Man in India,* Vol 77, Nos.2 and 3, June-September, pp.247-257.

Singh, K. S, 1990,'Environment, Technology and Management in Tribal Areas,' *Man in India,* Vol.70, pp. 123-129.

Srivastav, A.R.N., 1990. 'Rise of Ecological Studies in Cultural Anthropology,' *Man in India,* Vol.70, pp. 278-287.

Suryamani,M.,1969, 'The Significance of Groves in Soara Culture, *Folklore* 10:5 May, pp.187-92.

Suryanarayana, M.A., 1968, 'Note on a Few Significant Saoras Myths,' *Journal of Indian-Anthropological Society, 3: 1-2, March-Sept.,* pp. 153-6.

Tripathy, K.C., 1967, 'A Note on Fingerprints of the Sora (Lanjia) of Orissa', *Eastern Anthropologist,* 20:1, Jan.-April, pp. 64-70.

Vasumathi, S.,1992, 'Socio-Ecology of Bhils: A Community Adopting to Resources,' *Man in India*, Vol. 72, pp.353-358.

Venkaresan, D., 1992, 'Study of Island Cultures and Ecology: A Perspective', *Man in India,* Vol.72, pp.15-26.

Books

Alihan M. A., 1964, *SocialEcology: A Critical Analysis,* New York, Coopeer Square Publisher

Altman, I., and Chemans, 1984, *Culture and Environment,* Cambridge University Press.

Anderson Roberts and Wallet, Huber, 1986, *The Hour of the Fox: Tropical Forests, The World Bank and Indigenous People in Central India,* Washington University Press.

Anderson, Ralphe and I.R.L. Carter, 1990, *Human Behavior in the Social Environment: A Social Systems Approach,* New York, Aline de Gruyter.

Arnold, D., and R. Guha, (ed.), 1995. *Nature, Culture, Imperialism: Essays on the History of South Asia,* Delhi, Oxford University Press.

Bahuguna, Sunderlal, 1980, *Chipko-A Novel Movement for Establishment of Cordial Relationship Between Man and Nature,* Teherigarwal Chipko Information Centre.

Bailey, F.G., 1960, *Tribe, Caste and Nation: A Study of Political Activity and Political Change in Highland Orissa,* Manchester, Manchester University Press.

Baily, Robertic, 1991. *The Behavioural Ecology of Efe Pygmy Men in the Ituri Forest, Zaire,* Ann Arbor, Univ. of Michigan, Musem of Anthropology.

Behura, N.K., and J. Dash, 1985, 'Ecology and Development: The Dongria Kondhs of Orissa', K.L. Bhowmik (ed.), *Ecology and Development,* New Delhi: Inter India, pp. 49-59

Bennett, Olivia, (ed.), 1991, *Green War: Environment and Conflict*, Budapest, London, Panos.

Berry, J.W., et al.,1986, *On the Age of the Forest: Cultural Adaptation and Cognitive Developments in Central Africa*, Berwyn: Swets North America, Lisse: Swets and Zetbinger.

Bharragav, Gopal, 1992, *Environmental Challenges and Ecological Disaster*, New Delhi, Mital Publication.

Bhasin, Veena, 1989, Ecology, Culture and Change: Tribals of Sikkim Himalayas, New Delhi, Inter India Publications.

Bhattacharya, D.K., 1991, *Ecology and Social Formation in Ancient History*, Calcutta,

Bhowmick, P.K., 1992, *The Chenchus of the Forests and Plateaux: A Hunting-gathering Tribe in Transition*, Calcutta, Institute of Social Research aad Applied Anthropology.

Bonnie, J. McCay and James M.Acheson, (ed.), 1987, *The Question of the Commons: The Culture and Ecology of Communal Resources*, Arizoaiat Studies in Human Ecology, Tueson, Univ. Arizona Press.

Bookchin, Murray, 1989, *Remarking Society: Pathways to a Green Future*, Montreal: Blackrose Books.

Bookchin, Murray, 199O,*The Philosophy of Social Ecology: Essays on Dialectical Naturalism*, Montreal, Blackrose Books.

Bookchin, Murray, 1991,*Towards an Ecological Society*, Montreal: Blackrose Books.

Bookchin Murray, 1996, 'The Concept of SociaL Ecology', Carolyn Merchant (ed.), *Key Concept in Critical Theory: Ecology*, Jaipur & New Delhi, Rawat Publiation.

Bose, N.K., 1971, *Tribal Life in India*, Nalional Book Trust, New Delhi.

Buchanan, R.H., Emrys Jones and Desmand McCourt, (ed.), *Man and His Habitat: Essays Presented to EmyrEstyn Evans,* Randon Routledge and Kegain Paul.

Chakravati, P.K., 1984 , 'Habitat, Economy and Society: Aspects of Change in Sikkim', S.C. Joshi, D.R. Joshi and D.D.Dani (ed.), *Rural Development in- the Himalaya: Problems and Prospects,* Nainital: Gyanadayn Prakashan, pp.24-34.

Chaudhuri, A.B., 1993, *Trees and Environment: An Indian Scenario,* New Delhi, Ashish Publishing.

Chidyal, V.C., 1982, 'Tribe and Forest' K.S. Singh, (ed.), *Economics of Tribes and Their Transformation,* New Delhi, Concept Publication.

Croll, E., and David P., (ed.), 1992, *Bush Base Forest: Culture, Environment and Development,* London, Routledge.

D'Abreo, Desmand, 1952, *People and Forests: The Forest Bill and a New Forest Policy,* New Delhi, Indian Social Institute.

Danda, Dipali G., and Sanchita Ghatak, 1985, *The Semsa and Their Habitat,* Calcutta: Anthropological Survey of India.

Das, *J.C.,* and Negi, R.S., 1983, 'The Chipko Movement', K.S. Singh (ed.), *Tribal Movement in India,* Vol. 2, Delhi, Manohar Publishers and Distributors.

Das, K.B., 1953, *A Study of Orissa Folklore,* Santiniketan, Viswabharati.

Davis Michael G., 1996, *Ecology, Sociopolitical Organisation and Cultural Change on the Sourthen Plains: A Critical Treatise in the Sociocultural Anthropology of Native North America,* Kirksville; Thomas Jefferson Univ. Press.

Desai, A.R., 1978, 'Tribes in Transition', A. R. Desai (ed.), *Rural Sociology in India,* Bombay, Popular Prakashan.

Descola, Philippe, 1996, *In the Society of Nature: A Native Ecology in Amazonia,* translated by Nova Scott, Cambridge University Press.

Descola, Philippe and Gisli Palsso, (ed.), 1996, *Nature and Society: Anthropological Perspective,* London, NewYork: Routledge.

Doshi, S.L., 1976 'Forest and Excise Policy and Tribal Economic-Development', Hari Mohan Mathur (ed.), *Development Administration in Tribal Area,* Jaipur, The HCM State Institute of Public Administration.

Eder, Jasmes F., 1987, *On the Road to-Tribal Extinction: Depopulation, Decultaration, and Adoptive Well-being Among the Batak of the Philippines,* Berkeley, London: Univ. of California Press.

Elwin, V., 1991, *Leaves From the Jungle: Life in a Gond Village,* New Delhi, Oxford University press.

Elwin, V., 1964, *The Tribal World of Verrier Elwin: An Autobiography,* Bombay, Oxford University Press.

Elwin, V., 1955. *The Religion of an Indian Tribe,* Bombay, Oxford University Press.

Elwin, V., 1954. *Tribal Myths of Orissa,* Bombay.

Fairhead, James and Melissa Leach, 1996, *Misreading the African Landscape: Society and Ecology in a Forest-savanna Mosaic,* Cambridge University Press.

FAO, 1978, *Forestry for Local Community Development,* FAO, Rome, Forestry Paper No. 7.

FAO, 1981, *Forestry and Rural Development,* FAO, Rome, Forestry Paper No. 26.

Ferades, W., Menon, G., and Viegas, P., 1988, *Forest Environment and Tribal Economy: Deforestation, Impoverishment and Marginalisation in Orissa,* New Delhi, Indian Social Institute.

Fernandes, Walter and Geeta Menon, 1987, *Tribal Women and Forest Economy: Deforestation,Exploitation and Status Change,* New Delih, Indian Soial Institute.

Ferandes, W., Menon, G., and Vilogas, P., Chandy, K.T, 1985, *Forests, Environment and Forest Dweller Economy in Chattisgarh,* New Delhi, Indian Social Institute.

Forsyth, James, 1975, *The Highlands of Central India: Notes on Their Forest and Wild Tribes, Natural History and Sports,* New Delhi, Asian Publication Series.

Furer-Haimendrof, C., Von, 1985, *Tribes of India: The Struggle for Survival,* Delhi, Oxford University Press.

Gadgil, G., and Guha, R., 1995, *Ecology and Equity: The Use and Abuse of Nature in Contemporary India,* London and New York: Routledge.

Gaur Ranjan, 1987, *Environment and Ecology of Early Man in Northwest India: Geological and Palaeontological Evidences,* Delhi, B.R. Publishing.

Ghate, R.C., 1992, *Forest Policy and Tribal Development: A Study of Maharastra,* New Delhi, Concept Publication Company.

Gilmour, Dorald Alass, 1991, *Villagers Forests and Foresters: The Philosophy, Process and Practice of Community Forest in Nepal,* Katmandu, Sahayogi Press.

Government of India, 1982, *Report of the Committee on Forests and Tribals in India,* New Delhi, Ministry of Home Affairs, Tribal Development Division, Government of India

Government of India, 1972, *Interim Report of the National Commission on Agriculture and Production Forestry -Man Made Forestry,* New Delhi, Univ. of Agriculture.

Government of India (ed.) 1973, *The Tribal People of India,* New Delhi Publication Division.

Government of Orissa, 1983, *The Statistical Outline of Orissa Forests,* Cuttack: Dept. of Forest and Fisheries, Government of Orissa.

Grigson, W.V., 1938, *The Maria Gonds ofBaster,* Oxford University Press.

Guha, R.C., (ed.), *1994, Social Ecology,* Oxford University Press.

Guha, R.C., 1989, *The Unquiet Woods: Ecological Change and Peasant Resistance in the Himalayan,* Delhi, Oxford-University Press.

Guha, Ramchandra, *1996,* 'Radical Environmentalism: A Third World Critique', Carolyn Merchant (ed.), *Key Concept in Critical Theory: Ecology,* Jaipur & New Delhi, Rawat Publication.

Gupta, Ranjit and others, 1981, *Tribal Unrest and Forestry Management in Bihar,* Ahamdabad, IIM.

Geddes, Patrick, 1915, *Cites in Evolution*, New York, Oxford University Press.

Hannigna, John, 1995, *Environment Sociology: A Social Constructionist Perspective,* London, Routledge.

Hardiman, D., 1994, 'Power in the Forest: The Dangs, 1820-1940', D., Arnold and D. Hardiman, (ed.), *Subaltern Studies VII,* Delhi, Oxford University Press.

Hasnain, Nadeem, 1983, *Tribal India Today,* New Delhi, Harnan Publication.

Hivale, Shamrao, and Verrier Elwin, 1935, *The Songs From the Forest: The Folk Poetry of the Gonds,* London, Alen and Unain.

Hombor, A., 1996, 'Ecology as Semiotics: Outline of a Contexualist Paradigm for Human, Ecology' P. Descola and G. Palsson (ed.), *Nature and Society: Anthropological Perspective,* London and New York: Routledge.

Hutterer, Karl, L.A. Terry, and George Lovelace, (ed.), 1985, *Cultural Values and Human Ecology in Southeast Asia,* Ann Arbar, Michigam: Univ. of Michigan, Center for South and Southeast Asian Studies

Ingold, Tim, 1987, *The Appropriation ofNature: Essays on Human Ecology and Social Relations,* Manchester University Press.

Ives, J. and D.C. Pitt, (ed.), 1988, *Deforestation: Social Dynamics in Watersheds and Mountain Ecosystem,* Rouledge, 11, New Fetter Lane, London.

James, F. Edev, 1987, *On the Road to Tribal Extinction: Depopulation, Deculturation and Adoptive Well Being Among the Batak of the Philippines,* Berkeley, Univ. of California Press.

Jamison, A, 1996, 'The Shaping of the Global Environment Agenda: The Role of Non-Governmental Organisation', S. Lash, B. Szerszynski and B. Wynne (ed.), *Risk, Environment and Modernity: Towards a New Ecology,* New Delhi, Sage Publication.

John, McKinnon and Bernard Viee, 1989, *Hill Tribes Today: Problems in Change,* Paris, White Louts Orston.

Johnson, D. and David A. (ed.), 1988, *The Ecology of Survival: Case Studies from Northeast African History,* London, Lester Crook Academic, Boulder: Westview Press.

Julian, Burger, 1987, *Report from the Frontier: The State of the World's Indigenous Peoples,* Cultural Survival Report No. 28. London/ Cambridge, MA: Zed Books/ Cultural Survival.

Jurgen, Haberaias, 1996, 'Social and Cultural Origin of Environmental Movements', David Goldblatt, *Social Theory and Environment,* Oxford, Blackwell Publisher, PP. 112-153.

Karlsson, B.G., 1997, *Contested Belonging: An Indigenous People's Struggle for Forest and Identity in Sub-Himalayan Bengal,* Lund Monograph in Social Anthropology, Dept. of Sociology, Lund University.

Kelkar, Goviad and Dev Nathan, 1992, *Gender and Tribe: Women and Forest,* London: Zed Books.

Lal, Parmanand, 1997, *Great Nicobar Islands: A Study in Human Ecology,* Calcutta, Anthropological Survey of India.

Mahapatra, L.K., 1992, 'Social Movement Among Tribes of India', K.S.. Singh, (ed.), *Tribal Situation in India,* Shimla Indian Institute of Advance Studies.

Mahapatra, L. K., 1975, 'A Note on Sociology of the Resistance of Shifting. Cultivation in Soara Hill' *A Project Report for Soar a Area.*

Mann, R.S., (ed.), 1982, *Nature and Man Spirit Complex in Tribal India,* New Delhi, Concept Publication.

Martell, L., 1994, *Ecology and Society: An Introduction,* Polity Press in Association with Blackwell Publisher.

McCay, Bonnie M. and James M. Acheson, (ed.), 1987, *The Question of the Commons: The Culture and Ecology of Communal Resources,* Tueson: University of Arizona Press.

Meheta, B.H., 1968. 'Forestry and Tension in India', L.P. Vidyarthy *(ed.), Applied Anthropology in India,* Allahabad, Kitabmahal.

Merchant, C., (ed), 1996, *Key Concept in Critical Theory: Ecology,* Jaipur & New Delhi, Rawat Publication.

Milton, Kay, 1996, *Environmentalism and Cultural Theory: Exploring the Role of Anthropology in Environmental Discourse,* London, New York: Routledge.

Min, Mrinal, (ed.), 1993, *Continuity in Change in Tribal Society*, Shimla, Indian Institute of Advance Studies.

Mishra, Kamal K.,1985, 'Habitational Alienation and Cultural Disorganisation in Tribal Orissa', K.L Bhowmik, (ed.), *Ecology and Human Development,* New Delhi: Inter India.

Mishra, R.C., D. Sinha and J.W. Berry, 1996, *Ecology, Acculturation and Psychological Adoptation: A Study ofAdivasis in Bihar,* New Delhi, Sage Publication India Pvt. Ltd.

Mlinar, Zdravko and Henry, Telne, 1978, *The Social Ecology of Change: From Equilibrium to Development,* London, Sage Publication

Moore, H.L., and Megan Vaughan, 1994, *Cutting Down Trees: Gender, Nutrition andAgricultural Change in the Northern Province of Zambia 1890-1990,* Portsmouth, NH: Heinemann; London: James Currcy; Lusaka: University of Zambia Press.

Mukherjee, Radha Kamal, 1968, *Man and Habitation -A Study in Social Ecology,* Bombay, Popular Prakashan.

Mukherjee, R., 1994, 'An Ecological Approach to Sociology', Guha R., (ed.), *Social Ecology,* Oxford University Press.

Murida, Ratri, 1982 'Forest Development and Tribal Welfare-Analysis of Some Policy Issues', E.G. Hallswarth, (ed.), *Socio-economic Effect and Constraints in Tropical Forest Management,* John Willey and Sons Ltd. Oxford University Press.

Nanda, Sachchid and Anirudh Prasad, 1994, *Tribal Development and Voluntary Action: A Case Study of the Badlao Foundation,* New Delhi, Inter India Publications.

Padel, F., 1995, *The Sacrifice of Human Being: British Rule and Konds of Orissa,* Delhi, Oxford University Press.

Pandya, V., 1993, *Above the Forest: A Study of Andmanese Ethnoanemology, Cosmology and the Power of Ritual,* Delhi, Oxford University Press.

Parida, G., *Aculturation of Saura Children in Oriya Society,* Cuttack, Elite Publishing House.

Patel. M.S. and N.T. Patel, 1985, 'Ecology and Human Development in Tribal Gujrat', K. L. Bhowmik, (ed.), *Ideology and Human Development,* New Delhi, Inter India Publications.

Pathak. A., 1994, *Contested Domain: The State Peasants and Forest in Contemporary India,* New Delhi, Sage Publications.

Pathy, J , 1984, *Tribal Peasantry: Dynamics of Development,* New Delhi, Inter India Publications.

Patnaik, N., 1974, 'Social Cultural Background of Saora Personality', *Tribal Development and Administration Papers and Proceedings of the Workshop held at N.I.C.D.* Hydrabad, April 18-20.

Patnaik, Nitynanda, 1989, *The Saora,* Bhubaneswar, THRT Publication.

Pedoseyer, P. and Timofeyer T., (ed.), 1981, *Social Problems of Man's Environment: Who will Live and Work,* Moscow: Progressive Publisher.

Pennington, Ranee and Henry Harpending, 1993, *The Structure of an African Pastoralist Community: Demography, History and Ecology of the Ngamiland Herero,* Oxford, Clarendon Press.

Ramakant, 1990, *Tribes: A Study in Cultural Ecology and Tribal Dynamics of the Parahiya,* Delhi: Amar Publication.

Rekhel, Dohnateff, Gemio, 1996, *The Forest Within: The World View of the Tukano Amazonian Indias,* Totnes: Thermis Books.

Robert, S. Anderson and Walter Huber, 1988. *The Hour of the Fox: Tropical Forests, the World Bank and Indigenous People in Central India,* Seattle: University of Washington Press.

Roy Burman, B.K., 1968, 'Forest and Tribals in India' LP Vidyarthy (ed.), *Applied Anthropology in India,* New Delhi, Manohar Publishers and Distributors.

Roy Burman, B.K., 1979, 'Challanges and Response in Tribal India', M.S. Rao, (ed.), *Social Movements in India,* New Delhi, Manohar Publishers and Distributors.

Roy Burman, B.K., 1992, 'Homage to Earth' G. Sen, (ed.), *Indigenous Vision: People of India, Attitudes to the Environment,* New Delhi, Sage Publications.

Roy Burman, B.K., 1997, 'Social Process in the Hills of North-east: An Ecological Perspective', M.N. Srinivas, (ed.), *Dimensions of Social Change in India,* Bombay, Allied Publisher, pp. 405-18.

Roy Burman, B.K., 1968, 'Forest and Tribal in India', LP. Vidhyarthy (ed.), *Applied Anthropology in India,* Allahabad, Kitabmahal, pp. 170-207.

Sagreiga, K.P., 1982, *Forest and Forestry,* New Delhi, National Book Trust.

Sarkar, J., 1987, *Society Culture and Ecological Adoptation among Three Tribes of Arnuchal Pradesh,* Anthropological Survey of India, Ministry of HRD, Dept of Culture, Governrrtent of India.

Sarno Louis, 1994, *Songs from the Forest: My life Among the Ba-Benjella Pygmies,* Penguin.

Schwarts, Norman, B., 1990, *Forest Soceity: A Social History of Petern,* Guatemala, Philadelphia, University of Pennsylvassia Press.

Sen, G., (ed.), 1992, *Indigenous Vision-People of India: Attitudes to the Environment,* New Delhi, Sage Publications.

Sethi, Mohan Singh and Indrajeet Kaur Sethi, 1991, *Understanding Our Environment,* New Delhi, Common Wealth Publisher.

Shaha, A. M., B.S. Baviskar and E. A. Ramaswamy, (ed.), *Social Structure and Change: Development and Ethnicity,* Vol. 4, New Delhi, Sage Publications India Private Ltd.

Sharma, B.D., 1995, *Globalisation: The Tribal Encounter,* New Delhi, Hara Ananda Publications.

Sharma, H.S. and M.L. Sharma, (ed.), 1987, *Environmental Design and Development Conflict or Harmony: A Geographical Appraisal,* Jodhpur, Scientific Publisher.

Shashi, Shyam Singh, 1967, *Social Structure, Ecology, Economy of Gaddis in Himachal Pradesh,* New Delhi: Research Foundation.

Sheth, Pravin, 1997, *Environmentalism: Politics, Ecology and Development,* Jaipur, Rawat Publications.

Shigeru, K., 1994, *Our Land was a Forest: An Ainu Memoir,* forwaded by Mikiso Hane, Trans., Kyoko Selden and Lili Selden, Boulder, Oxford: Westview Press.

Shiva, Vandana, 1990, *Ecology and Politics of Survival: Conflicts Over Natural Resources in India,* New Delhi, Sage Publication.

Shiva, Vandana, 1988, *Staying Alive: Women, Ecology and Survival in India,* New Delhi, Panchashil Park.

Shiva, Vandana, 1996, Development, Ecology and Women, Carolyn Merchant, (ed.), *Key Concept in Critical Theory: Ecology,* Jaipur & New Delhi, Rawat Publications.

Shukla, Rohit et.al., 1990, *Forest and Tribal Life (Study of a Micro-Region)*, New Delhi, Concept Publishing Company.

Singh, B., 1984, *The Soara Highlander: Leadership and Development*, Bombay, Somaiya Publications.

Singh, K.S., (ed.), 1983, *Tribal Movements in India*, Vol. 2, New Delhi, Manohar Publisher and Distributors,

Singh, K S., 1993, *The Scheduled Tribes: People of India*, National Series, Vol. II, Anthropological Surveyof India, Oxford University.

Singh, K.S., 1983, 'A Forest Satyagraha', K.S. Singh, (ed.), *Tribal Movements in India*, VoL 2, Delhi, Manohar Publisher and Distributors.

Sinha, D., and R. Tripathy, et. al., 1982, *Towards an Ecological Framework of Deprivation in Deprivation : Its Social Roots and Psychological Consequences*, New Delhi, Concept Publishers.

Sinha, D.P., 1979, 'Cultural Ecology of the Birhor: A Methodological Utilisation', Ratish Srivastava, (ed.), *Social Anthropology in India*, New Delhi, Books Today, pp. 158-70.

Sinha, Surjit, et. al. (ed.), 1989, *Man and Environment: Biclogical and Cultural Perspective with Special Reference to India*, Calcutta, Indian Anthropological Society.

Sponsel, Lesliee, 1995. *Indigenous People and the Future of Amazonian: An Ecological Anthropology of an Endangered World*, Tucson: University of Arizona Press.

Susana, B.C. and Davalle, 1993, 'Beyond Ecology? Indigenous Territories and Natural Resources (Jarkhand, India)', Wolfgang L. Werner, (ed.), *Aspects of Ecological Problems and Environmental Awareness in South Asia*, New Delhi, Manohar Publisher and Distributors.

Singh, Y., 1997, *Social Stratification and Change in India*, New Delhi, Manohar Publishers and Distributors.

Singh, Y., 1988, *Modernizatoin of Indian Tradition: A Systematic Study of Social Change*, Jaipur, Rawat Publication.

Theoderson, (ed.), 1961, *Studies in Human Ecology, Evanston III.* Row, Perterson.

Thompson, M.M., Warburton and T, Hately, 1986, *Uncertainty on a Himalayan Scale: An Institutional Theory of Environmental Perception and a Strategic Framework for the Sustainable Development of the Himalayan*, London, Ethnographica.

Thusu, Kidarnath and Makhan Jha, 1972, *Ollar Gadba of Koraput,* Calcutta, Anthropological Survey of India.

Tim, Ingold, 1987, *The Appropriation of Nature: Essays on Human Ecology and Social Relation,* LowaCity, University of Lowa Press.

Tiwari, K.M., 1983, *Social Forestry for Rural Development,* DehraDun, International Book Distributors.

Troisi, Josep, 1979, 'Social Movements among Santhal', M.S.A. Rao (ed.), *Social Movement in India,* Delhi, Manohar Publisers & Distributors.

Viazzo, Pier Paolp, 1984, *Upland Communities: Environment, Population and Social Structure in the Alps Since the Sixteenth Century,* Cambridge: University Press.

Vidyarthi,L.P., 1963, *The Maler: A Study in Nature-Man Spirit Complex of a Hill Tribe in Bihar,* Calcutta, Bookland.

Vitebsky, P., 1993, *Dialogues with the Dead: The Discussion of Mortality Among the Soura of Eastern India,* Cambridge, Cambridge University Press.

Vitebsky, P., 1995, 'From Cosmology to Environmentalism Shamanism, as Local Knowledge in Global Setting', R. Fardon (ed.), *Counterworks: Managing the Diversity of Knowledge,* London, Routledge.

Vitebsky, P., 'A Farewell to Ancestors? Deforestation and Changing Spiritual Environment of the Soara', R. Grove (ed.), *Environment History of South and Southeast Asia,* (2 Vols.), Delhi, Oxford University Press.

Vyas, Ambalal, 1960, The Economic Problems of the Lanjia Saora, *Paper 6th Conference for Tribes and Tribal (Scheduled) Areas,* Delhi, Bhartiya Adimajati Sevak Sangh, pp. 48-52.

William, Nancy, M. and Graham Baines (ed.), 1993, *Traditional Ecological Knowledge: Wisdom for Sustainable Development,* Canberra: Centre for Resource and Environmental Studies, Australian National University.

Xaxa, V., 1992. 'Oraons: Religion, Customs and Environment', G. Sen (ed.), *Indigenous Visions: People of Indian, Attitudes to the Environment,* New Delhi, Sage Publications.

Index

A

African (traditional)
- family, living, 30
- society, 32

Agricultural rites, 167
Ainu Tribe, 19
- beliefs/rituals, 20

Alienation of Tribes, 9
All Party Hill Leaders Conference
- agitation, 113

Animals Habits
- observing, 25
- imitation, 33

Anthropologists
- contribution in analysis of tribes, 335
- view of culture, 16

Anthropology Today: Selections, 15
Anuak Kings, 107
Ashrams/Kanyashrams, 316
Attitude (Saoras) to education, 323

B

Bedouin Arabs, 234
Bhutias, 44-45
Biological Ecology, 17
Birinda (family), 86, 95, 247, 335
- ceremonies, 96
- marriage, 96
- descendency, 97
- changes, 336

Birth rituals, 146, 159-60
- Saora, 140
- Why, 161

Bourgeois society, 33
Breakdown of societies, 45
British period, 122
- and Gomangos, 122
- style of governance, 122
- different views, 122-23

Buyyas (priests), 85

C

Capitalism ecological costs, 33
Change/changes, 18
- and development, 52
- in Saora religion, 152
- and contradiction, 255

Classification of forest area (Orissa), 295
Compact tribal villages, 242
Community
- concept, 16
- ecological, 25

Communication System, 338
Conflict/rebellion, 107
Constitutional Safeguards SC/ST, 241, 279
Constitutional Rights (locals) violation, 12
Continuum Concept, 29
Crimes/disputes (dealing with), 27
Crisis rites, 159, 164
Critical Theory, 32-33
Crops (important) Saoras, 251
Cultivation rituals, 168

Culture, 48, 181
- tribes, 9
- viewing-geographer/ anthropologist, 16
- saoras, 51
- changes, 181
- concept, 182
- anthropological concept, 208
- scientific theory, 208
- change factors, influencing, 219

Cultural
- drift, 183
- ecology, 238
- protection by government, 223-25
- contradictions among Saora, 222
- change-studies/models, 220
- life (Orissa), 61-62
- differentiation, 62

Customary Law and Punishment, 124
Customs/taboos Saora, 188

D

Daily activities Saora, 209, 211
Darwin's Theory of Ecological Evolution, 46
Death rituals, 148
Deforestation in Orissa, 292
Degradation of Land, 10
Deities and Spirits Saora, 151
- order of, 151

Demographic Indicators (1951-94)
- of Orissa, 59

Dependency on Forests (tribal), 266
Depletion of Forest Resources/ Products
- effect, 264-67
- reason, 265

Descendency (Birinda), 97
Development projects
- sensitivity, 9

Development process, 41
- lessons, 43

Dhebar Commission, 328
Dialectic of Enlightenment, 34
Diffferences among Tribals, 242
Displacement of Tribes, 10
Division of Labour in Agriculture, 253
Divorce (Saora's), 90
Domestic Animals, 254
Domination of nature by man, 37
Dress and ornaments Saoras, 202
Durkheim Emill, 235
- Social structure, 78, 143

E

Early development of man, 23
Easton formula, 108
Ecology/Ecological approach, 15, 42
- concept, 14
- development, 43
- relationships, 22, 25
- perspectives, 48
- and Revolution, 35

Ecological
- Innocence age, 47
- and environmental problems, 47
- system-destruction, 45
- succession, 23

Ecologists parameter, 48
Eco-centric theorists, 35
Eco-system concept, 41-42
Economy Saora, 51, 243, 338
Economic Activities Saora, 232

- types of, 243

Economic Anthropology (Contemporary), 237

Economic development, 43
- of tribals, 241

Ecology (Saora), 61

Economic threat to forest, 12

Eco-society: A Historical study of Ecological Man, 20

Economic Society, 231

Education
- upliftment (Saora), 307
- meaning, 308
- tribals, 339
- backwardness causes, 326, 329
- and forests, 330

Environment
- concept, 15-16
- and organism, 15
- and culture, 16
- types, 131

Environmental conservation, 18

Environmental
- effects of man's activity, 18
- problems
  - solution, 18
  - India, 46-47
- Factors in Economics and Industrial Management, 45

Environmental Design and Development: Conflict or Harmony, 40

Eskimos, 234

Exploitation of natural resources by migrants, 11-12

Exposure to outside contacts (tribes), 11

F

Family and kinship
- Saora, 85, 91
- and household heads, 91
- types, 92
- size, 93
- Age and sex distribution, 94
- Religion, 95

Family types (Saora), 77

Festivity
- changes in, 171
- decline, 175
- effect of forest resource decline, 176

Feuds (in Nuers), 109
- and agnatic proximity, 109

Findings of study on forests, 340

Fire discovery of, 25

Folk culture, 192, 337

Folklore
- forest based, 11
- folk life studies, 190

Folk tale, 193

Folk and present economy, 238

Folk songs, 193
  of Saora, 194-95, 200, 337

Forest land degradation, dependence, 10

Forest based
- living (tribes), 10-11
- economic activity (types), 11

Forest (indirect benefits), 12

Forest eco-system threat, 12

Forest
- as source of living, 258
- role, 283
- burning, 46
- depredation, 46
- Orissa, 57
- and social structure, 99
- dependency, 259
- depletion, 262
- policy, 298

- economy, 338
- division, 339

Forest resources
protection by Panchayats, 129-30
- suggestion, 132

Forest (Orissa)
- social history, 290
- ex-princely/zamindars states, 290-91
- administration, 293
- government role in, 293
- protection, 294
- Department role, 297

Forest Dwellers/Officials relationships, 302
Fox, Robin
facts of life, 82
Funeral rites, 164
- rituals, 165
- Why, 166

G

Gamany (chief), 85
Garments preference Saoras, 216
General Economic History, 231
Gikuyu tribe
- society, 110
- rituals, 111
- Mao movement, 111
- Kenya domination, 111

Girl college (Rayagada), 320
God concept Saoras, 150, 178
Gomango, 115
- governance, 117-18
- changes, 336

Government measures for educational development, 327
Governance traditional system, 118
- occupational point of views, 119
- for sustenance of society, 121

Government schemes/imposition for development of forests, 298
- imapct, 300
- opinion on, 301

Green programme for change, 36
Greenhouse effect, 46
Guar ceremony (on death), 148
Gunupur educational profile, 321
Guahari, 28
Gunupur, 71
- literacy, 321

H

Headman (Savar/Saora), 115, 138
High School Enrollment 1990-96, 317
Hindu rituals and Saora, 63
Hippie ecology, 42
Historical analysis Orissa forest, 303
Homogenous tribal society, 242
House (Saoras), 187
Household pattern (Saoras), 77
Human Ecology: A Theory of Community Structure, 15
Human nature
- understanding, 32
- and non human nature, 32

Human beings and nature, 34
- relationship, 35

Hunting, 24
- adoption of, 24

I

Imitation
- and self preservation, 34

Indian tribes, 26
Industrialization effects, 23
Individuals needs (basic), 36
Indian tribes power and kinship

relations, 112
Integration principles, 235
Interview schedule of Respondents, 343-51
Irrigation
- Orissa, 57
- methods, 252

J

Jan Jatis, 9
Jokes and riddles Saora, 201
Judo-Christian ethic, 47

K

Kachins history, 107
Kaling war, 55
Kamui spirits, 20
Key Concept in Critical Theory: Ecology, 32
Kinship
- study, 81
- marriage rules, 336

Kinship and Marriage: An Anthropological Response, 82
Koraput
- district profile, 64-66, 115
- forest resources, 298

Kotas (of the Nilgiris), 112

L

Ladakh
- ecology and society, 38
- village, 39
- food-clothing, 39
- social grouping, 40

Lakes (Orissa), 57
Language, 58
Land utilization pattern (Raigada), 256
Life without forests, 271-72
Lanjia Saora tribe
- changes, 10
- study objectives, 13
- Legal/political system, 50
- structure, 50
- types, 72
- territory, 72
- traditional society structure, 84

Laps of Russia, 234
Leadership
- types, 114
- in tribal community, 114

Leisure
- concept, 205
- time spending ways, 209-10, 212

Levi Strauss, 79, 142
- and social structure, 79
- study of kinship, 81
- on marriage, 98

Life cycle of Saoras (egs), 149
Literacy Rate, 57
- category wise, 318
- statewise, 1971-91, 312
- Orissa, 60, 310-11
- district wise, 314

M

Magic
- significance in economic activities, 236

Man as social animal, 17
Man's Impact on Environment, 18
Man
- and nature, 34, 40
- and envionment, 43

Man and His Habitation: A Study in Social Ecology, 37
Manipuris, 112
Market Composition (Saoras), 273
Market dependency, 254
Marriage (Saoras), 86, 98, 102

• ceremony, 88
• modern trend, 98
• rituals, 162-63
Marx
on industrialization impact, 33
Matam (landed property), 247
Matrilineal basis, 149
Material culture of Saora, 201, 337
Men's style, 204
Migration (Saora), 338
Migration
• due to destruction, 269
• causes, 270
Mimesis and enlightenment, 34
Minor forest produces, 254
Money generation (institutionalization of), 235
Mukerjee, Prof. Radhakamal, 37
Music, 214
Mutual Aid, 21
Murdock, G. P., 78
Myth and symbol, 144
Mythology (Saoras), 186

N

Nagas, 112
Nature
• domination, 33
• and man, 34, 40, 41
• transforming, 44
• dependence, 233
Non human nature, 42-43
Non-material culture (Saoras) 181, 337
North Eastern region
• social structure, 112
• creation of states, 113
Nuer tribe (Africa)
• politics, 106-107, 110
• system, 109

O

Obligation activities, 206
Ollar Gadhe of Koraput, (ethnographic survey), 38
Orissa, 55
• history, 55
• location topography, 56
• lakes, 57
• forests, 57
• rainfall/irrigation, 57
• soil, 58
• minerals, 58
• demography, 58
• culture, 61
• scheduled tribes, list, 63-64
• tribes
population, 115
organisation, 115

P

Paleolithic/Maleolithic Age, 284
Panchayat
• activities Saora tribes, 125-27
• effect on tribal economy, 128
• forest resources protection, 129-30
suggestion, 132
Panchayat Raj introduction
• impact, 135
• and role decline views, 134
Peacock Dance (death ritual), 148
Peasant/Folk community, 239
Peasant Philosophy, 21
Personality development, 207
Perpetuation of species, 24
Pollution and environment, 46
Politics/governance
• organization, 106
• Saora tribes, 106
• African, 106
• Nuer tribe, 106

Political/legal system Saoras, 116
Polygamy (Saoras), 96
Population (Orissa), 58
- percentage distribution by sector of activity, 60

Post Independence
Saora tribe, 125
- governance–views, 125-126

Power, 114
Prayer reasons, 156
Priest
- importance, 167, 172
- in Puja, 170
- changing role, 171, 173-74

Primitive Government, 105
Primitive hunter–gatherer society, 285
Problems of tribals, 10
Primitive Society, 284
- relationship with nature, 286

Protection of forest, 277
Puja before going to forest (Saoras), 155
Puttasinghi
- village market, 273
- Panchayat, 326

Punishment for crimes, 28

R

Radcliffe, Brown
- theory of totemism, 19
- and social structure, 78

Radio listening frequency (Saora), 213
Rayagada
- district profile, 67-71
- district land utilization pattern, 256
- educational development, 319

Religion, 177
- tribals reason for, 153

Religion Saoras, 51, 95, 177
- system-importance, 141
- theoretical reflections, 142
- socio-economic cultural context, 143
- change, 152

Religious life characteristic structure, 143
Religious Rites, Rituals, 159
Religious belief system Saora,337
Religion-wise breakup, 255
Rituals
- causes for, 158
- in agriculture, 249

S

Sacred places and objects, 145
Safeguard of forests
- measures, 278

Sagada
- Panchayat, 326

Saora
- attitude to education, 322
- level of education, 325
- traditional religion, 146
- life cycle rituals, 146
- deities, 151
- traditional economy, 243
- traditional social structure, 84
- structure, 63
- political/legal system, 50, 116
- religion, 51
- culture, 51
- marriage, 86-89
- economy, ecology, development, 51
- social ecology forest resources, 52
- change/development, 52
- types, 72

• family types, 77
Saora culture (traditional), 185
Sanskriti, 181
Sarpanch Saoras, 133
Schools (categorywise), 319
Scheduled Tribes (Orissa), 63
List, 64
Scheduled Tribes population
India, 309
Self-reliance, 21
Sevashrams enrolment, 315
Shaman (diviner)
Summoning, 149
Shamanism, 151
Shifting cultivation, 11, 25, 244, 248, 279, 338
• area under, 246
• South East Asia, 286
Shona Tribe, 32
Sikkim tribals, 44
Slash and burn system (cultivation), 25
Socialization, 36
Social Anthropology, 105
Social Ecology, 47
Social Ecology, 283, 303
• definition, 48
• tasks, 48
• significance, 38
Social Structure, 231
concept, definition, 78-82
• Indian perspective, 83
• and forests, 99
Society, 78-79
Social domination, 37
Socio-cultural
• life of tribes, 9
• integration, 239
Socio-economic problems in forests, 12
Socio-economic situation (Orissa), 60
Social differentiation tibes (Orissa), 62
Social organizations, 184
Sowing cycle (Saora), 250
Spencer, 141, 233
Spirits deities, 20, 151
Storing of seeds, 252
Structure and Function in Primitive Society, 142
Study
• methodology, sample size, 49
• chapter scheme, 50
• findings, 52
Sustainable economy conditions, 36

T

Taboos (Saoras), 188-89
Talcott Parsons, 82
Technology
• impact, 41
• and nature, 44
Terrace cultivation, 244, 279
The Ainu Ecosystem: Environment and Group Structure, 19
The Ascent of Man, 234
The Interpretation of Culture, 208
Theories of primitive religion, 142
The Continuum Concept, 29
Theory of society and culture, 32
Totemism theory, 19
Traditionalism, 144
Traditional governance system changes, 135
• decline–views, 135
• likeness–views, 137
Traditional social structure Saora's, 84
Trees/Plants with food value (list

Orissa), 287-90
Tribes without Rulers, 108
Tribal education, 309
- Orissa, 311

Tribal/Modern
- music difference, 215
- garments difference, 217

Tribal communities, 9
- life, 26
- problems, 10
- dependence on forests, 10

Tribe and Clan, 25
Tribal solidarity, 26

U

Ukka and *Ersi* customs and taboos, 188
Universe of the study, 50
Unquiet Woods, 45
Urbanisation and forest relationship, 275

V

Value systems of tribes
- and development projects, 9

Vegetable eating by early man, 24
Vietnam war
- genocide/ecoside, 35

Village
- Saoras, 186
- community, 297

W

War against nature, 33
Western oversight of ecological degradation—causes, 47
Women status in tribes, 21-22
Women's wear (Saoras), 203
Work participation rate Orissa 1991, 61

Y

Ye'cuana
- tribe studies, 27
- structural unit of society, 27
- Guaharibo invasion on, 28
- Venezuelan penetration into, 29
- infant development in, 30
- life in, 30